THOMAS MERTON
Spiritual Master

THOMAS MERTON: SPIRITUAL MASTER

THE ESSENTIAL WRITINGS

EDITED, WITH AN INTRODUCTION
BY LAWRENCE S. CUNNINGHAM

FOREWORD BY
Patrick Hart, O.C.S.O.

PREFACE BY
Anne E. Carr

PAULIST PRESS
New York ◊ Mahwah, New Jersey

Copyright © 1992 by Lawrence S. Cunningham

Library of Congress Cataloging-in-Publication Data

Thomas Merton: spiritual master/edited with an introduction by
  Lawrence S. Cunningham: foreword by Patrick Hart; preface by
  Anne E. Carr.
      p. cm.
    Includes bibliographical references.
    ISBN 0-8091-3314-8 (pbk.)
      1. Merton, Thomas, 1915–1968.   2. Spiritual life—Catholic
  authors.   I. Cunningham, Lawrence S.
  BX4705.M542T495   1992
  271′.12502—dc20   92-9072
                                                                        CIP

Published by Paulist Press
997 Macarthur Boulevard
Mahwah, N.J. 07430

Printed and bound in the United States of America

CONTENTS

ACKNOWLEDGMENTS

"A Christian Looks at Zen" is taken from Thomas Merton, *Zen and the Birds of Appetite*, copyright © 1968 by The Abbey of Gethsemani, Inc. "Rain and the Rhinoceros" is taken from *Raids on the Unspeakable* by Thomas Merton, copyright © 1965 by The Abbey of Gethsemani, Inc. "Herakleitos the Obscure" is reprinted from Thomas Merton, *The Behavior of Titans*, copyright © 1961 by The Abbey of Gethsemani, Inc. The introduction to *The Wisdom of the Desert* by Thomas Merton is copyrighted © 1960 by The Abbey of Gethsemani, Inc. "Hagia Sophia" is taken from *Collected Poems of Thomas Merton*, copyright ©1963 by The Abbey of Gethsemani, Inc. "The General Dance" is reprinted from Thomas Merton, *New Seeds of Contemplation*, copyright © 1961 by The Abbey of Gethsemani, Inc. Selections from *The Asian Journal of Thomas Merton* are copyrighted © 1968, 1970, 1973 by The Trustees of the Merton Legacy Trust. All of the above are reprinted by permission of New Directions Publishing Corporation. Excerpts from *Conjectures of a Guilty Bystander* by Thomas Merton, copyright © 1966 by The Abbey of Gethsemani, and from *Contemplation in a World of Action* by Thomas Merton, copyright © 1965, 1969, 1970, 1971 by The Trustees of the Merton Legacy Trust, are reprinted by permission of Doubleday, a division of Bantam Doubleday Dell Publishing Group, Inc. "A Letter on the Contemplative Life" from *The Monastic Journey* is reprinted by permission of Sheed & Ward. "The Inner Experience" is reprinted by permission of Cistercian Studies. The excerpt from *The Seven Storey Mountain* by Thomas Merton, copyright 1948 by Harcourt Brace Jovanovich, Inc. and renewed 1976 by The Trustees of the Merton Legacy Trust is reprinted by permission of the publisher. The excerpt from *The Sign of Jonas* by Thomas Merton, copyright 1953 by The Abbey of Gethsemani and renewed 1981 by The Trustees of the Merton Legacy Trust is reprinted by permission of Harcourt Brace Jovanovich, Inc. The calligraphies by Thomas Merton that appear in this book are copyright © 1992 by The Trustees of the Merton Legacy Trust and used by permission. *Day of a Stranger* by Thomas Merton, copyright © 1981 by The Trustees of the Merton Legacy Trust, is used by permission. Acknowledgment is made to Farrar, Straus and Giroux, Inc. for permission to reprint "Learning to Live" from *Love and Living* by Thomas Merton, copyright © 1979 by The Trustees of the Merton Legacy Trust; diary entries from January to Easter, 1965, from *A Vow of Conversation* by Thomas Merton, copyright © 1988 by The Trustees of the Merton Legacy Trust; excerpts from "The Love of Solitude" from *Thoughts in Solitude* by Thomas Merton, copyright © 1956, 1958 by The Abbey of Our Lady of Gethsemani, renewed © 1986 by The Trustees of the Merton Legacy Trust.

FOREWORD

In making the selections for this volume, Lawrence Cunningham has wisely focused on Thomas Merton as a spiritual master. He has made a representative choice of texts from the voluminous corpus of the early and later Merton, the autobiographical writings as well as the works more specifically addressed to persons seeking spiritual insight.

I was particularly pleased to see Merton portrayed in this way, as I am convinced that it reveals the heart of Merton, the essential thrust of his life and writings as a monk of Gethsemani for twenty-seven years. It was from the monastic community that he drew much of his inspiration, especially in the early years. His wide reading and voluminous correspondence, of course, helped him to see social issues beyond the confines of the cloister, and enabled him to respond to the vexing problems facing a church and religious order undergoing rapid and profound changes in its structures.

During over half of his monastic life, the years from 1951 through 1965, Father Louis was either master of students or master of novices at Gethsemani. These years gave him the necessary experience he had previously lacked in dealing directly with persons who were embarking on the spiritual journey. His daily job was to respond to concrete spiritual problems posed to him by young monks, persons who had only recently entered the monastery and were in need of counsel by someone who had gone before them and was able to assist them during these early formative years. Merton proved himself equal to the task; as most of his former novices and students can testify, he was one of the best of spiritual masters.

Thomas Merton had an abhorrence of forming anything resembling a cult, of having a group of disciples or a "following" in the monastery. He preferred to be as helpful as he could, but his main goal was to lead other persons to Christ, and not to himself.

1

This aspect of his years as master of novices and students is remembered by all who have had the good fortune of his counsel and spiritual insights.

It is interesting that the editor of this volume sees Merton in the American tradition of Henry Thoreau and Emily Dickinson. I would heartily agree, and Merton had himself remarked on how proud he was to be in such a tradition, although toward the end of his life he had serious reservations about being an "American." This was due mainly to his dissatisfaction with the United States' policy in "keeping the world safe from communism" in Vietnam and Latin America in particular.

Merton became a citizen of the United States in June of 1951, and at the time he made a statement to the press which was picked up by a number of local newspapers, which bears quoting, as I have never seen it published elsewhere: "I do not consider myself to be really a foreigner in this country; I have always had an American outlook and American habits of thought. Naturalization for me is simply a formal affirmation of my love for America and my gratitude toward the land that has always been 'my country' " (*Lebanon Enterprise,* June 29, 1951).

The thirty-six year old monk continued the interview by spelling out what he considered his responsibility as a monk in such a country: "I want to serve America in a monastery. If God is the source and foundation of all liberty, it seems to me that there ought to be men in a democracy whose lives are entirely consecrated to God. These men can justly claim to be public servants in a special, spiritual sense. They are helping to preserve the nation's liberty by keeping the nation in contact with God, who is the giver of liberty."

Thomas Merton's early bohemian life and later conversion to the Catholic Church, and his later acceptance into the monastic life, burnt into the depths of his being a consciousness of the great mercy and love of God in his life. He experienced this so personally that he felt compelled to respond as totally as he could to God in return. As a poet and gifted writer, he was encouraged by his abbot to write his story, his personal journey, which acknowledged God's first having loved him. All his writings can be summed up as a proclamation of God's mercy in his life, the story of the ultimate triumph of grace in the heart of a monk.

Brother Patrick Hart, O.C.S.O.
Abbey of Gethsemani
Trappist, Kentucky
19 March 1991

PREFACE

Nearly twenty-five years after Thomas Merton's untimely, accidental death in December of 1968, most of his writings are still in print, in paperback editions that are eagerly read by students and senior citizens alike, by scholars and ordinary seekers, by religious persons and by those who claim no belief at all. How explain the extraordinary influence of the life and writings of this controversial monk on so many people? Poet and essayist, social critic and autobiographer, satirist and spiritual writer, biographer and literary analyst, translator and letter-writer, Merton continues to touch a wide range of readers. Perhaps one reason that the many who find the story of his life and his reflections on movements old and new, on persons past and present, and on places close and distant, so compelling is his bent toward what he called communion over mere communication. A writer by instinct, Merton paradoxically achieved authentic communion through his prodigious communication.

Professor Lawrence Cunningham's insightful introduction and judicious selection of writings rightly underscore Merton's unrivaled depth and skill as a "spiritual master." Cunningham points out that "master" in its traditional Christian context refers to greatness, not domination. That greatness includes broad knowledge of the spiritual resources of the past, of present questions, and future possibilities, surely. But beyond mere factual knowledge or information, that greatness implies a depth of perception, art, and imaginative power that we might call wisdom. And it is in Merton's particular calling as a monk that Cunningham finds the proper focus and framework for the spiritual wisdom that Merton communicates so well in his writing.

As a convert to Roman Catholic Christianity and especially as an aspiring Cistercian monk, Merton discovered a rich spiritual tradition that stressed the importance of solitude and contemplation. Such an emphasis not only suited his own temperament but was one that sounded an important new note for his readers. His retrieval of the writings of the monastic fathers and the mystics of the Christian tradition was part of the Catholic *ressourcement* or renascence of original texts and fresh studies of ancient and medieval religious writers, prior to Vatican Council II. This spiritual tradition was one which united head and heart, philosophy and contemplation—*theologia* in the older sense of the word; today it is called simply spirituality. Merton brought this tradition of spiritual theology into the present for his many readers and, through his evocative and imaginative language, enabled it to live in their hearts and minds.

As a monk, Merton sought to share the wisdom of the monastic and mystical traditions that he had incorporated into his own life, first with the ordinary American Christians outside the monastery, those who were not religious professionals of any sort, and then with an increasingly broad and international group of believers and religious seekers of all kinds. While Merton's earlier writing betrays some crude distinctions between monastery and city, church and world, the supernatural and the natural, his incarnational and sacramental vision, rooted in the ancient traditions of Christianity, led to an ever wider breadth and openness in his religious thought and writing. He moved from reflection on the Christian tradition in its depth to include study and intuitive appreciation of the contemplative dimensions of Shaker spirituality, Russian orthodoxy, Taoism, Buddhism, especially Zen, and Hinduism, Islamic Sufism, even the cargo cults of the south Pacific, all understood as part of the wisdom of the human family.

Because he recorded the story of his own life and intimate struggles at each stage of his personal journey, his several autobiographies, journals and notebooks comprise an important part of Thomas Merton's spiritual writing. But it is further true that all his many books, essays and poems register the immediacy and concreteness of personal engagement. And the reader is caught up into that close engagement. Merton lived through a period of turbulent change in the Roman Catholic Church. The Second Vatican Council and its aggiornamento had significant implications for Catholic Christianity and particularly for the monastic context that was Merton's own. The meaning of monasticism itself, and the solitude and contemplation that are its center, came to be questioned as authentic Christian life and witness in the twentieth century. But the monk insisted on the vital meaning of the monastic and mystical elements in the tradition for Christian life today. He spent the last years of his life as a hermit and, despite extensive travels, correspondence, and encounters with many friends, he searched for a place of greater contemplative solitude as he remained attached to his own monastery, Our Lady of Gethsemani, hidden in the thick forests and green hills of the knob country of Kentucky.

Professor Cunningham's introductory sketch describes Merton's colorful life so well that it is not necessary to point to this maverick monk's cosmopolitan origins and distinctive American context, the traumatic losses of his childhood and adolescence, his manifold intellectual interests, all of which found expression in his books and articles and poetry. Rather, it may be helpful to point to the center of Merton's continuing spiritual concern or the thread that connects the disparate strands in his constantly changing symbolic vision. Throughout his reflections on spirituality, from the earliest writings to the last, is the focus on authentic personal transformation. He understood interior transformation as the meaning and goal of monastic life and of its solitude and contemplation. Transformation of mind and heart is the issue whether Merton writes about his own life as monk and priest and hermit or the sayings of the desert fathers, the personalism of the ancient and medieval theologians, the German, Spanish, or English mystics, the problems of prayer and contemplation, the existential philosophers and theologians, the dehumanizing aspects of modern technology, or the provocations of Zen stories and *koans*. Personal transformation is the point whether Merton's voice is solemn and didactic, informal, colloquial and full of slang, or simply humorous, teasingly indirect and ironic.

What drew Thomas Merton to the authors he read and the movements he studied was the transformative human experience they suggested. Merton deeply believed in—indeed he knew from his own experience—the reality of sin. This sin was the sin of the world, sin in the human heart, not simply sins in the moralistic sense. His monastic tradition named it original sin, explained as the fall of the human person from contemplative union with God. At different times in his life Merton described this sin in various metaphors for the person. He wrote of the false, neurotic, empirical, exterior or merely superficial self, the masked or sham or masquerading self, the knotted cramp of the imagination or solipsistic bubble who understands itself as the center of the world, the "individual" who parades itself in disguise to impress the crowd, the phony that makes faces at itself as if in a mirror to prove its own reality, the Cartesian ego who thinks of itself as in control of all truth. This is the servile and anxious self who feels that it is walking a tightrope across an abyss of nothingness.

By contrast, there is the possibility of the true self who hides from ordinary consciousness like a shy, wild animal that emerges only when all is very quiet, when no one is present. The true, inner, hidden or real self is the "person" who is capable of genuine dialogue, encounter and communion with others because, in fact, that person is an irrelevant "nobody," a non-identity who has lost self-consciousness and self-importance. The Christian tradition testifies to the possibility of contemplative reunion with God, the restoration of humankind's lost likeness to God, the return from exile to paradise, the experience of the birth of Christ in the soul, Christ living in the self in such a way that the self is somehow "no longer I." The feared abyss is really the abyss of being, a fullness that awaits commitment, trust and self-forgetfulness. The real self is a liberated, free and autonomous person in union with God or with being in its deepest ground.

In his early writing, Merton suggests that the "key" to this reunion with God is contemplation as the experienced fullness of the supernatural meaning and goal of Christian life. This is the "superstructure" of Christianity that so deeply satisfied his own youthful search for and joyful discovery of spiritual reality. Even though contemplation is a gift, it can nevertheless seem to be accomplished through withdrawal into solitude and prayer. In his later work, Merton is less confident that there is a single "key" to the recovery of the lost or true self, to the maturity of transcultural integration that is the deepest truth of all the religious traditions of the world. Rather, the "night spirit" and "dawn breath" of their hidden wisdom suggest an uncovering of external encrustations, a return to one's homely, natural, ordinary self, to the simple, childlike "original face you had before you were born." Such a recovery is not the object of any human striving or technique as the methodical achievement of an egocentric subject. It is something beyond the categories of the subject/object distinction, transcending conceptual thought entirely. But concepts, images, and metaphors can point to it, as a finger points to the moon. The usual mistake, Merton believes, is to attend to the finger rather than the moon.

Merton's spiritual writings witness to his continuing conviction that the highest metaphysical and religious truth, including the truth of his own Christianity, is a matter of experience, not doctrine. While he surely respected religious doctrine and its methods and concepts, his interest lay in the practical and experiential dimensions of Christian tradition and the other religions he studied. And he studied seriously, consulting scholars and experts, reading voraciously, becoming immensely learned in the process. The focus of his massive research and writing, however, was not simply accurate historical and conceptual knowledge, important and necessary as these are, but the experience that was reflected in such knowledge. It was this concrete experience that Merton communicated in his writing, through the careful art of his published autobiographies and journals and the evocative metaphors of his essays and poetry.

Merton's concentration on the self and the experience of the self might seem to suggest narcissistic introversion. And it is true, as Cunningham points out, that a certain self-righteous tone, even priggishness, characterizes some of Merton's early reflections. But, as the reader soon discovers, this is not long the case. Merton's concern with Christian experience soon led him to reflection on the context of the self in the body of Christ, one's neighbors, the community, the church, the whole world. His early conflict about whether to serve the poor in Harlem or to seek monastic withdrawal is of a piece with his later writing about social issues, about race and the civil rights movement, about war and the peace movement, about technology and the natural environment. Prayer and politics came together in his life and thought. Merton embodied what the Latin American theologians today describe as a contemporary mystical-prophetic spirituality.

Moreover, although Merton called himself a Christian existentialist in his drive toward personal participation in and reflection on the experience of Christianity, he was consistently clear that the point was not to seek experience for its own sake. It was, he believed, a fatal error to interpret the revolutionary transformation of Christian "new birth" or "new creation" or the intuition and enlightenment of Zen *satori* as a new set of experiences to be added to ordinary awareness and enjoyed by the satisfied and fulfilled individual subject. Such concern with special experience as a kind of superconsciousness could all too easily cater to the avarice of modern commercialism for the new and "interesting" commodity to attract the bored consumer. In fact, he argued, the contemporary marketing society exploits the deep human need for renewal and rebirth, the human yearning for liberation of creative power, with its products. This need and yearning can really only be answered by religious wisdom with its note of grace, mercy, and spontaneity.

For the wisdom of the Christian monks and mystics, like that of the Sufis and the Zen teachers, taught a mysterious paradox about the self-discovery that is mature personal identity. Such personal maturity, Merton believed, is the basis for an authentic religious humanism in society and its institutions. Genuine autonomy is found only in self-forgetfulness: the inmost self is like a child or homely old man. It is naked, having relinquished its many disguises as a snake sheds its skin. It is found only when one stops searching. But this spiritual nakedness or poverty does not imply lazy or conformist obedience to the rules on the part of the monk or searcher, or mere adjustment on the part of the citizen. Rather, the human and religious quest is a continuing struggle to realize that apex of the spirit that is at once the inmost self, the truly human and the presence of God within. And mysteriously, this "virginal point" in the person is not a place or a thing but an event, an explosion, a happening that is beyond all rational categories. It is also a time, the *temps vierge,* compassionate time beyond the ego, one's own time, symbolized by the morning, when God opens the eyes of the birds. It is very simple and human, somehow familiar, ordinary, natural.

Ideas such as these could seem to corroborate the suspicion that Thomas Merton was so radical a thinker and seeker that he left Christianity, and his own monastic inheritance, far behind toward the end of his life. But as Cunningham rightly argues, this is a short-sighted perspective. Even as Merton's reading and teaching went beyond the approved list to include novels and plays, folk music and the myths of many religions, his later journals and letters testify that the Bible, the liturgy, and especially his vow of obedience remained central to his life. His attempts to speak his own convictions about peace with freedom and integrity as an intellectual during the era of the Vietnam war are matched by his struggle with obedience in the continuing conflict with monastic censors and superiors and with ecclesiastical authorities over his treatment of unpopular issues in his writing. Merton was conservative in many ways, preferring the Latin hymns of the divine office, Gregorian chant and the Latin rite for the mass to the new vernacular liturgy. And he worried that monastic renewal risked loss of important contemplative values in its rush to modernization, to changes that allowed cornflakes on the monastery breakfast table but might fail to preserve the deeper meaning of the monastic quest.

Merton brought those contemplative values of the monastic and mystical traditions of Christianity to his readers in his comments on Cassian, Meister Eckhart and John of the Cross, stressing the emptiness, desolation, loneliness and obscurity of the apophatic way that so engaged him. This way of "non-knowing" had powerful affinities, he thought, with the early desert tradition, with the cryptic and enigmatic expressions of Zen, and with the possibilities suggested in the mystical aspects of Hinduism and Islam. These insights were important not for the fulfillment of individuals with a taste for the esoteric but for a world on the brink of disaster. The anti-poetry of Merton's last years is a final and provocative witness to his conviction that western culture, and particularly American mass society, can only find salvation in a recovery of its own deepest humanism through dialogical communion with the wisdom of the world.

Despite his natural exuberance and love of life, Merton saw disaster threatening in the modern world. It was evident in the stockpiling of arms, the plans for fallout shelters, the manipulations of the mass media, America's racism and its concomitant belief in the myth of its own innocence. He interpreted these and similar issues as the loss of the self, the loss of the human, the loss of the natural, the loss of wisdom. Believing the monk to be a marginal person who embodied a critical attitude toward the world and its structures, he attempted, in his life and in his books and letters and conferences, to recover the wisdom of Christianity and the religions of the world both for persons and for society. Merton's personalism sought to integrate all the levels of human experience, from the loneliness and alienation of people everywhere to the problems of the young monks who came to the monastery to "find themselves," from the religious sisters who shared his concern for serious prayer to important cultural figures who led nations, institutions, and movements for change. Deeply serious about his life and work, Merton nevertheless often achieved communion with others through his impudence, sly humor, indirection and innuendo.

So, toward the end of his life, Merton reflected satirically on the Nazi victimization of the Jews, issued his allegiance to the new Latin American poets and commented on the comic strips and the astrology column in the newspaper as he flew over the Pacific on his journey to Asia. His last, self-prepared journal, *Vow of Conversation,* is deliberately entitled as a play on the words of the fifth Cistercian vow, the *conversio morum,* sometimes translated as "conversion of manners," to mean simply "pious" or "holy" comportment or, in more recent interpretation, as the promise to do the more perfect thing. Beyond just a promise to "stick around" a monastery for the rest of one's life, for Merton this vow meant commitment to progress in the mystical life, not to the achievement of extraordinary powers or visionary experiences but to inner transformation. For him, this "most mysterious" of the traditional monastic vows, which in some ancient Latin texts was spelled *conversatio morum,* could also suggest "conversation" in its ordinary meaning of personal exchange. Although a hermit, he continued to captivate readers with his conversation about his surroundings in his little cinderblock cottage, about the first frost, the pounding rain, the color of the clouds, the animals—or their footprints in the snow—who were his companions in the woods. His conviction that it was important that modern persons and society itself learn to "let life alone" in its recovery of wisdom is aptly symbolized in these simple reflections. For Merton, communion in the "hidden ground of love" was everywhere.

Lawrence Cunningham's splendid introduction and the representative selection of texts chosen for this volume offer a taste of Merton's "sapiential method," as one student of Merton's thought has put it, and of the dance of his thought and its continuing significance for our life and for our time. Thomas Merton continues to engage readers, in his life and writing. Despite his European provenance, his work represents one of the few distinctively American contemporary spiritual classics.

Anne E. Carr

INTRODUCTION

Please pray for me to Our Lord that
instead of merely writing something,
I may *be* something . . .

Thomas Merton to Étienne Gilson

The late Thomas Merton (1915–1968) liked to offer Henry David Thoreau and Emily Dickinson as exemplars of the solitary life in order to show that solitude could be both a virtue and a matrix out of which genuine spirituality could occur. It may also be that he cited those figures to establish the *bona fides* of the solitary life—a kind of life not immediately congenial either to his Cistercian confreres (who were traditionally ferocious in their community-mindedness) or to the larger American Catholic population who liked their clergy, and even their vowed religious, gregarious and accessible.

It was probably a good strategy on Merton's part to name some American exemplars in his defense since Thomas Merton himself could hardly appeal to his own deep American roots for such a justification. He could claim none of the New England solidity of either the poet of Amherst or the sage of Concord. Indeed, Merton's relationship to American life was not quite centered both because of the accidents of birth and the circumstances of his life (to say nothing of his own temperament). Indeed—and I think there is a great paradox here—the greatest spiritual master the American Catholic Church produced in this century (Dorothy Day might contest for the honor; there is no third) is best understood, in part, through the prism of this curious relationship to American culture.

He was not, of course, totally disengaged from American culture. Quite the contrary. Eldridge Cleaver, after all, in his classic memoir *Soul on Ice,* said that no white person wrote so feelingly of

15

the teeming vitality of black Harlem. Nor could Thomas Merton, in his monastic fastness in rural Nelson County, Kentucky, ignore the SAC bombers (one, ironically enough, would bring his body back from Asia after his death in Bangkok) flying overhead with their deadly cargo of atomic weapons. What other monk would give conferences to young scholastics on the fiction of William Faulkner? Was there ever a contemplative who worried more about civil rights or resistance to war? What other monk carried on a correspondence with a *soi-disant* hippie teenager in the 1960s or played Bob Dylan in an enclosed hermitage? If this monk was so detached from "our" world, why was he hiding those copies of *Newsweek* under his mattress in fear of abbatial visits to the hermitage? What was the folk singer Joan Baez doing visiting in his hermitage? How explain the steady rumble of buzzwords, advertising slang, Madison Avenue clichés, and other such verbal detritus in his poetry? And, most deliciously of all, how account for a monk whose poetry ended up being chanted in smoky nightclubs (complete with a stage German accent) by no less a non-monk than the late Lennie Bruce? From the late 1950s on, Merton's cell served as a conduit for many of the eddies of American cultural life, especially those currents which would give heft and definition to that period which we now call, simply, the Sixties.

Yet—and yet—his actual contacts with American life were modest in their beginnings and idiosyncratic in maturity. He was born in the south of France in 1915 of an American mother of Quaker stock and an artist father who came from New Zealand. The family ties to America were slim enough that when Merton's younger brother, John Paul, decided to enter the military at the onset of World War II, he chose the Canadian rather than the American services even though he had been studying at Cornell at the time.

Merton's mother Ruth died in 1921 in New York and his father Owen, a decade later, in England. It was all very peripatetic. In his later years the only family ties that Merton could claim were with elderly relatives who lived in New Zealand or close friends of his long dead maternal grandparents who still lived on Long Island.

Between Merton's birth in 1915 and his entrance into the monastery in 1941 at the age of twenty-six, he had gone to school in France and England with the only protracted stay in the United

States beginning in the mid 1930s when he left Cambridge University abruptly (there was a pregnant woman involved) for Columbia University in New York. In the years just before his decision to leave the secular world, he taught at Saint Bonaventure's College (later a university) in upstate Olean, New York. It is not sufficiently appreciated that his accidental death by electrocution outside Bangkok, Thailand in 1968 (Karl Barth, the magisterial Reformed theologian, died on the same day: December 10) occurred while Merton was on the first protracted stay outside the monastery which he had entered twenty-seven years before; in fact, it was twenty-seven years to the day.

Furthermore, the years in the monastery, especially in the 1940s and 1950s, were sealed off from the larger world. There were no radios, no televisions, no newspapers or secular magazines, and very limited contact with those outside the cloister. Life was tied to a round of prayer, agricultural labor, and study marked by the changing of the natural and liturgical seasons rather untouched by the events of the "world." Few visitors were permitted to the monastery, and mail—both incoming and outgoing—was severely restricted.

In a superficial sense, then, Thomas Merton was a marginal American. Only half-American by birth (he was naturalized as an American citizen only in the 1950s), he was bilingual by education, expatriate in his adolescence, an enclosed contemplative in his maturity. In the formative years of his monastic experience the war raged in Europe and the Pacific. It touched him only vicariously. His brother John Paul was killed in 1943, occasioning one of Merton's finest short poems "For My Brother" (CP 35–36)* which would be included in the only significant publication that came during the war years: *Thirty Poems* (1944).

After the extraordinary success of his autobiography *The Seven Storey Mountain* (1948), his was a household name in Catholic America and, quickly, abroad.[1] That fame was the engine power that soon had him churning out prefaces, essays, poems, books, and reviews at an astonishing rate. People, he once noted irritatingly (in *Vow of Conversation*), must think that "I perspire

---

* For a key to the works cited in the Introduction, see pp. 54–55.

articles." Even a cursory glance at the published bibliographies of his writings reflects an astonishing range of publications in journals ranging from the then Catholic avant-garde *Jubilee* and the radical *The Catholic Worker* to more enlightened purveyors of high culture like *The Sewanee Review*.[2] While his voice, understandably enough, spoke to American (especially Catholic American) culture, his intellectual roots were far more cosmopolitan. Not only did he read omnivorously in the ascetico-mystical literature of Christianity but he evinced a keen and protracted interest in the contemplative traditions of other faiths. Furthermore, his literary instincts were honed at Columbia (under the tutelage of Mark Van Doren) on the modernist canon which was largely, while not exclusively, non-American: Eliot, Joyce, Kafka, and so on. In his later years he had cultivated links with poets and writers in Central and Latin America, translating their words, contributing to their journals, and encouraging the spread of their work in the north. A quick perusal of his experimental journal *Monk's Pond* (it lasted, by design, four issues) shows the range of his literary contacts and interests,[3] but even toward the end of his life he saw the major influences upon him as either European or Latin American. In response to a letter from a young Italian woman writing on his poetry, he listed "Thoreau, Faulkner, William Carlos Williams, Mark Van Doren, Emily Dickinson" as the American writers who most influenced him (RJ 349).

To that degree, at least, Merton had an intellectual viewpoint that was catholic in the most generic sense of the word. It tells in the languages he knew well: Latin, French, Spanish, Italian, and some German. He began to study Russian after beginning a correspondence with Boris Pasternak in the 1950s and made a desultory stab at Chinese because of his interest in Zen. His early education did not derive from any narrow parochialism, and his university experiences were urban, non-sectarian, and modernist. It was that background that equipped him to do what he was best able to do: articulate a deep longing for the Absolute and that deep hunger of meaning which has haunted the modern mind since the last century.

It is not accidental that he could read sympathetically a figure like Albert Camus because he himself had known the cold indifference of the sky and the concomitant drive for authenticity, engagement, and wholeness.[4] The discovery of God for Merton was a discovery made by someone fully at home in the secularized world of his time. In *The Seven Storey Mountain* Merton has some moving pages about his reading of Etienne Gilson's *The Spirit of Medieval Philosophy* with its analysis of God as Being Itself. It was, as Merton wrote, "something that was to revolutionize my life" (SSM 211). In that intellectual encounter, later to be transformed into an existential commitment, Merton was to find the deep center that gave heft and substance to his life.

One can make the case, it seems to me, that the phenomenal success of his autobiography was due in large part to his ability to spell out that sense of spiritual hunger, bewilderment, outrage, and longing that bedeviled so many in the period after the war. The wonder of it is that its censorious tone, its praise of the ascetical life, its sheer naked religiousness (and, to be balanced, its somewhat spiritually priggish tone) could find a sympathetic audience at a period when a good deal of American religious writing was almost indiscriminately upbeat. After all, Merton wrote at a time that would see religious best sellers like Rabbi Joshua Liebman's *Peace of Mind* (1948), Fulton Sheen's *Peace of Soul* (1949), the ineffably vulgar *The Power of Positive Thinking* (1952) by Norman Vincent Peale, and the best selling All-American Catholic novel *The Cardinal* (1950) by Henry Morton Robinson.

It was also a time—especially after the end of the war—when American Catholicism was in the full flush of growth, increasing acceptance in the culture (the high point being the presidential election of John Kennedy in 1960), and brimming with that self-confidence which was part of the putative "American century" so confidentally trumpeted by the publications of Henry Luce. One need only read the standard histories of Catholicism in this period to see, apart from a *Jubilee* reading elite, how peripheral monasticism was in the church of Cardinals Spellman and Cushing and Fathers Keller and Sheen. The *beau ideal* of the clergy was not a cloistered ascetic, but a robust Bing Crosby or a ruggedly compassionate Spencer Tracy. There is a good book to be written on the popular image of Catholicism in the film world of the post-war period. That book will have little to say of asceticism, contemplation, silence, hiddenness—the stock in trade of the monastic life.

Against that trend, Merton preached a quite different gospel of prophetic resistance to worldly values, an affirmation of asceticism, the necessity of contemplation, and a disdain for the consumerism of the booming middle class culture of the post-war period. Indeed, this censorious tone in the early Merton was so conspicuous that a fellow monk, the English Benedictine Aelred Graham, felt compelled to chide Merton in a national journal for his insistence on being a "modern man in reverse."[5] Merton himself, in his maturity, would see the justice of these complaints and satirize his younger persona as one who "spurned New York, spat on Chicago, and tromped on Louisville, heading for the woods with Thoreau in one pocket, John of the Cross in another, and holding the bible open to the Apocalypse" (CWA 159).

If his attitudes had matured over the years, Merton never repented of his conviction that his entrance into monastic life was not only to serve God; it was also a gesture of protest against what he felt were the demonic elements in modern culture. Writing an introduction to the Japanese version of *The Seven Storey Mountain* in 1963, fifteen years after its original publication, Merton insisted that his life was a *no* to concentration camps, aerial bombardments, staged political trials, judicial murders, racial injustices, economic tyrannies and so on, just as it was a *yes* to all that is "good in the world and in man . . . to all that is beautiful in the world . . . to all men and women who are my brothers and sisters in the world" (HR 65-66). Given that predisposition, it should not suprise us that Merton always felt a sympathy for those figures in American culture who were on the margins of the culture or at the edges of respectability. He felt, in short, a kinship with an outsider like Thoreau and a more than passing interest in the beatniks of the 1950s (the last place he stayed at before leaving the United States for his Asian trip was the City Lights Book Store as a guest of his friend Lawrence Ferlinghetti), and the hippies of the 1960s as well as a close tie with the social protest movement that gained such prominence in the waning years of the Eisenhower era and came into full blossom in the 1960s, the last decade of his life.

One way of looking at Merton, then, would be to say that he represented the religious wing of the cultural left, a kind of believing beatnik. Such a view, however, would be very nearly a parody.

In my estimation, it is Merton's monasticism that is the crucial key to understanding him as a public person, as a writer, and as a spiritual master. Thomas Merton, to be sure, evolved in his own appreciation of what it meant to be a monk and in what sense he was a monk. Nonetheless, if we are to approach him and his writings, it is through the monastic prism that we must look.

THE MONK

The monastic order Thomas Merton entered in 1941 is called the Order of Cistercians of the Strict Observance (O.C.S.O.), but these monks are familiarly known as Trappists. The word Trappist derives from an abbey in France, La Trappe, where the Abbé Armand-Jean de Rance (1626–1700) applied his rigorous approach to the Cistercian Order as a reform movement within monastic life. Rance's reforms were carried out within the confines of the Cistercian Order which had been founded in 1098 at Citeaux (Lat.: *Cistercium*) in France by Saint Robert of Molesme (1027?–1111). That pioneering effort began under Saint Robert because he had been unable to carry forth his reform ideas at the Benedictine abbey of Molesme where he had been the abbot. That reform was given definitive shape by the towering figure of Bernard of Clairvaux (1090–1153). Merton's order, then, was the beneficiary and heir of a religious tradition that ran back to the seventeenth century to the late eleventh, and, from there, to the beginnings of the western monastic life inspired by Saint Benedict of Nursia (480?–543). Benedict's own Rule, of course, did not originate with him. He was in debt to earlier sources ultimately traceable to the primitive rise of the monastic impulse which had emerged in the Christian church in the third century.

Western monastic life, with its characteristic round of common prayer, sacred reading, and work had behind it not only a long history but the slow and complex development of a monastic culture. Merton himself, in one of his essays, describes this culture in what is almost an afterthought (it is, in fact, a footnote) in his volume *Contemplative Prayer* where he gives it a characteristic interpretation: "It implies the development of a set of tastes and skills, of openness to certain monastic values in all the arts and disciplines that have relation to the monastic life in all its fullness. One could say for example that for a twentieth century Christian monk monastic culture would imply not only an education in all that is living and relevant in monastic theology, tradition, and literature as well as art, architecture, and poetry, etc. but also in other religious cultures. Hence, a certain knowledge of Zen, of Sufism, of Hinduism can rightly claim a place in the monastic culture of the modern monk of the West" (CPR 85).

In his twenty-seven years in the monastic life Thomas Merton not only absorbed great draughts of that culture but, in important and radical ways, added to it, rethought it, and provided new issues for it to consider. That is an important fact for contemporary monasticism itself but, more pertinently, it was Merton's capacity to mediate the essential insights of that culture to the non-monastic world and to find links to bond his monastic life with other religious traditions as diverse as the Sufis and the Shakers that kept him from being a figure who, to use an old southern expression, preached only to the choir.

What is monasticism all about?

At the outset we must disabuse ourselves of the notion that monasticism is some exotic accretion that grows somewhat uneasily on the body of historic Christianity. It is, in fact, a way of being a Christian that goes back into the primordial stages of early Christian development. On this point I would very much make my own the sentiments of the noted liturgical scholar, Aidan Kavanaugh, himself a Benedictine monk: "Monasticism was not the creation of medieval bishops but of early Christian lay people. It flowed directly into Christian life out of Jewish prophetic asceticism which received new focus through the lens of Jesus' own teaching. One must therefore take the continuing fact of organized asceticism in Christian life as a given which provides access to whole dimensions of Christian perception and being. The existence, furthermore, of specifically monastic asceticism is a theological datum which adheres closely to the very nerve center of Christian origins and growth. One cannot study Christianity without taking monasticism into account. One cannot live as a Christian without practicing the Gospel asceticism which monasticism is meant to exemplify and support. A Christian need not be a monk or nun but every monk and nun is a crucial sort of Christian, and there have been too many of these people over the centuries for their witness not to have considerable theological importance."[6]

Monasticism testifies to the Christian desire to live in community with a keen sense that we are in the time of "not-yet"—the time in which we are called upon to grow in the love of Christ, through whom we praise God, in order to express that Christian love which will never be fully realized "until he comes again" (1 Cor 11:26; Rev 22:20). The monastery, to borrow the laconic phrase of Saint Benedict's *Rule,* is the "School of the Lord's Service." Through the public prayer of the psalms, the lifetime reading of sacred scripture, and interior cultivation the monk embarks on a life of learning, growing, and spiritual development. One enters a monastery, in short, not because one is spiritually perfect but because one seeks some measure of Christian perfection. One becomes a monk, in short, "to seek God and not a perfect monasticism" (VC 132).

To understand that basic thrust of monasticism is to avoid a too romantic view of what monasticism is. It is very hard to avoid that romanticism precisely because we are the heirs of a popular tradition, going back as early as the eighteenth century, of equating monasticism with quiet cloister gardens around which cowled and tonsured figures silently tread in silent prayer. Such a picture dwells too much on what is epiphenomenal about the monastic life and not enough on monasticism as a prophetic way of being a Christian that stands in tension with other ways of being a Christian and, most certainly, with other ways of being in the world. It has been a commonplace of ecclesiastical history to see monasticism as an embodiment of certain religious values that are attractive in their own right and correctives to exaggerations in the church.

Thomas Merton entered Gethsemani in 1941 fully prepared to accept monastic life as he found it, but during his twenty-seven years in the monastery he deepened his own understanding of monasticism in an attempt (at times consciously; at other times in response to the exigencies of the moment) to free it and to free himself from any spirit of atemporal conformity. During the 1960s he wrote a good deal on monastic reform in general and the place of monasticism in the world in particular. To reread the collected essays in *The Monastic Journey* (1977), *Contemplation in a World of Action* (1973) and the letters on monasticism in *The School of Charity* (1990) is to see Merton's attempts to calibrate the position of the monk within his own monastic tradition, in other monastic traditions outside of Christianity, and with the vast world, Christian or not, that was not monastic.

Of Chaucer's young scholar in *The Canterbury Tales* the poet wrote "gladly wold he lerne and gladly teche." The same high encomium could be applied to Merton the monk. That he was a monastic teacher is patent. Not only did he have such formal positions as master of scholastics and master of novices in the monastery but the thick volumes of his conference notes testify to the energetic labors he put in to prepare himself for those roles. His published writings, from the earliest years (e.g. his history of the order: *The Waters of Siloe*) to his final days on earth, reveal him as a student and teacher of monasticism. We might recall, not to put too fine a point on it, his attitude as expressed in some words he jotted down for a conference just a month before he died: "I think we have now reached a stage of (long overdue) religious maturity at which it might be possible for someone to remain perfectly faithful to a Christian and Western monastic commitment and yet *to learn* in depth from, say, a Buddhist or Hindu discipline and experience. I believe some of us need to do this in order to improve the quality of our own monastic life and even to help in the task of monastic renewal which has been undertaken within the Western Church" (AJ 313; emphasis added).

Merton, in short, was perfectly at home in monastic culture, but, as we have noted, he was at pains to enlarge its scope. He immersed himself in his own tradition, but there was a way in which he wished to add to it. That is clear from the lines we cited above. It is a theme that he returned to time and again. A journal entry he made after a (rare) trip outside the monastery to visit the Zen scholar D. T. Suzuki is not atypical: "Literature, contemplative solitude, Latin America, Asia, Zen, Islam, etc., all these things come together in my life. It would be madness for me to attempt to create a monastic life for myself by excluding all these. I would be less a monk. Others may have their way of doing it but I have mine" (VC 62).[7]

The phrase "contemplative solitude" leaps out at anyone who knows Merton's life and writings. From his earliest days as a monk he felt a tug away from the community-mindedness to the quiet of the hermitage. His early writings (preeminently *The Sign of Jonas*) testify to his fascination with such eremetical orders as the Carthusians and the Camaldolese. In his last years at Gethsemani, with a persistence that caused some friction, he gradually got a cottage built away from the abbey where he spent days, and finally, in 1965, he made a permanent move to that hermitage; a year later he made a private vow before Abbot James Fox that bound him to the life of a hermit as long as his health would permit it. His struggle for a permanent hermitage was not a personal victory; it became a renewed feature of Cistercian monasticism which is still alive in the Order.

The eremetical side of Merton's life is a complicated one. There was the practical desire to simplify his life in order to pray and write with more focus. There was a quasi-visionary desire to reimagine a form of monasticism which would combine solitude with a kind of intellectual and spiritual service to the world. Finally, and most significantly, there was his desire to live out in actuality his deepest insights about the ascetic and spiritual value of solitude understood both as an exterior sign against the world and as an interior state in which a person cleanses away that which is false in order to stand naked before God.

That latter point deserves some emphasis. People may quarrel about how well Thomas Merton was suited for the eremetical life. They may point out, as many have done, that there was something dissonant in his desire for greater solitude at a time in his life when he sought greater human contact and expressed a desire for travel and absence from the abbey. It may well be, to paraphrase an observation of Teresa of Avila, that God's greatest penance for us comes when our prayers are answered. Merton got his hermitage in 1965 precisely at a time when he felt he needed opportunities to travel—a paradox not lost on his then abbot with whom he had any number of *contretemps* over that precise issue.

The main point is, I suspect, that it was the centrality of the concept of solitude, and not the manner in which it was lived out, that was of lasting significance in the writings of Thomas Merton. Whether it was in his spiritual writings (like *New Seeds of Contemplation* or *Thoughts in Solitude*) or in his essays on Camus, Merton always turned back to the critical need for self-appropriation: the need to understand the true self which, despite its irreducibly social character, was the solitary self. One could not, Merton argued over and over again, evade the reality of the self, especially as that self stood in relation to the Absolute.

To be a monk, let us remind ourselves, is to be radically alone (*monachos* comes from *monos,* i.e. alone). Merton's desire to hone his monastic life, first in community and later in the hermitage, was, in the last analysis, a desire to orient himself toward the reality of God. It is so easy, in reading Merton, to forget this basic orientation. We so quickly catalogue the many Mertons (essayist, historian, poet, activist, spiritual writer, diarist, etc.) that the first reason why he became a monk—the centrality of transcendence—can be forgotten in the welter of his written words.

It is a strange but basic paradox about the life of Thomas Merton that for all of the autobiographical orientation of his writings he was notoriously reticent about his own spiritual life as it was experienced. He wrote much on spiritual ideas and provided much spiritual advice, but one must read carefully to find those experiential moments or those flashing epiphanies that break through the reticence of his prose and poetry. They are there to be sure: we find those moments in places like the epilogue to *The Sign of Jonas* ("The Firewatch") or sections of his diaries and in a few places in his letters. When those moments occur, we discover that what he writes of is not pure discursive rumination but the result of experience deeply held. It is there that we find what was once called *theologia*—authentic speech about God.

It was only with the publication of his letters (still in process as of this writing) that we get a fuller picture of how deep his contemplative experience has been. One of the most revealing descriptions of his interior life comes from a letter that he wrote to an Islamic professor in Pakistan (that, in itself, says much about Merton) in response to a question about his own experience of prayer. In response Merton writes some lines which have been oft quoted but bear quoting again: "There is in my heart this great thirst to recognize totally the nothingness of all that is not God. My prayer then is a kind of praise rising up out of the center of Nothing and Silence. If I am still present 'myself' this I recognize as an obstacle about which I can do nothing unless He himself removes the obstacle. Such is my ordinary way of prayer, or meditation. It is not 'thinking about' anything but a direct seeking of the Face of the Invisible. I do not ordinarily write about such things and I ask you to be discreet about it. But I write this as a testimony of confidence and friendship" (HGL 64).

THOMAS MERTON AS THEOLOGIAN

It seems idiosyncratic to call Thomas Merton a theologian, but it seems less so if one can scrub away understandings of the word "theologian" that are too narrowly restrictive or too distant from the ancient tradition of theology in the Roman Catholic tradition. There is a way of using the term to describe Merton with some accuracy, and, increasingly, the term is being used of him.[8]

When Thomas Merton entered Gethsemani in 1941, he joined the novitiate of those who aspired to be choir monks and not lay brothers. That meant, according to the customs of the time, that were he to persevere in monastic life he would be ordained to the priesthood since, for centuries, the old idea that the monk was to be a lay person had given way to a clericalization of monastic life despite the hesitancy of the Rule of Saint Benedict about admitting priests to the monastic community.

Since Merton was destined for both the choir and the priesthood he was required to pursue the full course of theological education which had been mandated at the Council of Trent in the sixteenth century for all aspirants to sacerdotal ordination.

In those years (there have been some major changes since the period after the Second Vatican Council) the theological course consisted of a four year program of systematic and moral theology with lesser courses in the ancillary disciplines of scripture, canon law, church history, homiletics, pastoral theology, and so on, to be completed after one finished the undergraduate course of the university or its near equivalent.

It further needs to be said that when Merton studied theology in the 1940s, it was a discipline which was very much in the doldrums because of both the paralysis caused by the anti-modernist rigor of the church and the low level of theology as a discipline in the United States. Theology was restricted to clerical education in this country. It was a subject taught by priests to future priests. It consisted mainly of glosses on scholastic manuals written in Latin.

The manuals, in turn, were jejeune intellectually, heavily rational-istic in their use of scholastic syllogisms, and massively innocent of any historical context or hermeneutical rigor. In fact, it was only in the period when Merton began his theological studies that the first stirrings of theological vigor in the United States were appearing: The Catholic Biblical Association was founded in 1936 but its scholarly journal (the now highly regarded *Catholic Biblical Quar-terly*) did not begin publication until 1939; *Theological Studies,* the eminent Jesuit quarterly, began in 1940; the Catholic Theological Society of America was not founded until 1946.

It is also worthy of note that in *The Sign of Jonas,* the journal that covers the years leading up to his ordination, only rarely does Merton even allude to his formal theological studies, and when he does it is in the most laconic and unenthusiastic fashion: "We had a moral theology exam and then my chest was x-rayed" (SJ 52–53). "For a year and a half I have sat . . . listening to Father Macarius expound the mysteries of Sabetti's moral theology or Tanquerey's dogma" (SJ 73).[9]

By contrast, in the same period, it is striking how voraciously Merton was reading the monastic literature and that of the mystics —an intellectually *terra incognita* for the vast majority of seminar-ians. It is, as it were, that Merton was receiving two educations: one in scholastic theology legislated by the law of the church and the customs of the time and the other in the contemplative tradi-tion out of deep personal need and because of a monastic predisposition.

When one reads the letters now published in *The School of Charity* (on monastic life and religious renewal) it is clear that Merton saw the inadequacy of scholastic theology early on. In 1949 he wrote an *aide memoire* to Abbot Fox about his idea of develop-ing a center for monastic theology for students. In a letter to Dom Damasus Winzen (the founder of the primitive Benedictine priory of Mount Saviour in New York) he explicitly noted the tension between monastic formation and theological training for the priesthood: "It certainly seems crucial to me that monks should be first of all *monks* and that they should get their roots firmly sunk into the monastic life and that the studies for the priesthood and thoughts of the priesthood do, in fact, distract them from this when they are assumed at the wrong time" (SC 91). Seven years later, in 1962, in a letter to another Benedictine he speaks of a "pet project" which he describes as a "monastic pre-philosophy course which will have nothing to do with the manuals but will be a sort of lectio divina of texts from St. Anselm, St. Augustine, Boethius, and so on" (SC 155). Notions like this—circling around unhappiness with the "manuals" and a desire for a more authentic monastic theological education—run like a leitmotif through Merton's published works as well as his correspondence.

The limited impact that his formal theological education had on him is visible in the books which he wrote which are, with few exceptions, almost pristine in their lack of scholastic style or citation.[10] The one conspicuous exception is *The Ascent to Truth* (1951), his study of Saint John of the Cross, which is a rather scholastic analysis of the great Spanish Carmelite's mystical doctrine. The book had a modest success in its own day but Merton himself felt that casting it in the language of scholasticism held him back from expressing what he felt and in what he had to say as a result of his studies. He made those hesitations explicit in the prologue to *The Sign of Jonas* only a year after *Ascent* was published: "I found that in writing *The Ascent to Truth* that technical language, though it is universal and certain and accepted by theologians, does not reach the average man and does not convey what is personal and most universal in religious experience. Since my focus is not on dogmas as such, but only on their repercussions in the life of the soul in which they begin to find a concrete realization, I may be pardoned for using my own words to talk about my own soul" (SJ 18).

Thomas Merton was not to repent of that judgment. In fact, in 1958 a French version of the *Ascent,* edited by a French Carmelite with Merton's permission, was published. In Merton's introduction to that volume he wrote: "This book was written seven years ago. If I were to attack the same subject at the present day (and I very probably would not) I might approach it very differently. For one thing, the psychological aspects of the study would have to be completed by some discussion of man's unconscious drives and their possible intervention in the life of prayer. On the other hand, I would prefer to draw more on scripture and the Fathers and to concern myself less with scholasticism which *is not the true intellectual climate for a monk.* In a word, the book would be quite different from what it actually is" (HR 28; emphasis added).

What, then, is the true intellectual climate for the monk? When we describe Thomas Merton as a theologian we must retrieve an older and somewhat parallel tradition of theology which derives from the monastic milieu: theology as discourse about the *experience* of God's presence, love, and right to praise. That understanding of theology might be summed up in a phrase made famous by an early monastic writer, Evagrius of Pontus (346–399), which Merton frequently cited: the theologian is the person who prays; the person who prays is truly a theologian.[11]

As Jean Leclercq has shown, this understanding of theology, developed in the patristic period, was common right down to the twelfth century and, even after the rise of the schools, it perdured.[12] It was a theology that was less concerned with dialectics and more with experience, a theology developed not from the scholar's cathedra but on the kneeling bench, and, finally, it grows out of the ancient practice of uninterrupted study of the Bible—*lectio divina.* Thomas Merton came to an understanding about the desirability of doing that kind of theology very early in his life as a monk. In a 1949 letter to his friend Bob Lax he wrote: "I have suddenly woken up to the fact that somebody needs to be teaching theology the way St. Augustine did and not the way textbooks in seminaries do. Someone should be able to find the Living God in scripture—and this is his word—and then lead others to find him there and all theology properly ends in contemplation and love and union with God—not ideas about Him and a set of rules about how to wear your hat" (RJ 172).

Conventional wisdom has it that such theology, old-fashioned and conservative, was overtaken and rendered irrelevant by the marriage of dialectic to theology in the twelfth century—that Abelard, in short, had triumphed over Bernard of Clairvaux. Theology, this view would say, moved monodirectionally from the cloister to the university. There is no doubt that the new dialectical theology did flourish in the schools, producing, in the thirteenth century, such luminaries as Saint Albert the Great, Saint Thomas Aquinas, and Saint Bonaventure. But it is also true that monastic theology (not always called that) continued to thrive in its old setting and in some new ones. Thus, in the fourteenth century, scholastic theology was taught at Oxford while, at the same time, the cloisters were producing books such as *The Cloud of Unknowing* and *The Revelations* (of Julian of Norwich) and other masterpieces of mystical literature from the pens of Richard Rolle and Walter Hilton. At a later period, a writer like Saint John of the Cross would balance ecstatic mystical poetry with scholastic commentaries. Increasingly, in our own day, there is a genuine effort to bridge the gap between "theology" and "spirituality" in order to heal any alleged rift between heart and head.

It seems clear to me that Thomas Merton fits comfortably into that model of monastic theology. Indeed, one could argue (I would so argue) that he energized it and gave it a peculiar relevance for the contemporary world. What marked him off from other writers of this same stripe in our century (I am thinking of his fellow Cistercian, the late Eugene Boylan, or Benedictines like Columba Marmion or Hubert Von Zeller—all much read in their day) was his sensitivity to the modernist high culture of our time (one finds it hard to think of Columba Marmion discussing the painting of Paul Klee or the prose of André Gide) as well as his ability to communicate with those outside the world of faith (what would Eugene Boylan, say, have in common with his fellow Irishman, James Joyce?). Merton, in short, was capable of entering the larger world of cultural discourse while rooted in a tradition that gave a peculiar weight and a ring of authenticity to his words. At the same time, he was not an elitist who ignored the household of the faith or the needs of the ordinary person. If Merton was a monastic theologian, he was also a *catholic* one in the deepest (and most undenominational) sense of the word.

There is a further point. The best of monastic theology attempted to know the self in order to know God. This was true both of autobiographical writings in this tradition and those works that guided others along the path of perfection. Christian monasticism was not a pious form of self-actualization nor a self-absorbed species of navel-gazing. Its attention to the self is an instrumental one whose aim was to transform the self through ascesis and prayer and receptivity to the promptings of God and in the cultivation of virtue. Saint Augustine's famous *noverim me ut noverim Te* ("I would know myself in order to know Thee") in the *Confessions* can stand as an encapsulated statement of the monastic (indeed, Christian) ideal generally. Even a rudimentary glance at the literature of Christian spirituality demonstrates that fact. It would be out of place here, for example, to cite specifics of, say, the *ascent* motif in this literature (everywhere from Benedict's twelve steps of humility to the ladder of John Climacus to John of the Cross' ascent of Mount Carmel) but there is one thing they all hold in common: the need to grasp one's actual state of being by stripping away evasive masks in order to understand one's relationship to God.

There are many ways to undertake this journey. Some do it by perfect fidelity to their state of life; others through the terrors of human calamity; still others by selfless service to others. Merton chose the monastic life, at least in part, because he was disgusted with his earlier life and because he had an enormous thirst for God. In the monastery he learned, in time, to concentrate on the latter and accept forgiveness for, and distance from, the former. Nonetheless, it was in the monastery that he slowly learned these ideas because he knew, as Saint Benedict says, famously, in his Rule that the monastery is a school.

When he first entered Gethsemani, Merton intended to put behind him his earlier desire to teach and write. It was his first abbot who ordered him to take up his pen again. Merton continued to write partly because he wanted to be an obedient monk and partly (the abbot was a very wise man) because he had a natural facility and a profound need to write. In fact, the pen became a fundamental tool which Thomas Merton used to scrutinize himself and to find God. Merton, in short, was a monk by vocation, a theologian by conviction, and a writer by instinct.

MERTON AS WRITER

Merton wrote long before he became a monk. There was a spurt of juvenilia published in the *The Oakhamian,* the English school magazine of which he became an editor in 1931. In his Columbia University days there were book reviews for the Sunday review sections of the *New York Times* and the *Herald Tribune.* Merton contributed both art and articles to campus magazines and served as editor of the Columbia yearbook in his senior year. He kept a journal at the end of the decade (later published under the title *The Secular Journal*), worked on fiction (one novel, written in 1941 had the working title *The Journal of My Escape from the Nazis;* it was published in 1969 as *My Argument with the Gestapo*), and wrote some of his finest poetry. One poem, inspired by a visit to Cuba and the shrine of the Black Virgin of Cobre, begins with the lovely lines: "The white girls lift their heads like trees/The black girls go/Reflected like flamingos in the street" ("Song for Our Lady of Cobre"—CP 29).

After his entrance in Gethsemani Merton assumed that the early promise of a writer's career would be sacrificed as part of his desire to live as a contemplative monk. That, of course, would not be the case. Even before the publication of *The Seven Storey Mountain* in 1948 he did writing for internal consumption in the monastery, had published some of his poetry, and did translations which appeared without his name (he translated the widely read *The Soul of the Apostolate* by Dom Chautard). After the enormous success of his autobiography there was both pressure to write more and, on Merton's part, a legitimate reason for doing what was, in fact, something close to his heart.

It was only with the passage of time that Merton came to understand that his vocation as a monk was not antithetical to his need to be a writer. Indeed, he came to realize that being a monk also demanded that he be a monk who wrote. He felt the call to be a writer as one that shaped who he was. That becomes very clear when one considers some words he wrote after looking at twenty-five years of his own output as it appeared in a revised version of *The Thomas Merton Reader.* In a revealing paragraph in an introduction to that volume Merton wrote: "It is possible to doubt whether I have become a monk (a doubt I have to live with) but it is not possible to doubt that I am a writer, that I was born one and will most probably die as one. Disconcerting, disedifying as it is, this seems to be my lot and my vocation. It is what God has given to me that I might give it back to him" (TMR 17).

There came a time when Merton himself had to sort out what he had written and what it all meant. On February 6, 1967 Merton made a graph that was calibrated from "awful" to "best" with, in descending order, the rubrics "better," "good," "less good," "poor," and "very poor" as the median steps. He juxtaposed thirty books and, as it were, took their temperature.[13] He does not award himself a "best" but follows his books up and down the chart from "better" (e.g. the poetry volume *Tears of the Blind Lion*) to a steep plunge to "awful" (the pious hagiography *What Are These Wounds?*). Among the volumes to which he gave the rating of "better" are those which both critics and admirers also value: *The Seven Storey Mountain, The Sign of Jonas, New Seeds of Contemplation, Wisdom of the Desert, Chuang Tzu, Raids on the Unspeakable, Conjectures of a Guilty Bystander,* and some of his earliest collections of poetry.

That this exercise was not simply a way to pass the longeurs of a winter afternoon can be seen from other evidences of Merton's self-analysis. In a 1968 letter to an inquirer Merton divided his career as a writer into three periods with books that were characteristic of each. There was a time of youth and first fervor reflected in books like *Secular Journal, Thirty Poems, The Seven Storey Mountain,* and *Seeds of Contemplation.* A second phase of more intensely monastic and ascetical writing was represented by *The Sign of Jonas, Thoughts in Solitude,* and *The Silent Life.* The transitional work, Merton thought, was *Disputed Questions* (1960) which marked a turn that was more open to the problems of the world and the various currents of modern intellectual life. This third period is reflected in works from the 1960s like the more experimental journal *Conjectures of a Guilty Bystander* and essay collections like *Raids on the Unspeakable* or studies like *Chuang Tzu.*[14]

That 1968 judgment is not unlike one Merton made to himself in 1965 in one of his yet unpublished reading journals. Reflecting on an observation of Rilke that all art springs from necessity, Merton wrote that about one-third of his work sprung from that impulse—works very much like those that he would graph as "better" three years later. The rest, he writes dismissively, is trash, or rather, he quickly adds, "journalism," by which he means, one assumes, written for the moment.

Those self-criticisms and others that one can detect in the various prefaces he wrote to translations of his work are not exercises in either self-deception or vanity. Merton had read too much good literature in his life not to be sensitive to what was mere boilerplate and what sprung from Rilkean necessity. Interestingly enough, his judgments about his work are not that far from the critical consensus of those who have studied his corpus in depth and commented on it at length. One always hesitates to trust the judgment of writers about their own work (they often love a work that appears to others as odd or idiosyncratic), but, in preparation for the anthologized part of this volume, I wrote to a number of Merton scholars and asked them to list the indispensable essays or selections of books they would include were they doing this volume. When a synopsis was made of their suggestions they culled their titles from the books that Merton himself judged the best almost without exception.

Despite that unanimity, a critical judgment about the Merton corpus as a whole and parts of it in particular is a difficult one to make. In the first place, one must make some crucial distinctions about what Merton has left behind him as his literary legacy. It is not possible to sort all of this into neat literary piles, but there are some broad contours to be noted. To observe some economics of space, let me rehearse some arbitrary distinctions that seem useful to me:

(1) The "thinking out loud" or "Merton at play" items: This would include everything from his personal journals (still unpublished), personal letters (in the process of publication), and internal monastic memoranda as well as some of the ephemeral poetic exercises, doggerel, and concrete poems appended to the volume of his *Collected Poems*.

(2) The "written under holy obedience" or out of a sense of duty imposed on a "celebrity Catholic" items: Pamphlets explaining monastic life, translations of pious works, hagiographic potboilers, introductions to other people's work, and works of earnest piety.

(3) Works derived from the monastic vocation deeply felt and profoundly lived: A heterogeneous pile of material that ranges from

conferences to scholastics (many available on tape) to important historical studies and reflective essays on the meaning of monasticism. The cream of this material is in those works which were meant to refract the monastic experience to those outside the cloister, e.g. *New Seeds of Contemplation* and in the posthumous collection of essays collected under such titles as *Contemplation in a World of Action* and *The Monastic Journey.*

(4) Works from the pen of a literary person: They are to be found, for the most part, in one of two fat volumes: *The Literary Essays* or *The Collected Poems.* His novel may belong here but probably was published as a by-product of the celebrity status mentioned in (2) above. In this same general category belongs his various translations and his later, more experimental essays and blendings of essays with poetry as well as his editing of the experimental journal, *Monk's Pond.*

(5) Celebrations of the (true) self: The Whitmanesque rubric that I employ here is only partially ironic. If Whitman is best remembered for his enormously fecund outpouring of the self in his poetry, Merton's permanent reputation derives from the great stream of autobiographical writings whose chronological contours run from *The Secular Journal* and *The Seven Storey Mountain* through *The Sign of Jonas* and *Conjectures of a Guilty Bystander* to *A Vow of Conversation* and *The Asian Journal.*

It is that latter category that is crucial. Elena Malits, and others after her, have insisted that one of Merton's greatest contributions to contemporary theological spirituality was his giving the pronoun "I" a renewed respectability in spiritual writing.[15] It was in the published journal, especially, that one finds the most fecund of his spiritual insights. It is those books that will most endure not because they are interesting or timely but because they reflect the experiences of a person who was deeply centered and whose whole life was an exercise in absorbing knowledge in order to become a caring and wise person.

The published journals are not printed versions of random thoughts. They were the reworkings of the various private journals (reading notebooks; personal diaries; written meditations, etc.) which Merton kept in voluminous number. Like all autobiographical writings, they were constructed and, at least to that degree, they were fictions. One can see just how much Merton worked on his journals before their publication by making even a superficial comparison between, say, *Vow of Conversation* which he did prepare for publication and the journals of his last year which are now in print but which he did not get to edit for his satisfaction. *Thomas Merton in Alaska* and *Woods, Shore, Desert* are thinner, less textured, than the ones he rewrote for publication. They were, as it were, "working notebooks" from which, had he lived, more finished journals would appear. Careful comparisons of the published works with unpublished or "unworked over" journal entries indicate the degree to which Merton repented thoughts written in the heat of the moment from ideas to which he gave firmer allegiance.

Journals, like journeys, are attempts to make sense of place and the self. Indeed, the autobiographical journal is a genre quite close to the American heart. That is why there is a little more than surface truth to Anthony Padovano's comparison of Merton's journal trajectory and its earlier American antecedents. Padavano writes: "It is intriguing to realize how closely Merton's work follows the conventions of Puritan autobiography. These required a description of wanton youthfulness, an adolescent conversion that does not endure, a mature commitment to faith, and a need to give witness by a written account that is part journal, part confession, and thoroughly didactic. Puritan autobiography, like *The Seven Storey Mountain,* works to dissipate illusion and to describe worldly life in stern and hostile terms. . . . Puritans were obsessed, as was Merton, with the need to get beyond the shadow and the disguise, to achieve sincerity, to clarify their perceptions of the world."[16]

Writing, then, for Merton (and especially his journal writing) must be linked to that project which we mentioned earlier: the search for the true self not *qua* self but the self in relationship to God. Merton's writing then, *pace* some of his critics, was an extension of his own understanding of monasticism. The fact that his published journals are constructed after the fact simply means that he tests and seeks a deeper understanding of what happens to him in his negotiations with God. Thus, the famous epiphany which

Merton describes in *Conjectures of a Guilty Bystander* (CGB 156) in which he describes an almost mystical moment of love and solidarity with people that happened to him at "Fourth and Walnut" in downtown Louisville is dated as happening in September. From his journal, there is a much abbreviated version of the same event as occurring in March of that year (1958). Is the *Conjectures* account then a poetic amplification as Michael Mott suggests?[17] That is one explanation. Another one is that the *Conjectures* account is a reflection of Merton's understanding of what happened to him that day—"a drawing out of the broader implications of an experience whose meaning and significance grew as Merton reflected on it."[18]

The point in short, is that the journal entries—apart from those which are raw and unedited like *The Alaskan Journal*—quite often reflect an experience refracted through the writer's continual attempt at "making sense" of and a deepening of what occurs to him in his contemplative life. It is in that reflective exercise that the roles of theologian, mystic, and writer converge.

One cannot leave a discussion of Thomas Merton as writer without some consideration of his role as poet. Well before Merton entered the monastery he was already attracted to, and began to write, poetry. During his lifetime he published nine volumes of poetry apart from his many translations and single offerings to various journals. After his death New Directions published the hefty *Collected Poems* (1977), and since then limited editions of other poems have also been put into print.

It would be beyond the scope of this work to comment at any length on Merton's poetic corpus but a few generalizations may be assayed which would not be out of place.

First, when one looks at the early volumes of poetry, especially those written in the 1940s, it is clear that Merton was a child of literary modernism. One hears the poetic voice and sees the literary conceits of the seventeenth century poets so beloved of the period. There is also the underlying voice of Gerard Manley Hopkins who was to be the subject of his never completed doctoral thesis and that of William Blake who was the subject of his M.A. thesis at Columbia in 1939. Furthermore, like every poet of his generation, he was under the influence of T.S. Eliot (whom he was still reading in his monastic days), continental voices like Lorca and Rilke, and Americans like Emily Dickinson and Walt Whitman.

The poetry of that period obeyed the conventions of tight rhyme schemes, strained for the metaphysical conceit, and found its inspiration, more frequently than not, in the wellsprings of his monastic *lectio* and the cycles of monastic life. In the volume *Tears of the Blind Lions* (1949), dedicated to Jacques Maritain, one finds beautiful lines like these quatrains:

> Suppose the dead could crown their wit
> With some intemperate exercise,
> Spring wine from their ivory
> Or roses from their eyes?
>
> Or if the wise would understand
> And the world without heart
> That the dead are not yet dead
> And that the living live apart
>
> And the Wounded are healing,
> Though in a place of flame.
> The sick in a great ship
> Are riding. They are riding home.
> ("A Responsory, 1948" in CP 219)

Such lyricism directed toward explicitly religious themes and under such direct poetic influences (one sees both Blake and Eliot in the above lines as well as the talismanic invocation of "wit" which renders homage to the metaphysicals) would give way in the late 1950s and the 1960s to poetry which would become increasingly more experimental and whose subject matter would more directly engage the concerns of the world. The two short publications of 1962, *Original Child Bomb* and *Hagia Sophia,* would attempt to create poetry in a prose format with the former utilizing a strategy as old as John Dos Passos' use of fragments of newspapers and books to reflect Merton's savagely ironical comments on atomic warfare.

By the late 1960s Merton would be writing book-length poems like the highly complex *Cables to the Ace* and *The Geography of Lograire* (both published in 1968) which would contain a mosaic-like mixture of lyric, prose fragment, extended meditation, and arcane allusion to serve as a vehicle to condense his both omnivorous reading and his increasingly ecumenical cast of mind.

Of his poetry of social protest there is little need to comment. Merton, as we have noted, saw his life as a monk as a life of protest, so there is no reason to think that there was anything incongruous in his poetic vocation being directed toward the horrors of modern life. He wished to do what he could do best: which was to say "No!" both in his life and in his poetry.

But what of those more esoteric flights of poetic imagination? What did they mean to him? Merton himself saw them as part of the large poetic task in which a "poet spends his life in repeated projects, over and over again, attempting to build or to dream a world in which he lives" (GL 1).

There is a further clue, I think, to be found in something Merton wrote about some calligraphies which he did in the 1960s. These gestural works of pen and ink on paper were exhibited at a number of galleries. Merton commented on the "meaning" of these calligraphies or, as he variously called them, these abstractions or graffiti or writings by saying: "No need to characterize these marks. It is better if they remain unidentified vestiges, signatures of someone who is not around. If these drawings are able to persist in a certain autonomy and fidelity, they may continue to awaken possibilities, consonances; they may dimly help to alter one's perceptions. Or they may quietly and independently continue to invent themselves. Such is the 'success' they may aspire to. Doubtless there is more ambition than modesty in such an aim" (RU 182).

Such sentiments, teasingly Zenlike and cryptic in tone, allusive in character, and dense in possibility, seem to me just the note with which to approach the late poetry of Merton. In *Cables to the Ace* he said as much: "I think poetry must/I think it must/stay open all night/In beautiful cellars" (CP 431).

MERTON THE SOCIAL CRITIC

Much of the conventional wisdom about Thomas Merton insists that his greatest significance derives from his *persona* as a critic of racial injustice and as a spokesperson for peace and a voice against militarism and atomic warfare. In the 1960s he was increasingly identified with the civil rights movement and with many different facets of the anti-war and anti-nuclear groups that were active both in this country and abroad. It is worth noting that one of the first full-length dissertations written on his work (and while he was still alive) chose his role as a social critic as the focus of the study.[19]

By background and instinct, Merton was interested in these issues. His own mother was a Quaker. As a young man fresh out of Columbia he not only wanted to declare for the status of conscientious objector when faced with the draft but struggled in the same period over whether he should devote his energies to working with the poor in Harlem as a member of Catherine De Hueck's Friendship House. He, in fact, spent his last summer in New York working for the baroness in Harlem before entering the monastery.

In the 1960s, encouraged by the writings of Pope John XXIII (especially *Pacem in Terris*) and increasing church involvement with peace and racial justice issues (and not without resistance from ecclesiastical authorities both in and outside the order) Merton turned his pen more frequently to the burning social questions of the day. The first fruit of this interest can be seen in works he either wrote or edited. In the 1960s there came *Original Child Bomb* (1962), *Breakthrough to Peace* (1962), *Seeds of Destruction* (1964), *Gandhi on Non-violence* (1965), and *Faith and Violence* (1968), as well as any number of essays, broadsides, poems, and appeals which would see later publication.[20]

Along with his writing, Merton participated, as best he could given his cloistered life, with groups of peace activists, either by direct meeting or through correspondence. The first volume of his published correspondence under the title of *The Hidden Ground of Love* (1985) provides us with a panoramic view of his activities in this area. There are letters to activists, Vietnamese Buddhist monks, and public figures like Coretta Scott King, as well as a generous selection of his so-called "Cold War Letters" which was Merton's ruse (the use of circular letters to various and sundry people) to get around the publication restrictions placed upon him by those ecclesiastical authorities who found his writings in this area as unseemly for a cloistered religious. The "Cold War Letters" are, in short, a kind of religio-ethical *samidzat* not unlike the mimeographed essays circulated by Teilhard De Chardin (died 1955) when open publication was forbidden him by church superiors.

There is no need to rehearse Merton's involvement with these issues since they have been exhaustively chronicled in the standard biographies. What is important, however, is to emphasize something about this activity to which we made mention in the beginning of this essay: Merton did not understand (nor should we) this form of activism as peripheral to (much less incompatible with) his monastic vocation. Indeed, as he evolved and refined his understanding of what it meant to be a monk, he became more convinced that his very life should be an icon that both said something about the way one lives and about how one should not live.

Fuga mundi—the old ascetic notion that one should "flee the world"—may be understood as either a rejection of the world in order to live a life indifferent to it or it may be understood as a flight from the world as a way of protesting the way the world lives. If Merton entered the monastery with the former paradigm in mind (which he surely did), it was the latter that became more central to his thinking as he groped for a deeper understanding of what it meant to be a monk. In a 1966 letter to some Latin American students he wrote: "I live my own form of protest which is a matter of solitude and irony" (RJ 339). A year later, in a letter in response to an invitation to speak, he wrote to an American student in words that formally link his social action with his eremetical life: "I . . . am living as a hermit now, partly as a protest against the kind of society we have. For me to come out of the woods for public appearances would tend to neutralize that protest . . ." (RJ 259).

One might dismiss these sentiments as either quixotic or posturing if it were not for the fact that Merton had thought about these issues long and hard in terms of the monastic tradition in general and his own monastic vocation in particular. In the preface to his collection of essays entitled *Seeds of Destruction* he described the monastic flight from the world (*fuga mundi*) not as "a mere refusal to know anything about the world, but a total rejection of all standards of judgment which imply attachment to a history of delusion, egoism, and sin" (SD xii–xiii). In subsequent essays Merton attempts to think about the monk in terms of the modern Christian diaspora and the sign value of such a life when Christians themselves are increasingly at the periphery of culture. In a tribute to Gandhi he underscores how Gandhi's life—seemingly insignificant given the enormity of India's millions and Britain's colonial power—acted as a "small disquieting question mark" (SD 222).

The gestural power of a figure like Gandhi did not exist in isolation for Merton. Like others of like mind, he saw Gandhi in tandem with Tolstoy and Thoreau and, in his own day, with Martin Luther King, Jr. In those figures he recognized the power of witness and the deeper power of truth which gave witness its warrant.[21] Indeed, in many of his writings, Merton would look to these paradigmatic figures not only for the quality of their existential witness but because he saw in them the playing out of certain values (not excluding monastic ones) in which authentically converted lives were worked out. Here, for example, is Merton on Albert Camus: "The work of Camus is a humanism rooted in man as authentic value, in life which is to be affirmed in the face of suffering and death, in love, compassion, and understanding, the solidarity of men in revolt against the absurd, men whose comradeship has a certain purity because it is based on the renunciation of all illusions, all misleading ideals, all deceptive and hypocritical social forms" (LE 186).

To understand Thomas Merton as a social critic is one valid approach to his life and work, but it is a very incomplete one if that social criticism is made to stand as an independent career understood apart from his own firm, yet evolving, monastic commitment. It may well have taken Merton years to understand fully how he could merge his contemplative life with a deep compassion for the world, and it may be equally true that he came down overly hard on the contemplative separation from the world in the first flush of his monastic life. Nonetheless, it is equally true that he tried various strategies to overcome the gap. His problem was not uniquely his; it was a theological problem endemic in pre-conciliar Catholicism of how to understand the chasm and the bond between nature and super-nature. His early emphasis on *fuga mundi* does not belie the fact that he could forget the world. Commenting on Merton's *Secular Journal* (written prior to his entrance into Gethsemani but published long after he became a monk) Joseph Chinnici observes something with which I am in agreement: "Merton also expressed an intuition that the poor, the monastery, the hermitage, and the life of children were somehow interconnected in the life of holiness. It was in these places that 'angels appeared' and he clearly wanted to find a place where all these experiences could be united."[22]

In the intervening years the vocabulary and the social setting changed but Merton's basic orientation did not. He went to the monastery in 1941 at least partially out of disgust with the world (as well as self-disgust); he stayed the monastic course for the same reason, but later his concept of the world changed. His life was to be a "No!" to everything that hid the beauty of that world as it came from the hands of God and had been redeemed in Christ.

Merton's view of monasticism as a "No" to the world may seem terribly modern until one remembers that the first anchorites (*anchorein* means "to withdraw" in Greek) fled to the desert, at least in part, as a protest against the oppression and decadence of Roman culture. Merton may have been viewed as a "progressive" in his day but he was, in fact, in the process of retrieving something very primordial in the monastic tradition. Early monastic literature is filled with praise for the harmonic life of the desert as a contrast to the fleshpots of the city; it was a life, as Athanasius said in his famous *Life of Antony,* where people lived in peace with even the lower animals free of that living symbol of Roman decadence—the tax collector!

MERTON AND THE EAST

No discussion of Thomas Merton would be complete without some consideration of his deep interest in, and contacts with, the religious traditions of the east. Those interests were long-standing.

Readers of *The Seven Storey Mountain* will remember Merton's friendship with a Hindu ascetic M.B. Bramachari. It was Bramachari who answered Merton's queries about eastern mysticism with the suggestion that he begin with something closer to home by first acquainting himself with western classics like *The Confessions* of Saint Augustine and *The Imitation of Christ.* The circle of this friendship would not close until 1968 when Merton, on his fateful trip to Asia, attempted to meet Bramachari who he believed had an ashram near Calcutta. The meeting was not to be, but as late as 1965 he was in irregular contact with his early spiritual mentor.[23]

Merton's greatest interest, however, was in the Zen tradition of Buddhism, an interest which he explored through his contacts with the Christian Asian Studies expert, John C.H. Wu who taught at Seton Hall University in New Jersey and his long dialogue with the eminent Zen scholar, D.T. Suzuki. With the collaboration of the former, Merton did an "interpretation" of the Chinese writer Chuang Tzu [*The Way of Chuang Tzu* (New York: New Directions, 1965)] while the influence of the latter is evident in two volumes Merton published in this area: *Mystics and Zen Masters* (New York: Farrar, Straus, and Giroux, 1967) and *Zen and the Birds of Appetite* (New York: New Directions, 1968).

It is not difficult to see how an open person like Merton might become attracted to this tradition. Aesthetically, the Zen emphasis on spareness, simplicity, indirection, and purity would provide a natural gravitational pull to anyone attracted to the Cistercian aesthetic which, in its historical beginnings, stressed the same values as a protest against the phantasmagorical excesses of the Romanesque in general and Cluniac monasticism in particular. In fact, it is that very Cistercian aesthetic, I think, which provides a context for understanding Merton's love for the minimalist abstractions of his friend Ad Reinhardt as well as his appreciation for oriental calligraphy, Shaker architecture, and the gestural art of Paul Klee.[24]

Secondly, Zen, if it was nothing else, was contemplative in its worldview and, further, strongly biased toward that imageless strain of contemplation which has strong affinities with the apophatic tradition of the west. For Merton, this had a double attraction. First, Zen might well shed light on the western contemplative tradition from the point of view of technique alone. A good deal of Merton's writings dealt with correspondences between, for example, the Zen *koan* and the epigrammatic sayings of the desert fathers and mothers or the emptiness of the Zen experience and the mystical metaphysics of Meister Eckhart. Beyond that, the Zen desire for self-emptying might aid the Christian in understanding that self-emptying which is incumbent on every believer who wishes to follow "Christ in his kenosis" (WCT 15 *et passim*).[25]

When Merton made his fateful trip to the Far East in 1968 he had behind him nearly two decades of intense study of Buddhism, the Sufi tradition of Islam, and, to a lesser degree, Hinduism. We have already noted that he saw his own monastic life as inextricably bound up with his studious and existential dialogue with these great traditions. Indeed, I think I would be in agreement with those scholars who argue that at this stage of his life he was reaching for a deeper communion of mysticism that made him radically open to the presence of the Spirit in the world. His life was, to borrow the fine phrase of Walter Conn, in a state of "continual conversion" toward the absolute ground of existence as well as a sense of compassion for the world.[26]

Reading the *Asian Journal* might tempt the unwary reader into thinking that Merton had gone beyond Christianity into some kind of *philosophia perennis* decked out in Buddhist language and Christian allusions. Indeed, not a few commentators have seen him precisely as making that move. My own judgment is that such an interpretation is overly facile.[27] What does seem clear to me is that we have a new kind of monk who is in the process of extending the boundaries of the contemplative life. He recognizes levels of spiritual development which are "universally recognizable," yet "Cultural and doctrinal differences must remain, but they do not invalidate a very real quality of existential likeness" (AJ 312). In that search, Merton stands in the line of a entire tradition of twentieth century seekers (one thinks of Henri LeSaux, Bede Griffiths, Aelred Graham, William Johnston, Raimundo Panikkar, etc.) who have sought to bridge the spiritual traditions of the east and west.

It is that religious dimension of life that is "universally recognizable" after which Merton sought in his monastic life generally and on his Asian pilgrimage in particular. In a paragraph at the end of the talk he gave in Thailand, only hours before his death, he summed up in a few short sentences what that search was all about both for him and for his monastic tradition: "And I believe that by openness to Buddhism and Hinduism and to those other great Asian traditions, we stand a wonderful chance of learning more about the potentiality of our own traditions, because they have gone, from the natural point of view, so much deeper into this than we have. The combination of the natural techniques and the graces and the other things that have been manifested in Asia and the Christian liberty of the Gospel should bring all of us at last to that full and transcendent liberty which is beyond mere cultural differences and mere externals—and mere this and that. I will conclude on that note. I believe the plan is to have all the questions for this morning's lectures this evening at the panel. So I will disappear" (AJ 343).[28]

THE SPIRITUAL MASTER

Throughout these pages I have insisted that Thomas Merton is best understood from the starting point of his own monasticism. When, however, we respond to him—at least those of us who are not monks—it is not his monasticism but the quality of his life and his "teaching" (it is hard to separate those two things) that most attracts us. It is for that reason that I have borrowed the term "spiritual master" which Dom Flavian Burns, Merton's last abbot and now a hermit, ascribes to him. Dom Flavian had in mind the spiritual master or father who nourishes a younger aspirant in the way of the spiritual life.[29]

The term *master* is not to be understood in terms of dominance/dominated (e.g. Hegel's paradigm of "master/slave") but in the older, more etymologically correct understanding of master (Lat. *magister* perhaps ultimately from *magnus*—"great") as a teacher who—to give both meanings of the term—has mastered a body of doctrine or a way of life. In a sense, Merton did both: he mastered a way of living which is called monastic while, in turn, using his example and his pen as a way of passing on that life to others, both monks (remember that he was both *master* of novices and *master* of studies at the abbey in Gethsemani) and those who were not called to the cloister.

To be a master of novices or scholastics is, of course, a title of appointment, and Merton held those titles in his years at Gethsemani. What Flavian Burns was reaching for, however, is that deeper sense of the spiritual master: one who has learned the spiritual way with such experiential exactitude that he or she is able to guide others on that path and serve as an exemplar or paradigm for those committed to its journey.

To understand Merton as a spiritual master helps explain the wide-ranging influence that he had over people both in his own lifetime and now more than twenty years after his death. Anyone who has spoken at the many Merton conferences over the years (like those held on the tenth and twentieth anniversaries of his death or at the meetings of the International Thomas Merton Society) comes away amazed at the diversity of people who come and the reasons that bring them: there are religious who found their vocations through his example, people of varied religious persuasions who find in his writings an anchor for their spiritual life, creative folks—artists, musicians, poets—who feel nurtured by his example, and "seekers" who think that he may provide clues for a deeper and fuller life. Such people are, variously, committed to institutional forms of Christianity or at its margins or completely away from them. Merton speaks to them as he did in his own lifetime. One reads through his published correspondence to find him encouraging teenagers, sharing ideas of the spiritual life with a Pakistani Sufi, engaged in mutual encouragement with peace activists of every (and no) religious persuasion, exchanging poetry from people of different continents, in dialogue with fellow monastics, artists, theologians, and occasional writers.

In all this correspondence one hears, as a kind of *cantus firmus,* the traditional monastic preoccupations with the role of silence, the place of purity of intention, the need for contemplative study, and the constant refinement of the search for a deep center and ground for personal and social existence.

The very fact that these resonances are so deep in Merton's

writings made selections for this volume a difficult chore. One could argue that almost all of his published writing derives from his self-understanding as a monk/contemplative. That is the argument that was advanced above. Nonetheless, there are certain writings which are so patently engaged with the subject of the human relationship to God that they deserve pride of place in a volume such as this. There was no intention of attempting a general anthology of his writings. That was done, aided by Merton himself, in *The Thomas Merton Reader.*

We will say a word about each of the selections at the appropriate place, but we should say, at this place, that it is the concept of Merton as a spiritual master which underlies the selections in this work. We have reproduced little of his poetry and none of his letters (they are not, of this writing, fully published) and have been very sparing in representing his literary essays despite the vast bulk of them that make up the collected *Literary Essays* and the occasional pieces which he wrote on a variety of subjects. In all of those writings, as we have argued, one can detect—at times, faintly—the spiritual writer but our intention was to choose those essays which *ex professo* deal with the spiritual life and its implications.

On the positive side the criterion that was foremost was this: Does this piece represent Merton, the spiritual master, at his best? The danger in using that criterion is, as is obvious, that there were so many sides to Merton that his spiritual appeal may have come in a variety of genres. Fellow monastics may find more in his essays on that life than, say, a person of a literary bent who finds much in the *Collected Poems.*

My strategy, to combat idiosyncratic choices, was a simple if somewhat impressionistic one. I put down a list of essays/selections about which there would be general unanimity. The "Fire Watch" from *The Sign of Jonas,* for example, is singled out by every person who has read Merton (as it was by no less a personage than Jacques Maritain) as one of his most powerful prose compositions. It also seemed clear that a range of selections from the *ex professo* autobiographical writings was necessary since, as was noted earlier, he was profoundly an autobiographical writer. I then added to that list those essays to which I have always returned.

With that list in hand I turned both to recognized experts on Merton and to people whom I met on this or that occasion who read him and/or were influenced by his writings and showed them my selections. My queries would follow: Is this representative? What would you strike off? What would you add? Is there a selection which is missing which absolutely must be added? Is there anything that could be struck off in trade? It was from that first selection on my part and from the hospitable aid of many people that the final shape of these entries took place.

One final note on selection: I did not want to replicate, as I said, the estimable *A Thomas Merton Reader* which has served so well as a first introduction to Merton. That anthology has a far wider range of selections but many of them are very abbreviated. My goal was to produce a shorter list of longer selections focused almost exclusively on the spiritual life with the hope that the reader (a) will get a sense of the coherence of Merton's thought and (b) will abandon this anthology in order to read Merton whole.

I am left, then, with the happy task of giving due recognition to those who have aided me in my work while, at the same moment, absolving them of any responsibility for what appears in this volume.

First of all, I would like to thank the Trustees of the Thomas Merton Literary Trust for their cooperation while this work was in progress. Second, I would like to thank the monastic community of The Abbey of Our Lady of Gethsemani for their hospitality over the years. Third, I would like to thank the director of the Thomas Merton Study Center at Bellarmine College, Robert Daggy, for his friendship and help.

A special word of thanks must go to Brother Patrick Hart, O.C.S.O. who has been a true friend over the years. Monsignor William Shannon has been exceedingly generous with his advice on Merton matters. Conversations with Michael Mott and Ping Ferry have helped me enormously in understanding Merton, as have conversations with George Kilcourse, David Cooper, Paul Wilkes, Thomas O'Meara, O.P., E. Glenn Hinson, Dewey and Victor Kramer, Peter Kountz, Anthony Padovano, Richard Hauser, S.J., Bonnie Thurston, Doug Burton Christie, and Elena Malits, C.S.C.

I would also like to express my appreciation to the department of theology and its chair, Rev. Prof. Richard McBrien, for providing such a congenial place within which to work and teach.

Finally, a word of appreciation is extended to Kevin Lynch, the publisher of Paulist Press, Don Brophy, my editor, and the individuals who helped prepare this book for publication.

This volume, as always, is for the three women in my life: Cecilia, Sarah Mary, and Julia Clare.

Notes

1. The story of this publishing phenomenon has been brilliantly told in Robert Giroux's "Editing *The Seven Storey Mountain,*" *America* (October 22, 1988), pp. 273–276. Merton's book would eventually sell 600,000 copies in the American hardback edition. It was published in England under the title *Elected Silence* with cuts made by the English novelist, Evelyn Waugh.

2. The standard bibliography is Marquita Breit and Robert Daggy, eds., *Thomas Merton: A Comprehensive Bibliography—New Edition* (New York: Garland, 1986). The entries of "short prose" alone has 1,263 items! The Breit/Daggy bibliography replaces Frank Dell'Isola's *Thomas Merton: A Bibliography* (New York: Farrar, Straus, and Cudahy, 1956).

3. The four issues (rare items) have recently been reprinted: *Monk's Pond,* edited with an introduction by Robert E. Daggy (Lexington: University Presses of Kentucky, 1989). Among the contributors were Ad Reinhardt, Louis Zukovsky, Jack Kerouac, Wendell Berry, Hayden Carruth, and Robert Lax.

4. Written between 1966–1968, Merton's essays on Camus can be found in *The Literary Essays of Thomas Merton,* edited by Brother Patrick Hart (New York: New Directions, 1981), pp. 181–304. On the importance of these essays for Merton, see David D. Cooper, *Thomas Merton's Art of Denial: The Evolution of a Radical Humanist* (Athens: University of Georgia Press, 1989), pp. 208ff.

5. Aelred Graham, O.S.B., "Thomas Merton: A Modern Man in Reverse," *Atlantic* 191 (January 1953), pp. 70–74.

6. Aidan Kavanaugh, *On Liturgical Theology* (New York: Pueblo, 1983), pp. 6–7. For a history of Merton's own order, the standard work is Louis Lekai's *The Cistercians: Ideals and Reality* (Kent State: Kent State University Press, 1977). The handiest survey of Christian monasticism is still David Knowles' *Christian Monasticism* (New

York: McGraw-Hill, 1969); the classic study of monastic culture is Jean Leclercq's *The Love of Learning and the Desire for God: A Study of Monastic Culture,* 3rd edition (New York: Fordham University Press, 1985).

7. A fuller account of the visit between Merton and Suzuki may be found in *Encounter: Thomas Merton and D.T. Suzuki,* edited by Robert E. Daggy (Monterey: Larkspur, 1988).

8. I first unburdened myself on this topic in "Thomas Merton as Theologian: An Appreciation," *The Kentucky Review* VII (Summer 1987), pp. 90–97. There are also valuable suggestions in William Shannon's essay "Thomas Merton and the Living Tradition of Faith," *The Merton Annual* I (New York: AMS, 1988), pp. 79–102 and Anne Carr's *A Search For Wisdom and Spirit: Thomas Merton's Theology of the Self* (Notre Dame: University of Notre Dame Press, 1988), p. 3 *et passim.*

9. Luigi Sabetti's *Compendium Theologia Moralis* (1884) and Adolphe Tanquerey's *Synopsis Theologiae Dogmaticae* 2 vols. (1894) went through many editions and were used widely in American seminaries.

10. This is not to deny that Thomism and the metaphysics of Esse had a profound impact on him. It did, and his debt to writers like Jacques Maritain, Etienne Gilson, and his own teacher Daniel Walsh is often acknowledged by Merton, especially in his writings in the 1940s and 1950s. Philosophy is one thing; theology quite another.

11. The first instance of Merton's use of this quote that I have found is in his introduction to Raissa Maritain's *Notes on the Lord's Prayer* (New York: Kenedy, 1964).

12. Jean Leclercq, "Theologie traditionelle et theologie monastique," *Irenikon* XXXVII (1964), pp. 50–74. A summary of that article, by the same author, may be found in the article "Theology and Prayer," *New Catholic Encyclopedia* XIV (Washington, D.C.: The Catholic University of America, 1967), pp. 64–65. In the glossary to Irenee Hausherr's *Spiritual Direction in the Christian East* (Kalamazoo: Cistercian Publications, 1990), *theologia* is defined "in the mystical sense, the contemplation of things divine, the highest degree of the spiritual life (ascent), after *praxis* and *theoria physike* (natural understanding, or an understanding of creation, in God)." For a full discussion of this tradition, see: Andrew Louth, *The Origins of the Christian Mystical Tradition* (Oxford: Clarendon, 1981).

13. A reproduction of this graph may be found in the second appendix of

Robert Daggy's edition of Merton's prefaces recently reprinted under the title *Honourable Reader: Reflections on My Work* (New York: Crossroad, 1989).

14. I am grateful to Monsignor William Shannon for pointing out this letter to me (as of this writing, unpublished) and the reading journal entry discussed with it.

15. Elena Malits, *The Solitary Explorer: Thomas Merton's Transforming Journey* (San Francisco: Harper and Row, 1980), especially pp. 139ff. On this theme, two other excellent works should be cited: William H. Shannon, *Thomas Merton's Dark Path,* rev. ed. (New York: Farrar, Straus, and Giroux, 1987); Anne E. Carr, *A Search For Wisdom and Spirit: Thomas Merton's Theology of the Self* (Notre Dame: University of Notre Dame Press, 1988).

16. Anthony Padovano, *The Human Journey: Thomas Merton Symbol of a Century* (Garden City: Doubleday, 1982), pp. 5–6. Padovano also has some striking parallels to make with that most autobiographical of nineteenth century converts, John Henry Newman. Behind both figures, of course, is the *fons et origo* of the genre: Augustine's *Confessions.*

17. Mott, p. 311.

18. William H. Shannon, *Thomas Merton's Dark Path,* 2nd edition (New York: Farrar, Straus, & Giroux), p. xiii.

19. Originally a dissertation at the Florida State University, it was later published as a book: James Baker, *Thomas Merton: Social Critic* (Lexington: University of Kentucky Press, 1971). Baker first knew Merton while he was a student at the Southern Baptist Seminary in Louisville. His book, the first full-length study of Merton, was read by the monk in manuscript.

20. The most useful collection of Merton writings in this area is *Thomas Merton: The Nonviolent Alternative,* edited by Gordon Zahn (New York: Farrar, Straus, and Giroux, 1980). Also, see Frederic Joseph Kelly, S.J., *Man Before God: Thomas Merton on Social Responsibility* (Garden City: Doubleday, 1974).

21. See the fine study of Brother John Albert, O.C.S.O., "Lights Across the Ridge: Henry David Thoreau and Thomas Merton," in *The Merton Annual* I (New York: AMS, 1988), pp. 271–320, esp. pp. 298ff. on this tradition of dissent.

22. Joseph P. Chinnici, O.F.M., *Living Stones: The History and Structure of Catholic Spiritual Life in the United States* (New York: Macmillan, 1989), p. 207. Chinnici is commenting on Merton's indeci-

sion in 1941 about whether he should enter a monastery or work at a Harlem Settlement House.

23. One letter from Merton to Bramachari survives from the 1960s (see RJ 122–123). The monk's name is correctly spelled *Brahmacari* but I follow the usage of Merton and his circle who invariably spell it as I have it in the text. Merton mentions seeking out his ashram in Calcutta in AJ 131.

24. See Lawrence S. Cunningham, "The Black Painting in the Hermit Hatch: A Note on Thomas Merton and Ad Reinhardt," *The Merton Seasonal* 11 (Autumn 1986), pp. 10–12. Merton's aesthetic was, however, a complex and not always consistent one, as David Cooper's *Thomas Merton's Art of Denial* (Athens: University of Georgia, 1989), pp. 89ff, amply demonstrates.

25. On kenosis, see Mott, pp. 507ff and Carr, pp. 79ff.

26. Walter Conn, *Christian Conversion* (Mahwah: Paulist, 1986), pp. 158–268. These final chapters of Conn's work constitute a detailed study of Merton's spiritual growth under the rubric of developmental theory. They repay a close reading.

27. See Lawrence S. Cunningham, "Crossing Over in the Late Writings of Thomas Merton," in *Towards an Integrated Humanity: Thomas Merton's Journey,* edited by M. Basil Pennington, O.C.S.O. (Kalamazoo: Cistercian Publications, 1987), pp. 192–203.

28. The phrases "natural point of view" and "natural techniques" indicate that either (a) Merton was still imprisoned in the old nature/supernature language of late scholasticism or (b) he did not want to scandalize some of the more conservative members of his audience who were largely Christian contemplatives.

29. In his funeral homily for Merton's funeral, Abbot Flavian said, "Those of us who had the privilege and pleasure to deal with Father Louis [Merton's religious name] on intimate terms and submit our inner lives to his direction, knew that in him we had the best of spiritual masters." Quoted in the epilogue to *Thomas Merton, Monk,* edited by Patrick Hart, O.C.S.O. (Garden City: Doubleday Image, 1976), p. 219. For the historical background, see the classic work of Irenee Hausheer, S.J., *Spiritual Direction in the Early Christian East* (Kalamazoo: Cistercian Publications, 1990).

Works Cited in the Introduction

AJ   *The Asian Journal of Thomas Merton,* edited by Naomi Burton, Brothers Patrick Hart and James Laughlin (New York: New Directions, 1973)

CGB   *Conjectures of a Guilty Bystander* (Garden City: Image, 1968)

CP   *Collected Poems* (New York: New Directions, 1977)

CPR   *Contemplative Prayer* (Garden City: Image, 1971)

CWA   *Contemplation in a World Of Action* (Garden City: Image, 1973)

GL   *The Geography of Lograire* (New York: New Directions, 1968)

HGR   *The Hidden Ground of Love: The Letters of Thomas Merton on Religious Experience and Social Concern,* edited by William H. Shannon (New York: Farrar, Straus, and Giroux, 1985)

HR   *Honorable Reader: Reflections on My Work,* edited by Robert E. Daggy (New York: Crossroad, 1989)

LE   *The Literary Essays of Thomas Merton,* edited by Brother Patrick Hart (New York: New Directions, 1981)

RJ   *The Road to Joy: The Letters of Thomas Merton to Old and New Friends,* edited by Robert E. Daggy (New York: Farrar, Straus & Giroux, 1988)

RU   *Raids on the Unspeakable* (New York: New Directions, 1964)

SC   *The School of Charity: The Letters of Thomas Merton on Religious Renewal and Spiritual Direction,* edited by Patrick Hart, O.C.S.O. (New York: Farrar, Straus & Giroux, 1990)

SD   *Seeds of Destruction* (New York: Farrar, Straus & Giroux, 1964)

SJ   *The Sign of Jonas* (Garden City: Image, 1956)

SSM   *The Seven Storey Mountain* (Garden City: Image, 1970)

TMR   *The Thomas Merton Reader,* 2nd edition (Garden City: Image, 1974)

VC   *A Vow of Conversation* (New York: Farrar, Straus & Giroux, 1988)

WCZ   *The Way of Chaung Tzu* (New York: New Directions, 1965)

CHRONOLOGY OF MERTON'S LIFE

1915	Born to Owen Merton and Ruth Jenkins Merton on January 31 in Prades, France.
1918	John Paul Merton born on November 2 in Flushing, New York where family had moved in 1916.
1921	Ruth Jenkins Merton dies in Bellevue Hospital (New York) of stomach cancer on October 3.
1922	Owen Merton takes his son, Thomas, to Bermuda.
1925	After a brief return to New York, Thomas Merton returns to France with his Father. He is enrolled in a French school at Montaubon (*Lycee Ingres*).
1928	Owen Merton removes Thomas from school and leaves for England where he has some success in selling his paintings.
1929	Enrolled in Oakham—an English public school.
1931	Owen Merton dies in Middlesex Hospital (London) on January 18.
1932	Wins a scholarship for entrance to Clare College at the University of Cambridge.
1933	Makes a summer tour to Rome and a visit to the United States; matriculates to Cambridge for the fall term.
1934	Leaves Cambridge (and England) abruptly after some mysterious events which probably involved an (unnamed) pregnant woman.
1935	Enters Columbia University in New York City. Begins to write for *Jester* and later becomes its art editor. Begins friendship with Robert Lax, Edward Rice, Ad Reinhardt and Sy Freedgood.
1936	Maternal grandfather dies.
1937	Paternal grandfather dies. Becomes editor of Columbia University Yearbook.
1938	Receives BA from Columbia in February; begins study

for an MA with a proposed thesis on William Blake. In the fall, enrolls in a course in St. Thomas Aquinas under Dan Walsh. At the suggestion of a Hindu guru Bramachari, begins to read *The Confessions* of Saint Augustine and *The Imitation of Christ*. On November 16 he is received into the Catholic Church at Corpus Christi Parish in New York City; Ed Rice is his sponsor.

1939   Receives MA in February. Makes plans to go on for doctorate with a dissertation on Gerard Manley Hopkins. Tries, without success, to publish a novel. Thinks about studying for the priesthood; takes first steps to join Franciscans. April/May '40, leaves for a trip in Cuba.

1940   Is turned down as a candidate for the Franciscans (due to his Cambridge past?). Accepts a job as an instructor in English at Saint Bonaventure's College (later a university) for the fall term.

1941   Spends Holy Week in retreat at the Trappist monastery of Our Lady of Gethsemani at the suggestion of Dan Walsh. Works at Friendship House in Harlem under the inspiration of Baroness Catherine de Hueck (Doherty) during the summer. John Paul, his brother, joins the Royal Canadian Air Force in Toronto. On December 10, he enters Gethsemani to become a postulant in the Order of Cistercians of the Strict Observance.

1942   On February 21 receives the habit of a choir-monk novice and is given the religious name of M(ary) Louis. John Paul visits the monastery and is received into the Catholic Church after a short period of instruction.

1943   His brother is killed in action over Mannheim.

1944   Takes simple vows on the feast of Saint Joseph (March 19). *Thirty Poems* is published under his secular name. Given writing assignments by the abbot. A new foundation from Gethsemani is begun in Conyers, Georgia.

1946   Begins to think of a lyrical work but not "pure autobiography" to which he had already given the title *The Seven Storey Mountain* as a tribute to his love for

Dante. A manuscript is sent to his friend and agent, Naomi Burton, in October.

1947   Pronounces solemn vows on March 19. Rewrites his autobiography at suggestion of Robert Giroux; works on other books.

1948   *The Seven Storey Mountain* is published; by the following year it is a best seller and would eventually sell 600,000 copies in the American hardback edition.

1949   Ordained to the priesthood on Ascension Thursday, May 26.

1951   Appointed master of scholastics. Becomes an American citizen.

1952   Makes a private vow never to become a prior or an abbot of a monastery.

1953   *The Sign of Jonas* published. Interest in moving to a more contemplative life with Carthusians or Camaldolese increases as Gethsemani becomes more crowded and "busy" with work.

1955   Becomes master of novices.

1956   Begins intense interest in Latin American literature spurred by a possible foundation in Ecuador. Ernesto Cardenal, the Nicaraguan poet, is a novice under Merton's direction. Reads widely in Russian mystical literature.

1958   Experiences an "epiphany" at the corner of "Fourth and Walnut" (immortalized in *Conjectures of a Guilty Bystander*) in which he turns from a world-denying mysticism to one that embraces the needs of the world. In the autumn a correspondence with the Russian novelist Boris Pasternak begins.

1960   Hermitage built on monastery grounds to be used by Merton occasionally and to shelter retreatants for ecumenical discussions encouraged by events on the eve of the Second Vatican Council. Uses hermitage (for a few hours) on Saint Lucy's day, December 13, nineteen years after he entered Gethsemani as a postulant.

1961   Increasing interest in racial issues and pacifism (publishes prose-poem *Original Child Bomb*); rewrites what would be one of his spiritual classics, *New Seeds of*

Contemplation. Intensifies study of oriental religious thought and Shaker culture.

1963   Awarded an honorary doctorate of letters from the University of Kentucky which was accepted for him by his friend (and printer of some of his smaller books), Victor Hammer. The Merton Collection is opened at Bellarmine College in Louisville.

1964   Travels to New York to visit with the Zen scholar D.T. Suzuki. Begins experiments in calligraphy with encouragement of his old Columbia classmate, the abstract painter Ad Reinhardt. Organizes and participates in a retreat at Gethsemani on non-violence sponsored by the Fellowship of Reconciliation. Spends first full days/nights at hermitage. Pursues an interest in photography with encouragement of his friend John Howard Griffin.

1965   On the feast of Saint Bernard (August 20) moves permanently to hermitage; resigns as novice master. Involved with Catholic peace groups in opposition to war in Vietnam.

1966   Brief but intense romantic interlude with a student nurse, three decades his junior, from Louisville who cared for him when he had a back operation. Buddhist monk, Thich Nhat Hanh, visits monastery and makes enormous impression on Merton and community. On September 8 makes a life commitment to the eremitical life. Jacques Maritain visits abbey in October.

1967   Extensive literary studies; works on long experimental poem published as *The Geography of Lograire*. Establishes a literary trust to put his works in order. His long-time friend and former teacher, Dan Walsh, ordained to the diocesan priesthood on Pentecost Sunday. Abbot James Fox announces his resignation as abbot.

1968   Produces four issues of a "little magazine" under title of *Monk's Pond*. His former student Flavian Burns is elected abbot; James Fox becomes a hermit. Martin Luther King assassinated before he is able to make a promised visit to Gethsemani. Visits California, New

Mexico, and Alaska to visit monasteries and scout possible locations for new hermitages. Leaves abbey on September 10 on first leg of trip which would take him to the Far East for a meeting on interreligious monastic life in Bangkok. Visits Dalai Lama in northern India and great Buddhist shrines in Sri Lanka. On December 10 gives his paper at a session of the monastic meeting; that afternoon he is found dead of an apparent heart attack after having been accidentally electrocuted by a defective fan. It was twenty-seven years to the day after his departure from New York to enter Gethsemani. Funeral is held at Gethsemani on December 17 after his body had been brought back from Asia in an Air Force plane.

Autobiographical Writings

THE SEVEN STOREY MOUNTAIN

This selection from The Seven Storey Mountain, *chronicling Merton's life to the point where he seeks instruction in Catholicism, is valuable for its emphasis on themes which would be central to Merton's later life: the place of literature as a source of spiritual nourishment, the importance of his friends (especially Robert Lax) and his mentor Mark Van Doren, his deep concept of God as Being Itself (learned from Gilson), and his early introduction to mysticism both through Aldous Huxley's* Ends and Means *and, more importantly, through the saintly figure of Bramachari who would figure in Merton's later life.*

One also notes in this longish passage some of the criticisms which Merton himself would make of his earlier writings: a certain judgmental character about the world and an apologetic approach to Catholicism (natural enough in a convert). Be that as it may, there is still much to admire in Merton's re-creation of his college years in the tempetuous period before the Second World War.

Readers may wish to follow the friendship of Merton and Mark Van Doren by reading their correspondence; see Merton's letters in The Road to Joy, *edited by Robert Daggy (New York: Farrar, Straus, and Giroux, 1989) and the wonderful exchanges between Merton and Lax in* A Catch of Anti-Letters *(Kansas City: Sheed, Andrews, and McNeel, 1978).*

*

Now I come to speak of the real part Columbia seems to have been destined to play in my life in the providential designs of God. Poor Columbia! It was founded by sincere Protestants as a college predominantly religious. The only thing that remains of that is the university motto: *In lumine tuo videbimus lumen*—one of the deepest and most beautiful lines of the psalms. "In Thy light, we shall see light." It is, precisely, about grace. It is a line that might serve as the foundation stone of all Christian and Scholastic learning, and which simply has nothing whatever to do with the standards of education at modern Columbia. It might profitably be changed to *In lumine Randall videbimus Dewey.*

Yet, strangely enough, it was on this big factory of a campus that the Holy Ghost was waiting to show me the light, in His own light. And one of the chief means He used, and through which he operated, was human friendship.

God has willed that we should all depend on one another for our salvation, and all strive together for our own mutual good and our own common salvation. Scripture teaches us that this is especially true in the supernatural order, in the doctrine of the Mystical Body of Christ, which flows necessarily from Christian teaching on grace.

"You are the body of Christ and members one of another. . . . And the eye cannot say to the hand: I need not thy help: nor again the head to the feet, I have no need of you. . . . And if one member suffer anything, all the members suffer with it; and if one member glory all the others rejoice with it."

So now is the time to tell a thing that I could not realize then, but which has become very clear to me: that God brought me and a half a dozen others together at Columbia, and made us friends, in such a way that our friendship would work powerfully to rescue us from the confusion and the misery in which we had come to find ourselves, partly through our own fault, and partly through a complex set of circumstances which might be grouped together under the heading of the "modern world," "modern society." But the qualification "modern" is unnecessary and perhaps unfair. The traditional Gospel term, "the world," will do well enough.

All our salvation begins on the level of common and natural and ordinary things. (That is why the whole economy of the Sacraments, for instance, rests, in its material element, upon plain and ordinary things like bread and wine and water and salt and oil.) And so it was with me. Books and ideas and poems and stories, pictures and music, buildings, cities, places, philosophies were to be the materials on which grace would work. But these things are themselves not enough. The more fundamental instinct of fear for my own preservation came in, in a minor sort of a way, in this strange, half-imaginary sickness which nobody could diagnose completely.

The coming war, and all the uncertainties and confusions and fears that followed necessarily from that, and all the rest of the violence and injustice that were in the world, had a very important part to play. All these things were bound together and fused and vitalized and prepared for the action of grace, both in my own soul and in the souls of at least one or two of my friends, merely by our friendship and association together. And it fermented in our sharing of our own ideas and miseries and headaches and perplexities and fears and difficulties and desires and hangovers and all the rest.

I have already mentioned Mark Van Doren. It would not be exactly true to say that he was a kind of nucleus around whom this concretion of friends formed itself: that would not be accurate. Not all of us took his courses, and those who did, did not do so all at the same time. And yet nevertheless our common respect for Mark's sanity and wisdom did much to make us aware of how much we ourselves had in common.

Perhaps it was for me, personally, more than for the others, that Mark's course worked in this way. I am thinking of one particular incident.

It was the fall of 1936, just at the beginning of the new school year—on one of those first, bright, crazy days when everybody is full of ambition. It was the beginning of the year in which Pop was going to die and my own resistance would cave in under the load of pleasures and ambitions I was too weak to carry: the year in which I would be all the time getting dizzy, and in which I learned to fear the Long Island railroad as if it were some kind of a monster, and to shrink from New York as if it were the wide-open mouth of some burning Aztec god.

That day, I did not foresee any of this. My veins were still bursting with the materialistic and political enthusiasms with which I had first come to Columbia and, indeed, in line with their general direction, I had signed up for courses that were more or less sociological and economic and historical. In the obscurity of the strange, half-conscious semi-conversion that had attended my retreat from Cambridge, I had tended more and more to be suspicious of literature, poetry—the things towards which my nature drew me—on the grounds that they might lead to a sort of futile estheticism, a philosophy of "escape."

This had not involved me in any depreciation of people like Mark. However, it had just seemed more important to me that I should take some history course, rather than anything that was still left of his for me to take.

So now I was climbing one of the crowded stairways in Hamilton Hall to the room where I thought this history course was to be given. I looked in to the room. The second row was filled with the unbrushed heads of those who every day at noon sat in the *Jester* editorial offices and threw paper airplanes around the room or drew pictures on the walls.

Taller than them all, and more serious, with a long face, like a horse, and a great mane of black hair on top of it, Bob Lax meditated on some incomprehensible woe, and waited for someone to come in and begin to talk to them. It was when I had taken off my coat and put down my load of books that I found out that this was not the class I was supposed to be taking, but Van Doren's course on Shakespeare.

So I got up to go out. But when I got to the door I turned around again and went back and sat down where I had been, and stayed there. Later I went and changed everything with the registrar, so I remained in that class for the rest of the year.

It was the best course I ever had at college. And it did me the most good, in many different ways. It was the only place where I ever heard anything really sensible said about any of the things that were really fundamental—life, death, time, love, sorrow, fear, wisdom, suffering, eternity. A course in literature should never be a course in economics or philosophy or sociology or psychology: and I have explained how it was one of Mark's great virtues that he did not make it so. Nevertheless, the material of literature and especially of drama is chiefly human acts—that is, free acts, moral acts. And, as a matter of fact, literature, drama, poetry, make certain statements about these acts that can be made in no other way. That is precisely why you will miss all the deepest meaning of Shakespeare, Dante, and the rest if you reduce their vital and creative statements about life and men to the dry, matter-of-fact terms of history, or ethics, or some other science. They belong to a different order.

Nevertheless, the great power of something like *Hamlet, Coriolanus,* or the *Purgatorio* or Donne's *Holy Sonnets* lies precisely in the fact that they are a kind of commentary on ethics and psychology and even metaphysics, even theology. Or, sometimes, it is the other way 'round, and those sciences can serve as a commentary on these other realities, which we call plays, poems.

All that year we were, in fact, talking about the deepest springs of human desire and hope and fear; we were considering all the most important realities, not indeed in terms of something alien to Shakespeare and to poetry, but precisely in his own terms, with occasional intuitions of another order. And, as I have said, Mark's balanced and sensitive and clear way of seeing things, at once simple and yet capable of subtlety, being fundamentally scholastic, though not necessarily and explicitly Christian, presented these things in ways that made them live within us, and with a life that was healthy and permanent and productive. This class was one of the few things that could persuade me to get on the train and go to Columbia at all. It was, that year, my only health, until I came across and read the Gilson book.*

It was this year, too, that I began to discover who Bob Lax was, and that in him was a combination of Mark's clarity and my confusion and misery—and a lot more besides that was his own.

To name Robert Lax in another way, he was a kind of combination of Hamlet and Elias. A potential prophet, but without rage. A king, but a Jew too. A mind full of tremendous and subtle intuitions, and every day he found less and less to say about them, and resigned himself to being inarticulate. In his hesitations, though without embarrassment or nervousness at all, he would often curl his long legs all around a chair, in seven different ways, while he was trying to find a word with which to begin. He talked best sitting on the floor.

And the secret of his constant solidity I think has always been a kind of natural, instinctive spirituality, a kind of inborn direction

---

* *The Spirit of Medieval Philosophy* (ed.).

to the living God. Lax has always been afraid he was in a blind alley, and half aware that, after all, it might not be a blind alley, but God, infinity.

He had a mind naturally disposed, from the very cradle, to a kind of affinity for Job and St. John of the Cross. And I now know that he was born so much of a contemplative that he will probably never be able to find out how much.

To sum it up, even the people who have always thought he was "too impractical" have always tended to venerate him—in the way people who value material security unconsciously venerate people who do not fear insecurity.

In those days one of the things we had most in common, although perhaps we did not talk about it so much, was the abyss that walked around in front of our feet everywhere we went, and kept making us dizzy and afraid of trains and high buildings. For some reason, Lax developed an implicit trust in all my notions about what was good and bad for mental and physical health, perhaps because I was always very definite in my likes and dislikes. I am afraid it did not do him too much good, though. For even though I had my imaginary abyss, which broadened immeasurably and became ten times dizzier when I had a hangover, my ideas often tended to some particular place where we would hear this particular band and drink this special drink until the place folded up at four o'clock in the morning.

The months passed by, and most of the time I sat in Douglaston, drawing cartoons for the paper-cup business, and trying to do all the other things I was supposed to do. In the summer, Lax went to Europe, and I continued to sit in Douglaston, writing a long, stupid novel about a college football player who got mixed up in a lot of strikes in a textile mill.

I did not graduate that June, although I nominally belonged to that year's class: I had still one or two courses to take, on account of having entered Columbia in February. In the fall of 1937 I went back to school, then, with my mind a lot freer, since I was not burdened with any more of those ugly and useless jobs on the fourth floor. I could write and do the drawings I felt like doing for *Jester*.

I began to talk more to Lax and to Ed Rice who was now drawing better and funnier pictures than anybody else for the magazine. For the first time I saw Sy Freedgood, who was full of a fierce and complex intellectuality which he sometimes liked to present in the guise of a rather suspicious suavity. He was in love with a far more technical vocabulary than any of the rest of us possessed, and was working at something in the philosophy graduate school. Seymour used consciously to affect a whole set of different kinds of duplicity, of which he was proud, and he had carried the *mendacium jocosum* or "humorous lie" to its utmost extension and frequency. You could sometimes gauge the falsity of his answers by their promptitude: the quicker the falser. The reason for this was, probably, that he was thinking of something else, something very abstruse and far from the sphere of your question, and he could not be bothered to bring his mind all that way back, to think up the real answer.

For Lax and myself and Gibney there was no inconvenience about this, for two reasons. Since Seymour generally gave his false answers only to practical questions of fact, their falsity did not matter: we were all too impractical. Besides his false answers were generally more interesting than the truth. Finally, since we knew they were false anyway, we had the habit of seeing all his statements, in the common factual order by a kind of double standard, instituting a comparison between what he had said and the probable truth, and this cast many interesting and ironical lights upon life as a whole.

In his house at Long Beach, where his whole family lived in a state of turmoil and confusion, there was a large, stupid police dog that got in everybody's way with his bowed head and slapped-down ears and amiable, guilty look. The first time I saw the dog, I asked: "What's his name?"

"Prince," said Seymour, out of the corner of his mouth.

It was a name to which the beast responded gladly. I guess he responded to any name, didn't care what you called him, so flattered was he to be called at all, being as he knew an extremely stupid dog.

So I was out on the boardwalk with the dog, shouting: "Hey, Prince; hey, Prince!"

Seymour's wife, Helen, came along and heard me shouting all this and said nothing, imagining, no doubt, that it was some way I had of making fun of the brute. Later, Seymour or someone told me that "Prince" wasn't the dog's name, but they told me in such a way that I got the idea that his name was really "Rex." So for some time after that I called him: "Hey, Rex; hey, Rex!" Several months later, after many visits to the house, I finally learned that the dog was called nothing like Prince nor Rex, but "Bunky."

Moral theologians say that the *mendacium jocosum* in itself does not exceed a venial sin.

Seymour and Lax were rooming together in one of the dormitories, for Bob Gibney, with whom Lax had roomed the year before, had now graduated, and was sitting in Port Washington with much the same dispositions with which I had been sitting in Douglaston, facing a not too dissimilar blank wall, the end of his own blind-alley. He occasionally came in to town to see Dona Eaton who had a place on 112th Street, but no job, and was more cheerful about her own quandary than the rest of us, because the worst that could happen to her was that she would at last run completely out of money and have to go home to Panama.

Gibney was not what you would call pious. In fact, he had an attitude that would be commonly called impious, only I believe God understood well enough that his violence and sarcasms covered a sense of deep metaphysical dismay—an anguish that was real, though not humble enough to be of much use to his soul. What was materially impiety in him was directed more against common ideas and notions which he saw or considered to be totally inadequate, and maybe it subjectively represented a kind of oblique zeal for the purity of God, this rebellion against the commonplace and trite, against mediocrity, religiosity.

During the year that had passed, I suppose it must have been in the spring of 1937, both Gibney and Lax and Bob Gerdy had all been talking about becoming Catholics. Bob Gerdy was a very smart sophomore with the face of a child and a lot of curly hair on top of it, who took life seriously, and had discovered courses on Scholastic Philosophy in the graduate school, and had taken one of them.

Gibney was interested in Scholastic Philosophy in much the same way as James Joyce was—he respected its intellectuality, particularly that of the Thomists, but there was not enough that was affective about his interest to bring about any kind of a conversion.

For the three or four years that I knew Gibney, he was always holding out for some kind of a "sign," some kind of a sensible and tangible interior jolt from God, to get him started, some mystical experience or other. And while he waited and waited for this to come along, he did all the things that normally exclude and nullify the action of grace. So in those days, none of them became Catholics.

The most serious of them all, in this matter, was Lax: he was the one that had been born with the deepest sense of Who God was. But he would not make a move without the others.

And then there was myself. Having read *The Spirit of Medieval Philosophy* and having discovered that the Catholic conception of God was something tremendously solid, I had not progressed one step beyond this recognition, except that one day I had gone and looked up St. Bernard's *De Diligendo Deo* in the catalogue of the University Library. It was one of the books Gilson had frequently mentioned: but when I found that there was no good copy of it, except in Latin, I did not take it out.

Now it was November 1937. One day, Lax and I were riding downtown on one of those busses you caught at the corner of 110th Street and Broadway. We had skirted the southern edge of Harlem, passing along the top of Central Park, and the dirty lake full of rowboats. Now we were going down Fifth Avenue, under the trees. Lax was telling me about a book he had been reading which was Aldous Huxley's *Ends and Means*. He told me about it in a way that made me want to read it too.

So I went to Scribner's bookstore and bought it, and read it, and wrote an article about it, and gave the article to Barry Ulanov who was editor of *Review* by that time. He accepted the article with a big Greek smile and printed it. The smile was on account of the conversion it represented, I mean the conversion in me, as well as in Huxley, although one of the points I tried to make was that perhaps Huxley's conversion should not have been taken as so much of a surprise.

Huxley had been one of my favorite novelists in the days when I had been sixteen and seventeen and had built up a strange, ignorant philosophy of pleasure based on all the stories I was reading. And now everybody was talking about the way Huxley had changed. The chatter was all the more pleasant because of Huxley's agnostic old grandfather—and his biologist brother. Now the man was preaching mysticism.

Huxley was too sharp and intelligent and had too much sense of humor to take any of the missteps that usually make such conversions look ridiculous and oafish. You could not laugh at him, very well—at least not for any one concrete blunder. This was not one of those Oxford Group conversions, complete with a public confession.

On the contrary, he had read widely and deeply and intelligently in all kinds of Christian and Oriental mystical literature, and had come out with the astonishing truth that all this, far from being a mixture of dreams and magic and charlatanism, was very real and very serious.

Not only was there such a thing as a supernatural order, but as a matter of concrete experience, it was accessible, very close at hand, an extremely near, an immediate and most necessary source of moral vitality, and one which could be reached most simply, most readily by prayer, faith, detachment, love.

The point of his title was this: we cannot use evil means to attain a good end. Huxley's chief argument was that we were using the means that precisely made good ends impossible to attain: war, violence, reprisals, rapacity. And he traced our impossibility to use the proper means to the fact that men were immersed in the material and animal urges of an element in their nature which was blind and crude and unspiritual.

The main problem is to fight our way free from subjection to this more or less inferior element, and to reassert the dominance of our mind and will: to vindicate for these faculties, for the spirit as a whole, the freedom of action which it must necessarily have if we are to live like anything but wild beasts, tearing each other to pieces. And the big conclusion from all this was: we must practice prayer and asceticism.

Asceticism! The very thought of such a thing was a complete revolution in my mind. The word had so far stood for a kind of weird and ugly perversion of nature, the masochism of men who had gone crazy in a warped and unjust society. What an idea! To deny the desires of one's flesh, and even to practice certain disciplines that punished and mortified those desires: until this day, these things had never succeeded in giving me anything but goose-flesh. But of course Huxley did not stress the physical angle of mortification and asceticism—and that was right, in so far as he was more interested in striking to the very heart of the matter, and showing the ultimate positive principle underlying the need for detachment.

He showed that this negation was not something absolute, sought for its own sake: but that it was a freeing a vindication of our real selves, a liberation of the spirit from limits and bonds that were intolerable, suicidal—from a servitude to flesh that must ultimately destroy our whole nature and society and the world as well.

Not only that, once the spirit was freed, and returned to its own element, it was not alone there: it could find the absolute and perfect Spirit, God. It could enter into union with Him: and what is more, this union was not something vague and metaphorical, but it was a matter of real experience. What that experience amounted to, according to Huxley, might or might not have been the nirvana of the Buddhists, which is the ultimate negation of all experience and all reality whatever: but anyway, somewhere along the line, he quoted proofs that it was and could be a real and positive experience.

The speculative side of the book—its strongest—was full, no doubt, of strange doctrines by reason of its very eclecticism. And the practical element, which was weak, inspired no confidence, especially when he tried to talk about a concrete social program. Huxley seemed not to be at home with the Christian term "Love" which sounded extraordinarily vague in his contexts—and which must nevertheless be the heart and life of all true mysticism. But out of it all I took these two big concepts of a supernatural, spiritual order, and the possibility of real, experimental contact with God.

Huxley was thought, by some people, to be on the point of entering the Church, but *Ends and Means* was written by a man who was not at ease with Catholicism. He quoted St. John of the Cross and St. Teresa of Avila indiscriminately with less orthodox Christian writers like Meister Eckhart: and on the whole he preferred the Orient. It seems to me that in discarding his family's tradition of materialism he had followed the old Protestant groove back into the heresies that make the material creation evil of itself, although I do not remember enough about him to accuse him of formally holding such a thing. Nevertheless, that would account for his sympathy for Buddhism, and for the nihilistic character which he preferred to give to his mysticism and even to his ethics. This also made him suspicious, as the Albigensians had been, and for the same reason, of the Sacraments and Liturgical life of the Church, and also of doctrines like the Incarnation.

With all that I was not concerned. My hatred of war and my own personal misery in my particular situation and the general crisis of the world made me accept with my whole heart this revelation of the need for a spiritual life, an interior life, including some kind of mortification. I was content to accept the latter truth purely as a matter of theory: or at least, to apply it most vociferously to one passion which was not strong in myself, and did not need to be mortified: that of anger, hatred, while neglecting the ones that really needed to be checked, like gluttony and lust.

But the most important effect of the book on me was to make me start ransacking the university library for books on Oriental mysticism.

I remember those winter days, at the end of 1937 and the beginning of 1938, peaceful days when I sat in the big living room at Douglaston, with the pale sun coming in the window by the piano, where one of my father's water-colors of Bermuda hung on the wall.

The house was very quiet, with Pop and Bonnemaman gone from it, and John Paul away trying to pass his courses at Cornell. I sat for hours, with the big quarto volumes of the Jesuit Father Wieger's French translations of hundreds of strange Oriental texts.

I have forgotten the titles, even the authors, and I never understood a word of what they said in the first place. I had the habit of reading fast, without stopping, or stopping only rarely to take a note, and all these mysteries would require a great deal of thought, even were a man who knew something about them to puzzle them out. And I was completely unfamiliar with anything of the kind. Consequently, the strange great jumble of myths and theories and moral aphorisms and elaborate parables made little or no real impression on my mind, except that I put the books down with the impression that mysticism was something very esoteric and complicated, and that we were all inside some huge Being in whom we were involved and out of whom we evolved, and the thing to do was to involve ourselves back in to him again by a system of elaborate disciplines subject more or less to the control of our own will. The Absolute Being was an infinite, timeless, peaceful, impersonal Nothing.

The only practical thing I got out of it was a system for going to sleep, at night, when you couldn't sleep. You lay flat in bed, without a pillow, your arms at your sides and your legs straight out, and relaxed all your muscles, and you said to yourself:

"Now I have no feet, now I have no feet . . . no feet . . . no legs . . . no knees."

Sometimes it really worked: you did manage to make it feel as if your feet and legs and the rest of your body had changed into air and vanished away. The only section with which it almost never worked was my head: and if I had not fallen asleep before I got that far, when I tried to wipe out my head, instantly chest and stomach and legs and feet all came back to life with a most exasperating reality and I did not get to sleep for hours. Usually, however, I managed to get to sleep quite quickly by this trick. I suppose it was a variety of auto-suggestion, a kind of hypnotism, or else simply muscular relaxation, with the help of a little work on the part of an active fancy.

Ultimately, I suppose all Oriental mysticism can be reduced to techniques that do the same thing, but in a far more subtle and advanced fashion: and if that is true, it is not mysticism at all. It remains purely in the natural order. That does not make it evil, *per se,* according to Christian standards: but it does not make it good, in relation to the supernatural. It is simply more or less useless, except when it is mixed up with elements that are strictly diabolical: and then of course these dreams and annihilations are designed to wipe out all vital moral activity, while leaving the personality in control of some nefarious principle, either of his own, or from outside himself.

It was with all this in my mind that I went and received my diploma of Bachelor of Arts from one of the windows in the Registrar's office, and immediately afterwards put my name down for some courses in the Graduate School of English.

The experience of the last year, with the sudden collapse of all my physical energy and the diminution of the brash vigor of my worldly ambitions, had meant that I had turned in terror from the idea of anything so active and uncertain as the newspaper business. This registration in the graduate school represented the first remote step of a retreat from the fight for money and fame, from the active and worldly life of conflict and competition. If anything, I would now be a teacher, and live the rest of my life in the relative peace of a college campus, reading and writing books.

That the influence of the Huxley book had not, by any means, lifted me bodily out of the natural order overnight is evident from the fact that I decided to specialize in eighteenth century English Literature, and to choose my subject for a Master of Arts Thesis from somewhere in that century. As a matter of fact, I had already half decided upon a subject, by the time the last pile of dirty snow had melted from the borders of South Field. It was an unknown novelist of the second half of the eighteenth century called Richard Graves. The most important thing he wrote was a novel called the *Spiritual Quixote,* which was in the Fielding tradition, a satire on the more excited kind of Methodists and other sects of religious enthusiasts in England at that time.

I was to work under Professor Tyndall, and this would have been just his kind of a subject. He was an agnostic and rationalist who took a deep and amused interest in all the strange perversions of the religious instinct that our world has seen in the last five hundred years. He was just finishing a book on D. H. Lawrence which discussed, not too kindly, Lawrence's attempt to build up a synthetic, home-made religion of his own out of all the semi-pagan spiritual jetsam that came his way. All Lawrence's friends were very much annoyed by it when it was published. I remember that in that year one of Tyndall's favorite topics of conversation was the miracles of Mother Cabrini, who had just been beatified. He was amused by these, too, because, as for all rationalists, it was for him an article of faith that miracles cannot happen.

I remember with what indecision I went on into the spring, trying to settle the problem of a subject with finality. Yet the thing worked itself out quite suddenly: so suddenly that I do not remember what brought it about. One day I came running down out of the Carpenter Library, and passed along the wire fences by the tennis courts, in the sun, with my mind made up that there was only one possible man in the eighteenth century for me to work on:

the one poet who had least to do with his age, and was most in opposition to everything it stood for.

I had just had in my hands the small, neatly printed Nonesuch Press edition of the *Poems of William Blake,* and I now knew what my thesis would probably be. It would take in his poems and some aspect of his religious ideas.

In the Columbia bookstore I bought the same edition of Blake, on credit. (I paid for it two years later.) It had a blue cover, and I suppose it is now hidden somewhere in our monastery library, the part to which nobody has access. And that is all right. I think the ordinary Trappist would be only dangerously bewildered by the "Prophetic Books," and those who still might be able to profit by Blake, have a lot of other things to read that are still better. For my own part, I no longer need him. He has done his work for me: and he did it very thoroughly. I hope that I will see him in heaven.

But oh, what a thing it was to live in contact with the genius and the holiness of William Blake that year, that summer, writing the thesis! I had some beginning of an appreciation of his greatness above the other men of his time in England: but from this distance, from the hill where I now stand, looking back I can really appreciate his stature.

To assimilate him to the men of the ending eighteenth century would be absurd. I will not do it: all those conceited and wordy and stuffy little characters! As for the other romantics: how feeble and hysterical their inspirations seem next to the tremendously genuine and spiritual fire of William Blake. Even Coleridge, in the rare moments when his imagination struck the pitch of true creativeness, was still only an artist, an imaginer, not a seer; a maker, but not a prophet.

Perhaps all the great romantics were capable of putting words together more sensibly than Blake, and yet he, with all his mistakes of spelling, turned out the greater poet, because his was the deeper and more solid inspiration. He wrote better poetry when he was twelve than Shelley wrote in his whole life. And it was because at twelve he had already seen, I think, Elias, standing under a tree in the fields south of London.

It was Blake's problem to try and adjust himself to a society that understood neither him nor his kind of faith and love. More than once, smug and inferior minds conceived it to be their duty to take this man Blake in hand and direct and form him, to try and canalize what they recognized as "talent" in some kind of a conventional channel. And always this meant the cold and heartless disparagement of all that was vital and real to him in art and in faith. There were years of all kinds of petty persecution, from many different quarters, until finally Blake parted from his would-be patrons, and gave up all hope of an alliance with a world that thought he was crazy, and went his own way.

It was when he did this, and settled down as an engraver for good, that the Prophetic Books were no longer necessary. In the latter part of his life, having discovered Dante, he came in contact, through him, with Catholicism, which he described as the only religion that really taught the love of God, and his last years were relatively full of peace. He never seems to have felt any desire to hunt out a priest in the England where Catholicism was still practically outlawed: but he died with a blazing face and great songs of joy bursting from his heart.

As Blake worked himself into my system, I became more and more conscious of the necessity of a vital faith, and the total unreality and unsubstantiality of the dead, selfish rationalism which had been freezing my mind and will for the last seven years. By the time the summer was over, I was to become conscious of the fact that the only way to live was to live in a world that was charged with the presence and reality of God.

To say that, is to say a great deal: and I don't want to say it in a way that conveys more than the truth. I will have to limit the statement by saying that it was still, for me, more an intellectual realization than anything else: and it had not yet struck down into the roots of my will. The life of the soul is not knowledge, it is love, since love is the act of the supreme faculty, the will, by which man is formally united to the final end of all his strivings—by which man becomes one with God.

On the door of the room in one of the dormitories, where Lax and Sy Freedgood were living in a state of chaos, was a large grey picture, a lithograph print. Its subject was a man, a Hindu, with wide-open eyes and a rather frightened expression, sitting cross-legged in white garments. I asked about it, and I could not figure out whether the answer was derisive or respectful. Lax said someone had thrown a knife at the picture and the knife had bounced back and nearly cut all their heads off. In other words, he gave me to understand that the picture had something intrinsically holy about it: that accounted for the respect and derision manifested towards it by all my friends. This mixture was their standard acknowledgment of the supernatural, or what was considered to be supernatural. How that picture happened to get on that door in that room is a strange story.

It represented a Hindu messiah, a savior sent to India in our own times, called Jagad-Bondhu. His mission had to do with universal peace and brotherhood. He had died not very long before, and had left a strong following in India. He was, as it were, in the role of a saint who had founded a new religious Order, although he was considered more than a saint: he was the latest incarnation of the godhead, according to the Hindu belief in a multiplicity of incarnations.

In 1932 a big official sort of letter was delivered to one of the monasteries of this new "Order," outside of Calcutta. The letter came from the Chicago World's Fair, which was to be held in the following year. How they ever heard of this monastery, I cannot imagine. The letter was a formal announcement of a "World Congress of Religions." I am writing this all from memory but that is the substance of the story: they invited the abbot of this monastery to send a representative to Congress.

I get this picture of the monastery: it is called Sri Angan, meaning "the Playground." It consists of an enclosure and many huts or "cells," to use an Occidental term. The monks are quiet, simple men. They live what we would call a liturgical life, very closely integrated with the cycle of the seasons and of nature: in fact, the chief characteristic of their worship seems to be this deep, harmonious identification with all living things, in praising God. Their praise itself is expressed in songs, accompanied by drums and primitive instruments, flutes, pipes. There is much ceremonial dancing. In addition to that, there is a profound stress laid on a form of "mental prayer" which is largely contemplative. The monk works himself into it, by softly chanting lyrical aspirations to God and then remains in peaceful absorption in the Absolute.

For the rest, their life is extremely primitive and frugal. It is not so much what we would call austere. I do not think there are any fierce penances or mortifications. But nevertheless, the general level of poverty in Hindu society as a whole imposes on these monks a standard of living which most Occidental religious would probably find unlivable. Their clothes consist of a turban and something thrown around the body and a robe. No shoes. Perhaps the robe is only for travelling. Their food—some rice, a few vegetables, a piece of fruit.

Of all that they do, they attach most importance to prayer, to praising God. They have a well-developed sense of the power and efficacy of prayer, based on a keen realization of the goodness of God. Their whole spirituality is childlike, simple, primitive if you like, close to nature, ingenuous, optimistic, happy. But the point is, although it may be no more than the full flowering of the natural virtue of religion, with the other natural virtues, including a powerful natural charity, still the life of these pagan monks is one of such purity and holiness and peace, in the natural order, that it may put to shame the actual conduct of many Christian religious, in spite of their advantages of constant access to all the means of grace.

So this was the atmosphere into which the letter from Chicago dropped like a heavy stone. The abbot was pleased by the letter. He did not know what the Chicago World's Fair was. He did not understand that all these things were simply schemes for accumulating money. The "World Congress of Religions" appeared to him as something more than the fatuous scheme of a few restless, though probably sincere, minds. He seemed to see in it the first step towards the realization of the hopes of their beloved messiah, Jagad-Bondhu: world peace, universal brotherhood. Perhaps, now, all religions would unite into one great universal religion, and all men would begin to praise God as brothers, instead of tearing each other to pieces.

At any rate, the abbot selected one of his monks and told him that he was to go to Chicago, to the World Congress of Religions.

This was a tremendous assignment. It was something far more terrible than an order given, for instance, to a newly ordained Capuchin to proceed to a mission in India. That would merely be a matter of a trained missionary going off to occupy a place that had been prepared for him. But here was a little man who had been born at the edge of a jungle told to start out from a contemplative monastery and go not only into the world, but into the heart of a civilization the violence and materialism of which he could scarcely evaluate, and which raised gooseflesh on every square inch of his body. What is more, he was told to undertake this journey *without money.* Not that money was prohibited to him, but they simply did not have any. His abbot managed to raise enough to get him a ticket for a little more than half the distance. After that heaven would have to take care of him.

By the time I met this poor little monk who had come to America without money, he had been living in the country for about five years, and had acquired, of all things, the degree of Doctor of Philosophy from the University of Chicago. So that people referred to him as Doctor Bramachari, although I believe that Bramachari is simply a generic Hindu term for monk—and one that might almost be translated: "Little-Brother-Without-the-Degree-of-Doctor."

How he got through all the red tape that stands between America and the penniless traveller is something that I never quite understood. But it seems that officials, after questioning him, being completely overwhelmed by his simplicity, would either do something dishonest in his favor, or else would give him a tip as to how to beat the various technicalities. Some of them even lent him fairly large sums of money. In any case he landed in America.

The only trouble was that he got to Chicago after the World Congress of Religions was all over.

By that time, one look at the Fair buildings, which were already being torn down, told him all he needed to know about the World Congress of Religions. But once he was there, he did not have much trouble. People would see him standing around in the middle of railway stations waiting for Providence to do something about his plight. They would be intrigued by his turban and white garments (which were partly concealed by a brown overcoat in winter). They observed that he was wearing a pair of sneakers, and perhaps that alone was enough to rouse their curiosity. He was frequently invited to give lectures to religious and social clubs, and to schools and colleges, and he more than once spoke from the pulpits of Protestant churches. In this way he managed to make a living for himself. Besides, he was always being hospitably entertained by people that he met, and he financed the stages of his journey by artlessly leaving his purse lying open on the living room table, at night, before his departure.

The open mouth of the purse spoke eloquently to the hearts of his hosts, saying: "As you see, I am empty," or, perhaps, "As you see, I am down to my last fifteen cents." It was often enough filled up in the morning. He got around.

How did he run into Sy Freedgood? Well, Seymour's wife was studying at Chicago, and she met Bramachari there, and then Seymour met Bramachari, and Bramachari came to Long Beach once or twice, and went out in Seymour's sailboat, and wrote a poem which he gave to Seymour and Helen. He was very happy with Seymour, because he did not have to answer so many stupid questions and, after all, a lot of the people who befriended him were cranks and semi-maniacs and theosophists who thought they had some kind of a claim on him. They wearied him with their eccentricities, although he was a gentle and patient little man. But at Long Beach he was left in peace, although Seymour's ancient grandmother was not easily convinced that he was not the hereditary enemy of the Jewish people. She moved around in the other room, lighting small religious lamps against the intruder.

It was the end of the school year, June 1938, when Lax and Seymour already had a huge box in the middle of the room, which they were beginning to pack with books, when we heard Bramachari was again coming to New York.

I went down to meet him at Grand Central with Seymour, and it was not without a certain suppressed excitement that I did so, for Seymour had me all primed with a superb selection of lies about Bramachari's ability to float in the air and walk on water. It was a long time before we found him in the crowd, although you would think that a Hindu in a turban and a white robe and a pair of Keds would have been a rather memorable sight. But all the people we asked, concerning such a one, had no idea of having seen him.

We had been looking around for ten or fifteen minutes, when a cat came walking cautiously through the crowd, and passed us by with a kind of a look, and disappeared.

"That's him," said Seymour. "He changed himself into a cat. Doesn't like to attract attention. Looking the place over. Now he knows we're here."

Almost at once, while Seymour was asking a porter if he had

seen anything like Bramachari, and the porter was saying no, Bramachari came up behind us.

I saw Seymour swing around and say, in his rare, suave manner:

"Ah, Bramachari, how are you!"

There stood a shy little man, very happy, with a huge smile, all teeth, in the midst of his brown face. And on the top of his head was a yellow turban with Hindu prayers written all over it in red. And, on his feet, sure enough: sneakers.

I shook hands with him, still worrying lest he give me some kind of an electric shock. But he didn't. We rode up to Columbia in the subway, with all the people goggling at us, and I was asking Bramachari about all the colleges he had been visiting. Did he like Smith, did he like Harvard? When we were coming out into the air at 116th Street, I asked him which one he liked best, and he told me that they were all the same to him: it had never occurred to him that one might have any special preference in such things.

I lapsed into a reverent silence and pondered on this thought.

I was now twenty-three years old and, indeed, I was more mature than that in some respects. Surely by now it ought to have dawned on me that places did not especially matter. But no, I was very much attached to places, and had very definite likes and dislikes for localities as such, especially colleges, since I was always thinking of finding one that was altogether pleasant to live and teach in.

After that, I became very fond of Bramachari, and he of me. We got along very well together, especially since he sensed that I was trying to feel my way into a settled religious conviction, and into some kind of a life that was centered, as his was, on God.

The thing that strikes me now is that he never attempted to explain his own religious beliefs to me—except some of the externals of the cult, and that was later on. He would no doubt have told me all I wanted to know, if I had asked him, but I was not curious enough. What was most valuable to me was to hear his evaluation of the society and religious beliefs he had come across in America: and to put all that down on paper would require another book.

He was never sarcastic, never ironical or unkind in his criticisms: in fact he did not make many judgements at all, especially adverse ones. He would simply make statements of fact, and then burst out laughing—his laughter was quiet and ingenuous, and it expressed his complete amazement at the very possibility that people should live the way he saw them living all around him.

He was beyond laughing at the noise and violence of American city life and all the obvious lunacies like radio-programs and billboard advertising. It was some of the well-meaning idealisms that he came across that struck him as funny. And one of the things that struck him as funniest of all was the eagerness with which Protestant ministers used to come up and ask him if India was by now nearly converted to Protestantism. He used to tell us how far India was from conversion to Protestantism—or Catholicism for that matter. One of the chief reasons he gave for the failure of any Christian missionaries to really strike deep into the tremendous populations of Asia was the fact that they maintained themselves on a social level that was too far above the natives. The Church of England, indeed, thought they would convert the Indians by maintaining a strict separation—white men in one church, natives in a different church: both of them listening to sermons on brotherly love and unity.

But all Christian missionaries, according to him, suffered from this big drawback: they lived too well, too comfortably. They took care of themselves in a way that simply made it impossible for the Hindus to regard them as holy—let alone the fact that they ate meat, which made them repugnant to the natives.

I don't know anything about missionaries: but I am sure that, by our own standards of living, their life is an arduous and difficult one, and certainly not one that could be regarded as comfortable. And by comparison with life in Europe and America it represents a tremendous sacrifice. Yet I suppose it would literally endanger their lives if they tried to subsist on the standard of living with which the vast majority of Asiatics have to be content. It seems hard to expect them to go around barefoot and sleep on mats and live in huts. But one thing is certain: the pagans have their own notions of holiness, and it is one that includes a prominent element of asceticism. According to Bramachari, the prevailing impression among the Hindus seems to be that Christians don't know what asceticism means. Of course, he was talking principally of Protestant missionaries, but I suppose it would apply to anyone coming to a tropical climate from one of the so-called "civilized" countries.

For my own part, I see no reason for discouragement. Bramachari was simply saying something that has long since been familiar to readers of the Gospels. Unless the grain of wheat, falling in the ground, die, itself remaineth alone: but if it die, it bringeth forth much fruit. The Hindus are not looking for us to send them men who will build schools and hospitals, although those things are good and useful in themselves—and perhaps very badly needed in India: they want to know if we have any saints to send them.

There is no doubt in my mind that plenty of our missionaries are saints: and that they are capable of becoming greater saints too. And that is all that is needed. And, after all, St. Francis Xavier converted hundreds of thousands of Hindus in the sixteenth century and established Christian societies in Asia strong enough to survive for several centuries without any material support from outside the Catholic world.

Bramachari was not telling me anything I did not know about the Church of England, or about the other Protestant sects he had come in contact with. But I was interested to hear his opinion of the Catholics. They, of course, had not invited him to preach in their pulpits: but he had gone into a few Catholic churches out of curiosity. He told me that these were the only ones in which he really felt that people were praying.

It was only there that religion seemed to have achieved any degree of vitality, among us, as far as he could see. It was only to Catholics that the love of God seemed to be a matter of real concern, something that struck deep in their natures, not merely pious speculation and sentiment.

However, when he described his visit to a big Benedictine monastery in the Mid-West he began to grin again. He said they had showed him a lot of workshops and machinery and printing presses and taken him over the whole "plant" as if they were very wrapped up in all their buildings and enterprises. He got the impression that they were more absorbed in printing and writing and teaching than they were in praying.

Bramachari was not the kind of man to be impressed with such statements as: "There's a quarter of a million dollars' worth of stained glass in this church . . . the organ has got six banks of keys and it contains drums, bells and a mechanical nightingale . . . and the retable is a genuine bas-relief by a real live Italian artist."

The people he had the least respect for were all the borderline cases, the strange, eccentric sects, the Christian Scientists, the Oxford Group and all the rest of them. That was, in a sense, very comforting. Not that I was worried about them: but it confirmed me in my respect for him.

He did not generally put his words in the form of advice: but the one counsel he did give me is something that I will not easily forget: "There are many beautiful mystical books written by the Christians. You should read St. Augustine's *Confessions,* and *The Imitation of Christ.*"

Of course I had heard of both of them: but he was speaking as if he took it for granted that most people in America had no idea that such books ever existed. He seemed to feel as if he were in possession of a truth that would come to most Americans as news—as if there was something in their own cultural heritage that they had long since forgotten: and he could remind them of it. He repeated what he had said, not without a certain earnestness:

"Yes, you must read those books."

It was not often that he spoke with this kind of emphasis.

Now that I look back on those days, it seems to me very probable that one of the reasons why God had brought him all the way from India, was that he might say just that.

After all, it is rather ironical that I had turned, spontaneously to the east, in reading about mysticism, as if there were little or nothing in the Christian tradition. I remember that I ploughed through those heavy tomes of Father Wieger's with the feeling that all this represented the highest development of religion on earth. The reason may have been that I came away from Huxley's *Ends and Means* with the prejudice that Christianity was a less pure religion, because it was more "immersed in matter"—that is, because it did not scorn to use a Sacramental liturgy that relied on the appeal of created things to the senses in order to raise the souls of men to higher things.

So now I was told that I ought to turn to the Christian tradition, to St. Augustine—and told by a Hindu monk!

Still, perhaps if he had never given me that piece of advice, I would have ended up in the Fathers of the Church and Scholasticism after all: because a fortunate discovery in the course of my work on my M.A. thesis put me fairly and definitely on that track at last.

That discovery was one book that untied all the knots in the problem which I had set myself to solve by my thesis. It was Jacques Maritain's *Art and Scholasticism.*

The last week of that school year at Columbia had been rather chaotic. Lax and Freedgood had been making futile efforts to get their belongings together and go home. Bramachari was living in their room, perched on top of a pile of books. Lax was trying to finish a novel for Professor Nobbe's course in novel-writing, and all his friends had volunteered to take a section of the book and write it, simultaneously: but in the end the book turned out to be more or less a three-cornered affair—by Lax and me and Dona Eaton. When Nobbe got the thing in his hands he could not figure it out at all, but he gave us a B-minus, with which we were more than satisfied.

Then Lax's mother had come to town to live near him in the last furious weeks before graduation and catch him if he collapsed. He had to take most of his meals in the apartment she had rented in Butler Hall. I sometimes went along and helped him nibble the various health-foods.

At the same time, we were planning to get a ride on an oil barge up the Hudson and the Erie Canal to Buffalo—because Lax's brother-in-law was in the oil business. After that we would go to the town where Lax lived, which was Olean, up in that corner of New York state.

On "Class Day" we leaned out the window of Lax's room and drank a bottle of champagne, looking at the sun on South Field, and watching the people beginning to gather under the trees in front of Hamilton, where we would all presently hear some speeches and shake hands with Nicholas Murray Butler.

It was not my business to graduate that June at all. My graduation was all over when I picked up my degree in the registrar's office last February. However, I borrowed the cap and gown with which Dona Eaton had graduated from Barnard a year before, and went and sat with all the rest, mocking the speeches, with the edge of my sobriety slightly dulled by the celebration that had just taken place with the champagne in Furnald.

Finally we all got up and filed slowly up the rickety wooden steps to the temporary platform to shake hands with all the officials. President Butler was a much smaller man than I had expected. He looked intensely miserable, and murmured something or other to each student, as he shook hands. It was inaudible. I was given to understand that for the past six or seven years people had been in the habit of insulting him, on these occasions, as a kind of a farewell.

I didn't say anything. I just shook his hand, and passed on. The next one I came to was Dean Hawkes who looked up with surprise, from under his bushy white eyebrows, and growled:

"What are *you* doing here, anyway?"

I smiled and passed on.

We did not get the ride on the oil barge, after all, but went to Olean on a train, and for the first time I saw a part of the world in which I was one day going to learn how to be very happy—and that day was not now very far away.

It is the association of that happiness which makes upper New York state seem, in my memory, to be so beautiful. But it is objectively so, there is no doubt of that. Those deep valleys and miles and miles of high, rolling wooded hills: the broad fields, the big red barns, the white farm houses and the peaceful towns: all this looked more and more impressive and fine in the long slanting rays of the sinking sun after we had passed Elmira.

And you began to get some of the feeling of the bigness of America, and to develop a continental sense of the scope of the country and of the vast, clear sky, as the train went on for mile after mile, and hour after hour. And the color, and freshness, and bigness, and richness of the land! The cleanness of it. The wholesomeness. This was new and yet it was old country. It was mellow country. It had been cleared and settled for much more than a hundred years.

When we got out at Olean, we breathed its health and listened to its silence.

I did not stay there for more than a week, being impatient to get back to New York on account of being, as usual, in love.

But one of the things we happened to do was to turn off the main road, one afternoon on the way to the Indian reservation, to look at the plain brick buildings of a college that was run by the Franciscans.

It was called St. Bonaventure's. Lax had a good feeling about the place. And his mother was always taking courses there, in the evenings—courses in literature from the Friars. He was a good friend of the Father Librarian and liked the library. We drove in to the grounds and stopped by one of the buildings.

But when Lax tried to make me get out of the car, I would not.

"Let's get out of here," I said.

"Why? It's a nice place."

"It's O.K., but let's get out of here. Let's go to the Indian reservation."

"Don't you want to see the library?"

"I can see enough of it from here. Let's get going."

I don't know what was the matter. Perhaps I was scared of the thought of nuns and priests being all around me—the elemental fear of the citizen of hell, in the presence of anything that savors of the religious life, religious vows, official dedication to God through Christ. Too many crosses. Too many holy statues. Too much quiet and cheerfulness. Too much pious optimism. It made me very uncomfortable. I had to flee.

When I got back to New York, one of the first things I did was to break away, at last, from the household in Douglaston. The family had really practically dissolved with the death of my grandparents, and I could get a lot more work done if I did not have to spend so much time on subways and the Long Island train.

One rainy day in June, then, I made a bargain with Herb, the colored taximan at Douglaston, and he drove me and all my bags and books and my portable vic and all my hot records and pictures to put on the wall and even a tennis racquet which I never used, uptown to a rooming-house on 114th Street, just behind the Columbia library.

All the way up we discussed the possible reasons for the mysterious death of Rudolph Valentino, once a famous movie star: but it was certainly not what you would call a live issue. Valentino had died at least ten years before.

"This is a nice spot you got here," said Herb, approving of the room I was renting for seven-fifty a week. It was shiny and clean and filled with new furniture and had a big view of a pile of coal, in a yard by the campus tennis courts, with South Field and the steps of the old domed library beyond. The panorama even took in a couple of trees.

"I guess you're going to have a pretty hot time, now you got away from your folks," Herb remarked, as he took his leave.

Whatever else may have happened in that room, it was also there that I started to pray again more or less regularly, and it was there that I added, as Bramachari had suggested, *The Imitation of Christ* to my books, and it was from there that I was eventually to be driven out by an almost physical push, to go and look for a priest.

July came, with its great, misty heats, and Columbia filled with all the thousands of plump, spectacled ladies in pink dresses, from the Middle-West, and all the grey gents in seersucker suits, all the dried-up high-school principals from Indiana and Kansas and Iowa and Tennessee, with their veins shrivelled up with positivism and all the reactions of the behaviorist flickering behind their spectacles as they meditated on the truths they learned in those sweltering halls.

The books piled higher and higher on my desk in the Graduate reading room and in my own lodgings. I was in the thick of my thesis, making hundreds of mistakes that I would not be able to detect for several years to come, because I was far out of my depth. Fortunately, nobody else detected them either. But for my own part, I was fairly happy, and learning many things. The discipline of the work itself was good for me, and helped to cure me, more than anything else did, of the illusion that my health was poor.

And it was in the middle of all this that I discovered Scholastic philosophy.

The subject I had finally chosen was "Nature and Art in William Blake." I did not realize how providential a subject it actually was! What it amounted to, was a study of Blake's reaction against every kind of literalism and naturalism and narrow, classical realism in art, because of his own ideal which was essentially mystical and supernatural. In other words, the topic, if I treated it at all sensibly, could not help but cure me of all the naturalism and materialism in my own philosophy, besides resolving all the inconsistencies and self-contradictions that had persisted in my mind for years, without my being able to explain them.

After all, from my very childhood, I had understood that the artistic experience, at its highest, was actually a natural analogue of mystical experience. It produced a kind of intuitive perception of reality through a sort of affective identification with the object contemplated—the kind of perception that the Thomists call "connatural." This means simply a knowledge that comes about as it were by the identification of natures: in the way that a chaste man understands the nature of chastity because of the very fact that his soul is full of it—it is a part of his own nature, since habit is second nature. Non-connatural knowledge of chastity would be that of a philosopher who, to borrow the language of the *Imitation,* would be able to define it, but would not possess it.

I had learned from my own father that it was almost blasphemy to regard the function of art as merely to reproduce some kind of a sensible pleasure or, at best, to stir up the emotions to a transitory thrill. I had always understood that art was contemplation, and that it involved the action of the highest faculties of man.

When I was once able to discover the key to Blake, in his rebellion against literalism and naturalism in art, I saw that his Prophetic Books and the rest of his verse at large represented a rebellion against naturalism in the moral order as well.

What a revelation that was! For at sixteen I had imagined that Blake, like the other romantics, was glorifying passion, natural energy, for their own sake. Far from it! What he was glorifying was the transfiguration of man's natural love, his natural powers, in the refining fires of mystical experience: and that, in itself, implied an arduous and total purification, by faith and love and desire, from all the petty materialistic and commonplace and earthly ideals of his rationalistic friends.

Blake, in his sweeping consistency, had developed a moral insight that cut through all the false distinctions of a worldly and interested morality. That was why he saw that, in the legislation of men, some evils had been set up as standards of right by which other evils were to be condemned: and the norms of pride or greed had been established in the judgement seat, to pronounce a crush-

ing and inhuman indictment against all the normal healthy strivings of human nature. Love was outlawed, and became lust, pity
was swallowed up in cruelty, and so Blake knew how:

> The harlot's cry from street to street
> Shall weave old England's winding-sheet.

I had heard that cry and that echo. I had seen that winding
sheet. But I had understood nothing of all that. I had tried to resolve
it into a matter of sociological laws, of economic forces. If I had
been able to listen to Blake in those old days, he would have told me
that sociology and economics, divorced from faith and charity,
become nothing but the chains of his aged, icy demon Urizen! But
now, reading Maritain, in connection with Blake, I saw all these
difficulties and contradictions disappear.

I, who had always been anti-naturalistic in art, had been a pure
naturalist in the moral order. No wonder my soul was sick and torn
apart: but now the bleeding wound was drawn together by
the notion of Christian virtue, ordered to the union of the soul
with God.

The word virtue: what a fate it has had in the last three
hundred years! The fact that it is nowhere near so despised and
ridiculed in Latin countries is a testimony to the fact that it suffered
mostly from the mangling it underwent at the hands of Calvinists
and Puritans. In our own days the word leaves on the lips of cynical
high-school children a kind of flippant smear, and it is exploited in
theaters for the possibilities it offers for lewd and cheesy sarcasm.
Everybody makes fun of virtue, which now has, as its primary
meaning, an affectation of prudery practiced by hypocrites and the
impotent.

When Maritain—who is by no means bothered by such trivia-
lities—in all simplicity went ahead to use the term in its Scholastic
sense, and was able to apply it to art, a "virtue of the practical
intellect," the very newness of the context was enough to disinfect
my mind of all the miasmas left in it by the ordinary prejudice
against "virtue" which, if it was ever strong in anybody, was strong
in me. I was never a lover of Puritanism. Now at last I came around
to the sane conception of virtue—without which there can be no
happiness, because virtues are precisely the powers by which we

can come to acquire happiness: without them, there can be no joy, because they are the habits which coordinate and canalize our natural energies and direct them to the harmony and perfection and balance, the unity of our nature with itself and with God, which must, in the end, constitute our everlasting peace.

By the time I was ready to begin the actual writing of my thesis, that is, around the beginning of September 1938, the groundwork of conversion was more or less complete. And how easily and sweetly it had all been done, with all the external graces that had been arranged, along my path, by the kind Providence of God! It had taken little more than a year and a half, counting from the time I read Gilson's *The Spirit of Medieval Philosophy* to bring me up from an "atheist"—as I considered myself—to one who accepted all the full range and possibilities of religious experience right up to the highest degree of glory.

I not only accepted all this, intellectually, but now I began to desire it. And not only did I begin to desire it, but I began to do so efficaciously: I began to want to take the necessary means to achieve this union, this peace. I began to desire to dedicate my life to God, to His service. The notion was still vague and obscure, and it was ludicrously impractical in the sense that I was already dreaming of mystical union when I did not even keep the simplest rudiments of the moral law. But nevertheless I was convinced of the reality of the goal, and confident that it could be achieved: and whatever element of presumption was in this confidence I am sure God excused, in His mercy, because of my stupidity and helplessness, and because I was really beginning to be ready to do whatever I thought He wanted me to do to bring me to Him.

But, oh, how blind and weak and sick I was, although I thought I saw where I was going, and half understood the way! How deluded we sometimes are by the clear notions we get out of books. They make us think that we really understand things of which we have no practical knowledge at all. I remember how learnedly and enthusiastically I could talk for hours about mysticism and the experimental knowledge of God, and all the while I was stoking the fires of the argument with Scotch and soda.

That was the way it turned out that Labor Day, for instance. I went to Philadelphia with Joe Roberts, who had a room in the same house as I, and who had been through all the battles on the Fourth

Floor of John Jay for the past four years. He had graduated and was working on some trade magazine about women's hats. All one night we sat, with a friend of his, in a big dark roadhouse outside of Philadelphia, arguing and arguing about mysticism, and smoking more and more cigarettes and gradually getting drunk. Eventually, filled with enthusiasm for the purity of heart which begets the vision of God, I went on with them into the city, after the closing of the bars, to a big speak-easy where we completed the work of getting plastered.

My internal contradictions were resolving themselves out, indeed, but still only on the plane of theory, not of practice: not for lack of good-will, but because I was still so completely chained and fettered by my sins and my attachments.

I think that if there is one truth that people need to learn, in the world, especially today, it is this: the intellect is only theoretically independent of desire and appetite in ordinary, actual practice. It is constantly being blinded and perverted by the ends and aims of passion, and the evidence it presents to us with such a show of impartiality and objectivity is fraught with interest and propaganda. We have become marvelous at self-delusion; all the more so, because we have gone to such trouble to convince ourselves of our own absolute infallibility. The desires of the flesh—and by that I mean not only sinful desires, but even the ordinary, normal appetites for comfort and ease and human respect, are fruitful sources of every kind of error and misjudgement, and because we have these yearnings in us, our intellects (which, if they operated all alone in a vacuum, would indeed, register with pure impartiality what they saw) present to us everything distorted and accommodated to the norms of our desire.

And therefore, even when we are acting with the best of intentions, and imagine that we are doing great good, we may be actually doing tremendous material harm and contradicting all our good intentions. There are ways that seem to men to be good, the end whereof is in the depths of hell.

The only answer to the problem is grace, grace, docility to grace. I was still in the precarious position of being my own guide and my own interpreter of grace. It is a wonder I ever got to the harbor at all!

Sometime in August, I finally answered an impulsion that had been working on me for a long time. Every Sunday, I had been going out on Long Island to spend the day with the same girl who had brought me back in such a hurry from Lax's town Olean. But every week, as Sunday came around, I was filled with a growing desire to stay in the city and go to some kind of a church.

At first, I had vaguely thought I might try to find some Quakers, and go and sit with them. There still remained in me something of the favorable notion about Quakers that I had picked up as a child, and which the reading of William Penn had not been able to overcome.

But, naturally enough, with the work I was doing in the library, a stronger drive began to assert itself, and I was drawn much more imperatively to the Catholic Church. Finally the urge became so strong that I could not resist it. I called up my girl and told her that I was not coming out that week-end, and made up my mind to go to Mass for the first time in my life.

The first time in my life! That was true. I had lived for several years on the continent, I had been to Rome, I had been in and out of a thousand Catholic cathedrals and churches, and yet I had never heard Mass. If anything had ever been going on in the churches I visited, I had always fled, in wild Protestant panic.

I will not easily forget how I felt that day. First, there was this sweet, strong, gentle, clean urge in me which said: "Go to Mass! Go to Mass!" It was something quite new and strange, this voice that seemed to prompt me, this firm, growing interior conviction of what I needed to do. It had a suavity, a simplicity about it that I could not easily account for. And when I gave in to it, it did not exult over me, and trample me down in its raging haste to land on its prey, but it carried me forward serenely and with purposeful direction.

That does not mean that my emotions yielded to it altogether quietly. I was really still a little afraid to go to a Catholic church, of set purpose, with all the other people, and dispose myself in a pew, and lay myself open to the mysterious perils of that strange and powerful thing they called their "Mass."

God made it a very beautiful Sunday. And since it was the first time I had ever really spent a sober Sunday in New York, I was surprised at the clean, quiet atmosphere of the empty streets uptown. The sun was blazing bright. At the end of the street, as I came out the front door, I could see a burst of green, and the blue river and the hills of Jersey on the other side.

Broadway was empty. A solitary trolley came speeding down in front of Barnard College and past the School of Journalism. Then, from the high, grey, expensive tower of the Rockefeller Church, huge bells began to boom. It served very well for the eleven o'clock Mass at the little brick Church of Corpus Christi, hidden behind Teachers College on 121st Street.

How bright the little building seemed. Indeed, it was quite new. The sun shone on the clean bricks. People were going in the wide open door, into the cool darkness and, all at once, all the churches of Italy and France came back to me. The richness and fulness of the atmosphere of Catholicism that I had not been able to avoid apprehending and loving as a child, came back to me with a rush: but now I was to enter into it fully for the first time. So far, I had known nothing but the outward surface.

It was a gay, clean church, with big plain windows and white columns and pilasters and a well-lighted, simple sanctuary. Its style was a trifle eclectic, but much less perverted with incongruities than the average Catholic church in America. It had a kind of a seventeenth-century, oratorian character about it, though with a sort of American colonial tinge of simplicity. The blend was effective and original: but although all this affected me, without my thinking about it, the thing that impressed me most was that the place was full, absolutely full. It was full not only of old ladies and broken-down gentlemen with one foot in the grave, but of men and women and children young and old—especially young: people of all classes, and all ranks on a solid foundation of workingmen and -women and their families.

I found a place that I hoped would be obscure, over on one side, in the back, and went to it without genuflecting, and knelt down. As I knelt, the first thing I noticed was a young girl, very pretty too, perhaps fifteen or sixteen, kneeling straight up and praying quite seriously. I was very much impressed to see that someone who was young and beautiful could with such simplicity make prayer the real and serious and principal reason for going to church. She was clearly kneeling that way because she meant it, not in order to show off, and she was praying with an absorption which, though not the deep recollection of a saint, was serious enough to show that she was not thinking at all about the other people who were there.

What a revelation it was, to discover so many ordinary people in a place together, more conscious of God than of one another: not there to show off their hats or their clothes, but to pray, or at least to fulfil a religious obligation, not a human one. For even those who might have been there for no better motive than that they were obliged to be, were at least free from any of the self-conscious and human constraint which is never absent from a Protestant church where people are definitely gathered together as people, as neighbors, and always have at least half an eye for one another, if not all of both eyes.

Since it was summer time, the eleven o'clock Mass was a Low Mass: but I had not come expecting to hear music. Before I knew it, the priest was in the sanctuary with the two altar boys, and was busy at the altar with something or other which I could not see very well, but the people were praying by themselves, and I was engrossed and absorbed in the thing as a whole: the business at the altar and the presence of the people. And still I had not got rid of my fear. Seeing the late-comers hastily genuflecting before entering the pew, I realised my omission, and got the idea that people had spotted me for a pagan and were just waiting for me to miss a few more genuflections before throwing me out or, at least, giving me looks of reproof.

Soon we all stood up. I did not know what it was for. The priest was at the other end of the altar, and, as I afterwards learned, he was reading the Gospel. And then the next thing I knew there was someone in the pulpit.

It was a young priest, perhaps not much over thirty-three or -four years old. His face was rather ascetic and thin, and its asceticism was heightened with a note of intellectuality by his horn-rimmed glasses, although he was only one of the assistants, and he did not consider himself an intellectual, nor did anyone else apparently consider him so. But anyway, that was the impression he made on me: and his sermon, which was simple enough, did not belie it.

It was not long: but to me it was very interesting to hear this young man quietly telling the people in language that was plain, yet tinged with scholastic terminology, about a point in Catholic Doctrine. How clear and solid the doctrine was: for behind those words you felt the full force not only of Scripture but of centuries of a unified and continuous and consistent tradition. And above all, it was a vital tradition: there was nothing studied or antique about it. These words, this terminology, this doctrine, and these convictions fell from the lips of the young priest as something that were most intimately part of his own life. What was more, I sensed that the people were familiar with it all, and that it was also, in due proportion, part of their life also: it was just as much integrated into their spiritual organism as the air they breathed or the food they ate worked in to their blood and flesh.

What was he saying? That Christ was the Son of God. That, in Him, the Second Person of the Holy Trinity, God, had assumed a Human Nature, a Human Body and Soul, and had taken Flesh and dwelt amongst us, full of grace and truth: and that this Man, Whom men called the Christ, was God. He was both Man and God: two Natures hypostatically united in one Person or suppositum, one individual Who was a Divine Person, having assumed to Himself a Human Nature. And His works were the works of God: His acts were the acts of God. He loved us: God, and walked among us: God, and died for us on the Cross, God of God, Light of Light, True God of True God.

Jesus Christ was not simply a man, a good man, a great man, the greatest prophet, a wonderful healer, a saint: He was something that made all such trivial words pale into irrelevance. He was God. But nevertheless He was not merely a spirit without a true body, God hiding under a visionary body: He was also truly a Man, born of the Flesh of the Most Pure Virgin, formed of her Flesh by the Holy Spirit. And what He did, in that Flesh, on earth, He did not only as Man but as God. He loved us as God, He suffered and died for us, God.

And how did we know? Because it was revealed to us in the Scriptures and confirmed by the teaching of the Church and of the powerful unanimity of Catholic Tradition from the First Apostles, from the first Popes and the early Fathers, on down through the Doctors of the Church and the great scholastics, to our own day. *De Fide Divina.* If you believed it, you would receive light to grasp it, to understand it in some measure. If you did not believe it, you would never understand: it would never be anything but scandal or folly.

And no one can believe these things merely by wanting to, of his own volition. Unless he receive grace, an actual light and impulsion of the mind and will from God, he cannot even make an act of living faith. It is God Who gives us faith, and no one cometh to Christ unless the Father draweth him.

I wonder what would have happened in my life if I had been given this grace in the days when I had almost discovered the Divinity of Christ in the ancient mosaics of the churches of Rome. What scores of self-murdering and Christ-murdering sins would have been avoided—all the filth I had plastered upon His image in my soul during those last five years that I had been scourging and crucifying God within me?

It is easy to say, after it all, that God had probably foreseen my infidelities and had never given me the grace in those days because He saw how I would waste and despise it: and perhaps that rejection would have been my ruin. For there is no doubt that one of the reasons why grace is not given to souls is because they have so hardened their wills in greed and cruelty and selfishness that their refusal of it would only harden them more. . . . But now I had been beaten into the semblance of some kind of humility by misery and confusion and perplexity and secret, interior fear, and my ploughed soul was better ground for the reception of good seed.

The sermon was what I most needed to hear that day. When the Mass of the Catechumens was over, I, who was not even a catechumen, but only a blind and deaf and dumb pagan as weak and dirty as anything that ever came out of the darkness of Imperial Rome or Corinth or Ephesus, was not able to understand anything else.

It all became completely mysterious when the attention was refocussed on the altar. When the silence grew more and more profound, and little bells began to ring, I got scared again and, finally, genuflecting hastily on my left knee, I hurried out of the church in the middle of the most important part of the Mass. But it was just as well. In a way, I suppose I was responding to a kind of liturgical instinct that told me I did not belong there for the celebration of the Mysteries as such. I had no idea what took place in them:

but the fact was that Christ, God, would be visibly present on the altar in the Sacred Species. And although He was there, yes, for love of me: yet He was there in His power and His might, and what was I? What was on my soul? What was I in His sight?

It was liturgically fitting that I should kick myself out at the end of the Mass of the Catechumens, when the ordained *ostiarii* should have been there to do it. Anyway, it was done.

Now I walked leisurely down Broadway in the sun, and my eyes looked about me at a new world. I could not understand what it was that had happened to make me so happy, why I was so much at peace, so content with life for I was not yet used to the clean savor that comes with an actual grace—indeed, there was no impossibility in a person's hearing and believing such a sermon and being justified, that is, receiving sanctifying grace in his soul as a habit, and beginning, from that moment, to live the divine and supernatural life for good and all. But that is something I will not speculate about.

All I know is that I walked in a new world. Even the ugly buildings of Columbia were transfigured in it, and everywhere was peace in these streets designed for violence and noise. Sitting outside the gloomy little Childs restaurant at 111th Street, behind the dirty, boxed bushes, and eating breakfast, was like sitting in the Elysian Fields.

My reading became more and more Catholic. I became absorbed in the poetry of Hopkins and in his notebooks—that poetry which had only impressed me a little six years before. Now, too, I was deeply interested in Hopkins' life as a Jesuit. What was that life? What did the Jesuits do? What did a priest do? How did he live? I scarcely knew where to begin to find out about all such things: but they had started to exercise a mysterious attraction over me.

And here is a strange thing. I had by now read James Joyce's *Ulysses* twice or three times. Six years before—on one of those winter vacations in Strasbourg—I had tried to read *Portrait of the Artist* and had bogged down in the part about his spiritual crisis. Something about it had discouraged, bored and depressed me. I did not want to read about such a thing: and I finally dropped it in the middle of the "Mission." Strange to say, sometime during this summer—I think it was before the first time I went to Corpus Christi—I reread *Portrait of the Artist* and was fascinated precisely by that part of the book, by the "Mission," by the priest's sermon on hell. What impressed me was not the fear of hell, but the expertness of the sermon. Now, instead of being repelled by the thought of such preaching—which was perhaps the author's intention—I was stimulated and edified by it. The style in which the priest in the book talked, pleased me by its efficiency and solidity and drive: and once again there was something eminently satisfying in the thought that these Catholics knew what they believed, and knew what to teach, and all taught the same thing, and taught it with coordination and purpose and great effect. It was this that struck me first of all, rather than the actual subject matter of their doctrine—until, that is, I heard the sermon at Corpus Christi.

So then I continued to read Joyce, more and more fascinated by the pictures of priests and Catholic life that came up here and there in his books. That, I am sure, will strike many people as a strange thing indeed. I think Joyce himself was only interested in rebuilding the Dublin he had known as objectively and vitally as he could. He was certainly very alive to all the faults in Irish Catholic society, and he had practically no sympathy left for the Church he had abandoned: but in his intense loyalty to the vocation of artist for which he had abandoned it (and the two vocations are not *per se* irreconcilable: they only became so because of peculiar subjective circumstances in Joyce's own case) he meant to be as accurate as he could in rebuilding his world as it truly was.

Therefore, reading Joyce, I was moving in his Dublin, and breathing the air of its physical and spiritual slums: and it was not the most Catholic side of Dublin that he always painted. But in the background was the Church, and its priests, and its devotions, and the Catholic life in all its gradations, from the Jesuits down to those who barely clung to the hem of the Church's garments. And it was this background that fascinated me now, along with the temper of Thomism that had once been in Joyce himself. If he had abandoned St. Thomas, he had not stepped much further down than Aristotle.

Then, of course, I was reading the metaphysical poets once again—especially Crashaw—and studying his life, too, and his conversion. That meant another avenue which led more or less directly to the Jesuits. So in the late August of 1938, and September of that year, my life began to be surrounded, interiorly, by Jesuits. They were the symbols of my new respect for the vitality and coordination of the Catholic Apostolate. Perhaps, in the back of my mind, was my greatest Jesuit hero: the glorious Father Rothschild of Evelyn Waugh's *Vile Bodies,* who plotted with all the diplomats, and rode away into the night on a motorcycle when everybody else was exhausted.

Yet with all this, I was not yet ready to stand beside the font. There was not even any interior debate as to whether I ought to become a Catholic. I was content to stand by and admire. For the rest, I remember one afternoon, when my girl had come in to town to see me, and we were walking around the streets uptown, I subjected her to the rather disappointing entertainment of going to Union Theological Seminary, and asking for a catalogue of their courses which I proceeded to read while we were walking around on Riverside Drive. She was not openly irritated by it: she was a very good and patient girl anyway. But still you could see she was a little bored, walking around with a man who was not sure whether he ought to enter a theological seminary.

There was nothing very attractive in that catalogue. I was to get much more excited by the article on the Jesuits in the *Catholic Encyclopaedia*—breathless with the thought of so many novitiates and tertianships and what not—so much scrutiny, so much training. What monsters of efficiency they must be, these Jesuits, I kept thinking to myself, as I read and reread the article. And perhaps, from time to time, I tried to picture myself with my face sharpened by asceticism, its pallor intensified by contrast with a black cassock, and every line of it proclaiming a Jesuit saint, a Jesuit master-mind. And I think the master-mind element was one of the strongest features of this obscure attraction.

Apart from this foolishness, I came no nearer to the Church, in practice, than adding a "Hail Mary" to my night prayers. I did not even go to Mass again, at once. The following week-end I went to see my girl once again; it was probably after that that I went on the expedition to Philadelphia. It took something that belongs to history to form and vitalize these resolutions that were still only vague and floating entities in my mind and will.

One of those hot evenings at the end of summer the atmosphere of the city suddenly became terribly tense with some news that came out of the radios. Before I knew what the news was, I began to feel the tension. For I was suddenly aware that the quiet, disparate murmurs of different radios in different houses had imperceptibly merged into one big, ominous unified voice, that moved at you from different directions and followed you down the street, and came to you from another angle as soon as you began to recede from any one of its particular sources.

I heard "Germany—Hitler—at six o'clock this morning the German Army . . . the Nazis . . ." What had they done?

Then Joe Roberts came in and said there was about to be a war. The Germans had occupied Czechoslovakia, and there was bound to be a war.

The city felt as if one of the doors of hell had been half opened, and a blast of its breath had flared out to wither up the spirits of men. And people were loitering around the newsstands in misery.

Joe Roberts and I sat in my room, where there was no radio, until long after midnight, drinking canned beer and smoking cigarettes, and making silly and excited jokes but, within a couple of days, the English Prime Minister had flown in a big hurry to see Hitler and had made a nice new alliance at Munich that cancelled everything that might have caused a war, and returned to England. He alighted at Croydon and came stumbling out of the plane saying "Peace in our time!"

I was very depressed. I was beyond thinking about the intricate and filthy political tangle that underlay the mess. I had given up politics as more or less hopeless, by this time. I was no longer interested in having any opinion about the movement and interplay of forces which were all more or less iniquitous and corrupt, and it was far too laborious and uncertain a business to try and find out some degree of truth and justice in all the loud, artificial claims that were put forward by the various sides.

All I could see was a world in which everybody said they hated war, and in which we were all being rushed into a war with a momentum that was at last getting dizzy enough to affect my stomach. All the internal contradictions of the society in which I lived were at last beginning to converge upon its heart. There could not be much more of a delay in its dismembering. Where would it end? In those days, the future was obscured, blanked out by war as by a dead-end wall. Nobody knew if anyone at all would come out of it alive. Who would be worse off, the civilians or the soldiers? The distinction between their fates was to be abolished, in most countries, by aerial warfare, by all the new planes, by all the marvelous new bombs. What would the end of it be?

I knew that I myself hated war, and all the motives that led to war and were behind wars. But I could see that now my likes or dislikes, beliefs or disbeliefs meant absolutely nothing in the external, political order. I was just an individual, and the individual had ceased to count. I meant nothing, in this world, except that I would probably soon become a number on the list of those to be drafted. I would get a piece of metal with my number on it, to hang around my neck, so as to help out the circulation of red-tape that would necessarily follow the disposal of my remains, and that would be the last eddy of mental activity that would close over my lost identity.

The whole business was so completely unthinkable that my mind, like almost all the other minds that were in the same situation, simply stopped trying to cope with it and refixed its focus on the ordinary routine of life.

I had my thesis to type out, and a lot of books to read, and I was thinking of preparing an article on Crashaw which perhaps I would send to T. S. Eliot for his *Criterion.* I did not know that *Criterion* had printed its last issue, and that Eliot's reaction to the situation that so depressed me was to fold up his magazine.

The days went on and the radios returned to their separate and individual murmuring, not to be regimented back into their appalling shout for yet another year. September, as I think, must have been more than half gone.

I borrowed Father Leahy's life of Hopkins from the library. It was a rainy day. I had been working in the library in the morning. I had gone to buy a thirty-five-cent lunch at one of those little pious kitchens on Broadway—the one where Professor Gerig, of the graduate school of French, sat daily in silence with his ancient, ailing mother, over a very small table, eating his Brussels sprouts. Later in the afternoon, perhaps about four, I would have to go down to Central Park West and give a Latin lesson to a youth who was sick in bed, and who ordinarily came to the tutoring school run by my landlord, on the ground floor of the house where I lived.

I walked back to my room. The rain was falling gently on the empty tennis courts across the street, and the huge old domed library stood entrenched in its own dreary greyness, arching a cyclops eyebrow at South Field.

I took up the book about Gerard Manley Hopkins. The chapter told of Hopkins at Balliol, at Oxford. He was thinking of becoming a Catholic. He was writing letters to Cardinal Newman (not yet a cardinal) about becoming a Catholic.

All of a sudden, something began to stir within me, something began to push me, to prompt me. It was a movement that spoke like a voice.

"What are you waiting for?" it said. "Why are you sitting here? Why do you still hesitate? You know what you ought to do? Why don't you do it?"

I stirred in the chair, I lit a cigarette, looked out the window at the rain, tried to shut the voice up. "Don't act on impulses," I thought. "This is crazy. This is not rational. Read your book."

Hopkins was writing to Newman, at Birmingham, about his indecision.

"What are you waiting for?" said the voice within me again. "Why are you sitting there? It is useless to hesitate any longer. Why don't you get up and go?"

I got up and walked restlessly around the room. "It's absurd," I thought. "Anyway, Father Ford would not be there at this time of day. I would only be wasting time."

Hopkins had written to Newman, and Newman had replied to him, telling him to come and see him at Birmingham.

Suddenly, I could bear it no longer. I put down the book, and got into my raincoat, and started down the stairs. I went out into the street. I crossed over, and walked along by the grey wooden fence, towards Broadway, in the light rain.

And then everything inside me began to sing—to sing with peace, to sing with strength and to sing with conviction.

I had nine blocks to walk. Then I turned the corner of 121st Street, and the brick church and presbytery were before me. I stood in the doorway and rang the bell and waited.

When the maid opened the door, I said:

"May I see Father Ford, please?"

"But Father Ford is out."

I thought: well, it is not a waste of time, anyway. And I asked when she expected him back. I would come back later, I thought.

The maid closed the door. I stepped back into the street. And then I saw Father Ford coming around the corner from Broadway. He approached, with his head down, in a rapid, thoughtful walk. I went to meet him and said:

"Father, may I speak to you about something?"

"Yes," he said, looking up, surprised. "Yes, sure, come into the house."

We sat in the little parlor by the door. And I said: "Father, I want to become a Catholic."

FIRE WATCH, JULY 4, 1952

"Fire Watch" is the epilogue to Thomas Merton's monastic journal The Sign of Jonas *(1953). Michael Mott, Merton's biographer, has said that it may suffer a bit from being too celebrated but a rereading is still moving. Being "too celebrated" may derive from the fact that it is one of his most perfectly realized prose pieces (much of it reads like poetry) and, on close reading, one of his most dense.*

The custom of having a monk make the rounds of the monastery at night as a "fire man" was a sensible precaution in an old building with such a large population of people in it. Merton imagines the rounds of the fire watcher as an extended metaphor of the descent/ascent of the spiritual life. The images of descent are linked to the figure of Jonah who descends into the belly of the beast (and the New Jonah, Christ, who went into the belly of death) while the ascent pattern is linked to the watchman in the tower celebrated by Isaiah the prophet. The climax of the episode comes with the embrace of the night in the abbey tower before the return of the morning light.

For an extended analysis of the Fire Watch epilogue, see Lawrence S. Cunningham. "Thomas Merton: Firewatcher," The Merton Seasonal *XV (Spring 1990), pp. 6–11.*

⚜

Watchman, what of the night?

The night, O My Lord, is a time of freedom. You have seen the morning and the night, and the night was better. In the night all things began, and in the night the end of all things has come before me.

Baptized in the rivers of night, Gethsemani has recovered her innocence. Darkness brings a semblance of order before all things disappear. With the clock slung over my shoulder, in the silence of the Fourth of July, it is my time to be the night watchman, in the house that will one day perish.

Here is the way it is when I go on the fire watch:

Before eight o'clock the monks are packed in the belly of the great heat, singing to the Mother of God like exiles sailing to their slavery, hoping for glory. The night angelus unlocks the church and sets them free. The holy monster which is The Community divides itself into segments and disperses through airless cloisters where yellow lamps do not attract the bugs.

The watchman's clock together with the watchman's sneakers are kept in a box, together with a flashlight and the keys to various places, at the foot of the infirmary stairs.

Rumors behind me and above me and around me signalize the fathers going severally to bed in different dormitories. Where there is cold water some stay to drink from celluloid cups. Thus we fight the heat. I take the heavy clock and sling it on its strap over my shoulder. I walk to the nearest window, on my silent feet. I recite the second nocturn of Saturday, sitting outside the window in the dark garden, and the house begins to be silent.

One late Father, with a change of dry clothes slung over his shoulder, stops to look out the window and pretends to be frightened when he sees me sitting around the corner in the dark, holding the breviary in the yellow light of the window, saying the Psalms of Saturday.

It is ten or fifteen minutes before there are no more feet echoing along the cloisters, shuffling up the stairs. (When you go late to the dormitories you have to take off your shoes and make your way to bed in socks, as if the others were already sleeping in such weather!)

At eight-fifteen I sit in darkness. I sit in human silence. Then I begin to hear the eloquent night, the night of wet trees, with moonlight sliding over the shoulder of the church in a haze of dampness and subsiding heat. The world of this night resounds from heaven to hell with animal eloquence, with the savage innocence of a million unknown creatures. While the earth eases and cools off like a huge wet living thing, the enormous vitality of their music pounds and rings and throbs and echoes until it gets into everything, and swamps the whole world in its neutral madness which never becomes an orgy because all things are innocent, all things are pure. Nor would I have mentioned the possibility of evil, except that I remember how the heat and the wild music of living things can drive people crazy, when they are not in monasteries, and make them do things which the world has forgotten how to lament. That is why some people act as if the night and the forest and the heat and the animals had in them something of contagion, whereas the heat is holy and the animals are the children of God and the night was never made to hide sin, but only to open infinite distances to charity and send our souls to play beyond the stars.

Eight-thirty. I begin my round, in the cellar of the south wing. The place is full of naked wires, stinks of the hides of slaughtered calves. My feet are walking on a floor of earth, down a long catacomb, at the end of which there is a brand-new locked door into the guest wing that was only finished the other day. So I punch the clock for the first time in the catacomb, I turn my back on the new wing, and the fire watch is on.

Around one corner is a hole in the wall with a vat where they stew fruit. Under this vat Dom Frederic told me to burn all the letters that were in the pigeonholes of the room where he had been Prior. Around another corner is an old furnace where I burned the rest of the papers from the same room. In this musty silence which no longer smells of wine (because the winery is now in another building) the flashlight creates a little alert tennis ball upon the walls and floor. Concrete now begins under the watchman's cat-feet and moonlight reaches through the windows into a dark place with jars of prunes and applesauce on all the shelves.

Then suddenly, after the old brooding catacomb, you hit something dizzy and new: the kitchen, painted by the brother novices, each wall in a different color. Some of the monks complained of the different colored walls, but a watchman has no opinions. There is tile under the shining vats and Scripture close to the ceiling: "Little children, love one another!"

There are blue benches in the scullery, and this one room is cool. Sometimes when you go up the stairs making no noise, a brother comes in late from the barns through the kitchen door and runs into you by surprise in the darkness, blinded by the flashlight, and (if a novice) he is probably scared to death.

For a few feet, the way is most familiar. I am in the little cloister which is the monastery's main stem. It goes from the places where the monks live to the places where they pray. But now it is empty, and like everything else it is a lot nicer when there is nobody there. The steps down to the tailor shop have a different sound. They drum under my rubber soles. I run into the smell of duck and cotton, mixed with the smell of bread. There is light in the bakery, and someone is working late, around the corner, behind the oven. I punch the clock by the bakery door: it is the second station.

The third station is the hottest one: the furnace room. This time the stairs don't drum, they ring: they are iron. I fight my way through a jungle of wet clothes, drying in the heat, and go down by the flanks of the boiler to the third station which is there up against the bricks, beneath an engraving of the Holy Face.

After that, I am in the choir novitiate. Here, too, it is hot. The place is swept and recently painted and there are notice boards at every turn in the little crooked passageways where each blue door is named after a saint. Long lists of appointments for the novices' confessions and direction. Sentences from the liturgy. Fragments of severe and necessary information. But the walls of the building have their own stuffy smell and I am suddenly haunted by my first days in religion, the freezing tough winter when I first received the habit and always had a cold, the smell of frozen straw in the dormitory under the chapel, and the deep unexpected ecstasy of Christmas—that first Christmas when you have nothing left in the world but God!

It is when you hit the novitiate that the fire watch begins in earnest. Alone, silent, wandering on your appointed rounds through the corridors of a huge, sleeping monastery, you come around the corner and find yourself face to face with your monastic past and with the mystery of your vocation.

The fire watch is an examination of conscience in which your task as watchman suddenly appears in its true light: a pretext devised by God to isolate you, and to search your soul with lamps and questions, in the heart of darkness.

God, my God, God Whom I meet in darkness, with You it is always the same thing! Always the same question that nobody knows how to answer!

I have prayed to You in the daytime with thoughts and reasons, and in the nighttime You have confronted me, scattering thought and reason. I have come to You in the morning with light and with desire, and You have descended upon me, with great gentleness, with most forbearing silence, in this inexplicable night, dispersing light, defeating all desire. I have explained to You a hundred times my motives for entering the monastery and You have listened and said nothing, and I have turned away and wept with shame.

Is it true that all my motives have meant nothing? Is it true that all my desires were an illusion?

While I am asking questions which You do not answer, You ask me a question which is so simple that I cannot answer. I do not even understand the question.

This night, and every night, it is the same question.

There is a special, living resonance in these steep hollow stairs to the novitiate chapel, where You are all alone, the windows closed tight upon You, shutting You up with the heat of the lost afternoon.

Here, when it was winter, I used to come after dinner when I was a novice, heavy with sleep and with potatoes, and kneel all the time because that was the only period in which we were allowed to do what we liked. Nothing ever happened: but that was what I liked.

Here, on Sunday mornings, a crowd of us would try to make the Way of the Cross, jostling one another among the benches, and on days of recollection in summer we would kneel here all afternoon with the sweat running down our ribs, while candles burned all around the tabernacle and the veiled ciborium stood shyly in the doorway, peeping out at us between the curtains.

And here, now, by night, with this huge clock ticking on my right hip and the flashlight in my hand and sneakers on my feet, I feel as if everything had been unreal. It is as if the past had never existed. The things I thought were so important—because of the effort I put into them—have turned out to be of small value. And the things I never thought about, the things I was never able either to measure or to expect, were the things that mattered.

(There used to be a man who walked down the back road singing, on summer mornings, right in the middle of the novices' thanksgiving after Communion: singing his own private song, every day the same. It was the sort of song you would expect to hear out in the country, in the Knobs of Kentucky.)

But in this darkness I would not be able to say, for certain, what it was that mattered. That, perhaps, is part of Your unanswerable question! Only I remember the heat in the beanfield the first June I was here, and I get the same sense of a mysterious, unsuspected value that struck me after Father Alberic's funeral.

After the novitiate, I come back into the little cloister. Soon I stand at the coolest station: down in the brothers' washroom, at the door of the ceramic studio. Cool winds come in from the forest through the big, wide-open windows.

This is a different city, with a different set of associations. The ceramic studio is something relatively new. Behind the door (where they burnt out one kiln and bought a new one) little Father John of God suddenly made a good crucifix, just a week ago. He is one of my scholastics. And I think of the clay Christ that came out of his heart. I think of the beauty and the simplicity and the pathos that were sleeping there, waiting to become an image. I think of this simple and mysterious child, and of all my other scholastics. What is waiting to be born in all their hearts? Suffering? Deception? Heroism? Defeat? Peace? Betrayal? Sanctity? Death? Glory?

On all sides I am confronted by questions that I cannot answer, because the time for answering them has not yet come. Between the silence of God and the silence of my own soul, stands the silence of the souls entrusted to me. Immersed in these three silences, I realize that the questions I ask myself about them are perhaps no more than a surmise. And perhaps the most urgent and practical renunciation is the renunciation of all questions.

The most poignant thing about the fire watch is that you go through Gethsemani not only in length and height, but also in depth. You hit strange caverns in the monastery's history, layers set down by the years, geological strata: you feel like an archeologist suddenly unearthing ancient civilizations. But the terrible thing is that you yourself have lived through those ancient civilizations. The house has changed so much that ten years have as many different meanings as ten Egyptian dynasties. The meanings are hidden in the walls. They mumble in the floor under the watchman's rubber feet. The lowest layer is at once in the catacomb under the south wing and in the church tower. Every other level of history is found in between.

The church. In spite of the stillness, the huge place seems alive. Shadows move everywhere, around the small uncertain area of light which the sanctuary light casts on the Gospel side of the altar. There are faint sounds in the darkness, the empty choirstalls creak and hidden boards mysteriously sigh.

The silence of the sacristy has its own sound. I shoot the beam of light down to Saint Malachy's altar and the relic cases. Vestments are laid out for my Mass tomorrow, at Our Lady of Victories altar. Keys rattle again in the door and the rattle echoes all over the church. When I was first on for the fire watch I thought the church was full of people praying in the dark. But no. The night is filled with unutterable murmurs, the walls with traveling noises which seem to wake up and come back, hours after something has happened, to gibber at the places where it happened.

This nearness to You in the darkness is too simple and too close for excitement. It is commonplace for all things to live an unexpected life in the nighttime: but their life is illusory and unreal. The illusion of sound only intensifies the infinite substance of Your silence.

Here, in this place where I made my vows, where I had my hands anointed for the Holy Sacrifice, where I have had Your priesthood seal the depth and intimate summit of my being, a word, a thought, would defile the quiet of Your inexplicable love.

Your Reality, O God, speaks to my life as to an intimate, in the midst of a crowd of fictions: I mean these walls, this roof, these arches, this (overhead) ridiculously large and unsubstantial tower.

Lord, God, the whole world tonight seems to be made out of paper. The most substantial things are ready to crumble or tear apart and blow away.

How much more so this monastery which everybody believes in and which has perhaps already ceased to exist!

O God, my God, the night has values that day has never dreamed of. All things stir by night, waking or sleeping, conscious of the nearness of their ruin. Only man makes himself illuminations he conceives to be solid and eternal. But while we ask our questions and come to our decisions, God blows our decisions out, the roofs of our houses cave in upon us, the tall towers are under-mined by ants, the walls crack and cave in, and the holiest buildings burn to ashes while the watchman is composing a theory of duration.

Now is the time to get up and go to the tower. Now is the time to meet You, God, where the night is wonderful, where the roof is almost without substance under my feet, where all the mysterious junk in the belfry considers the proximate coming of three new bells, where the forest opens out under the moon and the living things sing terribly that only the present is eternal and that all things having a past and a future are doomed to pass away!

This, then, is the way from the floor of the Church to the platform on the tower.

First I must make a full round of the house on the second floor. Then I must go to the third-floor dormitories. After that, the tower.

Cloister. Soft feet, total darkness. The brothers have torn up the tent in the cloister garden, where the novices were sleeping two winters ago, and where some of them got pneumonia.

Just yesterday they put a new door on Father Abbot's room, while he was away with Dom Gabriel, visiting the foundations.

I am in the corridor under the old guest house. In the middle of the hallway a long table is set with knives and forks and spoons and bowls for the breakfast of the postulants and family brothers. Three times a day they eat in the corridor. For two years there has been no other place to put them.

The high, light door into the old guest wing swings back and I am on the stairs.

I had forgotten that the upper floors were empty. The silence astonishes me. The last time I was on the fire watch there was a retreat party of fifty lined up on the second floor, signing their names in the guest register in the middle of the night. They had just arrived in a bus from Notre Dame. Now the place is absolutely empty. All the notices are off the walls. The bookshelf has vanished from the hall. The population of holy statues has been diminished. All the windows are wide open. Moonlight falls on the cool lino-leum floor. The doors of some of the rooms are open and I see that they are empty. I can feel the emptiness of all the rest.

I would like to stop and stand here for an hour, just to feel the difference. The house is like a sick person who has recovered. This is the Gethsemani that I entered, and whose existence I had almost forgotten. It was this silence, this darkness, this emptiness that I walked into with Brother Matthew eleven years ago this spring. This is the house that seemed to have been built to be remote from everything, to have forgotten all cities, to be absorbed in the eternal years. But this recovered innocence has nothing reassuring about it. The very silence is a reproach. The emptiness itself is my most terrible question.

If I have broken this silence, and if I have been to blame for talking so much about this emptiness that it came to be filled with people, who am I to praise the silence any more? Who am I to publicize this emptiness? Who am I to remark on the presence of so many visitors, so many retreatants, so many postulants, so many tourists? Or have the men of our age acquired a Midas touch of their own, so that as soon as they succeed, everything they touch becomes crowded with people?

In this age of crowds in which I have determined to be solitary, perhaps the greatest sin would be to lament the presence of people on the threshold of my solitude. Can I be so blind as to ignore that solitude is itself their greatest need? And yet if they rush in upon the desert in thousands, how shall they be alone? What went they out into the desert to see? Whom did I myself come here to find but You, O Christ, Who have compassion on the multitudes?

Nevertheless, Your compassion singles out and separates the one on whom Your mercy falls, and sets him apart from the multitudes even though You leave him in the midst of the multitudes. . . .

With my feet on the floor I waxed when I was a postulant, I ask these useless questions. With my hand on the key by the door to the tribune, where I first heard the monks chanting the psalms, I do not wait for an answer, because I have begun to realize You never answer when I expect.

The third room of the library is called hell. It is divided up by wallboard partitions into four small sections full of condemned books. The partitions are hung with American flags and pictures of Dom Edmond Obrecht. I thread my way through this unbelievable maze to the second room of the library, where the retreatants used to sit and mop their brows and listen to sermons. I do not have to look at the corner where the books about the Carthusians once sang to me their siren song as I sail past with clock ticking and light swinging and keys in my hand to unlock the door into the first room of the library. Here the scholastics have their desks. This is the upper Scriptorium. The theology books are all around the walls. Yonder is the broken cuckoo clock which Father Willibrod winds up each morning with a gesture of defiance, just before he flings open the windows.

Perhaps the dormitory of the choir monks is the longest room in Kentucky. Long lines of cubicles, with thin partitions a little over six feet high, shirts and robes and scapulars hang over the partitions trying to dry in the night air. Extra cells have been jammed along the walls between the windows. In each one lies a monk on a straw mattress. One pale bulb burns in the middle of the room. The ends are shrouded in shadows. I make my way softly past cell after cell. I know which cells have snorers in them. But no one seems to be asleep in this extraordinary tenement. I walk as softly as I can down to the far west end, where Frater Caleb sleeps in the bell-ringer's corner. I find my station inside the door of the organ loft, and punch the clock, and start off again on soft feet along the other side of the dormitory.

There is a door hidden between two cells. It leads into the infirmary annex, where the snoring is already in full swing. Beyond that, steep stairs to the third floor.

One more assignment before I can climb them. The infirmary, with its hot square little chapel, the room that contains the retreats I made before all the dates in my monastic life: clothing, professions, ordinations. I cannot pass it without something unutterable coming up out of the depths of my being. It is the silence which will lift me on to the tower.

Meanwhile I punch the clock at the next station, at the dentist's office, where next week I am to lose another molar.

Now the business is done. Now I shall ascend to the top of this religious city, leaving its modern history behind. These stairs climb back beyond the civil war. I make no account of the long lay-brothers' dormitory where a blue light burns. I hasten to the corridor by the wardrobe. I look out the low windows and know that I am already higher than the trees. Down at the end is the doorway to the attic and the tower.

The padlock always makes a great noise. The door swings back on swearing hinges and the night wind, hot and gusty, comes swirling down out of the loft with a smell of ancient rafters and old, hidden, dusty things. You have to watch the third step or your feet go through the boards. From here on the building has no substance left, but you have to mind your head and bow beneath the beams on which you can see the marks of the axes which our French Fathers used to hew them out a hundred years ago. . . .

And now the hollowness that rings under my feet measures some sixty feet to the floor of the church. I am over the transept crossing. If I climb around the corner of the dome I can find a hole once opened by the photographers and peer down into the abyss, and flash the light far down upon my stall in choir.

I climb the trembling, twisted stair into the belfry. The darkness stirs with a flurry of wings high above me in the gloomy engineering that holds the steeple together. Nearer at hand the old clock ticks in the tower. I flash the light into the mystery which keeps it going, and gaze upon the ancient bells.

I have seen the fuse box. I have looked in the corners where I think there is some wiring. I am satisfied that there is no fire in this tower which would flare like a great torch and take the whole abbey up with it in twenty minutes. . . .

And now my whole being breathes the wind which blows through the belfry, and my hand is on the door through which I see the heavens. The door swings out upon a vast sea of darkness and of prayer. Will it come like this, the moment of my death? Will You open a door upon the great forest and set my feet upon a ladder under the moon, and take me out among the stars?

The roof glistens under my feet, this long metal roof facing the forest and the hills, where I stand higher than the treetops and walk upon shining air.

Mists of damp heat rise up out of the fields around the sleeping abbey. The whole valley is flooded with moonlight and I can count the southern hills beyond the watertank, and almost number the trees of the forest to the north. Now the huge chorus of living beings rises up out of the world beneath my feet: life singing in the watercourses, throbbing in the creeks and the fields and the trees, choirs of millions and millions of jumping and flying and creeping things. And far above me the cool sky opens upon the frozen distance of the stars.

I lay the clock upon the belfry ledge and pray cross-legged with my back against the tower, and face the same unanswered question.

Lord God of this great night: do You see the woods? Do You hear the rumor of their loneliness? Do You behold their secrecy? Do You remember their solitudes? Do You see that my soul is beginning to dissolve like wax within me?

Clamabo per diem et non exaudies, et nocte et non ad insipientiam mihi!

Do You remember the place by the stream? Do You remember the top of the Vineyard Knob that time in autumn, when the train was in the valley? Do You remember McGinty's hollow? Do You remember the thinly wooded hillside behind Hanekamp's place? Do You remember the time of the forest fire? Do You know what has become of the little poplars we planted in the spring? Do You observe the valley where I marked the trees?

There is no leaf that is not in Your care. There is no cry that was not heard by You before it was uttered. There is no water in the shales that was not hidden there by Your wisdom. There is no concealed spring that was not concealed by You. There is no glen for a lone house that was not planned by You for a lone house. There is no man for that acre of woods that was not made by You for that acre of woods.

But there is greater comfort in the substance of silence than in the answer to a question. Eternity is in the present. Eternity is in the palm of the hand. Eternity is a seed of fire, whose sudden roots break barriers that keep my heart from being an abyss.

The things of Time are in connivance with eternity. The shadows serve You. The beasts sing to You before they pass away. The solid hills shall vanish like a worn-out garment. All things change, and die and disappear. Questions arrive, assume their actuality, and also disappear. In this hour I shall cease to ask them, and silence shall be my answer. The world that Your love created, that the heat has distorted, and that my mind is always misinterpreting, shall cease to interfere with our voices.

Minds which are separated pretend to blend in one another's

language. The marriage of souls in concepts is mostly an illusion. Thoughts which travel outward bring back reports of You from outward things: but a dialogue with You, uttered through the world, always ends by being a dialogue with my own reflection in the stream of time. With You there is no dialogue unless You choose a mountain and circle it with cloud and print Your words in fire upon the mind of Moses. What was delivered to Moses on tables of stone, as the fruit of lightning and thunder, is now more thoroughly born in our own souls as quietly as the breath of our own being.

The hand lies open. The heart is dumb. The soul that held my substance together, like a hard gem in the hollow of my own power, will one day totally give in.

Although I see the stars, I no longer pretend to know them. Although I have walked in those woods, how can I claim to love them? One by one I shall forget the names of individual things.

You, Who sleep in my breast, are not met with words, but in the emergence of life within life and of wisdom within wisdom. You are found in communion: Thou in me and I in Thee and Thou in them and they in me: dispossession within dispossession, dispassion within dispassion, emptiness within emptiness, freedom within freedom. I am alone. Thou art alone. The Father and I are One.

The Voice of God is heard in Paradise:

"What was vile has become precious. What is now precious was never vile. I have always known the vile as precious: for what is vile I know not at all.

"What was cruel has become merciful. What is now merciful was never cruel. I have always overshadowed Jonas with My mercy, and cruelty I know not at all. Have you had sight of Me, Jonas My child? Mercy within mercy within mercy. I have forgiven the universe without end, because I have never known sin.

"What was poor has become infinite. What is infinite was never poor. I have always known poverty as infinite: riches I love not at all. Prisons within prisons within prisons. Do not lay up for yourselves ecstasies upon earth, where time and space corrupt, where the minutes break in and steal. No more lay hold on time, Jonas, My son, lest the rivers bear you away.

"What was fragile has become powerful. I loved what was most frail. I looked upon what was nothing. I touched what was without substance, and within what was not, I am."

There are drops of dew that show like sapphires in the grass as soon as the great sun appears, and leaves stir behind the hushed flight of an escaping dove.

CONJECTURES OF A GUILTY BYSTANDER

Conjectures of a Guilty Bystander *(1966) marks a departure from Merton's earlier journals. He wanted* Conjectures *to be more allusive; less connected to rigid journal entries; more filled with reflections on his reading, his love for nature, his deeper entry into the contemplative life of the liturgy.*

The excerpt below, the third part of the journal, is most remembered for the famous moment of conversion at the corner of "Fourth and Walnut" in which Merton affirms his great love and solidarity with all who live in the world. Many commentators have seen that moment as axial: Merton's working out of the relationship between his contemplative vocation and the demands of being a witness for social justice.

Less well known is the closing prayer written on the eve of Pentecost. Merton's writings are studded with prayers and prayer fragments. This is one of the longer ones, and its sentiments, redolent of praise of God, artfully combine his love of nature and deepening sense of the human community at prayer.

❊

THE NIGHT SPIRIT AND THE DAWN AIR

We must love them both, those whose opinions we share and those whose opinions we reject. For both have labored in the search for truth and both have helped us in the finding of it.   —St. Thomas Aquinas

When devils drive the reasonable wild
They strip the adult century so bare,
Love must be regrown from the sensual child.
                    —W. H. Auden

121

How the valley awakes. At two-fifteen in the morning there are no sounds except in the monastery: the bells ring, the office begins. Outside, nothing, except perhaps a bullfrog saying "Om" in the creek or in the guesthouse pond. Some nights he is in Samadhi; there is not even "Om." The mysterious and uninterrupted whooping of the whippoorwill begins about three, these mornings. He is not always near. Sometimes there are two whooping together, perhaps a mile away in the woods in the east.

The first chirps of the waking day birds mark the "*point vierge*" of the dawn under a sky as yet without real light, a moment of awe and inexpressible innocence, when the Father in perfect silence opens their eyes. They begin to speak to Him, not with fluent song, but with an awakening question that is their dawn state, their state at the "*point vierge.*" Their condition asks if it is time for them to "be." He answers "yes." Then, they one by one wake up, and become birds. They manifest themselves as birds, beginning to sing. Presently they will be fully themselves, and will even fly.

Meanwhile, the most wonderful moment of the day is that when creation in its innocence asks permission to "be" once again, as it did on the first morning that ever was.

All wisdom seeks to collect and manifest itself at that blind sweet point. Man's wisdom does not succeed, for we are fallen into self-mastery and cannot ask permission of anyone. We face our mornings as men of undaunted purpose. We know the time and we dictate terms. We are in a position to dictate terms, we suppose: we have a clock that proves we are right from the very start. We know what time it is. We are in touch with the hidden inner laws. We will say in advance what kind of day it has to be. Then if necessary we will take steps to make it meet our requirements.

For the birds there is not a time that they tell, but the virgin point between darkness and light, between nonbeing and being. You can tell yourself the time by their waking, if you are experienced. But that is your folly, not theirs. Worse folly still if you think they are telling you something you might consider useful—that it is, for example, four o'clock.

So they wake: first the catbirds and cardinals and some that I do not know. Later the song sparrows and wrens. Last of all the doves and crows.

The waking of crows is most like the waking of men: querulous, noisy, raw.

Here is an unspeakable secret: paradise is all around us and we do not understand. It is wide open. The sword is taken away, but we do not know it: we are off "one to his farm and another to his merchandise." Lights on. Clocks ticking. Thermostats working. Stoves cooking. Electric shavers filling radios with static. "Wisdom," cries the dawn deacon, but we do not attend.

We are now in the most perfect days of the Appalachian spring, late April: days of dogwood and redbud blossoms. Cool clear days with every delicate shade of green and red in the thinly budding branches of the oaks and maples. Later, in the burnt haze of summer, Kentucky's soaked green will be monotonous as a jungle, turning brown in the heat. Now it is France, or England. The hills suddenly look like the Cotswolds.

Yesterday I got a letter from one of the last Shaker eldresses, at their community in New Hampshire. It was an answer to an inquiry, and she enclosed a rather touching little leaflet about how the Shakers now faced extinction without concern, convinced that they had not been a failure, that they had done what the Lord had asked of them. I find this easy to believe. The Shakers have been something of a sign, a mystery, a strange attempt at utter honesty which, in trying perhaps to be too ideally pure, was nevertheless pure—with moments of absurdity.

They were absolutely loyal to a vision that led nowhere: but which seemed to them to point to a definitive eschatological goal. And perhaps they were not as deceived as one might think. Can such definitive visions really be pure illusion? Even in leading "nowhere," are they perhaps not significant? Could the Shakers do the perfect work they did (in their furniture, for instance) if their vision were not real? The witness of their craftsmanship is certainly most impressive.

The poems of Bertolt Brecht are like sackcloth and brown

bread. To what extent is their healthy disillusionment itself an artifice? I think he is genuine. But if so, how does he believe what he
seems to believe? Or does he believe it? Or is his Marxism a matter
of convenience? It would be silly to suppose that a Marxist poet
with official backing could not be also a good poet. I don't know
how much of a Marxist Brecht really is. But I like him, in any case:
and I like his poems better than his plays. I like his poetry better
than that of the esoteric American pontiffs of the day. Brecht is a
most individual poet, more so than many who are intensely
conscious of their individuality.

It is curious that the growth of anti-Semitism in medieval Germanic Christendom went hand in hand with a kind of practical
Judaizing of Christianity. The consciousness of Germanic Christendom in the eighth to eleventh centuries was increasingly levitical and military. The God of Charlemagne was the Lord of Hosts
who anointed him emperor. Liturgy and theology became allegori-
cal and midrashic. Germanic medieval culture appealed spontaneously to the Old Testament rather than to the New to justify its
instinctive tendencies. So also in some measure did the Celtic
Church, with its penitential tariffs. The altar of the Christian
Church became once again the altar of the temple, in the holy of
holies, the hidden sanctuary, served by a levitical priesthood. The
theology of baptism in this cultural and religious climate turned
back to look again at circumcision (says Chenu).

The theology of suffering is strongly tinged with ideas of punishment, and morality becomes a morality of obedience rather than
love. In this aggressive, solemn, dark and feudal Christianity in
which the emperor is nearer and more real than the Pope, in which
the bishop is at once a high priest and a general and monks are
fighting Levites, there grows up the hatred and contempt of the
Jew, whose role is more and more that of the theological Christ-
killer on whom the curse has fallen. But perhaps there was in this a
deep unconscious guilt for Christians who did not truly understand
Christ. St. Paul was still read, and there must have been something
of a consciousness of a return to the Law which is, in the eyes of
Paul, the confession that one has failed to understand Christian
faith and has secretly abandoned it.

It is interesting to note the creeping anti-Semitism in the Liturgical Easter Trope, which turns into a real drama, with comic characters and villains. This development is seen for example at St. Gall, where an odious and comic Jewish villain, Rufus, comes to play a more and more important part in the Crucifixion scenes, for the Easter play, as we advance into the Middle Ages, becomes more and more a Passion play. It is with the dramatizing of the Passion that the image of the Jew as villain and "Christ-killer" becomes fixed in the European mind.

In the theology of the time, the transition from Old to New Testament was more and more the esoteric privilege of those who, understanding the "mystical sense" of the Old Testament types, were able to see the Charity and the Spirit of Christ in the "carnal figures" of the Old Testament. But since this mystical understanding implied, in fact, not only a very special culture, but also a highly developed spirituality, it was not the affair of many. The fact that in monasteries there were many monks who could not transcend in this way the Old Testament symbolism and ritual of the monasteries constituted something of a problem. Blessed Guerric of Igny, the Cistercian, in his Christmas sermons (which like all his sermons are very Pauline) upbraids these severe and rather pessimistic monks and calls them "the Jews." Thus again there was a renewal of a very bad conscience among those who were thought and supposed to be the best of Christians. If many of these were still "no better than Jews," what about the Jews themselves, down at the bottom of the social scale? (Note, as the Middle Ages went on Cistercian monasteries were often heavily in debt to Jews. (See Knowles, *Monastic Order in England*)

John of Salisbury, the School of Chartres, and St. Thomas Aquinas, in creating a new climate of philosophy and theology, changed this somewhat. The School of St. Victor at the beginning of the twelfth century returned to the literal interpretation of Scripture with much friendly consultation of rabbis. St. Anselm and his group were open to a more tolerant and reasonable dialogue with the Jew as well as the Muslim. But the Crusades did much to destroy this spirit of openness and toleration.

The greatness of the Old Testament is beginning to be fully evident in some of the fine Old Testament theologies written by Protestant scholars like Von Rad, Eichrodt, and others. The universe of the Old Testament is a praising universe, of which man is a living and essential part, standing shoulder to shoulder with the angelic hosts who praise Yahweh: and praise is the surest manifestation of true life. The characteristic of *Sheol,* the realm of the dead, is that there is no praise in it. The Psalms then are the purest expression of the essence of life in this universe: Yahweh is present to His people when the Psalms are sung with triumphant vigor and jubilation (not just muttered and mediated in the individual beard). This presence and communion, this *coming into being* in the act of praise, is the heart of Old Testament worship as it is also of monastic choral praise. Living praise is the fullness of man's being with God and the "mystery of the spirit" (Von Rad). But it also has a historical dimension: faith in the power of Yahweh and in His great works of mercy as well as in His promises makes history present to the singer as a theological reality and fact (again Von Rad). The theological realization of these great acts of the Lord is *felt and experienced in their beauty;* the magnificent power of the radiance of the Lord revealed in His saving acts takes hold entirely on the worshiper. Hence the "transported" quality of the Psalms which we priests miss entirely when we simply mumble our way through the breviary, with no taste left for words like *cantate, jubilate, exultate. . . .* (I remember when Dom Baron came to Gethsemani and was teaching us chant: he finally got us really going in the Introit of the fourth Sunday after Easter and I thought we were going to rock the roof off the Church. But that was only once—no, we nearly did it again on the following Ascension Day. The text was perfect for it: *Jubilate Deo omnis terra,* "Sing your joy to God all the earth.") *Jubilate:* it is a joy one *cannot contain.* Where is that in our liturgy today? This is the true liturgical shout of triumph, the triumph we know when divine and angelic beauty possess our whole being, in the joy of the risen Christ!

Returning to my previous section on the "Old Testament" quality of early Germanic Christendom and monasticism: we must not be too one-sided about it. One cannot read the monastic Fathers, whether you take Paschasius Radbertus, or Rupert of Deutz, or St. Bernard, or Guerric of Igny, or Odo of Cluny, or Peter the Venerable, without realizing that this sense of being transported with praise came to life in the monasteries of the early Middle Ages: but perhaps after the years it was deadened (and then we get the bawdy and despairing songs of the wandering, lost, beat monks, the Goliards).

The beauty of God is best praised by the men who *reach and realize their limit* knowing that their praise cannot attain to God. It is then that the inarticulate, long *jubilus* takes over in Gregorian chant: some of the extended melismatic developments of the alleluia in the Easter Liturgy, particularly those of the seventh tone. Gregorian has a special grace for bringing out this experience of praise that reaches its limit, fails, and yet continues in a new dimension.

In this way praise reaches not only the heart of God but also the heart of creation itself, finding everywhere the beauty of the righteousness of Yahweh.

Bishop Nanayakkara of Kandy in Ceylon was here last week. He said that he got to know St. John of the Cross when the books were sent to him as a present by a poor working woman in the United States. He is glad to have the Little Brothers of Jesus in his diocese, and says he told one of them, who is a shoemaker, that if the other shoemakers have a party and invite him, he ought to go: for if he is not able to go he is betraying his vocation!

The Ox Mountain parable of Mencius: Note the importance of the "night spirit" and the "dawn breath" in restoring to life the forest that has been cut down.

Even though the Ox Mountain forest has been cut to the ground, if the mountain is left to rest and recuperate in the night and the dawn, the trees will return. But men cut them down, cattle browse on the new shoots: no night spirit, no dawn breath—no rest, no renewal—and finally one is convinced that there never were any woods on the Ox Mountain. So, Mencius concludes, with human nature. Without the night spirit, the dawn breath, silence, passivity, rest, man's nature cannot be itself. In its barrenness it is no longer *natura:* nothing grows from it, nothing is born of it any more.

Lewis Mumford says, in his *City in History,* that the earliest cities were cities of the dead. The necropolis, the cemetery, antedates the city of the living. This is clear in Genesis. Abraham lives in tents and is on the move all the time—until he dies. There is one fixed place only: the place where you finally stop and "rest" or "sleep with the Fathers." This place may be selected (or indeed hallowed by the tombs of generations), and one may die far from it: but one's body must then be transported there. The beginning of the world as we know it is the beginning of fixed cities for the living, growing up next to the cities of the dead, under the shadow of the ancestors. The metropolis. But the metropolis, with all its affluence and all its bursting pride of apparent life, is a center for death. Even the architecture of a city like modern Washington is the architecture of a necropolis (compare the even more tomblike government buildings erected by Hitler, Mussolini, Stalin). Among the big white tombs, vast dark areas of slums, through which one travels without seeing them: the permanence of death, sickness, vice in the world of the poor who remain imprisoned in their poverty, nailed to one place by it!

Why all this? In spite of our myths about him, Stone Age man was not a man of war. He was concerned with hunting, agriculture, domesticating animals, the home. The city is the place where the mythology of power and war develop, the center from which the magic of power reaches out to destroy the enemy and to perpetuate one's own life and riches—interminably if only it were possible. But it is never possible. Hence, the desperate need to placate the gods, to have the gods on our side, to win: for this, the most drastic and "effective method" is human sacrifice. Wars have to be won in order to keep the gods of the city supplied with the blood of conquered victims. The dead also demand the blood of the living. This is the answer of Minerva justifying the war of Troy (Simone Weil). Once you have four dead heroes you have four unanswerable reasons why a whole army must shed its blood until the enemy is destroyed and the heroes are avenged. Urban culture is then committed to war "as to the elixir of sovereign power and the most effective purgation of sovereign discontent with that power" (Mumford).

We live, of course, in the most advanced of all urban cultures.

Czeslaw Milosz has sent some of his translations of Zbigniew Herbert—a fantastically good poet—along with a letter in which he challenges me on my love of nature, my optimistic attitude toward it, my not reflecting how cruel nature is, and so on. In other words, he thinks I am not Manichaean enough: do I have a right at a time like this to be, (or to imagine myself), immune to certain poisons? (Others are convinced that I am too Manichaean, but I have never taken them seriously.)

Should I really experience nature as *alien* and *heartless?* Should I be prepared to imagine that this alienation from nature is real, and that an attitude of sympathy, of oneness with it, is only imaginary? On the contrary—we have a choice of projections. Our attitude toward nature is simply an extension of our attitude toward ourselves, and toward one another. We are free to be at peace with ourselves and others, and also with nature.

Or are we?

There is this problem: it was the swine in the SS who most loved nature, and who turned to "her" as a relief from their orgies, to keep themselves, after all, human in the midst of the hell they had created for themselves by creating it for others. They would torture others, and then turn around and be at peace with nature! The problem is this: that since in fact it is those who are most beastly who often tend to speak in the simplest and most innocent terms of the happiness of life, does it follow that one should not permit himself to be happy in such a time as ours, because the mere fact of enjoying life, or any aspect of life, automatically puts one in connivance with those who are systematically ruining it?

In any case, there is certainly a trite and completely false naturalism that is part of the totalitarian myth—or simply part of the mentality of mass society (campers, national parks, driving to the beach, etc., etc.). But does that mean that one cannot retain any claim to honesty and authenticity without making a cult of the ugly, the irrelevant?

Sartre's meditation on the root in *La Nausée* seems to me to be just as forced and just as trite as any romantic effusion of Lamartine on a moonlit landscape . . . just as pitiable as the cry of a kid on the waterfront promenade at Bouville when the lighthouse turned on: this cry which made the hero of *La Nausée* turn in disgust from the Sunday crowd.

(Where I meet Roquentin, the dour hero of *La Nausée,* is in the cafe, listening to "Some of These Days!" Here I identify with him. I wonder if Sartre realized the full impact of this voice of the distant Negro singer *abolishing* the absolute loneliness of Roquentin by making it universal and showing it to be shared by all!)

I wonder if it is a sin against poverty to read St. John Perse. His poems abound in all kinds of magnificence, in every sort of rich words. To read such poems is to live and move in splendor. Your heart becomes a tropical palace, opening out on the seven seas and all the continents, with spice ships coming to you from everywhere, and the soft voices of the Antilles speaking from the heart of the sun.

The democratic primaries are coming up. There is a man running for jailer who ought to know the job well. He has been in jail four times as a moonshiner. He is a "good Catholic" too. Everything recommends him for the office.

Flycatchers, shaking their wings after the rain.

This morning there was a theological conference in Chapter. Father A—came slowly out with a dignity befitting his years and, after a very long silence, began reading what he had written on the backs of envelopes. As the general tittering subsided and everyone sank into a blank, clock-watching resignation, Father A. went on persistently and almost unintelligibly, developing his chosen theme. I settled back, got myself sitting straight, and started some yoga breathing. Five or six pranayamas. Some square breathing, then concentrated on the stream of air entering my nostrils and followed it in and out of the lungs. The time passed painlessly enough with this and the Jesus prayer. At the end, however, when Father A— got his envelopes back together again and returned to his place, instead of getting out of there as fast as we decently could we had to sit through a question period. Everyone was so mad that there were very few questions, except one from Father B—, who complained that Father A— had not quoted from any of the Fathers of the Church. I had not been struck by this oversight myself, and cannot say that I cared. Then Father C— got up and read two or three authoritative declarations of Councils, Popes, etc., and Father D—, the moderator, as usual, said that the conference was really very good, but he added that he had hoped it would be longer.

In any normal gathering this statement would have been unpopular enough to merit boos and catcalls, if not a near riot. We just stood up and chanted the De Profundis.

If you ask me, that was significant enough!

A satanic theology—which Rimbaud had learned somewhere, and France and Belgium used to be full of it—hides Christ from us altogether, and makes Him so impossibly beautiful that He must remain infinitely remote from our wretchedness.

"He was a man like you and me: or rather He was a man, but *not like you,* because He was 'The God-Man.' If He suffered, it was almost as if He only seemed to suffer, because He could stop suffering when He wished (which *you* cannot do!) and because even in His suffering He had the beatific vision. God can cheat like that and get away with it. But *you* can't get away with anything.

"On the contrary: His suffering has become *your* condemnation to suffer without reprieve. All sorts of authorities can now point to the Cross as the ultimate reason why you should submit to arbitrary punishment now and forever! Please do not protest or contradict! To do so is now blasphemy!

"He knew He was God. He knew He was *not like you.* He thought of this and was secretly pleased all the time. He thought: I am God, I am *not like them.*" (As if He had never preached the parable of the Pharisee and the publican. It is Satan's theology to make Christ the most perfect of all the Pharisees, so that the publicans will all despair while the Pharisees will come to Him and be confirmed in their self-righteousness.)

"All His life long, then, He was looking around at the men He had come to save, knowing He was *not like them.* Death could not hold Him. He did not really have to pray. He just pretended. And by pretending, He set a trap for man. He made all suffering final and inexorable!"

That is a tragedy of Rimbaud's meditations, the brave despair of one forever alienated by the beautiful, satanic hypocrisy of a gnostic incarnation! The despair of one who feels that to be poor and miserable is automatically to be damned: He accepts his poverty and misery fully, he empties himself, in full consciousness of what he is doing, because the only alternative is the self-deception of pretending to come close to the Beautiful Pure One Who is forever inaccessible! With only a little less contempt on his lips, Rimbaud would have the face of a saint, and who is to say what his heart was? Who will say that the bitterness was his fault?

"There is in Him no comeliness." Christ came on earth, not to wear the awful cold beauty of a holy statue, but to be numbered among the wicked, to die as one of them, condemned by the pure, He Who was beyond purity and impurity. If Christ is not really my brother with all my sorrows, with all my burdens on His shoulder and all my poverty and sadness in His heart, then there has been no redemption. Then what happened on the Cross was only magic, and the miracles were magic without purpose. We have trouble understanding the Albigensians? But the world is full of them, Rimbaud, Surrealists, Beats ... not only poor Simone Weil! Whose fault, I wonder?

Both in Malraux and in Orwell it is there—the obsession with immortality. You find it everywhere. Orwell comes out with it several times, in essays: He will say, in passing, that this is the "great question." Immortality. "The major problem of our day is the decay of the belief in personal immortality." Such are his words. The Ministry of Truth has its own way of dealing with that question. Indeed, the great question, among totalitarians. And Berken, in Malraux's *Royal Way* (a poor book), seeking to remain immortal among dead cities in Cambodia!

Julien Green continually asks himself: can a novelist be a saint? Can a novelist save his soul? But perhaps the salvation of his soul depends precisely on his willingness to take that risk, and to be a novelist. And perhaps if he refused to challenge and accepted something that seemed to him more "safe," he would be lost. "He that will save his life must lose it."

I believe, with Diadochos of Photike, that if at the hour of my death my confidence in God's mercy is unfaltering, I will pass the frontier without trouble and get by the dreadful array of my sins as if they were not there, because of God's grace and the Precious Blood of Christ the Lamb of God, and the compunction He gives to the repentant. And I will, by His mercy, leave them behind forever.

"Des hommes comme Saint Seraphim, Saint François d'As-

sise et bien d'autres, ont accompli dans leur vie l'union des Eglises." *

This profound and simple statement of an Orthodox Metropolitan, Eulogius, gives the key to ecumenism for monks, and indeed for everyone.

If I do not have unity in myself, how can I even think, let alone speak, of unity among Christians? Yet, of course, in seeking unity for all Christians, I also attain unity within myself.

The heresy of individualism: thinking oneself a completely self-sufficient unit and asserting this imaginary "unity" against all others. The affirmation of the self as simply "not the other." But when you seek to affirm your unity by denying that you have anything to do with anyone else, by negating everyone else in the universe until you come down to *you:* what is there left to affirm? Even if there were something to affirm, you would have no breath left with which to affirm it.

The true way is just the opposite: the more I am able to affirm others, to say "yes" to them in myself, by discovering them in myself and myself in them, the more real I am. I am fully real if my own heart says *yes* to *everyone.*

I will be a better Catholic, not if I can *refute* every shade of Protestantism, but if I can affirm the truth in it and still go further.

So, too, with the Muslims, the Hindus, the Buddhists, etc. This does not mean syncretism, indifferentism, the vapid and careless friendliness that accepts everything by thinking of nothing. There is much that one cannot "affirm" and "accept," but first one must say "yes" where one really can.

If I affirm myself as a Catholic merely by denying all that is Muslim, Jewish, Protestant, Hindu, Buddhist, etc., in the end I will find that there is not much left for me to affirm as a Catholic: and certainly no breath of the Spirit with which to affirm it.

I had been waiting for an opportunity to say Mass for Louis Massignon and for his project for African boys, under the patronage of Blessed Charles Lwanga. I happened in a curious and almost

---

* Men like St. Seraphim, Saint Francis of Assisi, and others like them, have accomplished, in their lives, the union of the Churches.

arbitrary manner to pick June 3d, and only today did I discover by accident that June 3d is the Feast of the Uganda Martyrs (and of Blessed Charles Lwanga among them). Meanwhile, Louis Massignon writes that nonviolence is mocked in Paris and opposed by the hierarchy.

Festival of a martyr (Saint Antonin, September 2).

Through the martyr in whose town I knew thee, O Christ, whose sanctuary I did not enter, though as a child I danced at his festival.

Through the great merits of this martyr bring me to truth and to the suffering of reality, which is my joy.

Thy martyr, O Christ, has a deep green river, and a limestone bridge of unequal arches, reflected in the placid water.

Thy martyr, O Christ, has cliffs and woods, and, as I understand, no longer any train.

Sometimes, O Lord, I pray best to the saints, and sometimes best of all to this one who had a clarinet and a gramophone. (I was reproved for sticking my head into the horn of the gramophone, which was playing "Tea For Two" and not for one.) The people of the town, O Lord! They have not changed. The Germans probably did not come there, or not very much, though there must have been *maquis* in the forest where the wild boars once were, where we danced at the forester's wedding. Wine barrels, berets, *tabliers, l'accent du midi,* and singing in the stinking dark streets, walking slowly! (Watch your step by the old tannery!)

Thy martyr's town, O Lord, still walks at the pace of the ox cart.

Some charitable and some harsh, some beautiful and some ugly. The smell of the hair lotions from the barbershops, and of rabbit stewed in wine in many houses. How could I forget the people of this martyr, laughing over the wine glasses?

Or the girl in the dark dress, the solemn one, who served me beer in the Hotel Luffaut and told me: "Arnold Bennett slept here."

For Marxian humanism, man does not yet exist. Man is alienated by the society he lives in. He does not yet know what he will be when he becomes himself. But alienated man must be wiped out, and then man as he really ought to be will come into existence.

It is both dangerous and easy to hate man as he is because he is not "what he ought to be." If we do not first respect what he *is* we will never suffer him to become what he ought to be: in our impatience we will do away with him altogether. Strange that Marx at first toyed with an idea of what man *is* and then rejected it, confessing the sin of "idealism": he had wasted time thinking about an "essence." For Communism, this is the great philosophical sin.

But if you deny man his essence, you refuse him at the same time the respect that is due to his existence. It is of little avail to deify man if at the same time you do not allow that he is real: if at the same time he remains simply a fluid nonentity, the shadow of the situations into which he is maneuvered by history. What matter if he takes charge of history if history, after all, really determines him anyway? If, in the end, he is only the reflection of his own work?

The great question, then, is the ambivalence of Marxian humanism.

Let us walk along here, says my shadow, and compose a number of sentences, each one of which begins: "You think you are a monk, but . . ."

Perhaps I am stronger than I think.

Perhaps I am even afraid of my strength, and turn it against myself, thus making myself weak. Making myself secure. Making myself guilty.

Perhaps I am most afraid of the strength of God in me. Perhaps I would rather be guilty and weak in myself, than strong in Him whom I cannot understand.

Beauty of sunlight falling on a tall vase of red and white carnations and green leaves on the altar of the novitiate chapel. The light and dark. The darkness of the fresh, crinkled flower: light, warm and red, all around the darkness. The flower is the same color as blood, but it is in no sense whatever "as red as blood." Not at all! It is as red as a carnation. Only that.

This flower, this light, this moment, this silence: *Dominus est.* Eternity. He passes. He remains. We pass. In and out. He passes.

We remain. We are nothing. We are everything. He is in us. He is gone from us. He is not here. We are here in Him.

All these things can be said, but why say them?

The flower is itself. The light is itself. The silence is itself. I am myself. All, perhaps, illusion. But no matter, for illusion is the shadow of reality and reality is the grace and gift that underlies all these lights, these colors, this silence. Underlies? Is that true? They are simply real. They themselves are His gift.

The simplicity that would have kept these flowers off this altar is perhaps less simple than the simplicity which enjoys them there, but does not need them to be there.

And for the rest, whatever is said about it is nothing.

Louis Massignon is a man with a rare and important vocation: the dialogue with Islam. Not a dressed-up dialogue over teacups or on TV: but the dialogue as compassion, substitution, identification, taking upon himself the effects of what "our own" have done, knowingly or otherwise, to "them," whether in North Africa, the Near East, or anywhere else.

Better than anyone, Massignon understands the peculiar arrogance of an apostolate which, without seeking to understand in depth the meaning of *Tawhid,* bursts in upon the faith of the Muslim with the accusation that he is inferior, with the demand that he betray his highest conception of the purity and oneness of God the Holy: in favor of what we assert to be more holy. He thinks that we are trying to substitute something for the One God and persuade him that the One God is not yet holy enough! Small wonder that he does not betray a truth that, after all, we ourselves are supposed to die for.

Heavy snow. It is a cold winter and there is a flu epidemic. There was one warm moment the other day after dinner, in which transient warmth I heard a song sparrow out in the fields beyond the enclosure wall. Sunlight played on the dead yellow grass in the Mill Bottom and lied that spring was coming. Not yet!

There is yellow grass all over the big dirt dam. Behind it, the dark and wooded wall of the Forty Acre Knob.

Flu. People stumble out of the night office and go back to bed. Indulgences in refectory. It is now beginning to get so bad that they are taking sick monks out of the dormitory and putting them, six or eight together, in the big rooms of the old guest house. One novice is sleeping in the novitiate typing room, where it is warm. A postulant arrived in the middle of the plague and immediately got it.

Brother Wilfrid, the assistant infirmarian, complains: "All Father Abbot can talk about is temperatures and eggs. I could set fire to the hen house and then we'd have plenty of both."

Room 5 in the old guesthouse is full of novices, therefore full of dissipation, pillow fights, and even some talking, so I am informed.

Brother Lawrence (Cardenal—the Nicaraguan poet) lies in bed with the blanket drawn up to his chin. Asked how he feels he smiles broadly and says: "Very bad."

Two brothers push a wagon up and down the long hall, bringing soup and fruit juice to the victims.

The other night they moved one of the novices, who snores, into a room with some professed. He woke up in the morning and looked around. All the other beds were empty. The wise and prudent had moved to the new guesthouse. Another, with the simplicity of the dove, had gone to sleep on the floor of the scriptorium.

Everyone says the Northern Lights were seen all over the sky early this morning (around three, when we were in choir).

Looking out of the novitiate, when the winter sun is rising on the snowy pastures and on the pine woods of the Lake Knob, I am absorbed in the lovely blue and mauve shadows on the snow and the indescribably delicate color of the sunlit patches under the trees. All the life and color of the landscape is in the snow and sky, as if the soul of winter had appeared and animated our world this morning. The green of the pines is dull, verging on brown. Dead leaves still cling to the oaks and they also are dull brown. The cold sky is very blue. The air is dry and frozen. Instead of the mild, ambivalent winter of Kentucky, I breathe again the rugged cold of upstate New York.

Yang and Yin: the rock and earth, for Chinese artists, would be *feminine*. The light and austerity of color in the snow and sky, *masculine*. Yet there is a great deal of pastel softness in the blue and purple shadows. There is no art that has anything to say about this and art should not attempt it. The Chinese came closest to it with their Tao of painting, and what they painted was not landscapes but Tao. The nineteenth-century European and American realists were so realistic that their pictures were totally unlike what they were supposed to represent. And the first thing wrong with them was, of course, precisely that they were pictures. In any case, nothing resembles reality less than the photograph. Nothing resembles substance less than its shadow. To convey the meaning of something substantial you have to use not a shadow but a sign, not the imitation but the image. The image is a new and different reality, and of course it does not convey an impression of some object, but the mind of the subject: and that is something else again.

Man is the image of God, not His shadow. At present, we have decided that God is dead and that we are his shadow. . . . Take a picture of that, Jack!

A postulant from Colombia, who came to us from the Franciscan seminary, told me about his experiences when Rojas Pinilla's troops were firing tear gas into the Church of the Portiuncula in Bogota. Tanks in the crowded street. Crowds surging out of the church and into the friars' enclosure, for refuge, everyone of course in tears.

Gabriel Marcel says that the artist who labors to produce effects for which he is well known is unfaithful to himself. This may seem obvious enough when it is badly stated: but how differently we act. We are all too ready to believe that the self that we have created out of our more or less inauthentic efforts to be real in the eyes of others is a "real self." We even take it for our identity. Fidelity to such a nonidentity is of course infidelity to our real person, which is hidden in mystery. Who will you find that has enough faith and self-respect to attend to this mystery and to begin by accepting himself as *unknown?* God help the man who thinks he knows all about himself.

Today (February 14) is the Feast of the Cistercian hermit, Blessed Conrad—a great embarrassment to the entire Order. I would not be surprised if they did away with him, finally. He even bothered me a bit when I was a novice, and later when I was given the job of writing those absurd lives of saints that, thank God, never got published. Now I find that I have a great love for him. I even think I understand him a little. He is perhaps my favorite saint in the Order—a choice which can only be interpreted as very perverse.

I doubt if I even included him in the "lives" I wrote *in illo tempore.* He seemed to be an odd-ball and a failure. This, of course, is what almost any genuine hermit *must* seem, until such time as he becomes a completely impossible legend (or, more likely, is totally forgotten). Blessed Conrad apparently got nowhere: as if his life, a series of incomprehensible accidents, ended in midair. This last fact is taken, in desperation, by the breviary to justify what was in fact not comprehensible. "He was on his way home because he heard St. Bernard was dying." But of course he did not get home. He died on the way. "In a crypt." He was not even traveling, he was staying in this crypt. Outside Bari, in Italy. It was the people of Bari who venerated him, not the monks (until much later).

Blessed Conrad enjoys the unique distinction of being a monk of the Order who was *permitted by St. Bernard* to become a hermit. This is certainly, in itself, almost a miracle. In addition, it is thought that Blessed Conrad was one of the group that started out for the Holy Land with Abbot Arnold of Morimond, traditionally treated as an apostate. . . .

Obviously none of the really interesting and important things about Conrad are known, except that he was a hermit in Palestine for many years, and then returned, dying as a pilgrim hermit in a crypt outside Bari, dedicated to Our Lady.

But in any event, my Mass on his feast today was certainly festive and splendid. Sun poured in the novitiate chapel onto the altar and a glory of reflected lights from the hammered-silver chalice splashed all over the corporal and all around the Host. Deep and total silence. And the Gospel: "Fear not little flock . . ."

Those who love solitude have a special claim on Providence and must rely on God's love for them even more blindly than anyone else.

Massignon has some deeply moving pages in the *Mardis de Dar-es-Salam:* About the desert, the tears of Agar, the Muslims, the "*point vierge*" of the spirit, the center of our nothingness where, in apparent despair, one meets God—and is found completely in His mercy.

At the Little Sisters of the Poor in Louisville: the beauty of the Church is evident in the charity of her children, and especially her daughters.

The "Good Mother" is transparent, simple, of no age, both child and mother, and hence something like Mary. Perhaps the complicated names of nuns (which I can never remember) are in the end no names at all, as if nuns could not have names anyway. As if only God could know their names. Yet how real they are as *persons!* How much more real (often enough) than people who have "big names" in the world. One does not need to idealize the Sisters. They have their problems. Often they have to struggle with a difficult "system." Yet their faith and their love give them greatness.

As for the old people: the beauty of the Church shines also in those who are helped and who have nothing to give except the fact that they can be helped: which is a great gift to the Church! It makes them most important in the Church. Thus, for instance: one old man playing the piano and another old man dancing. The one who danced was turning around and stamping the floor with one foot, apparently unaware that he no longer had the use of the muscles that make for tap dancing. The old man at the piano was banging away with a disastrous abandon and God knows what he was playing, though it was certainly better than rock 'n' roll.

One would certainly have to admit that it was antidancing accompanied by nonmusic. Nor would it be enough to say that one could approve it as a manifestation of "good will"—an expense of effort intended in some way *ad majorem Dei gloriam.* Better than that: I think God was glorified not by the intention, but by the nonmusic itself. Simply by what it was—as a concrete existential fact. Here is where the "beauty of the Church" comes to us: it was she who made this possible. At moments one gets a flash of Zen in the midst of the Church! There should, in reality, be much more. But we frustrate it by reasoning too much about everything.

The old Negro people were especially attractive: a sweet, dignified, and ancient Negro lady told me she had long worked for our doctor in New Haven (now dead). And another old, beat, Negro lady with wisps of white beard, sunk in her blank dream, slowly came out of it, out of some mental ocean, when spoken to. Another old lady who had both legs cut off (it sounds like the title of a child's weird story), and yet another old lady who still thought of herself as a little girl, curtsied and made a speech.

Then in this hierarchic world there were the girl auxiliaries, school girl volunteer helpers in blue and white uniforms, who sang a song about playing the piano and playing the violin and playing the triangle. One of them enters the postulancy this week. I wonder if she will stay.

Here is an impressive statement from Vinoba Bhave, in his *Talks on the Gita.* "The action of the person who acts without desire should be much better than that of the person who acts with desire. This is only proper, for the latter is attracted to the fruit and part, much or little, of his time and attention will be spent on thoughts and dreams of the fruit. But all the time and all the strength of the man who has no desire for fruit is devoted to the action." This neatly disposes of the myth that "spirituality" is not practical! But perhaps what some people really mean by spirituality is "spiritual desire"—and that is a worse error than action driven by desire: the awful illusion of a supposed "contemplation" that is nothing but mute desire feeding on itself!

There was once a certain Monsignor Hulst, who, before his death, is reported to have said something like this: "I have never denied God a moment of my time: I HOPE HE WILL TAKE THAT INTO ACCOUNT . . . !"

I was comforted to find almost the same thing on the lips of one of Job's friends, in the Bible de Jerusalem:
> Ta piété ne te donne-t-elle pas confiance,
> Ta vie intègre ne fait elle pas ton assurance?

What's the trouble, Job? Aren't you one of us?

I am thoroughly committed to the position that the words of Eliphas are a blasphemy. Even if I had done some good works to trust in, I would not want to trust in them.

Julien Green says: "Religion is not understood. Those who wish themselves pious, in order to admire themselves in this state, are made stupid by religion. What is needed is to lose ourselves completely in God; what is needed is perfect silence, supernatural silence. Pious talk has something revolting about it."

There is precisely a revolt against this kind of "religion" even among the most earnest of present-day Christians. The word "religion" itself comes to be used equivocally, since it has been made profoundly ambiguous by religious people themselves.

"Religion," in the sense of something emanating from man's nature and tending to God, does not really change man or save him, but brings him into a false relationship with God: for a religion that starts in man is nothing but man's wish for himself. Man "wishes himself" (magically) to become godly, holy, gentle, pure, etc. His wish terminates not in God but in himself. This is no more than the religion of those who wish themselves to be in a certain state in which they can live with themselves, approve of themselves: for they feel that, when they can approve of themselves, God is at peace with them. How many Christians seriously believe that Christianity itself consists of nothing more than this? Yet it is anathema to true Christianity.

The whole meaning of Paul's anger with "the Law" and with "the elements of this world" is seen here. Such religion is not saved by good intentions: in the end it becomes a caricature. It must. For otherwise we would never see the difference between this and the "religion" which is born in us from God and which perhaps ought not to be called religion, born from the devastation of our trivial "self" and all our plans for "our self," even though they be plans for a holy self, a pure self, a loving, sacrificing self.

This is one of the deep problems that Eliot suggests at the end of *Murder in the Cathedral,* where Thomas is faced with the realization that he may be gladly admitting martyrdom into a political and religiously ambitious scheme for himself: punishing the wicked and making himself a saint by treading down his enemies, stepping upon their heads into heaven. It is in this sense that the fear of the Lord is the beginning of wisdom—and of true religion. This fear questions our own religiosity, our own ambition to be good. It begins to see with horror the complacency of speeches that "know all about" piety, possess the right method of pleasing God and infallibly winning Him over to our side, etc. This "fear" is what imposes silence. It is the beginning of the "supernatural silence" Green asks for.

Last night I was on the night watch. It rained heavily. Between rounds I went into the little shelter in the middle of the cloister court, which is traditionally called by the French name of *préau* here. Rain poured down on the walls of the building, on the four big maples, on the roof of the shelter. I was sleepy, and sat in the chair, nodding in the dark. Hanging on the edge of sleep I could hear the rain around me like a huge aviary full of parrots: but just as the aviary became "real" I would wake up, rescue myself from this strange world of sound, until gradually I would fall into it again. I did not fall asleep, because I could never sleep in a chair anyway, no matter how the rain sounded, no matter how inviting the strange universe of birds created by it!

I had to go to Louisville to see about printing the new postulants' guide. I was driven in by one of the neighbors, a young man called Yvo who lives up the road and works at the monastery. Interesting conversation—particularly on the way home, for when we were in town he went to see "some kin folks" and came away from them much more voluble and lively than he had been before. His driving was even more exciting. He zigzagged madly through traffic, jamming on his brakes just in time to avoid climbing over the car in front or flying through red lights. Meanwhile, of course, he talked about the accidents that other drivers for the monastery have had. Joe Carrol, the family brother, had a historic one at the bottom of the hill in High Grove, when the brakes of a dump truck full of cement bags failed and he piled up in the front yard of one of the houses. He was unhurt, but entirely covered with cement. The punch line of the story (which I remember because Yvo repeated it several times) is the description by the lady of the house, of Joe sitting in the ruins of the truck:

> "He tried to whistle and he couldn't whistle.
> He tried to sing and he couldn't sing.
> He tried to talk and he couldn't talk.
> He couldn't do nothing and he looked like a nigger with all
>   that cement all over him."

I could not match the classic flavor of this with my lame account of Dom Frederic and Senator Dawson skidding off the road into a creek near Mount Washington. I wasn't there. Nobody was there but the angels. It happened in ice and fog when Dom Frederic was supposed to be going to New Melleray for the funeral or the installation of an abbot.

More of Yvo's oracles. Concerning Father Gettlefinger, the pastor in New Haven, he said: "When Father Gettlefinger works in that field he works like he was killing snakes."

Concerning, on the other hand, those who follow a golf ball around a golf course, he had this to say. On the way through Bardstown in the morning, Yvo expressed contempt for golfers, and as we passed the golf club, he said: "You wait, when we come back tonight, *they'll be there.*" Sure enough, when we came back in the evening, they were. "See," said Yvo triumphantly, "*there they are!*" It was as if he had fiercely and rightly predicted in the morning that by evening the town would be completely infiltrated by Communists.

In Louisville, at the corner of Fourth and Walnut, in the center of the shopping district, I was suddenly overwhelmed with the realization that I loved all those people, that they were mine and I theirs, that we could not be alien to one another even though we were total strangers. It was like waking from a dream of separateness, of spurious self-isolation in a special world, the world of renunciation and supposed holiness. The whole illusion of a separate holy existence is a dream. Not that I question the reality of my vocation, or of my monastic life: but the conception of "separation from the world" that we have in the monastery too easily presents itself as a complete illusion: the illusion that by making vows we become a different species of being, pseudo-angels, "spiritual men," men of interior life, what have you.

Certainly these traditional values are very real, but their reality is not of an order outside everyday existence in a contingent world, nor does it entitle one to despise the secular: though "out of the world" we are in the same world as everybody else, the world of the bomb, the world of race hatred, the world of technology, the world of mass media, big business, revolution, and all the rest. We take a different attitude to all these things, for we belong to God. Yet so does everybody else belong to God. We just happen to be conscious of it, and to make a profession out of this consciousness. But does that entitle us to consider ourselves different, or even *better,* than others? The whole idea is preposterous.

This sense of liberation from an illusory difference was such a relief and such a joy to me that I almost laughed out loud. And I suppose my happiness could have taken form in the words: "Thank God, thank God that I *am* like other men, that I am only a man among others." To think that for sixteen or seventeen years I have been taking seriously this pure illusion that is implicit in so much of our monastic thinking.

It is a glorious destiny to be a member of the human race, though it is a race dedicated to many absurdities and one which makes many terrible mistakes: yet, with all that, God Himself gloried in becoming a member of the human race. A member of the human race! To think that such a commonplace realization should suddenly seem like news that one holds the winning ticket in a cosmic sweepstake.

I have the immense joy of being *man,* a member of a race in which God Himself became incarnate. As if the sorrows and stupidities of the human condition could overwhelm me, now I realize what we all are. And if only everybody could realize this! But it cannot be explained. "There is no way of telling people that they are all walking around shining like the sun."

This changes nothing in the sense and value of my solitude, for it is in fact the function of solitude to make one realize such things with a clarity that would be impossible to anyone completely immersed in the other cares, the other illusions, and all the automatisms of a tightly collective existence. My solitude, however, is not my own, for I see now how much it belongs to them—and that I have a responsibility for it in their regard, not just in my own. It is because I am one with them that I owe it to them to be alone, and when I am alone they are not "they" but my own self. There are no strangers!

Then it was as if I suddenly saw the secret beauty of their hearts, the depths of their hearts where neither sin nor desire nor self-knowledge can reach, the core of their reality, the person that each one is in God's eyes. If only they could all see themselves as they really *are.* If only we could see each other that way all the time. There would be no more war, no more hatred, no more cruelty, no more greed. . . . I suppose the big problem would be that we would fall down and worship each other. But this cannot be *seen,* only believed and "understood" by a peculiar gift.

Again, that expression, *le point vierge,* (I cannot translate it) comes in here. At the center of our being is a point of nothingness which is untouched by sin and by illusion, a point of pure truth, a point or spark which belongs entirely to God, which is never at our disposal, from which God disposes of our lives, which is inaccessible to the fantasies of our own mind or the brutalities of our own will. This little point of nothingness and of *absolute poverty* is the pure glory of God in us. It is so to speak His name written in us, as our poverty, as our indigence, as our dependence, as our sonship. It is like a pure diamond, blazing with the invisible light of heaven. It is in everybody, and if we could see it we would see these billions of points of light coming together in the face and blaze of a sun that would make all the darkness and cruelty of life vanish completely. . . . I have no program for this seeing. It is only given. But the gate of heaven is everywhere.

Palm Sunday.

Father John of the Cross is one of the few men in this monastery who have anything to say in a sermon. When it is his turn to preach, everybody listens. What he preaches is really the Gospel, not words about the Gospel or knowledge of the Gospel, or yet knowledge of Christ. It is one thing to preach Christ, another to preach that one knows Christ. I know the integrity of this man is very costly to him. He suffers very much in order to be true to his own heart, that is to the heart which God has given him, and which has in it a mysterious command that no one here is able to understand.

Will he be disloyal to this heart? Some will try to make him disloyal, in the name of other kinds of loyalty with which they themselves are more at home: the more comfortable kind. Since in any case he is true to the command that is in him (the command that most of us spend our lives trying not to hear) he does not betray the truth by fitting it into popular and easy formulas. Nor does he trifle with it in any way, to win people to himself in order that they may then hear "his truth." It is not "his" truth that he is preaching, it is just truth.

Speaking of friendship with Christ, he said that in all friendship there is first a stage at which we see the acts of our friend and come, by them, to know who he is. But after we have come to know who he is, then we see his acts differently, only in the light of *who he is*. Then even acts that would otherwise disconcert us and would seem ambiguous in themselves are accepted because we know who he is. The transition point comes when we know the inmost desires of our friend's heart. So, in the Passion of Jesus and in His apparent failure, His yielding to destruction, when He could have saved Himself: the inmost desire of His Heart is to love the Father and to be about the Father's business. Therefore we do not need to know and understand all about the Cross, the Kingdom or the way to the Kingdom. What we need to know is the inmost desire in the heart of Christ, which is that we should come to the Kingdom with Him. He alone knows the way, which is that of the Cross. I would perhaps add, on my own, that the inmost desire in the heart of Christ makes itself somehow present in us in the form of that little point of nothingness and poverty in us which is the "point" or virgin eye by which we know Him!

Holy Thursday evening, after the evening Mass and Communion, I was standing in the novitiate garden looking at the gray skies and the hills, when the Colombian postulant came up behind me and said in Spanish that the view without doubt offered poetic inspiration, to which I readily agreed. We talked a little about climates, earthquakes, and what-not, and the "terrible cliffs" along some of the roads in Colombia. (I have heard of them, in Caldas, for example. You look over into the canyons and see the ruins of cars and trucks five hundred feet below.)

Then a moment later he said: "Why would not you, Father Merton, leave here and come to South America and start a totally new kind of monastic order, one that would appeal more to men of modern times?"

I could not tell him how much I would like to try it, or how impossible it would be to make any such attempt without leaving the Order, and how impossible it would be for me to try to leave the Order.

I suppose this is a platitude by now, and one that would irritate many: but it represents the area where I disagree with Barth, for instance. I am aware that the Easter Vigil retains many vestiges of primitive nature rites, and I am glad of it. I think this is perfectly proper and Christian. The mystery of fire, the mystery of water. The mystery of spring—*Ver sacrum.* Fire, water, spring, made sacred and explicit by the Resurrection, which finds in them symbols that point to itself. The old creation is made solely for the new creation. The new creation (of life out of death) springs from the old, even though the pattern of the old is the falling away of life in death.

Instead of stamping down the force of the new life rising in us by our very nature (and so turning it into Leviathan, the dragon in the unsanctified waters), let the new life be sweetened, sanctified by the bitterness of the Cross, which destroys death in the waters and makes the waters the laver of life. Water then becomes the dwelling not of Leviathan but of the spirit of life. We are no longer marked like Cain, but signed with the Blood of the Paschal Lamb.

A visiting abbot declared in Chapter that the contemplative life consisted in clinging by main force to an idea one had on entering the novitiate. An incredible statement: I mean, incredible that such a statement could be seriously proposed by such a person and in such a place. No one seems to have felt there was anything strange about it. The mere concept of *effort* justifies everything. It doesn't matter what you do so long as you work at it with all your might—I almost said work like the devil.

*Audite et intelligite traditiones quas Deus dedi vobis.** There are traditions which God has given us. They are so to speak a *memory* we are born with and into which we are born: a store of meanings, of symbols, of signs. What is born in us is the connatural ability to understand these great buried signs as soon as they are manifested to us. What is given us in society is a more or less authentic manifestation of the signs. If society loses its "memory," if it forgets its language of traditional symbol, then the individuals who make it up become neurotic, because their own memories are corrupted by uninterpreted, unused meanings. Then traditions themselves become mere dead conventions—worse than that, obsessions—collective neuroses. To replace one set of conventions

---

* "Hear and understand the traditions which I, God, have given you."

with another, however new, does nothing to revive a truly living sense of meaning and of life. This is our present condition.

Saints of the fifteenth century.

In the collapse of medieval society, amid the corruption of the clergy and the decadence of conventual life, there arose men and women of the laity who were *perfectly obedient to God.* Nicholas of Flue, for instance, and Joan of Arc. They were simple and straight-forward signs of contradiction in the middle of worldliness, preju-dice, cruelty, despair, and greed. They were *not rebels* at all. They were meek and submissive instruments of God who, while being completely opposed to the corrupt norms around them, gave every man and every authority his due. They show clearly and convinc-ingly what it is to be not a rebel, but obedient to God as a sign to men—a sign of mercy, a revelation of truth and power. We are spontaneously drawn to these signs of God with all the love of our hearts. We naturally trust them, believe in their intercession, knowing that they live on in the glory of God and that God would not give us such love for them if they were not still "sacraments" of His mercy to us.

"For what, in that world gigantic horror, was tolerable except the slighter gestures of dissent?" So wrote E. M. Forester discussing his satisfaction on reading the early Eliot during World War I.

World War I, that distant, relatively civilized war, in which it took weeks to mobilize the armies, in which it was not yet possible to annihilate entire civilian populations with firestorms and TNT . . . yet that was already and very truly a "gigantic horror." The horror we have come to know in the forty years since then, the even greater horror we have come to anticipate, has made the World War I seem like a very tame brawl.

"The slighter gestures of dissent." For anything slight, we have now only contempt. Indeed dissent itself has come to look like crime, madness, or at least subversion.

Even those strange ones who still see fit to dissent, tend to think now that massive protest is more valid. Yet the more massive a movement is, the more it is doctored and manipulated. The more it tends to be a mass lie, a front. As if protest itself were useless unless supported and patronized by some inhuman power.

Genuine dissent must always keep a human measure. It must be free and spontaneous. The slighter gestures are often the more significant, because they are unpremediated and they cannot be doctored beforehand by the propagandist.

And so perhaps it is saner and nobler to expect effective protest from the individual, from the small unsponsored group, than from the well-organized mass movement. It is better that the "slighter gestures" never find their way into the big papers or onto the pages of the slick magazines. It is better not to line up with the big, manipulated group.

True, he who dissents alone may confine his dissent to words, to declarations, to attitudes, to symbolic gestures. He may fail to act. Gestures are perhaps not enough. They are perhaps too slight.

On the other hand what seems to be "action" on the mass scale may be nothing more than a political circus, or an organized disaster. Such action is often nothing more than the big absurd lie, the blown-up puerility which, by its own emptiness, ends in a cataclysm of frustration and destructive rage.

Against the empty and debased rhetoric of the giant demonstration, even the smallest, genuine idea, the slightest of sincere and honest protests is not only tolerable but to be admired.

(All this is to be qualified in view of the spontaneous, very effective, very telling power of the Civil Rights movement in America. The thing that it is *not* is what its enemies claim that it is—a front for Communism.)

I have great admiration for the simple, austere, Russian figure of Staretz Sylvan, who died on Mount Athos in 1938. He had been a monk of the Russikon, or St. Panteleimon, since 1892.

He was a tall man with a shaggy beard, and a true hesychast, avid for solitude and for prayer, humble, outwardly ordinary, a hard worker—in fact he was "steward," or cellarer, of his monastery and had two hundred workmen under him. He identified himself with them in all their troubles and sorrows. They were very aware of this and loved him deeply. His compassion for them was an element in his recollection and in his interior silence. He said: "I became steward as an act of obedience blessed by the Abbot, so I pray better at my task than I prayed at the Old Rossikon [where he had a solitary hut] where I asked to go for the sake of interior silence. If the soul loves and pities the people, prayer is not interrupted."—from *The Undistorted Image,* biography of Staretz Sylvan, by Archimandrite Sophrony.

In his inner conflicts and sorrows he found a strange answer and a still stranger way of prayer. The Lord said to him: "Keep thy soul in hell and despair not." At first it sounds a bit dreadful, or perhaps at best eccentric. Yet to me it is in a strange way comforting. Men still share deeply and silently the anguish of Christ abandoned by His Father (to be abandoned by God is to be "in hell") and they "despair not." How much better and saner it is to face despair and not give in than to work away at keeping up appearances and patching up our conviction that a bogus spirituality is real! That we are not really facing dread! That we are all triumphantly advancing "getting somewhere" (where?), accomplishing great things for Christ, and changing the face of the world!

We can still choose between the way of Job and the way of Job's friends, and we have to have the sense (I say sense, not courage) to choose the way of Job: it takes far more than courage to start out on a way that obviously leads to the far end of nothing, and to walk over the abyss of our own absurdity in order to be found and saved by God, who has called us to walk that way. It takes sense to see that if He calls us, it is the only way. As to courage, He will provide: and of course He will provide it more in the form of *hope* than as plain fortitude. We must not expect to glance at ourselves and see "courage," and take comfort from this. Christ alone, on the Cross and in darkness, but already victorious, is our comfort.

"The saints," said Bernanos, "are not resigned, at least in the sense that the world thinks. If they suffer in silence those injustices which upset the mediocre, it is in order better to turn against injustice, against its face of brass, all the strength of their great souls. Angers, daughters of despair, creep and twist like worms. Prayer is, all things considered, the only form of revolt that stays standing up."

This is very true from all points of view. A spirituality that preaches resignation under official brutalities, servile acquiescence in frustration and sterility, and total submission to organized injustice is one which has lost interest in holiness and remains concerned only with a spurious notion of "order." On the other hand, it is so easy to waste oneself in the futilities of that "anger, the daughter of despair," the vain recrimination that takes a perverse joy in blaming everyone else for our failure. We may certainly fail to accomplish what we believed was God's will for us and for the Church: but simply to take revenge by resentment against those who blocked the way is not to turn the strength on one's soul (if any) against the "brass face of injustice." It is another way of yielding to it.

There may be a touch of stoicism in Bernanos' wording here, but that does not matter. A little more stoic strength would not hurt us, and would not necessarily get in the way of grace!

Steinmann's book on St. Jerome is interesting and well done, but I am sick of Jerome, sick of his querulous sensitivity, his rage, his politics. And I am sick of Steinmann's anti-Origenism. It is too insistent. I am for John Chrysostom, and especially for Rufinus. These are quarrels about which no monk can be indifferent. We are all implicated in their absurdity.

Music is being played to the cows in the milking barn. Rules have been made and confirmed: only sacred music is to be played to the cows, not "classical" music. The music is to make the cows give more milk. The sacred music is to keep the brothers who work in the cow barn recollected. For sometime now sacred music has played to the cows in the milking barn. They have not given more milk. The brothers have not been any more recollected than usual. I believe the cows will soon be hearing Beethoven. Then we shall have classical, perhaps worldly milk and the monastery will prosper. (Later: It was true. The hills resounded with Beethoven. The monastery has prospered. The brother mainly concerned with the music, however, departed.)

If you call one thing vile and another precious, if you praise success and blame failure, you will fill the world with thieves, soldiers, and businessmen. I have praised the saints and I have told at what cost they strove to surpass lesser men. What madness have I not preached in sermons!

Is Christian ethics merely a specific set of Christian answers to the question of good and evil, right and wrong? To make it no more than this is to forget that man's fall was a fall *into* the knowledge of good and evil, reinforced by the inexorable knowledge of a condemning law, and that man's restoration in Christ is a restoration to freedom and grace, to a love that needs no law since it knows and does only what is in accord with love and with God. To imprison ethics in the realm of division, of good and evil, right and wrong, is to condemn it to sterility, and rob it of its real reason for existing, which is *love.* Love cannot be reduced to one virtue among many others prescribed by ethical imperatives. When love is only "a virtue" among many, man forgets that "God is love" and becomes incapable of that all-embracing love by which we secretly begin to know God as our Creator and Redeemer—who has saved us from the limitations of a purely restrictive and aimless existence "under a law."

So Bonhoeffer says very rightly: "In the knowledge of good and evil man does not understand himself in the reality of the destiny appointed in his origin, but rather in his own possibilities, his possibility of being good or evil. He knows himself now as something apart from God, outside God, and this means that he now knows only himself and no longer knows God at all. . . . The knowledge of good and evil is therefore separation from God. Only against God can man know good and evil."

It is clear that an exclusively *ethical* emphasis on right and wrong, good and evil, in Christian education, *breeds doubt and not faith.* The more we insist that Catholicism must consist in the avoidance of sin (especially in the realm of sex), in "being good" and in doing one's duty, the more we make it difficult for men to really believe, and the more we make faith into a mental and spiritual problem, contingent on a certain ethical achievement. The only way faith continues to be humanly possible in such a situation is for it to be understood as a virtue and duty among other virtues and duties. One believes because one is *told to believe,* not because of a living and life-giving aspiration to know the living God. Faith itself becomes shot through with an existential doubt which, nevertheless, one ignores out of duty, while going about one's business of avoiding evil and doing good.

The tension generated by this struggle of doubt and duty eventually seeks a natural release in crusades and in the persecution of heretics, in order that we may prove ourselves "good" and "right" by judging and condemning evil and error in those who are unlike ourselves.

Existentialist ethics, while trying to escape the iron necessity of objective duty imposed by the ethic of law and of good and evil, simply pushes the logic of the fall to its further conclusion. To know good and evil is to know oneself as the subject of choice confronted with indefinite possibilities. The possibilities are meaningless; good and evil are fictitious; all that remains is the subject as the source and origin of his own choices. It is the honesty and authenticity of *the choice* that endows our possibilities with a semblance of "good" (if one would take the trouble to call it that).

The resentment of (atheist) existentialism against the frustrating limits and obstacles imposed by a legalist ethic still imparts no freedom. It tries to transcend good and evil, but it is imprisoned in its own spurious transcendence. *Choice cannot be free from the frustrating, tormenting division between good and evil. Hence subjective choice cannot be an absolute.* There is no way of understanding freedom as long as it is seen only as the power to choose between good and evil. And if one abolishes good and evil, in order to make freedom simply the power to choose, then the difficulty is further compounded by ambiguity and mystification.

Then we come around in a full circle: in bourgeois society, the good and respectable were considered *ipso facto* justified. Now it is considered quite sufficient to stand Protestantism on its head and to speak as if all one needed to be justified was to be wicked: the sicker, the more unfaithful, the more revolting your life is, the more justified you are. Thus Sartre's Protestantism in reverse canonizes the good thief Genet since the ability to canonize good thieves puts one automatically in the position of an admittedly secular Christ. This is very entertaining and no one begrudges Sartre his jokes at the expense of conventional Christianity. But things begin to complicate themselves when conventional Christianity itself adopts the gospel of Sartre, and goes around singing that God is dead, alleluia, that we are all alone in the world, that we might as well make the best of it, smoke pot and make our own rules. That is just it: a new set of rules, which we ourselves have decreed! A whole new canon of respectability, a whole new human system of justification, a new ethic that is easy to learn because all it asks is that where the squares say "yes" you say "no" and vice versa.

The religious genius of the Protestant Reformation, as I see it, lies in its struggle with the problem of justification in all its depth. The great Christian question is the conversion of man and his restoration to the grace of God in Christ. And this question, in its simplest form, is that of the conversion of the wicked and the sinful to Christ. But Protestantism raised this same question again in its *most radical form*—how about the much more difficult and problematic conversion, that of the pious and the good? It is relatively easy to convert the sinner, but the good are often completely unconvertible simply because they do not see any need for conversion.

Thus the genius of Protestantism focused from the beginning on the ambiguities contained in "being good" and "being saved" or "belonging to Christ." For conversion to Christ is not merely the conversion from bad habits to good habits, but *nova creatura,* becoming a totally new man in Christ and in the Spirit. Obviously the works and habits of the new man will correspond with his new being. There is nothing un-Catholic in this, quite the contrary. Yet Catholic perspectives, in emphasizing good works, sometimes lead to a neglect of the new being, life in Christ, life in the Spirit. And when Protestantism is unfaithful to its gift, it first plays down even the "new being" and the radical depth of conversion, in order to emphasize the pure grace and gift of Christ's pardon (hence we remain essentially wicked), or else, later, forgetting the seriousness of the need to convert the good, bogs down in the satisfied complacency of a rather superficial and suburban goodness—the folksy togetherness, the hand-shaking fellowship, the garrulous witness of moral platitudes. (In this of course Protestants are often outdistanced by the more complex and sometimes more vulgar inanities of the "good Catholic.")

Here is where *fides sola* may have proved to be dangerous. For the faith that justifies is not just any faith, or even the faith that, at revival time, *feels* itself justified. In the end an insufficient faith is not belief in Christ and obedience to His word, but only a question of believing we believe because we are found acceptable in the eyes of other believers. What matters then is to cultivate this quality of acceptance in a sociological milieu, and then (as in the deep South) even objectively unjust works can be counted virtuous and Christian, since they are approved by those who are locally certified as "good." Truly the great problem is the salvation of those who, being good, think they have no further need to be saved and imagine their task is to make others "good" like themselves!

Those who are faithful to the original grace (I should not say genius) of Protestantism are precisely those who, in all depth, see as Luther saw that the "goodness" of the good may in fact be the greatest religious disaster for a society, and that the crucial problem is the *conversion of the good to Christ.* Kierkegaard sees it, so does Barth, so does Bonhoeffer, so do the Protestant existentialists.

As a Catholic I firmly hold of course to what the Church teaches on justification and grace. One cannot be justified by a faith that does not do the works of love, for love is the witness and evidence of "new being" in Christ. But precisely this love is primarily the work of Christ in me, not simply something that originates in my own will and is then approved and rewarded by God. It is faith that opens my heart to Christ and His Spirit, that He may work in me. No work of mine can be called "love" in the Christian sense, unless it comes from Christ. But "the good" are solely tempted to believe in their own goodness and their own capacity to love, while one who realizes his own poverty and nothingness is much more ready to surrender himself entirely to the gift of love *he knows* cannot come from anything in himself.

It is with this in mind that I will, in the next section, consider the ambiguities of "doing good," knowing that when one is firmly convinced of his own rightness and goodness, he can without qualm perpetrate the most appalling evil. After all, it was the righteous, the holy, the "believers in God" who crucified Christ, and they did so in the name of righteousness, holiness, and even of God (John 10:32).

Note that one of the deep psychological motives of Christian anti-Semitism is, I believe, an attempt to evade this. The Gospel teaches us precisely that human holiness and goodness alone do not prevent us from betraying God and that the "good men" who crucified Christ are the paradigm of all the "good" whose "goodness" is merely a fidelity to ethical prescriptions. But to evade the implications of this we have changed it to read as follows: Christ was crucified by wicked and unbelieving men who loved sin precisely because they were Jews and cursed by God. This overlooks the following facts: the Jews were and remain the people especially chosen and loved by God. The Pharisees were austere and virtuous men who devoted themselves with great energy to doing good as they saw it. They devoutly studied the word of God with deep concern about the coming of the Messiah.

Anti-Semitism conveniently helps the Christian who thinks himself austere, virtuous, concerned with doing good and obeying God, etc., to avoid every occasion of realizing that he may himself be the exact replica of the Pharisee. When will we learn that "being good" may easily mean having the mentality of a "Christ-killer?"

One thing above all is important: the "return to the Father."

The Son came into the world and died for us, rose and ascended to the Father; sent us His Spirit, that in Him and with Him we might return to the Father.

That we might pass clean out of the midst of all that is transitory and inconclusive: return to the Immense, the Primordial, the Source, the Unknown, to Him Who loves and knows, to the Silent, to the Merciful, to the Holy, to Him Who is All.

To seek anything, to be concerned with anything but this is only madness and sickness, for this is the whole meaning and heart of all existence, and in this all the affairs of life, all the needs of the world and of men, take on their right significance: all point to this one great return to the Source.

All goals that are not ultimate, all "ends of the line" that we can see and plan as "ends," are simply absurd, because they do not even begin. The "return" is the end beyond all ends, and the beginning of beginnings.

To "return to the Father" is not to "go back" in time, to roll up the scroll of history, or to reverse anything. It is a going forward, a going beyond, for merely to retrace one's steps would be a vanity on top of vanity, a renewal of the same absurdity in reverse.

Our destiny is to go on beyond everything, to leave everything, to press forward to the End and find in the End our Beginning, the ever-new Beginning that has no end.

To obey Him on the way, in order to reach Him in whom I have begun, who is the key and the end—because He is the Beginning.

The optimistic radicalism of the thirties is dead and buried and judged. It is most important to realize this, for an attempt to recapture the illusion at the present moment would certainly be disastrous. We cannot forget the mistakes of FDR. Yet at the same time there is a new radicalism and a new optimism which has gone beyond the fears and fanaticisms of the McCarthy era and is breaking through to new areas of dialogue and concern. It is a radicalism that is far less doctrinaire, less concerned with sweeping political programs, more intent on certain immediate practical ends, especially civil rights and disarmament. There is a new generation and a new spirit here, and perhaps it will turn out to have been much more serious and much more effective than anything I can remember from my own youth. I think this new radicalism may be the decisive force and hope of the sixties—or it may simply be the catalyst that will bring on our transformation into something very disagreeable and stupid, a permanently organized warfare state, blind and dedicated to the forceful resolution of imaginary problems.

We have been putting off, rather than solving, the problem of the hideous tabernacle in the novitiate chapel by hiding it under a veil (which the Cistercian Ritual frowns on). I also spirited away the square nightclubish candle holders. And I am afraid Frank Kacmarcik is right: our walnut altar does look a bit like a bar. I am afraid the new tabernacle veil is too jazzy, with its Matisse foliage (in brown). But in general the chapel is simple and even austere. I am glad to feel that it now looks *only a little* vulgar. It used to look like an ecclesiastical pawnshop.

Father S—, who had to go to the doctor in Louisville, came back with a clipping about a man out in the Kentucky mountains, an old coal miner who, for thirteen years, has lived as a hermit with his dog in a pitiful little shack without even a chimney. He used an old car seat for his bed. When he was asked why he chose to live such a life he replied: "Because of all these wars." A real desert father, perhaps. And probably not too sure how he got there.

Reading Chuang Tzu, I wonder seriously if the wisest answer (on the human level, apart from the answer of faith) is not beyond both ethics and politics. It is a hidden answer, it defies analysis and cannot be embodied in a program. Ethics and politics, of course: but only in passing, only as a "night's lodging." There is a time for action, a time for "commitment," but never for total involvement in the intricacies of a movement. There is a moment of innocence and *kairos,* when action makes a great deal of sense. But who can recognize such moments? Not he who is debauched by a series of programs. And when all action has become absurd, shall one continue to act simply because once, a long time ago, it made a great deal of sense? As if one were always getting somewhere? There is a time to listen, in the active life as everywhere else, and the better part of action is waiting, not knowing what next, and not having a glib answer.

Brother G—, a postulant who has come to the end of his rope and wants to leave, but who has been dissuaded (not by me), stands in the novitiate library leafing through a book called *Relax and Live.* Sooner or later it comes to that.

A basic temptation: the flatly unchristian refusal to love those whom we consider, for some reason or other, unworthy of love. And, on top of that, to consider others unworthy of love for even very trivial reasons. Not that we hate them of course: but we just refuse to accept them in our hearts, to treat them without suspicion and deal with them without inner reservations. In a word, we reject those who do not please us. We are of course "charitable toward them." An interesting use of the word "charity" to cover and to justify a certain coldness, suspicion, and even disdain. But this is punished by another inexorable refusal: we are bound by the logic of this defensive rejection to reject any form of happiness that even implies acceptance of those we have decided to reject. This certainly complicates life, and if one is sufficiently intolerant, it ends by making all happiness impossible.

This means that we have to get along without constantly apply-
ing the yardstick of "worthiness" (who is worthy to be loved, and
who is not). And it almost means, by implication, that we cease to
ask even indirect questions about who is "justified," who is worthy
of acceptance, who can be tolerated by the believer! What a preposterous idea that would be! And yet the world is full of "believers"
who find themselves entirely surrounded by people they can hardly
be expected to "tolerate," such as Jews, Negroes, unbelievers, heretics, Communists, pagans, fanatics, and so on.

God is asking of me, the unworthy, to forget my unworthiness
and that of all my brothers, and dare to advance in the love which
has redeemed and renewed us all in God's likeness. And to laugh,
after all, at all preposterous ideas of "worthiness."

The basic sin, for Christianity, is rejecting others in order to
choose oneself, deciding *against* others and deciding *for* oneself.
Why is this sin so basic? Because the idea that you can choose
yourself, approve yourself, and then offer yourself (fully "chosen"
and "approved") to God, applies the assertion of yourself over
against God. From this root of error comes all the sour leafage and
fruitage of a life of self-examination, interminable problems and
unending decisions, always making right choices, walking on the
razor edge of an impossibly subtle ethic (with an equally subtle
psychology to take care of the unconscious). All this implies the
frenzied conviction that one can be his own light and his own
justification, and that God is there for a purpose: to issue the stamp
of confirmation upon my own rightness. In such a religion the
Cross becomes meaningless except as the (blasphemous) certifica-
tion that because you suffer, because you are misunderstood, you
are justified twice over—you are a martyr. Martyr means witness.
You are then a witness? To what? To your own infallible light and
your own justice, which you have *chosen.*

This is the exact opposite of everything Jesus ever did or
taught.

Hitler regarded the power of his madness as a divine power
because he felt inspired. The Communists regard the power of their
collective obsession as "divine" (ultimate, or absolute) because it is
not inspired, but blessed with the infallibility of science. All power

politicians proceed on the assumption that *their* power is somehow ultimate, an expression of historic, or cosmic, or divine forces, of eternal laws, ultimate principles. And they say they have no religion? Their very religion is their "absolute corruption" by power.

Last evening at Vespers, singing the Magnificat antiphon of the Invention of the Holy Cross, I was happy with the splendor of the Gregorian setting, its rhythm, its verve, its strength and *entrain*. Only when we were singing the last alleluia did I realize that this was probably the last time we would ever have this antiphon. The feast has been done away with. In memory of many sunny May afternoons in which I have sung this, and the hymn, I thought I would make of the antiphon a short English poem:

O Cross, more splendid than all the stars,
Glorious to the world,
Greatly to be loved by men,
More holy than all things that are,
Thou who alone wast worthy to weigh the gold of the world's
    ransom,
Sweet tree, beloved nails,
Bearing the Love-Burden,
Save us who have come together here, this day,
In choirs for Thy Praise!
Alleluia, alleluia, alleluia!

It is important to realize when you do not need to know any more, or do any more. But to know when one acts just enough, one needs more (or less) than the reflective and planned knowledge by which one watches one's own acts. He who acts enough, and no more than enough, is also probably less than aware that he has acted. He does not reflect that he has acted just enough.

To know about it would add something unnecessary to the action itself. To stop when there has been enough is, then, to stop before one knows there was even the question of "enough, or too much" (Blake). And, of course, "enough" in this sense is not a limit, but a change of pace. There is nothing but the dynamism, and really one does not stop at all, one moves in another dimension. To have clear knowledge of a preconceived and arbitrary limit, and then to impose it, is to frustrate and falsify vital action. However, sometimes this has to be done: but we are then in another world, not that of life itself.

Harmony is not bought by parsimony.

To stop in the right way is to go on, to spend more (but not to buy anything, simply to give more).

To cling to something, to know one has it, to want to use it more, to squeeze all the enjoyment out of it: to do this consciously is to stop really living. It is to stop, to fix one's attention and one's hunger on what cannot satisfy it. But life itself "goes on," and as long as there is no "stopping," then it is always content with itself (but does not know that it is so).

To leave things alone at the right time: this is the right way to "stop" and the right way to "go on."

To leave a thing alone before you have had anything to do with it, (supposing that you ought to use it, ought to have something to do with it) this is also stopping before you have begun. Use it to go on.

To be great is to go on
To go is to be far
To be far is to return.
—Lao Tzu

A Prayer to God the Father on the Vigil of Pentecost.

Today, Father, this blue sky lauds you. The delicate green and orange flowers of the tulip poplar tree praise you. The distant blue hills praise you, together with the sweet-smelling air that is full of brilliant light. The bickering flycatchers praise you with the lowing cattle and the quails that whistle over there. I too, Father, praise you, with all these my brothers, and they give voice to my own heart and to my own silence. We are all one silence, and a diversity of voices.

You have made us together, you have made us one and many, you have placed me here in the midst as witness, as awareness, and as joy. Here I am. In me the world is present, and you are present. I am a link in the chain of light and of presence. You have made me a kind of center, but a center that is nowhere. And yet also I am "here," let us say I am "here" under these trees, not others.

For a long time I was in darkness and in sorrow, and I suppose my confusion was my own fault. No doubt my own will has been the root of my sorrow, and I regret it, merciful Father, but I do not regret it merely because this formula is acceptable as an official answer to all problems. I know I have sinned, but the sin is not to be found in any list. Perhaps I have looked too hard at all the lists to find out what my sin was, and I did not know that it was precisely the sin of looking at all the lists when you were telling me that this was useless. My "sin" is not on the list, and is perhaps not even a sin. In any case, I cannot know what it is, and doubtless there is nothing there anyway.

Whatever may have been my particular stupidity, the prayers of your friends and my own prayers have somehow been answered, and I am here, in this solitude, before you, and I am glad because you see me here. For it is here, I think, that you want to see me and I am seen by you. My being here is a response you have asked of me, to something I have not clearly heard. But I have responded, and I am content: there is little more to know about it at present.

Here you ask of me nothing else than to be content that I am your Child and your Friend. Which means simply to accept your friendship because it is your friendship and your Fatherhood because I am your son. This friendship is Sonship, and is Spirit. You have called me here to be repeatedly born in the Spirit as your son. Repeatedly born in light, in knowledge, in unknowing, in faith, in awareness, in gratitude, in poverty, in presence, and in praise.

If I have any choice to make, it is to live here and perhaps die here. But in any case it is not the living or the dying that matter, but speaking your name with confidence in this light, in this unvisited place: to speak your name of "Father" just by being here as "son" in the Spirit and the Light which you have given, and which are no unearthly light but simply this plain June day, with its shining fields, its tulip tree, the pines, the woods, the clouds, and the flowers everywhere.

To be here with the silence of Sonship in my heart is to be a center in which all things converge upon you. That is surely enough for the time being.

Therefore, Father, I beg you to keep me in this silence so that I may learn from it the word of your peace and the word of your mercy and the word of your gentleness to the world: and that through me perhaps your word of peace may make itself heard where it has not been possible for anyone to hear it for a long time.

To study truth here and learn here to suffer for truth.

The Light itself, and the contentment and the Spirit, these are enough.

Amen.

A VOW OF CONVERSATION

A Vow of Conversation: Journals 1964–1965 were published twenty years after Thomas Merton's death. He had not done the final editing of them in his lifetime and some feared that they were "thin" in comparison with both the earlier and later journals. Now that they have seen light, we can see that this was an unwarranted hesitation.

A Vow of Conversation creates a natural link between Conjectures and the Asian Journal. The entries mark the period in Merton's life when he was slowly disengaging himself from the community life of the monastery in order to take up his solitary existence in the hermitage built for him. The entries included here (January to Easter 1965) reflect the momentous events happening outside the monastery: the conclusion of the Second Vatican Council in Rome, the increasing violence connected with the civil rights movement in America, and the escalating war in Vietnam. One hears Merton's reactions to these events against his sharp sense of the world of nature and the rhythms of the liturgical and spiritual life to which he has committed himself in his new life of solitude.

*

January 1

I woke up this morning with the vague feeling that something was walking around the hermitage. It was the rain again. So begins the imagined New Year. Yet it is too well imagined, and the date, 1965, on the new ordo confounds me. My Mass was fine and so was the Thanksgiving afterward. The last thing I read before going to bed in the old year was a letter of Peter Damian to hermits, recently republished by Dom Leclercq. They wanted to be buried, when they died, at their hermitage and nowhere else. I can well agree with that!

165

I got a fine letter from John Wu and a chapter of his new book (in progress), *The Golden Age of Zen,* a good chapter on Hui Neng. Also a letter from Webster College, where they will want the exhibit of drawings in April. A card from the Polish Marxist who was here with a group from Indiana University. When was it?

I had a long talk with Brother Basil McMurray, who thinks he will leave here when his simple vows run out, to go to Mount Savior, but on a special basis.

It seems to be a mistake to read in uninterrupted succession in the refectory one speech after another by Pope Paul, just as it was a mistake to try to read all the Council interventions. One becomes very oppressed with the jargon, the uniform tone of official optimism and inspirationalism and so forth. Yet the Pope did say a few good things both at Bombay and in his Christmas message on peace, emphasizing the need for disarmament, speaking against nationalism, the arms race, and the stockpiling of overkill weapons.

January 4
    Even worse than Council speeches in the refectory was Archbishop O'Boyle's "explanation" of the last two agitated days of the Council. And then, after that, the *Time* story on the murder of hostages in Stanleyville, Congo, last November. A tragic thing. But the *Time* story, equally tragic, assumes fantastic perspectives. No indication that anybody could possibly be wrong except the African rebels, and that the Tshombe Belgian–American intervention is the only thing that could possibly be reasonable, human, etc. Were the hostages martyrs to a Red plot or also to the greed of the people who want to hold on to the mines in Katanga? The trouble is that indignation and horror swept the community (and they should) but with them also a complete conviction that of course the implied judgment and interpretation of *Time* were both satisfactory and final.

When you think that in all the country it is this way, about Cuba, Vietnam, the Congo, etc., what can possibly become of it but one dirty adventure and war on top of another?

Use of torture in Vietnam by our side is admitted, without apology, as something quite reasonable.

January 6

Yesterday was extraordinary. I had planned to take a whole day of recollection out in the hills around Edelin's hollow to explore the place and get some idea of where it goes and what is around it. Fortunately, Edelin came along with Brother Colman, who drove me out in the Scout, to show me where one could get into his property from the top of the hills on the west. It was wonderful wild country and I had a great day.

We left the monastery about 8:15, started back into the knobs to the southwest of New Hope and climbed the narrow country road that clings to the steep hillside above Old Coon Hollow, not to be confused, says Edelin, with Coon Hollow.

At the top of the rise we got into a rolling tableland of scrub oak and sassafras, with deep hollows biting into it. A very old road runs along the watershed between the Rolling Fork valley and the other valley where Edelin's house used to be. It is a magnificent wild, scrubby, lost road. The sun was bright and the air was not too cold.

I got off near where the woods slope down, about a mile, into Bell Hollow at the top, amid the thick tangle of trees and wild grapevines near a collapsed house. In a half-cleared area, there are still pear trees and Edelin says the deer like to come and eat the pears. Here too in a gully is a spring which feeds the stream running through Edelin's pasture. Actually, one of several streams that join there.

Edelin and Brother Colman left me there and I went down to the spring, found it without trouble. Wonderful clear water pouring strongly out of the cleft in the mossy rock. I drank from it in my cupped hands and suddenly realized it was years, perhaps twenty-five or thirty years, since I had tasted such water. Absolutely pure and clear and sweet with the freshness of untouched water. No chemicals.

I looked up at the clear sky and the tops of the leafless trees shining in the sun and it was a moment of angelic lucidity. I said the Psalms of Tierce with great joy, overflowing joy, as if the land and woods and spring were all praising God through me. Again the sense of angelic transparency of everything: of pure, simple and total light.

The word that comes closest to pointing to it is "simple." It was all so simple, but with a simplicity to which one seems to aspire, only seldom to attain it. A simplicity that is and has and says everything just because it is simple.

After that I scrambled around a bit on the steep rocky hillside in the sun to get oriented and then started through the thick sassafras out on a long wooded spur which I guessed would overlook Bell Hollow: and it did.

After about a half mile through very thick brush with vines and creepers and brambles and much young growth, bigger trees being damaged by fire, I came to the end. I could see the hollow in haze against the sun. I could see the point of the pasture on the hillside a mile or so away where the three walnut trees grow and, of course, the other side of the valley and the county road. Most of the view was of knobs and woods. A sea of sun and haze, silence and trees.

I sat there a long time, said Sext, read a letter from Milosz (an important letter too) and had a marvelous box lunch which Leone Gannon at the ladies' guesthouse got up for me. (She is Brother Colman's mother.) And as time went on I was more and more under the spell of the place until finally about twelve the sky began to cloud over.

The SAC planes. I forgot to mention that when I was at the spring after Tierce, when I was about to leave, the huge SAC plane announced its coming and immediately swooped exactly overhead, not more than two or three hundred feet above the hilltops. It was fantastic and sure enough I could see the trap door of the bomb bays. The whole thing was an awesome part of the "simplicity," a sign and an "of course." It had a great deal to do with all the rest of the day.

During the day, in fact, five SAC planes went over all on the same course, swooping over the hills. Not all exactly over this particular hollow but all visible from it, i.e., very close, within a mile. Otherwise, one could not see them flying so low with so many hills around. Only the first and the last went directly over me, but directly so that I was looking right up at the bomb. This was quite fantastic. Of course, the mere concept of fear was utterly meaningless, out of the question. I felt only an intellectual and moral intuition, a sort of "of course," which seemed to be part of the whole day and of its experience.

Near the collapsed house on the ridge is a clearing with rubbish lying around, beer cans with bullet holes in them, a pair of shoes, chewing-gum wrappers, etc. It used to be, said Edelin, a "dance hall," a place where people from the hollows came up to get drunk and raise hell. It is near the spring but far from the hollow. Of this particular area, incidentally, Freddie Hicks, who lives on the other side of the road down by New Hope, says: "When you get beyond this road, you leave civilization!"

I went down a logging trail. Many trees were cut this fall and winter. A beautiful wet trail into the hollow, full of tall beech trees and other hardwoods. Most of the mature oaks had just been cut.

A lovely silent walk with streams full of clear water and I suddenly came out into Edelin's pasture in Bell Hollow at the bottom. The place just took my breath away. I had seen it before in September but without this angelic light. Now the sun was hidden and the sky overcast but there was a sense of blessed silence and joy. And once again that perfect simplicity.

I wandered up and down the hollow in the empty pasture, tasting the void, silence and peace, went up the hillside where the two knob hawks came out screaming and wheeled over to the other side of the valley. I found the old half-burnt barn, belonging to one of Edelin's neighbors in a branch of the hollow. I began the Office of Epiphany in the open space where there are still stones from the foundations of the slaves' house. I could use them as foundations for a house of my own.

I went back to my place, sat on a felled white oak and looked down at the hollow until I had to go. The last SAC plane went over again, right overhead, and the bomb pointed to the chosen place. I read a blessing over the valley from the breviary. Never has a written prayer meant so much. I know one day there will be hermits here, or men living alone, but I think the hollow is already blessed because of the slaves that were there. Perhaps one or other of them was very holy.

So I went back up the logging trail and met Brother Colman and Edelin in the Scout on the ridge, coming along the old road. Never was there such a day.

January 8

When I got back and calmed down the other evening, I realized that I was being very enthusiastic and unreasonable. All day Epiphany I had a sort of emotional hangover from that day out in Bell Hollow. I sat at the top of the field next to the hermitage looking down at the cottage and I tried to meditate sanely in the sun. I came out of it much quieter and cooked myself some supper, a thin potato soup made out of dust from an envelope.

Then, as the sun was setting, I looked up at the end of the field where I had sat in the afternoon and suddenly realized that there were beings there—deer. In the evening light they were hard to descry against the tall brown grass, but I could pick out at least five.

They stood still looking at me and I stood looking at them. A lovely moment that stretched into ten minutes or more. They did not run, though kids could be heard shouting somewhere down by the waterworks, but eventually they walked quietly away into the tall grass and bushes and, for all I know, they slept there. When they walked they seemed to multiply, so that in the end I thought there must be at least ten of them.

As for the SAC plane, it is perfectly impartial. Yesterday afternoon, as I was saying Office on the walk below the novitiate before going to see the abbot, the planes swooped by right over my hermitage. I would say it was hardly one hundred and fifty feet above the treetops.

I spoke to Father Abbot about Bell Hollow and he said there could be no question of anybody going there until the monastery had title to the land. He is also thinking of buying other property next to Edelin's so that the place will be protected. He seems quite intent on eventually having hermitages there. It is clearly not yet time to be thinking of moving there myself, and I am very doubtful whether I should really think of that at all: I have this place now and I have just begun to really live in it. Brother Joachim is slowly getting it wired up for electric light, etc., and there is an old beat-up electric stove to cook my soup on when it has current to work with.

January 9

Again last night in the warm dark, before the plentiful rain, a plane again—though perhaps smaller than the big SAC—came right over the hermitage in the dark, a cross of four lights, a technological swan.

> *La espesa rueda de la tierra*
> *Su llanto húmedo de olvido*
> *Hace rodar, cortando el tiempo*
> *En mitades inaccesibles.* (Neruda)

> *Its wet complaint of forgetting*
> *Is what makes turn the world's thick wheel,*
> *Cutting time*
> *Into inaccessible halves.*

I am full of rice which I found a new good way of cooking. Peace, silence.

January 10

Jaspers says (and this is analogous to a basic principle of J. Ellul also): "Once I envision world history or life's entirety as a kind of finite totality, I can act only on the basis of sham knowledge, in distortion of actual possibilities, far from reality, vague about facts, achieving nothing but confusion and advancing in directions altogether different from those I wanted" (*Nietzsche and Christianity*). This applies also to monastic reform.

Jaspers again: "Whenever my knowledge is chained to total concepts, whenever my actions are based on a specific world view, I am distracted from what I am really able to do. I am cheated of the present for the sake of something imagined, past or future, rather than real which has not been actually lived and has never been realized."

(Note that in "monastic ideals," this is precisely the problem.

One assumes that the ideal was once fully real and actually lived in a golden age and, thus, one claims to have every reason for resentment at the unrealization of what cannot be and *never was* real. In actual fact, the true monks had a reality which was quite different and fitted in entirely and precisely with their own special and fully accepted circumstances.)

Another quote from Jaspers: "The man who keeps faith with reality wants to act truthfully in the here and now, not to derive a secondhand here and now from a purpose."

There is a problem of false, so-called Christian historicism which sets up history as a unity that "can be comprehended." Nietzsche did and did not see this danger. He may have fallen into it himself, but he said that *because of this* change of focus centered on history, "God was dead" and his death was the fault of Christianity.

Nietzsche also made his classic analysis of Christian morality and the Christian will to truth being, in the end, self-destructive. The ultimate end of Christian will to truth was to destroy even itself by doubts, said Nietzsche. (Thus, Christianity ends in nihilism.)

We certainly see something of this in monasticism today. With the breakdown of confidence in authority and the insatiable thirst for an "authentic ideal," monks are becoming incapable of accepting and resting in anything. Yet they do not really seek God, they seek a perfect monasticism.

All that Nietzsche said about Christianity immediately becomes true as soon as one puts anything else before God, whether it be history or culture or science or contemplation or liturgy or reform or justice. But Jaspers has a brilliant insight into the real possibilities of Nietzsche. If all is permitted, then there is an alternative to the nihilism of despair: the nihilism of strength, "drawn from the vastness of the encompassing and able to do without ties to supposedly finite objectives, maxims and laws." Is not this Christianity?

"It needs no such ties because from the depths of the encompassing, it will always come upon what is true and what is to be done. It will know historically and with the tranquility of eternity."

Maybe. But it seems to me that the Gospel says this and the Gospel remains necessary if men are to attain this freedom rightly, not fall into the fanaticism and arbitrariness which are rooted in despair.

In any case, Jaspers certainly shows the difference between the popular residue of Nietzsche's anti-Christianity and its really profound implication. He ends with Nietzsche's curse on his own admirers: "To this mankind of today, I will not be light nor be called light! Those I will blind!"

Thank God that after NCWC reports of this or that speech of the Pope in the refectory, we are finally getting back to Meriol Trevor's biography of Newman. I have missed it for three months. It is a very good book.

January 11
I spoke too soon. The NCWC reports started all over again yesterday, Sunday.

A little Nietzsche is stimulating, no doubt, but what I really like to read is Isaac of Nineveh in the hermitage or Zen Masters in the fields.

I like to say Lauds of the Little Office of the Blessed Virgin by heart when I am coming down through the woods by starlight with everything there, stars and light, frost and cold, ice and snow, trees, earth, hills and, cozy in the lighted monastery, the sons of men.

January 17
Brilliant night, deep snow sparkling in the moon. Difficult to get this ball-point pen to write, it is so cold; but a good fire keeps the front room of the hermitage fairly warm and I think it will be wonderful walking down to the monastery in an hour or so. The snow began in the early morning yesterday and by the time I started down to the monastery it was blowing in my eyes so that I had to keep them half closed. It blew and snowed all day.

In the monastery after dinner, I played to the novices Brother Antoninus' record *The Tongs of Jeopardy.* It is remarkably good. A meditation on the Kennedy assassination. Brother Antoninus was speaking about this when he was here and I was quite struck by his ideas at that time. They cannot be summed up as "Jungian" but he has remarkable and sensitive poetic insight into the state of the American mind—better than anything else I know. For instance, how much deeper than Paul Goodman's *Growing Up Absurd,* which I have just recently read. More than Jungian, the *Tongs* meditation is deeply Biblical; and his intuition of the Cain idea, the drive to fratricide as the great weakness in the American psyche, is most impressive and I think great.

Illtud Evans is coming here to preach the retreat and I will talk to him about this.

I am tempted to review Brother Antoninus' *Tongs of Jeopardy* for *Blackfriars.*

Showing how the Kennedy assassination moved people, rightly or wrongly, sanely or otherwise, one of our brothers did a drawing, nothing to do with the Antoninus record, of a crucifixion and on the cross was Jacqueline Kennedy (!!). A failure of taste and full of implication. A concept that to me is unintelligible. She, of course, was central in the whole thing. Brother Antoninus had little to say of her in *Tongs.* I wonder why. Perhaps the Irish keening at the end was meant to carry what could not be articulated about her and her grief.

My feeling was that the relationship to her, in which we all ended up, was the most significant thing of all, as if she had redeemed us from all the evil of the murder and of the national sin. (Of course, I suppose that was the idea of the brother who did the drawing.)

She stood out as a presence of love, nobility, truth and decision; as one who chose to be as she was and to forgive inexplicably and be loved and admired and yet to stand above all relationships and bear witness to a kind of deep truth in the whole thing which enabled the mind of the nation to get itself back together again, to collect itself again, relate itself once again to identity and truth.

In other words, it was she who did the greatest thing of all and the noblest thing: disinterestedly and without strings, deciding on her own with great courage and intuition to point to the truth and allow everybody else to see what she was pointing to and decide accordingly. Thanks to the TV presentation of it, I understand, very many people did come up with a noble and honest and contrite decision. But, on the other hand, many did not. Dallas remained "without sin."

Brother Antoninus contrasted the funeral rites of Kennedy with the mendacity of conventions and the lying quality of so much in American life. In any case, Jacqueline Kennedy gave America a sense of being *true* which we seldom get in public life.

When I step out on the porch the bristles in my nose instantly freeze up and the outdoor jakes is a grievous shock. The temperature must be zero or below.

Inside the house the thermometer by the door says forty-five but it is unreliable. I am warm close to the fire but have plenty of clothes on. The whole valley is bright with moonlight and snow and perfectly silent.

Last week I wrote the preface to Phil Berrigan's book *No More Strangers,* in which there are some fine ideas and some bad writing.

January 19

Very cold again. Snow still fairly deep but a bright day. Father Illtud Evans began our retreat last night. Sister Luke came over with him from Loretto yesterday. She is now on a subcommittee working on Schema 13 for the Council, one of the first women to be in such a position, and she wanted to talk about the work of the committee and the schema. I gave her what ideas I had, and I think that as long as they don't take account of the real problem posed by technology, anything they say or do will be beside the point.

January 21

I spent another good day in Bell Hollow. Snow, sun, peace. This was yesterday.

I explored a little more, climbed back up the gully to the spring and came down again by the logging trail. All was undisturbed snow except for the tracks of dogs and rabbits, though at the top of the ridge, on the old wagon road to Howardstown, were the steps of a man who had been there probably the day before. Father Abbot came out there with Brother Nicholas and I ran into him, which I did not particularly want to do. The talk got around to electric fences, boundary lines, snakes, etc. He is very interested in the place and, first of all, acquiring the place. He is full of ideas and deals. And Edelin is dealing with somebody whose name sounds like Cruise, getting ready to trade something for something else. The big trees have been cut off Cruise's land and the tops are lying around all over the place. Cruise, it is said, buys only in order to sell and so on. Cruise owns the valley where the ruined barn is and this is right next to Edelin's, so that, if we wanted to be fully protected, we would have to have it. Besides, his valley would be good for hermitages too. I saw it yesterday and it goes back deep into the hills.

But when I think of all this dealing and organizing and planning and so on and the institution that might finally result, the whole thing becomes much less interesting. Would I be a fool if I went along with all this? Perhaps I would. Would it not be much wiser and simpler to stay where I am and make the best of it for the moment? I am clearly on my own and I no longer have to make any more plans and I am arousing no comment in the community and I am, above all, dependent upon no one. My hermitage is a very decent and beautiful solitude which no longer arouses any comment, is not particularly criticized, gives nobody any trouble, enables me to take care of myself without relying on anybody else, it is close to the monastery, I can get what I need at any moment, nobody has to bring things to me, whereas, if I went to Bell Hollow, I would be completely dependent on others coming out there, unless they gave me a jeep: in which case there would be a great deal of running around. All this is something to think of.

January 22

Vintila Horia sent me his novel about Plato in French. Horia is a Romanian novelist. I find it extraordinarily beautiful, a sustained tone of wisdom with all kinds of modern undertones. Very actual.

Plato says in the novel: "I saw the world rushing into stupidity with such natural self-assurance that it caused me to suffer keenly, as if I had been personally responsible for it, while the people around me saw the future as a new pleasure to be expected from a certain joy: as if by being born into the world they acquired a right to this" (p. 101).

Meanwhile, an ex-novice, Bill Grimes, sent a copy of the *Kiplinger News Letter* which wound up 1964 with the gift of prophecy, peering into the glad future of 1980. Millions more people but no nuclear war, no world war but more, more, more of everything. More superhighways, more cities rebuilt, more suburbs, more money.

He ignores the question whether all these more people will have more jobs.

More recreation, more fun, more colleges and even, with all the money around, a boom in art, music and literature.

(I just can't wait to be sixty-five, still not fully able to believe I will make it to fifty in nine days' time.) Will I see this glorious future in which he does, nevertheless, hint at the possibility of problems?

What a total lack of imagination! The prophecy is unimaginative enough to be perhaps even *true,* but how intolerable. Nothing to look forward to but the same inanities, falsities, clichés, and pretenses. But there will surely be more frustration, therefore more madness, violence, degeneracy, addiction. The country will be one vast asylum.

I have higher hopes. I dare to hope for *change,* not only quantitative but qualitative too; such change must come through darkness and crisis, not joyous and painless adventure. Perhaps I say that out of habit.

January 25

Father Illtud has been preaching a good retreat. We took a couple of walks together and had some long conversations on gray windy afternoons. Talked about Cambridge and *Blackfriars* and the new colleges and the Hebrides. (On Rum now they allow no one to live except those protecting the wildlife and trying to restore the original ecology. This is wonderful.)

January 27

The retreat ended yesterday. Father Illtud tired with a cold. John Howard Griffin came to see Illtud and I saw John briefly. He spoke of a bombing in Youngstown, Ohio, the house of some Ne-

groes who moved into a white neighborhood. Now it all moves
North. He says my stuff on the race issue was by no means too
pessimistic. Some reviewers are indignantly stating that it is.

There was a concelebrated Mass at the end of the retreat, the
first one we have had here after some difficulties with the bishop,
not just obstruction but meticulous observation. It was solemn and
impressive and I think a very great grace for the community and a
fine ending for the retreat. I was not one of the concelebrants, as I
preferred to watch this time, and I also wanted to be sure not to
exclude someone else who is more keen on the liturgy than I am.
The number this time was limited. I am near the top of the list, so I
might exclude one of the junior priests if I signed up for it. Actually,
only three priests senior to me got in on it, Fathers Joseph, Ray-
mond and Roger. But it was a great festival. A little overlong due to
excessive slowness and delay, for instance, purifying patens, cha-
lices, etc., at the end.

The Communion of the concelebrants went extremely slowly,
still it was quite impressive.

After the Mass, I came out into a high wind and a strange
mauve fog, a dust storm from somewhere. The infirmary refectory
was full of dust at the dinner. A swinging window was smashed and
fell in the elevator shaft, where there are still windows. The fire
alarm went off and everything was in confusion. I was buried under
the avalanche of mail they had obligingly saved up over the retreat.

Best thing in the mail, two books from Nicanor Parra. I would
love to translate some of it. Maybe I will do a book of translations
from Parra and Pessõa and call it "Two Anti-Poets." I think I will
write Laughlin about this. But I will not neglect Chuang Tzu.

January 30

A cold night. I woke up to find the night completely filled with
the depth and silence of snow. I stayed up here (at the hermitage)
for supper last night, but having cooked soup, cut up a pear and a
banana for dessert, and made toast, I finally came to the conclusion
that it was all much too elaborate. If there were no better reason for
fasting, the mere fact of saving time would be a good enough reason. The bowl and saucepan have to be washed and I have only a

bucket of rainwater for washing them in, etc. Taking only coffee for breakfast makes a lot of sense because then I can read quietly and sip my mug of coffee at leisure and it really suffices for the morning.

There is a great need for discipline in meditation. Reading helps, the early-morning hours are good, though, in the morning meditation, I am easily distracted by the fire. An hour is not much, but I can be more meditative in the hours of reading which follow and which go much too fast. This can be two hours if I go down later to the monastery, which on Sundays I do. In the afternoon, work takes up so much time and there can be so much of it. Just keeping the place clean is already a big task. Then there is wood to be chopped, etc. The fire is voracious but it is pleasant company.

Today I sent off to *Holiday* a revised version of "Rain and the Rhinoceros" (which is also being censored).

A telegram came yesterday from New Orleans that my drawings had not arrived there.

The vigil of my fiftieth birthday. A bright snowy afternoon. Delicate blue clouds of snow blowing down off the frozen trees. I forcibly restrained myself from much work around the hermitage, made sure of my hour's meditation and will do more later. How badly I need it. I realize how great is the tempo and pressure of work I have been in down at the community, with too many irons in the fire.

True, I have there gained the knack of dropping everything, completely relaxing my attention and forgetting the work by going out and looking at the hills. And the novitiate work is not exceedingly absorbing. My biggest trouble now is letter writing.

Shall I look at the past as if it were something to analyze and think about? Rather, I thank God for the present, not for myself in the present but for the present which is His and in Him. As for the past, I am inarticulate about it now. I can remember irrelevant moments of embarrassment here and there and my joys seemed to have been, to a great extent, meaningless. Yet, as I sit here in this wintry, lonely, quiet place, I suppose I am the same person as the eighteen-year-old riding alone back into Bournemouth in a bus out of the New Forest, where I had camped a couple of days and nights alone. I suppose I regret most my lack of love, my selfishness, my glibness, which covered a profound shyness and an urgent need for love. My glibness with girls who after all did love me, I think, for a time. My fault was my inability to believe it and my efforts to get complete assurance and perfect fulfillment.

I suppose I am still the person that lived for a while at 71 Bridge Street, Cambridge, and had Sabberton for my tailor. He made me that strange Alphonse Daudet coat and the tails I wore perhaps twice. Once to the Boat-race Ball, where I was very selfish and unkind to Joan. And Clare was my college and I was a damned fool, sitting on the steps of the boathouse late at night with Sylvia . . . things like that. Adventures.

What I find most in my whole life is illusion, wanting to be something of which I have formed a concept. I hope I will get free of all that now, because that is going to be the struggle and yet I have to be something that I ought to be. I have to meet a certain demand for order and inner light and tranquility, God's demand, that is, that I remove obstacles to His giving me all these.

Snow, silence, the talking fire, the watch on the table, sorrow. What would be the use of going over all this? I will just get cleaned up (my hands are dirty) and say the Psalms of my birthday:

> *Yet you drew me out of the womb*
> *you entrusted me to my mother's breasts*
> *placed on your lap from my birth*
> *from my mother's womb you have been my God.*
> (Ps. 21 [22])

No matter what mistakes and delusions have marked my life, most of it I think has been happiness and, as far as I can tell, truth. There were whole seasons of insecurity, largely when I was under twenty-one and followed friends who were not really my own kind. But in my senior year at Columbia things got straight.

I can remember many happy and illumined days and whole blocks of time that were fruitful. There were a few nightmare times in my childhood, but at Saint-Antonin life was a real revelation. Then again at so many various times and places. In Sussex, at Rye, in the country, at Olean to spend Christmas with Lax. Arrivals and departures on the Erie were generally great. The cottage on the hill too. Then Cuba, wonderful days there. All this I have said before and the whole world knows it.

Here? The profoundest and happiest times of my life have been in and around Gethsemani, but also some of the most terrible. Mostly, the happy moments were in the woods and fields along with the sky and the sun and up here at the hermitage and with the novices afternoons at work. Good moments, too, with Protestants coming here, especially the Hammers and, of course, on one or two visits to Lexington.

Good visits with J. Laughlin, Ping Ferry, good days in Louisville with Jim Wygal; but the deepest happiness has always been when I was alone, either here in the hermitage or in the novice master's room (that wonderful summer of the gardenias and Plato), or simply out in the fields.

Of course, there was the old vault too, and I must mention many happy moments with the students when I was their Father Master. Also a couple of good days in the hospital when I was well enough to go out and walk around near the grotto.

I could fill another page just with names of people I have loved to be with and loved to hear from. Lax, above all, and Mark Van Doren and all the old friends, Ad Reinhardt and so on. Naomi and Bob Giroux, and all my Latin American friends—Ernesto Cardenal and Pablo Antonio Cuadra. So many students and novices especially, for some reason, the group that came in 1960 and 1961. Brothers Cuthbert, Dennis, Basil and so forth; so many others that have left, like Father John of the Cross. Why go on? Thank God for all of them.

January 31

I can imagine no greater cause for gratitude on my fiftieth birthday than that, on it, I woke up in a hermitage. Fierce cold all night, certainly down to zero, but I have no outdoor thermometer.

Inside the house, it almost froze, though embers still glowed under the ashes in the fireplace. The cold woke me up at one point, but I adjusted the blankets and went back to sleep. What more do I seek than this silence, this simplicity, this "living together with wisdom"? For me, there is nothing else, and to think that I have had the grace to taste a little of what all men really seek without realizing it! All the more obligation to have compassion and love, and to pray for them.

Last night before going to bed I realized momentarily what solitude really means. When the ropes are cast off and the ship is no longer tied to land but heads out to sea without ties and without restraint, not the sea of passion, but the sea of purity and love that is without care. The vastness that loves God alone immediately and directly in Himself as the All, and the seeming nothing that is all. The unutterable confusion of those who think that God is a mental object and that to "love God alone" is to exclude all other objects and concentrate on this one! Fatal. Yet that is why so many misunderstand the meaning of contemplation and solitude and condemn it.

But I see too that I no longer have the slightest need to argue with these people. I have nothing to justify, nothing to defend. I need only defend this vast simple emptiness from my own self and the rest is clear.

The beautiful jeweled shining of honey in the lamplight. Festival!

A thought that came to me during meditation: The error of racism is the logical consequence of an essentialist style of thought. Finding out what a man is and then nailing him down to his definition so that he can never change. A white man is a white man and that is it. A Negro, even though he be three parts white, is a Negro with all that our rigid definition predicates of a Negro. And so the logical machine can grind him down and devour him because of his essence.

Do you think that, in an era of existentialism, this will get any better? On the contrary, definitions, more and more schematic, are fed into computers. The machines are meditating on the most arbitrary and rudimentary of essences punched into IBM cards and defining you and me forever without appeal. "A priest, a Negro, a Jew, a socialist." (Problem of the Mexican intellectual and editor García Torres and his passport trouble because some idiot in an embassy punched his card as "Red.")

February 2

Again it is very cold. On the 31st, it went down to about four below. This morning it is about zero. Yesterday it was warmer. It went up all the way to twenty-eight and there was more snow.

A great deal of wood I have for the fire is wet or not sufficiently seasoned to burn well, though finally, this morning, I got a pretty hot fire going with a big cedar log on top of it. This is some of the coldest weather we have had in the twenty-three years I have been here, but sleeping was fine, certainly no worse than anywhere else. In fact, I was very snug under a big pile of blankets.

It is hard but good to live according to nature, with a primitive technology of wood-chopping and fires, rather than according to the mature technology which has supplanted nature, creating its own weather. Yet there are advantages too in a warmed house and a self-stoking furnace. There is no need to pledge allegiance to either of these systems. Just get warm in any way you can and love God and pray.

I see more and more that now I must desire nothing else than to be "poured out as a libation" to give and surrender my being without concern. The cold woods make this more real; and so does the loneliness.

Coming up last night at the time of a very cold sunset, I found two little birds still picking at crumbs I had left for them on the frozen porch. Everywhere else, snow.

In the morning, coming down, all the tracks covered by snow blown over the path by the wind except tracks of the cat that hunts around the old sheep barn.

Solitude; being aware that you are one man in this snow where there has been no one else but one cat.

February 4

The cold weather finally let up a bit today, the first time in about a week that it has been above freezing. Zero nights or ten above, very cold, sometimes even in bed.

I had the night watch in the monastery last night and came back through the frozen woods to a very cold cottage. But today the snow melted in part and ran loquaciously from the gutters of my roof into buckets. Water again for dishwashing. The bucket I had collected last time was nearly finished.

In my fireplace, I am burning shelves from the old monastic library: not the chestnut shelves, but the sides of poplar. They are dry and quickly make a good hot blaze.

The new library was formally opened in the former brothers' novitiate building on Sunday, my birthday. I was very happy with it. The stacks are well lighted, a big pleasant room with desks was formerly a dormitory, and the reading room upstairs is pleasant too. It is too far for me to go often, but I am glad of the change.

Last night I had a curious and moving dream about a "black mother." I was in a place somewhere I had been as a child. I could not recognize it, but also there seemed to be some connection with Bell Hollow and I realized that I had come there for a reunion with a Negro foster mother whom I had loved in my childhood in the dream. Indeed it seemed, in the dream, that I owed my life to her, to her love for me, so that it was really she and not my natural mother who had given me life, as if from her had come a new life. And there she was. Her face was ugly and severe, yet a great warmth came from her to me and we embraced with love. I felt deep gratitude, and what I recognized was not her face but the warmth of her embrace and of her heart, so to speak. Then we danced a little together, I and my black mother.

Finally I had to continue the journey that I was on in my dream. I cannot remember any more about this journey or any incidents connected with it. The comings and goings, the turning back and so forth.

Today, besides a good letter from Gordon Zahn and other pleasant things in the mail, came a fantastic present from Daisetz Suzuki. A scroll with some of his calligraphies superbly done. The scroll in a perfect little box, the whole thing utterly splendid. I never saw anything so excellent. It will be wonderful in the hermitage, but I have no clue to what the characters say.

Also there was a letter from John Pick saying he wanted my

drawings for exhibit for Marquette in Milwaukee. They are now at Xavier University in New Orleans.

February 9

I must admit that I am still very much moved by Horace, as, for instance, a quote from the Second Epode which I ran across by chance when leafing through the *Liber Confortatorius* of Goscelin in the eleventh-century letter to a recluse. The structure and clarity and music of Horace are great. He is *not* trite (I used to think he was!). There is, it seems to me, real depth there and this is shown by the sustained purity and strength of his tone. Something quite untranslatable.

Rereading the issue of *La Vie Spirituelle* on solitude in 1952, I am struck by the evident progress that has been made. In those days, the tone was not one of real hope, simply a statement of the deplorable fact that the hermit life had practically ceased to exist and that religious superiors could not be brought to see its meaning and importance. Now, on the contrary, it is once again a fact and we are moving beyond the stage where it was thought necessary for a monk to get exclaustrated in order to be a solitary. In other words, beyond the time when it was necessary for a monk to leave the monastic order in order to fulfill his monastic vocation. I am working on a paper about this for a meeting of canonists (to which I will certainly not be going) at New Melleray this spring.

February 11

There has been depressing news from Vietnam. Because of the successful guerrilla attacks of the Vietcong on American bases in South Vietnam, there has been bombing of towns and bases in North Vietnam and signs today are going around the monastery that there was a big bombing evidently of a city by our planes. Perhaps Hanoi has been bombed.

All I can feel is disgust and hopelessness. Have people no understanding left and not even a memory? Haven't they enough imagination to see how totally useless and absurd the whole thing is, even if they lack the moral sense to see the injustice of it? The whole effect of this will be to make America more hated, just as the Russians were hated after the Hungarian revolt in 1956. There is no better way than this to promote Communism in Asia. We are driving people to it instead of "liberating" them from it.

Today I finished the first draft of my paper on eremitism.

Rain all day. I did not get back to the hermitage until after supper. It seems that everything looks favorable for my moving up here when Father Callistus gets back from Rome. But now there is doubt about Father Flavian taking the novice master's job because he wants to go to the Camaldolese, of all things, which sounds foolish to me.

Nightfall. Wind from the west. The porch shines with rain and low dark rags of clouds blow over the valley. The rain becomes more furious and the air is filled with voices and with what might sound like confused radio music in another building—but there is no other building. The sound seems to be coming to a brassy crescendo and ending, but it does not end.

Also the jet planes. High in the storm are jet planes.

Today I got the censor's approval for "Rain and the Rhinoceros," written in December. But the rain is different this time, more serious, less peaceful, more talkative. A very great deal of talk.

February 14

The other day a letter came from Godfrey Diekmann asking me to participate in an ecumenical meeting at Collegeville together with Father Häring, Dom Leclerq, Father Barnabas Ahern and, on the other side, Douglas Steere and nine others. I asked Father Abbot and this permission, which in the circumstances I think any other superior would have granted, was refused.

It is not that I had my heart set on going, about that I can be indifferent. I would have liked to go because I think, for one thing, it would have done me good and I would have learned a lot. I would have had the grace of having done something for the Church and of having participated in a dialogue that would be evidently blessed and fruitful.

It was not possible to discuss anything about this with the abbot. In fact, there was no discussion of why I should *not* go. No real reasons were given, just emotion on the part of the abbot.

He got that look compounded of suffering and stubbornness, interpretable in so many ways, but which oh this occasion made him look as if I were stealing something from him, as though I were making away with the key to his office, for example. A look of vulnerability and defiance. A man threatened in his belly or somewhere, with the determination that I should *not* get away with it, I should *never* get away with it.

Thus the confused motives ("It is not our vocation to travel and attend meetings") become clear in ways other than words. (After all, our Father Chrysogonus is traveling all over the place, attending all kinds of things, and his stay in Europe has already been prolonged twice.)

Dom James regards this invitation to Collegeville as a personal threat to himself, to his prestige, to his very existence as father image and icon. If he were invited, he would probably attend. After refusing my Japanese permission, he himself took off for Norway. I am sure he is not aware of this himself. It appears to him only in the most acceptable terms. He thinks my humility would be deflowered by this meeting with experts, like Dom Leclercq. He detests Dom Leclercq, Dom Winandy, Dom Damasus Winzen and all these wicked Benedictines.

Well, I have to learn to accept this without resentment. Certainly not easy to do. So far, I have hardly tried, and to tell the truth, it angers and distracts me. So that is the vow of obedience. You submit yourself also to somebody else's prejudice and to his myths and to the worship of *his* fetishes.

Well, I have made the vow and will keep it, and will see why I keep it, and will try at the same time not to let myself be involved in the real harm that can come from a wrong kind of submission. There are several wrong kinds, and the right kind is not always easy to find.

In other words, I do not agree with those who say that *any* submission will do.

February 16

I must admit that over Sunday I was troubled by the whole business of that refused permission.

Father Abbot preached a long impassioned sermon on vanity, ambition, using one's gifts for one's own glory, etc., etc., on Sunday morning in Chapter, and I could see he was still very upset. There was a great deal of emotion. His voice was trembling in the beginning, his breathing was not altogether under control, and so on. Obviously this had something to do with my request. This is the way he usually operates and I thought it was quite unfair if it was.

I too was irritated and finally depressed, sitting there in a position of total helplessness and unable to respond or do anything about it. The feeling of powerlessness and frustration and most of all humiliation over the fact that I should feel it so much and be forced by my feelings to think about it all day. How absurd.

And yet the efforts I made to see it rationally, to see it as trifling and laughable, would not quite come off. Nor did the religious arguments and the repeated acceptance of it as a cross and humiliation in the depths of my will. Nothing seemed to make any difference, and finally I lay awake at night, the first time this has happened in the hermitage.

At last I wrote a note to Father Abbot saying I was sorry I had offended him, that his sermon had made me miserable but that my writing, etc., was not pure ambition and vanity, though obviously there was some vanity involved in it, and that I wished he would accept me realistically and not expect me to be something I can never be.

He replied that the sermon had had nothing to do with me, that he had no intention of hurting me, was most concerned, etc. Maybe it was an illusion, but anyway, there it was. I was relieved that it was all settled. A tantrum. I am surely old enough to be beyond that. (I don't really believe his reply.)

Yesterday, in the morning, when I went out for a breath of air before my novice conference, I saw men working on the hillside beyond the sheep barn. At last the electric line is coming. All day they were working on holes, digging and blasting the rock with small charges. Young men in yellow helmets, good, eager, hard-working guys with machines. I was glad of them and of American technology, pitching in to bring light as they would for any farmer in the district. And it was good to feel part of this, which is not to be despised but admirable, which does not mean that I hold any brief for the excess of useless developments in technology.

Afternoon. Landscape of stylites. The REA men all over the hillside, one on top of each pole. Brand-new copper wire swinging and shining, yellow hats all over the place. The light is coming.

1:30 p.m. They came in the morning and the first pole was already up by 9. I hope it may be finished by tonight. I was talking to some of them and they are real nice guys, open and friendly and without guile.

Evening. About 2:45, the red-faced foreman of the REA team, a very good simple man, came and set up my meter, and I put on the switch and had light. I was in the middle of translating some Pessõa poems for Suzuki in return for the calligraphy he sent me recently. The light is a great blessing.

The New Mexican mask at the end of the lattices shows up well and so does the black ink on Suzuki's scroll.

The icons look presentable, though they are much better in ordinary daylight, when the light is outside and they are in the shade of the room. An icon is meant to be seen in shadow and candlelight.

I celebrated the great event, the Epiphany and the coming of the REA, with a good supper of potato soup cooked on an old beat-up electric stove which Brother Joachim gave me. It works all right, so it is an evening of alleluia.

February 17

Early morning. I must admit that the light is a great help. It simplifies things. It makes prayer less complicated. There is no fussing with matches, candles, flashlight.

The electric heater is a help when the morning is not actually freezing, so that I do not have to light the fire and get into all the distraction of logs and pokers.

I am conscious of the fact that the light comes through others. I am part of a collectivity, a rural cooperative, the Salt River RECC.

This is significant and consoling. In this light I am united to the people of the countryside who share the same source as I. But I am not on the same line as the monastery, which is on the big utility company, KU. I am with the poor farmers on REA.

I have been rereading the remarkable notes by S. in *La Vie Spirituelle* of 1952 on solitude. One thing I know now that I could not realize then. It is not enough to be a part-time hermit, living mostly in community, for he says: "Quand il faut composer entre les deux esprits, on partage ses forces entre deux tiédeurs" (When one has to compromise between the two spirits, one divides one's forces between two mediocrities). And this is perfectly true.

Hence I must keep working toward the day of a complete solitude, perhaps when I do not even go down to the conventual Mass. Still, I think it continues to make sense to take dinner down there so as to avoid the fuss of cooking. But as long as I am master of novices, I am obviously going to be tied down.

Father Flavian, my confessor, says it remains a duty of charity to be present with the community for at least a few things.

One of the things I liked about the REA foreman yesterday was that, after asking whether I saw a deer around here, he said, "I don't think I could ever kill a deer." And he said he thought probably a deer would come around here "because they know they would be safe." That was nice. But I told him that I had to chase hunters out of here all the time, even though it is supposed to be a wildlife refuge.

February 24

I have to go in to Dr. Scheen again today. The skin of my hands has erupted once more, leafed and cracked, and deep holes in the skin are quite painful. It interferes with work. Even tying shoes is painful. I had to wear gloves to make my bed. What a mess!

Brother Joachim was up yesterday to put some finishing touches on his electrical work and Brother Clement brought me a big glossy refrigerator which came Saturday, or was installed here that day. It immediately became a big distraction and in many ways

I wish I did not have to have it, but in summer it will be necessary. The first couple of nights I was annoyed by the noise it makes when it wakes up to cool itself, and each time it did this, I woke up too. But I set myself to learn sleeping again and by the grace of God it worked. I might as well forget about being guilty, the thing is too splendid. But local people have such and they have TV too.

Everything about this hermitage fills me with gladness.

There are lots of things that could have been far more perfect one way or the other, ascetically or domestically, but it is the place God has given me after so much prayer and longing and without my deserving it, and it is a delight. I can imagine no other joy on earth than to have such a place to be at peace in. To live in silence, to think and write, to listen to the wind and to all the voices of the wood, to struggle with a new anguish, which is, nevertheless, blessed and secure, to live in the shadow of a big cedar cross, to prepare for my death and my exodus to the heavenly country, to love my brothers and all people, to pray for the whole world and offer peace and good sense among men. So it is my place in the scheme of things and that is sufficient. Amen.

I am reading some studies on St. Leonard of Port Maurice and his *retiro* and the hermitage of the *incontro*. How clearly Vatican II has brought into question all the attitudes he and his companions took completely for granted, such as the dramatic barefoot procession from Florence to the *incontro* in the snow, the daily half-hour discipline in common, etc. This used to be admired, if prudently avoided, by all in the Church. This was thought to be "the real thing" even if only few could do it. Now we have come to be openly doubtful of the intrinsic value of such practices. The sincerity was there and it obviously meant a great deal to them, but depth psychology and so forth have made these things forever questionable. They belong to another age and to another kind of consciousness. They presuppose a certain unawareness of the unconscious. But it is in the unconscious that the true purification and repentance have to reach down and happen. Artificially austere practices have a tendency to prevent this deeper change. They can be a substitute for change in depth, although it is not necessarily true that they can *never* be associated with a deep change. But can they in our time?

Nevertheless, there has to be a certain amount of hardness, difficulty and rigor in the solitary life. The hardness is there all by itself. It does not need to be put there. The cold, the solitude, the loneliness, the labor, the need for poverty to keep everything simple and manageable, the need for discipline, for long meditation in silence; but no dramas, no collective exercises of self-chastisement, into which there can come so much that is spurious and question-able. Indeed, it is good to have a solitary life without this collective dimension. Even though it may be dangerous, it is better.

Evening of February 24

It has been a strange day. I end it by writing with dermal gloves on, as rain pelts down on the cottage.

I was supposed to go to town with Bernard Fox, but he had left when I arrived at the gatehouse at 8:03. As a result, while I was waiting for another ride, the brothers in the store were making signs to me. "It's a good thing that that fellow that wanted to kill you has gone away." Apparently, some nut in the guesthouse was breathing fire and brimstone on my account. In the mail too, there are some letters from some fanatics of varying degrees, who don't like me.

I rode into town with Bobby Gill, who is afraid to drive in city traffic and who, in fact, had never driven in Louisville before. He lives back in the woods the other side of New Hope in a little cabin with his family. He got me to the Medical Arts Building all right and slept peacefully in the parking lot while I was in the doctor's office.

The doctor does not know what is causing this dermatitis. He took bits of skin for a lab test. I wear dermal gloves. My hands *hurt*.

Riding back, about noon, we made good time. If I had been with Bernard and the others, it would have meant lunch in Louis-ville. As it was, Bobby Gill wanted only the sandwiches he had left from his job with Brother Christopher. I got some food at the su-permarket in Bardstown and ate lunch at the hermitage.

Then at the end of the afternoon I went back to the monastery. I had a couple of direction sessions in the novitiate and went to the infirmary kitchen to stock up on sugar.

Over the public-address system from the Chapter Room, they were reading a stern reproof of the hermit life in a book by a Benedictine. Father Roger, who was standing there, told me that Brother Gerard had received the last sacraments at 6 p.m. and was very low.

Coming up in the rain, I thought peacefully of death and accepted the fact that very possibly some madman might come up here one night and do me in and, if that is the way it is to be, I am glad to accept it from God's hand. He will give me the grace to die pleasing to Him.

Bobby Gill is now living at the entrance to the back road that leads to Edelin's place. Bell Hollow is its proper name. Keith Hollow branches northeast from it. So, if I go to live in Bell Hollow, Bobby Gill could possibly be my contact man with the monastery.

Malcolm X, the Negro radical, has been murdered. I am sorry to hear it. Now there is fighting among different factions of black nationalists.

February 26

I see more and more that solitude is not something to play with. It is deadly serious, and much as I have wanted it, I have not been serious enough about it. It is not enough just to "like solitude" or love it even. Even if you like it, solitude can wreck you, I believe, if you desire it only for your own sake.

So I go forward, and I don't believe I could ever go back (even interiorly I have reached a point of no return), but I go on in fear and trembling and often with a sense of lostness, trying to be careful what I do because I am beginning to see that every false step is paid for dearly.

Hence, I fall back on prayer or try to. Yet no matter; there is great beauty and peace in the life of silence and emptiness. But to merely fool around with it brings awful desolation. When one is trifling, even the beauty of the life suddenly becomes implacable. Solitude is a stern mother who brooks no nonsense. And the question arises—am I so full of nonsense that she will cast me out? I pray that she will not and I suppose that is going to take much prayer.

I must admit that I like my own cooking. Rice and pinto beans today, for instance, with apple sauce from the monastery and some peanuts. A nice supper.

I read an excellent Pendle Hill pamphlet. Douglas Steere sent it. It is by Edward Brooke. Three letters on the situation in South Africa. They are hopeful in a Christian sense but I wonder if that hope will, in fact, be realized in history. Certainly it is important to understand South Africa if we want to get a real perspective on our own racial problem.

February 27

The solitary life makes sense only when it is centered entirely on the love of God. Without this, everything is triviality. Love of God in Himself, for Himself, sought only in His will in total surrender. Anything but this in solitude is nausea and absurdity.

But outside of solitude, one can be occupied in many things that seem to have a meaning of their own; and their meaning can be and is accepted, at least provisionally, as something that must be reckoned with until such time as one can come to love God perfectly. This is all right in a way, except that, while doing things theoretically "for the love of God," one falls, in practice, into complete forgetfulness and ignorance and torpor. This happens in solitude, too, of course but in solitude, where distraction is evidently vain, forgetfulness brings conscious nausea. In society, forgetfulness can bring a certain kind of comfort. It is therefore a great thing to be completely vulnerable and feel at once, with every weakening of faith, a total loss. In that way, one has to struggle against the weakening.

Things that in community are legitimate concerns are seen in solitude to be also temptations, tests and questionings. For instance, the skin trouble on my hand.

March 2, Shrove Tuesday

Light rain, Forty Hours [devotion]. A pleasant vigil last night with the novices in church. But it took a long time for the church to calm down after everyone had gone to bed. The sacristans were running around for half an hour.

I am reading a good biography of Simone Weil which I have to review for *Peace News* in London. I am finally getting to know her. I have a lot of sympathy for her, although I cannot agree with some of her attitudes and ideas.

Basically: I wonder what disturbs me about her. Something does. In her experience of Christ, for example: is it Gnostic rather than mystical? But, one has to admit, she seems to have seen this herself and she did not cling to what was wrong. "The attic" was a place she had to leave behind. Her mystique of action and the world is her true climate, now familiar and, I think, more authentic. For a time, I think Catholics were running to Simone Weil to learn this, but now they have forgotten and Teilhard de Chardin is the prophet of this cosmic Christianity.

(And yet, what about St. Francis?)

One thing the hermitage is making me see is that the universe is my home and I am nothing if not part of it. Destruction of the self that seems to stand outside the universe. Get free from the illusion of solipsism.

Only as part of the world's fabric and dynamism can I find my true being in God, who has willed me to exist in the world. This, I discover here in the hermitage, not mentally only but in depth and wholeness, especially, for instance, in the ability to sleep. At the monastery, frogs kept me awake. There are frogs here but they do not keep me awake. They are a comfort, an extension of my own being. Now the hum of the electric meter near my bed is nothing, though in the monastery it would have been intolerable. So there is an acceptance of nature and even of technology in my true habitat. I do not have to work the thing out *theoretically.* It is working itself out in practice in a way that does not need to be explained or justified.

March 3, Ash Wednesday

Though I may be uncomfortable with Simone Weil's imaginative description of her experience with Christ, I think her mysticism has something basically authentic about it. Though I cannot accept her dogmatic ambiguities, I think her reasons, her *personal* and subjective reasons for not joining the Church, are quite sincere. They are profound as well as challenging. Furthermore, I can also see that these might be from God and therefore they may have a special reference to the Church, a special relevance to the predicament of the Church in our time. They are perhaps a kind of accusation of the Church, an accusation which might be seen as coming indirectly from God Himself.

What does impress me in Simone Weil is her intuition of suffering and love: her insistence on being identified with the unfortunate and with the unbeliever. The realization that God's love must break the human heart.

And finally this: "Blessed are they who suffer, in the flesh, the suffering of the world itself in their epoch. They have the possibility and function of knowing its truth, contemplating its reality, its suffering of the world. But unfortunate are they who, having this function, do not fulfill it." Another quote: "We have to discard the illusion of being in possession of time." So says Simone Weil. And this implies consenting to be "human material" molded by time under the eye of God.

March 4

Simone Weil has to be taken as a whole and in her context. Individual and independent as she was, the whole meaning of her thought is to be found, not by isolating it, but by situating it in her dialogue with her contemporaries. The way to dispose of her uncomfortable intuitions is not to set her apart and look at her as if she were a totally isolated phenomenon. Her non-conformism and mysticism are, on the contrary, an essential element in our time. Without her contribution, we would be less human.

Take, for instance, the special importance of her critique of shallow personalism.

See also her prophetic remarks about the Americanization of Europe after the war, which would deaden the Oriental roots of contact with the East in Europe. Her intuition of America as purely non-Oriental and rootless. Her vision of a world threatened with rootlessness through Americanization. This is quite a thought. Consider the symbolic meaning of Vietnam and the burning Buddhists. South America (and this is my addition) is more Oriental as well as more European than North America and this is perhaps the hope of the world, a bridge, a remedy.

Simone Weil thought France should substitute cultural exchange for colonial domination.

She concludes that the exposure of America to the shock of misfortune may make America see the need for roots. But there are no signs of this so far!

Evening—lots of wet snow.

I had to spend the whole day in the monastery, as I had a conference, directions and so forth, and then in the afternoon a long meeting of the building committee (from which I wish I could decently resign) about the project for the new church.

I came briefly up to the hermitage after dinner to sweep, pick up the water bottle to refill and also to read a few pages of a new book, Nishida Kitaro's *Study of the Good,* which Suzuki sent and which is just what I am looking for at the moment. It is magnificent.

But the rest of the day was dreary enough—a test of patience and resignation. Really, I don't care too much. It was wonderful to get back to the hermitage and silence in the evening, to see the trees full of snow outside the bedroom window.

This morning, I said a Requiem Mass for Simone Weil and also spoke of her in the conference to the novices and juniors, reading Herbert's poem on love, which she liked.

The magazine *Holiday* paid me a thousand dollars for "Rain and the Rhinoceros," which they have changed into "The Art of Solitude." (Later, they changed it back to the original title.) Otherwise, there has been no editing except my own, though maybe they edited out the SAC plane. I must look again when the magazine comes. The galleys were here a few days ago.

March 5

Nishida Kitaro is just what I am looking for. For example, I see my objection to the cliché about "meaningful experience" as if it were meaningfulness that made experience somehow real and worthwhile. "Experience" is thought to be made "meaningful" by being referred to something else—a system, or perhaps a report of someone else's experience—and therefore its quality is diminished. So the ambiguity of "meaningfulness" is exposed. When experience becomes "meaningful," it also, in some sense, becomes unreal or less real. To live always outside of experience as if it were the fullness of experience! This is one of the basic ambiguities of Western thought.

A curious thing! Finishing the book on Simone Weil, I discover that it was Tom Bennett, my godfather and guardian, who tried to treat her in the Middlesex Hospital and had her transferred to Ashford because she refused to eat and rejected his care. Funny that she and I have this in common! We are both problems to this good man.

March 9

Several days of rain, mist, damp, cold.

It is flu weather and there is flu in the monastery.

A postulant left and another one came. This one was a Carthusian for a few months at Parkminster (which does not mean that *this* is the best place for him!). We had a meeting about him yesterday and decided to give him a chance.

Father Timothy is on retreat for diaconate, so I spend more time in the novitiate and it was pleasant being there yesterday for Lenten reading.

The place is quiet and peaceful—almost a hermitage itself.

It seems to me that since I have been more often in the hermitage the novices themselves have become much quieter and more serious. I have never done less work with them and never had them so good.

My conclusion is: there is much, too much, anxiety on the part of superiors to interfere with and "direct" their subjects.

Yesterday I sent off the review of the Simone Weil book to *Peace News* and finished some translations of a few poems of Nicanor Parra, who is excellent: sharp, hard, full of solid irony. He is one of the best South American poets, a no nonsense anti-poet with a deep sense of the futility and corruption of social life, a sense which has now been taken over entirely by poets and writers.

I sent the Pessõa poems to Suzuki. Dan [Walsh] said that he had read some of them to his class at Bellarmine.

The new Mass began Sunday and there are good things about it but it is obviously transitional. I will miss the prologue of St. John at the end of the Mass but I am saying it in my Thanksgiving. After all, that is what it was intended for, anyway. Actually, I did not realize how much this "Last Gospel" had drawn to itself and soaked up all the associations of all the joys of fourteen years of Mass and priesthood for me.

All those simple quiet Masses—nine years and more of them in the novitiate chapel. Summer mornings—saying the Last Gospel with the open window looking out toward the green woods of Vineyard Knob. The text itself is one of the most wonderful in the Bible. Certainly ideal for contemplation.

March 10

There is no question now that the Mass ends too abruptly. One has to go more slowly and deliberately, perhaps with a few discreet pauses, or one is suddenly unvesting, as it were, in the middle of Communion.

Of course, a whole new attitude toward the "shape" of the Mass is now required. This attitude is implicit in the new rite; but one must feel it and bring it out. One needs to see the Mass celebrated by priests who have thought out the new implications and experienced their meaning. So far, after all, it is only four days; we here seem to be dutifully setting out the bare fragments of a liturgy in a new arrangement, without having grasped the organic significance of what is going on.

After four or five grim, wet days, cold and dark, suddenly we have bright spring. Cold, clear blue sky with a very few, clean, well-washed clouds, thin and full of light. The wet earth is springy. Green moss shows in the short grass under the pines. The frogs sang for a moment, but it is still cold. The buds are beginning to swell. A flycatcher was playing in the woods near the stile, as I came up, and the pileated woodpecker, bright-combed, darted out, swinging up and down over the field to the east.

All day I have been uncomfortably aware of the wrong that is in me. The useless burden of pride I condemn myself to carry, and all that comes with carrying it. I know I deceive myself as a monk and a writer, but I cannot catch myself in the act. I do not see exactly where the deception lies. Perhaps it is a question of trying to do things that are beyond me, or trying to have something to say about everything. I do not have enough mistrust of my own opinion. Beyond that, there is my rebellious and nasty dissatisfaction with everything—with the country, with the Church, with the monastery, although not so much with the monastery now.

I am accepting it more peacefully and I see how foolish it is to rebel against what is, after all, human and normal and only to be expected. I am, unfortunately, very impatient with the uniformly benign, vague, public pronouncements of Pope Paul VI, as if he could be anything else. Perhaps he is trying earnestly to do something about Vietnam. I am impatient with biographies of new cardinals, read from the newspapers, in the refectory.

At the root of it all is a mean and childish impatience with myself and there is no way of dignifying it as a valid protest.

March 14, Second Sunday of Lent

The sense of wrong is still with me. I now see the negative and weak side of my intentions in writing *Seeds of Destruction,* an element that was invisible to me before, as if I wanted to make sure that I too was part of the human race and concerned in its concerns. Well, I am. There is nothing wrong with that. But for various reasons I do not understand, and because of all the usual ambiguities, I am too anguished and too excited, especially since I am out of touch with what goes on.

Because of this, the book, or at least the part on race, fails to make complete sense. It is not fully useful in the current situation. The part on war has, I think, greater value. The letters may, in some cases, be all right, but they also show the foolishness and futility I have got into with all my mail. Yet I cannot honestly say that I have wished this all on myself. The letters that come in *do* impose a certain obligation by themselves. I have to try to answer some of them and I have not, certainly, gone looking for them.

March 15

Yesterday afternoon it was cold and rainy. I read a little of Eric Colledge's essay on Mechthild of Magdeburg under the tall pine trees behind the hermitage before going in to shave and give my conference—the last conference on Ephrem—and then sing Vespers.

I love the Lenten hymns, all the hymns. What a loss it will be if they are thrown out.

In the evening it cleared, became cold. I came back up to the hermitage with the sun setting and the moon out. I looked out the bedroom window and saw two deer grazing quietly in the field, in the dim dusk and moonlight, barely twenty feet from the cottage. Once in a while, they would look up at the house with their big ears extended. Even a little movement would make them do this, but eventually I walked quietly out on the porch and stayed there and they remained peacefully, quietly, until finally I began moving about. Then they lifted up the white flag of their tails and started off in a wonderful, silent, bounding flight down the field only to stop a hundred yards away. I don't know what became of them after that, for it was my bedtime and I had not read my bit of Genesis (on Jacob's dream), so I read it and went to bed.

March 19, St. Joseph

Bright full moon, cold night. The moonlight is wonderful in the tall pines. Absolute silence of the moonlit valley. It is the twenty-first anniversary of my simple vows.

Last evening I was called over to the guesthouse for a conversation with Father Coffield, who is on his way back from the march at Selma and returning to Chicago. He is one who left Los Angeles in protest against Cardinal McIntyre.

He talked about the tensions and excitements of Selma, and described what it was like to be on the line facing the police at 3 a.m.

There was a legal and official march in Montgomery. Though everything is not yet over, there seems to have been a breakthrough, and the violence of the posse men seems to have had a great deal to do with bringing it about. The protest is going on all over the nation. It is very articulate, and Congress is intent on getting something done. This is due, in great part, to the fact that everyone saw everything on TV. From now on, I will be more careful about what I say against TV.

Father Coffield spoke of John Griffin, who has been very ill and is in the hospital again.

March 21, Third Sunday of Lent

On the afternoon of St. Joseph's, I went over to Edelin's valley with some novices and went to explore on my own a couple of thickly wooded hollows over the ridges south of Bell Hollow. They are both excellent snake pits and I would not want to go there in summer. Coming back over the ridge into Bell Hollow in very thick brush, I got hit in the eye by a branch of sapling. It wounded the cornea and, for two days, I have not been able to see properly out of that eye. It is only a little better today, though it hurts less, what with ointment and dark glasses.

I was able to do very little work yesterday except cooking, gathering wood, etc. I said Office and tried to read a bit with the left eye and wrote a letter to Nicanor Parra.

March 23

Hausherr remarks that in patristic times the theology of baptism was the theology also of Christian perfection, that is to say, it was spiritual theology. This is a more profound remark than it seems to be at first sight. By baptism, a man becomes another Christ and his life must be that of another Christ. The theology of baptism, therefore, teaches us who we are. The consequences are easy to deduce. The saint, or *hagios,* is one who is sanctified in the sense of sacrifice. Compare John 17:19.

In other words, martyrdom is the perfect response to the baptismal vocation. (Compare St. Ignatius of Antioch.)

At the same time, Origen, in the true spirit of non-violence, warns against the impure motive of self-love, which leads one to court death without consideration of the sin of those who would destroy us. We must also consider the importance of remembering the spiritual welfare of the persecutor himself. This has to be taken into account. The experience of the Deep South shows that the death of the martyr does not automatically redeem and convert the persecutor.

In any case, martyrdom can never be a mere improvisation. The only preparation for martyrdom is not some special technical training but the Christian life itself. Thus, eventually a truly Christian life, worthy to be consummated in martyrdom, is treated as almost equivalent to it. Then you get the ideal of the confessor and the monk. This is simply the life of true discipleship.

The mark of such discipleship is perfect love of the Saviour and of the Father's will. He who does not live according to his baptism and discipleship is living as a potential renegade from martyrdom.

My eye gets better only slowly. Ointments and even a black patch have been necessary for a couple of days. Only today am I able to read with it again and that makes it burn. But this has been a grace. I have been sobered by it. What was I doing charging through the woods on that godforsaken ridge? Trying to see if I would come out where I did. All right, but it was still useless. I would have been better off quietly praying, as I did yesterday afternoon in that lovely glen where I used to go twelve years ago.

I was preparing the sermon on St. Benedict, which I had to preach yesterday, and I was much struck by the idea of judgments of God. The thought took deep hold on me that what matters in our life is not abstract ideals but profound love and surrender to the concrete judgments of God. They are our life and our light. Inexhaustible source of purity and strength, but we can ignore them, and this is the saddest thing of all.

March 23, Evening

My eye is slightly better but not yet healed.

There was a high wind all day. It is my free day at the hermitage and in the middle of the afternoon a knock came on the door. It was my neighbor, Andy Boone. He wanted to talk about the fence line he is working on and a deal about three white oaks he wants to cut down. He offered me twenty-five dollars a month to pasture his cows in the field next to the hermitage and I said no, on account of the locust seedlings we put in there last spring, and so on. One very good thing came out of it.* He told me there was an excellent spring that had got filled in and buried some years ago. It is only fifty yards or so behind the hermitage through thick brush. I knew the place and did not realize there was a spring there, though water is running there now. We will clear it and perhaps pump it to the hermitage. Anyway, clear it.

I went out there and saw a dozen places in the thick brush where deer had been sleeping. They are my nearest dormitory neighbors—thirty or forty yards from my own bed or even less. How wonderful!

Andy Boone was full of all kinds of information and stories. For one thing, he said that the water from all these springs comes from the Lake Knob. He was told this by a geologist. He had the geologist here looking for uranium!

He has a lot of stories about chasing people from Elizabethtown out of the woods when they come to have wild parties by night near Dom Frederic's Lake. He talks about hunters who are too lazy to get out of their cars and sit in them by the roadside, shooting woodchucks in our field. He tells how Daniel Boone first came to Kentucky and spread the people around wherever there was water and then went off himself to Indiana. In Indiana, he had a hole that he hid in when the Indians were after him. He withdrew into it, pulled a stone over it, and they never found him. The hole was eight miles long and twelve feet high and nine feet wide and had a stream in it, and when a powder plant was being built on which Andy worked before World War II, a bulldozer disappeared in this hole and that is how it was discovered.

All this is typical Andy Boone talk. Andy Boone is an old farmer who has been living here all his life on the farm next door to the property where I live. He is always around the monastery and knows a lot about the monks and has an inexhaustible fund of stories that only a madman would take seriously. I know what it costs to believe him!

---

* This was not a good thing at all. It was a very bad thing! As the results proved. T.M.

March 26

Vile rain and fog.

I came up last night in very heavy rain with a cold beginning. As long as I stay in the hermitage and keep the fire going, the cold is not too bad. It was a bit bothersome in the community, where there is flu. The choir is overheated. You sweat and then get chilled. I wish I could simply stay up here at the hermitage and say Mass up here.

I have grapefruit juice in the icebox and that is a big help. I decided to take some bread with my coffee this morning instead of fasting on coffee only until dinner. The rye bread was good and so was the coffee.

Dan Walsh is giving his momentous talk at Catholic University today and I promised I would say a Mass of the Holy Spirit for the canonization of Duns Scotus. His talk is ostensibly about Duns Scotus and Anselm but also, and above all, consists in the development of his own ideas on the metaphysics of faith. I shall be very interested to hear it when he gets back.

Evening. The weather continued to be very foul all day. It is plague weather. I have not been able to see across the valley all day long. My cold is a little worse, but not much.

I sat out the conventual Mass alone in the back of the brothers' choir and could see a few good fathers look back disapprovingly from the monks' choir, as if there were a divine commandment to sit with the other invalids in the transept when you have a cold. Actually, it was quite impressive to follow the Mass from back there—a thing I had never done before. The main reason I was there was to be completely alone. I suppose that is what everybody resented.

After I got back to the hermitage, Andy Boone came by with a check for a hundred and twenty-five dollars for the trees he cut down on the fence line and he talked some more. Am I going to be in perceptual conversation with this man? He was talking of the connection of dogwood trees with the passion of Christ. And one of his favorite topics—how to tell the sex of cedar trees. Only the "she trees" make good Christmas trees, he says. He claims that our planting loblolly seedlings brought in the beetles which are killing cedars and Virginia pines. This I can well believe.

March 27

The moon is out, the sky is clearing at last. The air is drier and fresher. There is a very thin film of ice on the water buckets. Last end of the old moon. The new moon will be the moon of Easter.

March 29

The hope of better and drier weather died quickly yesterday. The sky darkened and at night there was thunder, lightning, heavy rain beating down and, half awake, I remembered that I had left my rubber boots down at the house and thought of my cold, which gets no better. Fortunately, I had a raincoat at the hermitage.

The fire alarm at the monastery went off at about 5:30 and the rain abated, so I went down. It was a false alarm. Water got into the warning system. It kept on raining all morning.

Then I received an anonymous letter from Alabama from a reader who desired to prove her sincerity by saying she was a mother and grandmother and who said my book *Seeds of Destruction* was appalling, spelled "appauling." Some clippings from the Alabama papers were enclosed. Nothing but righteous indignation and outrage. In fact, the same irrationality, the same ferocity that one saw in the Nazi press twenty years ago. One theme only—that some degraded and despicable people, "outside agitators," were simply defiling, insulting and gratuitously provoking the good people of Alabama; that such things were simply beyond comprehension and beyond pardon; that the thought of considering any apparent reason behind them was totally unacceptable; that Alabama had done and could do no wrong. Complete failure to face reality.

Another murder took place last week after the Montgomery marches.*

---

* That was probably the murder of Viola Liuzzo. T.M.

March 31

Better weather yesterday.

My biggest distraction these days is Andy Boone, who extracted from me a vague agreement that he ought to cut down some oaks at the top of the field east of the hermitage. His sons have been out there with chain saws making a frightful racket and sending the biggest white oaks (naturally) crashing down one on top of the other. By last evening, the woods were in a fine mess, with one big tree hung up in another and a third hanging on the one that is hung up. I persuaded him yesterday to direct his attention elsewhere and cut up the dead trees around the spring so that we can get in there and clean it up.

But my cold is better and I am trying to get back into some serious meditation. Serious, not just hanging around quietly and moodily. Here too, there is a spring to be cleared and I am not going deep enough these days.

April 3

This morning I finished the appendix to Nishida Kitaro's *Study of Good,* which gives some idea of the full scope of Nishida's thought. It is most satisfying. Happily, there is at least one other of his books in English. The *Study of Good* is his first. The development from here is not linear, but a special deepening of his basic intuition of pure experience, which becomes "absolute nothingness as the place of existence," and "eschatological everyday life," in which the person as a focus of absolute contradiction (our very existence opening onto death is a contradiction) can say with Rinzai, "Wherever I stand is all the truth." This hit me with great force. My meditation has been building up to this. (Awareness, for instance, that doubt arises from projection of the self into the future or from retrospection and not grasping the present. He who *grasps* the present does not doubt.)

To be open to the nothingness which I am is to grasp the All in whom I am.

Yesterday I marked the trees that Andy Boone is to cut down and I have to see that he cuts down *only* the trees that are marked. They are all in the hollow behind the hermitage, where the spring is.

What a tangle of brush, saplings, vines, fallen trees and honey-suckle! Marks of deer everywhere. A fire in there would be a disaster. I hope we can get a space of an acre or so good and clear between here and the spring and keep it clear and I can use the spring, for I need it.

All this wild area is the geographical unconscious of my hermitage. Out in front, the conscious mind, the ordered fields, the wide valley, tame woods. Behind, the unconscious, this lush tangle of life and death, full of danger, yet where beautiful beings move, the deer, and where there is a spring of sweet pure water buried.*

April 4, Passion Sunday
Light rain all night.
The need to keep working at meditation and going to the root. Mere passivity won't do at this point, but activism won't do either. A time of wordless deepening to grasp the inner reality of my nothingness in Him, who is.

Talking about it in these terms is absurd, nothing to do with the concrete reality that is to be grasped and is grasped. My prayer is peace and struggle in silence, to be aware and true, beyond myself. To go outside the door of myself, not because I *will* it but because I am *called* and must respond.

April 6
Tuesday in Passion Week.
A rainy, humid, stuffy day—as warm as summer. Had to go to town to see the eye doctor. My eye is still injured by that blow I got from the branch in the woods on March 19. I saw Dr. Flowers. It is the first time I have been in the new Medical Towers near all those new hospitals, which have so transformed Gray Street from the lazy Southern street it was ten years ago.

The windows of the Presbyterian Seminary are boarded up. The seminary has moved out of the old fake-Gothic building,

---

* It is sobering to reflect that the spring was not so pure! T.M.

Scotch Victorian Tudor or whatever it was. They are now up by Cherokee Park.

So I sweated in the doctor's waiting room and read copies of *Life* magazine—one more tedious than the other. Great emphasis on the mess in Vietnam, trying to make it look good, honest, reasonable, and so forth, which it is not.

Senator Cooper gave a good speech in the Senate against extending the war and I got a letter from him in reply to one I had written about it. He seems serious and sane about it.

April 9, Feast of Our Lady of Sorrows.
Friday in Passion Week.

Dawn is beginning (5:30) on a mild spring morning. Holy Week is about to open and I was never more conscious of its solemnity and its importance. I am a Christian and a member of a Christian community. I and my brothers are to put aside everything else and recognize that we belong, not to ourselves, but to God in Jesus Christ, that we have vowed obedience that is intended to unite us in Christ, obedient unto death, even the death of the cross. That, without our listening and attention and submission in total self-renunciation and love for the Father's will in union with Christ, our life is false and without meaning.

But insofar as we desire with Christ that the Father's will may be done in us as it is in heaven and in Jesus, then even the smallest and most ordinary things are made holy and great. Then, in all things, the love of God opens out and flowers. Then our lives are transformed. This transformation is an Epiphany and advent of God in the world.

It is unfortunate that so much of monastic obedience has become merely formal and trivial. There is no use in lamenting this, but nevertheless, renewal in this area must mean, above all, a recovery of the sense of *obedience to God in all things* and not just obedience to rules and superiors when obedience is *demanded:* and after that, go wool-gathering where you may!

A sad thing that formal obedience or non-disobedience is an expedient which, in practice, justifies us in self-will in harmless and futile matters. Thus our lives, in fact, become totally absorbed in futilities, which are licit and which are not subject to formal control. Instead of imitating Christ, we are content to parody Him.

One of the fruits of the solitary life is a sense of the absolute importance of *obeying God,* a sense of the need to obey and *to seek His will,* to choose freely, to see and accept what comes from Him, not as a last resort, but as one's daily supersubstantial bread. This means liberation from automatic obedience into the seriousness and gravity of a *free choice to submit;* but it is not always easy to see where and how.

April 13

Tuesday in Holy Week.

On Palm Sunday, everything was going well and I was getting into chants of the Mass when suddenly the Passion, instead of being solemnly sung on the ancient tone in Latin, was read in the extremely trite and pedestrian English version that has been approved by the American bishops. The effect was, to my mind, complete bathos, a total lack of nobility or of solemnity or of any style whatever. It became an utterly trivial act. I could not get away from the impression of a comedy. Not that English is not capable of serious liturgical use, but the total lack of imagination, of creativity, of any sense of worship in this pedestrian version! Yet many in the community were delighted, including the professor of liturgy.

In the evening conference, I talked (foolishly) of Angela of Foligno and then back to Philoxenos.

After supper and direction, I went up to bed in the hermitage feeling unwell. I woke up after an hour's sleep with violent diarrhea and vomiting, which went on for most of the night. Fortunately, the night was warm and moonlit. I was weak and nauseated all yesterday. I began to feel better in the evening and took a little supper. I slept last night in the infirmary and slept well too. Had a good breakfast of fried eggs and coffee. I felt a little weak this morning, but on the whole I seem to have got off easy, unless it starts up again after supper, which I suppose it might. While it lasted, it was a miserable experience.*

---

* First indication of what was in the water of the "pure" spring. T.M.

April 15, Holy Thursday

Obedient unto death.

Perhaps the most crucial aspect of Christian obedience to God today concerns the responsibility of the Christian, in technological society, toward creation and God's will for his creation. Obedience to God's will for nature and for man; respect for nature and love for man; awareness of our power to frustrate God's designs for nature and for man, to radically corrupt and destroy natural goods by misuse and blind exploitation, especially by criminal waste.

The problem of nuclear war is only one facet of an immense complex question.

A theologian writes: "It is the duty of the Christian to lead the world of nature to its natural perfection." And this is true in a sense, but it is written with a tone and with implications that are perhaps misleading. It assumes that technology is obviously doing something to perfect nature; it does not consider that technology might be squandering and abusing nature in the most irresponsible fashion.

There are then very grave problems in the implications of a certain kind of Christian outlook on the world. The crux of the matter seems to be to what extent a Christian thinker can preserve his independence from obsessive modes of thought about secular progress, behind which lies the anxiety for us and for the Church to be acceptable in a society that is leaving us behind in a cloud of dust.

In other words, where is our hope? If, in fact, our hope is in a temporal and secular messianism of technological and political progress, we find ourselves, in the name of Christ, joining in the stupidity and barbarism of those who are wrecking his creation in order to make money or to get power for themselves. But our hope must be in God.

Yesterday I got out of the infirmary at my own request, perhaps too soon, but I felt better and wanted to get back to the hermitage, though it tires me to come out here.

Last night I was restless and feverish, sweating a lot, and had to change my shirt three or four times. At the end of the night, I had some rather beautiful dreams and got up at three. My meditation wasn't much good, as I was feeling sick. But some superb tea that

Jack Ford gave me, Lapsang Souchong, made me feel much better. It is the most effective medicine I have taken in this sickness, a marvelous tea. That, with a slice of lemon and a couple of pieces of rye toast, made a fine breakfast, and after reading a bit, I am very alert and alive. But as heavy rain began about 4:30, I did not go down to the monastery for Chapter and some of the ceremonies.

The rain is slowing down now at 7:15. The valley is dark and beautifully wet. You can almost see the grass growing and the leaves pushing out of the poplars. There are small flowers on my redbuds and the dogwood buds are beginning to swell.

There is no question for me that my one job as a monk is to live this hermit life in simple direct contact with nature, primitively, quietly, doing some writing, maintaining such contacts as are willed by God and bearing witness to the value and goodness of simple things and ways, loving God in all of it. I am more convinced of this than of anything else in my life and I am sure it is what He asks of me. Yet I do not always respond with perfect simplicity.

April 16, Good Friday

Today, God disputes with his people. One of the rare times when he argues with man, enters the court and pleads his own cause. O my people, what have I done to you? Man blames God for evil, but it turns out that all the evil in the world has been done through man by the mysterious adversary of God. And all the evil has been done *to* God. He who need not have taken it upon Himself has done so in order to save man from evil and from his adversary. The adversary, and man allied with him, makes himself "be" by declaring himself to be real and God less real or unreal, trying to reduce God to nothing on the cross. But God, the abyss of being beyond all division of being and nothingness, can neither be made to be nor reduced to nothing.

The judgment: those who have turned their hate against God have in reality destroyed themselves in striving, in their own manner, to assert themselves. The way to "being" is then the way of non-assertion. This is God's way. Not that He has a way in Himself, but it is the way He has revealed for us, revealing Himself as the way. "I am the way," said Christ. And last night we went out of Chapter into the church for concelebration.

April 17, Holy Saturday
The great sin, the source of all other sin, is idolatry and never has it been greater, more prevalent, than now. Yet it is almost completely unrecognized precisely because it is so overwhelming and so total. It takes in everything. There is nothing else left. Fetishism of power, machines, possessions, medicines, sports, clothes, etc., all kept going by greed for money and power. The bomb is only one accidental aspect of the cult. Indeed, the bomb is not the worst. We should be thankful for it as a sign, a revelation of what all the rest of our civilization points to. The self-immolation of man to his own greed and his own despair. And behind it all are the principalities and powers whom man serves in this idolatry.

A warm bright spring day. I saw a palm warbler in the small ash tree behind the hermitage with his red-brown cap and bobbing tail. He is on his way to the north of Canada. Why do they call him a palm warbler?

April 18, Easter Sunday
The peace and beauty of Easter morning! Sunrise, deep green grass, soft winds, the woods turning green on the hills across the valley and here too.

I got up and said the old Office of Lauds and there was a wood thrush singing Fourth Tone mysteries in the deep ringing pine wood, the unconscious wood behind the hermitage. (The unconscious wood has a long moment of perfect clarity at dawn. From being dark and confused, lit from the east, it becomes all clarity, all distinct, seems to be a place of silence and peace with its own order and disorder. The fallen trees don't matter. They are part of it.)

Last night I went down to the Offices of the Easter Vigil by full moonlight, the woods being perfectly silent and the moon so strong one could hardly see any stars. I sat on the porch to make my Thanksgiving after Communion. I did not concelebrate, I only went to Communion.

DAY OF A STRANGER

In reply to a questioner from Latin America on how he spent his day, Thomas Merton wrote "Day of a Stranger." The piece went through several drafts, and one of them was published in Spanish in 1966 in a Venezuelan journal.

Merton wrote this essay in the summer of 1965 just as he had taken up residence in the cinder block hermitage built for him on the monastic property. "Day of a Stranger" allows him to celebrate this new style of eremetical living although, as he notes, he still went down to the main monastery each day.

This meditation, reproduced below in its entirety, is quintessential Merton. One reads in it a fusion of his liturgical, artistic, and contemplative interests as well as his ever present sense of the destructive capacity of the modern world symbolized here by the lofty presence of the Strategic Air Command (SAC) bombers which flew over the monastery carrying their load of atomic weapons.

It is instructive to compare this work with the previous "Fire Watch" selection from The Sign of Jonas *written fifteen years earlier. "Day of a Stranger" still reverberates with monastic and liturgical rhythms but the tone is more ironic, more playful, and more engaged with the world outside the cloister. The first flush of piety is gone from this piece (the spirituality is still there in an explicitly palpable form), replaced now with a sense of wry detachment which may well reflect both the author's maturity and the leavening effect of his encounter with Zen.*

The best analysis of this work is to be found in the introduction to its book publication written by Robert Daggy who also puts the work into the context of Merton's increasing contacts with thinkers and poets from Latin America. See Thomas Merton, Day of a Stranger, *with an Introduction by Robert E. Daggy (Salt Lake City: Gibbs M. Smith, 1981). "Day of a Stranger" was first published in* The Hudson Review *XX (Summer 1967), pp. 211–218, and reprinted many times in various anthologies and journals.*

*

The hills are blue and hot. There is a brown, dusty field in the bottom of the valley. I hear a machine, a bird, a clock. The clouds are high and enormous. Through them the inevitable jet plane passes: this time probably full of passengers from Miami to Chicago. What passengers? This I have no need to decide. They are out of my world, up there, busy sitting in their small, isolated, arbitrary lounge that does not even seem to be moving—the lounge that somehow unaccountably picked them up off the earth in Florida to suspend them for a while with timeless cocktails and then let them down in Illinois. The suspension of modern life in contemplation that *gets you somewhere!*

There are also other worlds above me. Other jets will pass over, with other contemplations and other modalities of intentness.

I have seen the SAC plane, with the bomb in it, fly low over me and I have looked up out of the woods directly at the closed bay of the metal bird with a scientific egg in its breast! A womb easily and mechanically opened! I do not consider this technological mother to be the friend of anything I believe in. However, like everyone else, I live in the shadow of the apocalyptic cherub. I am surveyed by it, impersonally. Its number recognizes my number. Are these numbers preparing at some moment to coincide in the benevolent mind of a computer? This does not concern me, for I live in the woods as a reminder that I am free not to be a number.

There is, in fact, a choice.

In an age where there is much talk about "being yourself" I reserve to myself the right to forget about being myself, since in any case there is very little chance of my being anybody else. Rather it seems to me that when one is too intent on "being himself" he runs the risk of impersonating a shadow.

Yet I cannot pride myself on special freedom, simply because I am living in the woods. I am accused of living in the woods like Thoreau instead of living in the desert like St. John the Baptist. All I can answer is that I am not living "like anybody." Or "unlike anybody." We all live somehow or other, and that's that. It is a compelling necessity for me to be free to embrace the necessity of my own nature.

I exist under trees. I walk in the woods out of necessity. I am both a prisoner and an escaped prisoner. I cannot tell you why, born in France, my journey ended here in Kentucky. I have considered going further, but it is not practical. It makes no difference. Do I have a "day"? Do I spend my "day" in a "place"? I know there are trees here. I know there are birds here. I know the birds in fact very well, for there are precise pairs of birds (two each of fifteen or twenty species) living in the immediate area of my cabin. I share this particular place with them: we form an ecological balance. This harmony gives the idea of "place" a new configuration.

As to the crows, they form part of a different pattern. They are vociferous and self-justifying, like humans. They are not two, they are many. They fight each other and the other birds, in a constant state of war.

There is a mental ecology, too, a living balance of spirits in this corner of the woods. There is room here for many other songs besides those of birds. Of Vallejo, for instance. Or Rilke, or René Char, Montale, Zukofsky, Ungaretti, Edwin Muir, Quasimodo or some Greeks. Or the dry, disconcerting voice of Nicanor Parra, the poet of the sneeze. Here also is Chuang Tzu whose climate is perhaps most the climate of this silent corner of woods. A climate in which there is no need for explanation. Here is the reassuring companionship of many silent Tzu's and Fu's; Kung Tzu, Lao Tzu, Meng Tzu, Tu Fu. And Hui Neng. And Chao-Chu. And the drawings of Sengai. And a big graceful scroll from Suzuki. Here also is a Syrian hermit called Philoxenus. An Algerian cenobite called Camus. Here is heard the clanging prose of Tertullian, with the dry catarrh of Sartre. Here the voluble dissonances of Auden, with the golden sounds of John of Salisbury. Here is the deep vegetation of that more ancient forest in which the angry birds, Isaias and Jeremias, sing. Here should be, and are, feminine voices from Angela of Foligno to Flannery O'Connor, Theresa of Avila, Juliana of Norwich, and, more personally and warmly still, Raissa Maritain. It is good to choose the voices that will be heard in these woods, but they also choose themselves, and send themselves here to be present in this silence. In any case, there is no lack of voices.

The hermit life is cool. It is a life of low definition in which there is little to decide, in which there are few transactions or none, in which there are no packages to be delivered. In which I do not bundle up packages and deliver them to myself. It is not intense. There is no give and take of questions and answers, problems and solutions. Problems begin down the hill. Over there under the water tower are the solutions. Here there are woods, foxes. Here there is no need for dark glasses. "Here" does not even warm itself up with references to "there." It is just a "here" for which there is no "there." The hermit life is that cool.

The monastic life as a whole is a hot medium. Hot with words like "must," "ought" and "should." Communities are devoted to high definition projects: "making it all clear!" The clearer it gets the clearer it has to be made. It branches out. You have to keep clearing the branches. The more branches you cut back the more branches grow. For one you cut you get three more. On the end of each branch is a big bushy question mark. People are running all around with packages of meaning. Each is very anxious to know whether all the others have received the latest messages. Has someone else received a message that he has not received? Will they be willing to pass it on to him? Will he understand it when it is passed on? Will he have to argue about it? Will he be expected to clear his throat and stand up and say "Well the way I look at it St. Benedict said. . . ?" Saint Benedict saw that the best thing to do with the monastic life was to cool it but today everybody is heating it up. Maybe to cool it you have to be a hermit. But then they will keep thinking that *you* have got a special message. When they find out you haven't . . . Well, that's their worry, not mine.

This is not a hermitage—it is a house. ("Who was that hermitage I seen you with last night? . . .") What I wear is pants. What I do is live. How I pray is breathe. Who said Zen? Wash out your mouth if you said Zen. If you see a meditation going by, shoot it. Who said "Love?" Love is in the movies. The spiritual life is something that people worry about when they are so busy with something else they think they ought to be spiritual. Spiritual life is guilt. Up here in the woods is seen the New Testament: that is to say, the wind comes through the trees and you breathe it. Is it supposed to be clear? I am not inviting anybody to try it. Or suggesting that one day the message will come saying NOW. That is none of my business.

I am out of bed at two-fifteen in the morning, when the night is darkest and most silent. Perhaps this is due to some ailment or other. I find myself in the primordial lostness of night, solitude, forest, peace, a mind awake in the dark, looking for a light, not totally reconciled to being out of bed. A light appears, and in the light an ikon. There is now in the large darkness a small room of radiance with psalms in it. The psalms grow up silently by themselves without effort like plants in this light which is favorable to them. The plants hold themselves up on stems which have a single consistency, that of mercy, or rather great mercy. *Magna misericordia.** In the formlessness of night and silence a word then pronounces itself: Mercy. It is surrounded by other words of lesser consequence: "destroy iniquity" "wash me" "purify" "I know my iniquity." *Peccavi.*** Concepts without interest in the world of business, war, politics, culture, etc. Concepts also often without interest to ecclesiastics.

Other words: Blood. Guile. Anger. The way that is not good. The way of blood, guile, anger, war.

Out there the hills in the dark lie southward. The way over the hills is blood, guile, dark, anger, death: Selma, Birmingham, Mississippi. Nearer than these, the atomic city, from which each day a freight car of fissionable material is brought to be laid carefully beside the gold in the underground vault which is at the heart of this nation.

"Their mouth is the opening of the grave; their tongues are set in motion by lies; their heart is void."

Blood, lies, fire, hate, the opening of the grave, void. Mercy, great mercy.

The birds begin to wake. It will soon be dawn. In an hour or two the towns will wake, and men will enjoy everywhere the great luminous smiles of production and business.

— Why live in the woods?
— Well, you have to live somewhere.

---

* [Great mercy.]
** [I have sinned.]

— Do you get lonely?
— Yes, sometimes.
— Are you mad at people?
— No.
— Are you mad at the monastery?
— No.
— What do you think about the future of monasticism?
— Nothing. I don't think about it.
— Is it true that your bad back is due to Yoga?
— No.
— Is it true that you are practising Zen in secret?
— Pardon me, I don't speak English.

All monks, as is well known, are unmarried, and hermits more unmarried than the rest of them. Not that I have anything against women. I see no reason why a man can't love God and a woman at the same time. If God was going to regard women with a jealous eye, why did he go and make them in the first place? There is a lot of talk about a married clergy. Interesting. So far there has not been a great deal said about married hermits. Well, anyway, I have the place full of ikons of the Holy Virgin.

One might say I had decided to marry the silence of the forest. The sweet dark warmth of the whole world will have to be my wife. Out of the heart of that dark warmth comes the secret that is heard only in silence, but it is the root of all the secrets that are whispered by all the lovers in their beds all over the world. So perhaps I have an obligation to preserve the stillness, the silence, the poverty, the virginal point of pure nothingness which is at the center of all other loves. I attempt to cultivate this plant without comment in the middle of the night and water it with psalms and prophecies in silence. It becomes the most rare of all the trees in the garden, at once the primordial paradise tree, the *axis mundi,* the cosmic axle, and the Cross. *Nulla silva talem profert.** There is only one such tree. It cannot be multiplied. It is not interesting.

It is necessary for me to see the first point of light which begins

---

* ["No forest produced such a tree," from the hymn *Vexilla Regis.*]

to be dawn. It is necessary to be present alone at the resurrection of Day, in the blank silence when the sun appears. In this completely neutral instant I receive from the Eastern woods, the tall oaks, the one word "DAY," which is never the same. It is never spoken in any known language.

Sermon to the birds: "Esteemed friends, birds of noble lineage, I have no message to you except this: be what you are: be *birds.* Thus you will be your own sermon to yourselves!"
Reply: "Even this is one sermon too many!"

Rituals. Washing out the coffee pot in the rain bucket. Approaching the outhouse with circumspection on account of the king snake who likes to curl up on one of the beams inside. Addressing the possible king snake in the outhouse and informing him that he should not be there. Asking the formal ritual question that is asked at this time every morning: "Are you in there, you bastard?"

More rituals. Spray bedroom (cockroaches and mosquitoes). Close all the windows on south side (heat). Leave windows open on north and east sides (cool). Leave windows open on west side until maybe June when it gets very hot on all sides. Pull down shades. Get water bottle. Rosary. Watch. Library book to be returned.
It is time to visit the human race.

I start out under the pines. The valley is already hot. Machines out there in the bottoms, perhaps planting corn. Fragrance of the woods. Cool west wind under the oaks. Here is the place on the path where I killed a copperhead. There is the place where I saw the fox run daintily and carefully for cover carrying a rabbit in his mouth. And there is the cement cross that, for no reason, the novices rescued from the corner of a destroyed wall and put up in the woods: people imagine someone is buried there. It is just a cross. Why should there not be a cement cross by itself in the middle of the woods?
A squirrel is kidding around somewhere overhead in midair. Tree to tree. The coquetry of flight.
I come out into the open over the hot hollow and the old sheep

barn. Over there is the monastery, bugging with windows, humming with action.

The long yellow side of the monastery faces the sun on a sharp rise with fruit trees and beehives. This is without question one of the least interesting buildings on the face of the earth. However, in spite of the most earnest efforts to deprive it of all character and keep it ugly, it is surpassed in this respect by the vast majority of other monasteries. It is so completely plain that it ends, in spite of itself, by being at least simple. A lamentable failure of religious architecture—to come so close to non-entity and yet not fully succeed! I climb sweating into the novitiate, and put down my water bottle on the cement floor. The bell is ringing. I have duties, obligations, since here I am a monk. When I have accomplished these, I return to the woods where I am nobody. In the choir are the young monks, patient, serene, with very clear eyes, then, reflective, gentle, confused. Today perhaps I tell them of Eliot's *Little Gidding,* analyzing the first movement of the poem ("Midwinter spring is its own season"). They will listen with attention thinking that some other person is talking to them about some other poem.

Chanting the *alleluia* in the second mode: strength and solidity of the Latin, seriousness of the second mode, built on the *Re* as though on a sacrament, a presence. One keeps returning to the *re* as to an inevitable center. *Sol-Re, Fa-Re, Sol-Re, Do-Re.* Many other notes in between, but suddenly one hears only the one note. *Consonantia:* all notes, in their perfect distinctness, are yet blended in one. (Through a curious oversight Gregorian chant has continued to be sung in this monastery. But not for long.)

In the refectory is read a message of the Pope, denouncing war, denouncing the bombing of civilians, reprisals on civilians, killing of hostages, torturing of prisoners (all in Vietnam). Do the people of this country realize who the Pope is talking about? They have by now become so solidly convinced that the Pope never denounces anybody but Communists that they have long since ceased to listen. The monks seem to know. The voice of the reader trembles.

In the heat of noon I return with the water bottle freshly filled, through the cornfield, past the barn under the oaks, up the hill, under the pines, to the hot cabin. Larks rise out of the long grass singing. A bumblebee hums under the wide shady eaves.

I sit in the cool back room, where words cease to resound, where all meanings are absorbed in the *consonantia* of heat, fragrant pine, quiet wind, bird song and one central tonic note that is unheard and unuttered. This is no longer a time of obligations. In the silence of the afternoon all is present and all is inscrutable in one central tonic note to which every other sound ascends or descends, to which every other meaning aspires, in order to find its true fulfillment. To ask when the note will sound is to lose the afternoon: it has already sounded, and all things now hum with the resonance of its sounding.

I sweep. I spread a blanket out in the sun. I cut grass behind the cabin. I write in the heat of the afternoon. Soon I will bring the blanket in again and make the bed. The sun is over-clouded. The day declines. Perhaps there will be rain. A bell rings in the monastery. A devout Cistercian tractor growls in the valley. Soon I will cut bread, eat supper, say psalms, sit in the back room as the sun sets, as the birds sing outside the window, as night descends on the valley. I become surrounded once again by all the silent Tzu's and Fu's (men without office and without obligation). The birds draw closer to their nests. I sit on the cool straw mat on the floor, considering the bed in which I will presently sleep alone under the ikon of the Nativity.

Meanwhile the metal cherub of the apocalypse passes over me in the clouds, treasuring its egg and its message.

THE ASIAN JOURNAL

The following three selections and Merton's prayer are excerpts from the posthumously published The Asian Journal of Thomas Merton (1973). As the editors of that journal show in their introduction, this journal was done en route while Merton was making his fateful 1968 trip to the Far East. His accidental death outside Bangkok precluded his working over the writings which make up the volume as we now have it.

The first selection, an excerpt from his journal, is now famous. On a visit to the Polonnaruwa Buddhist sculptures in Ceylon (renamed, after 1972, Sri Lanka), Merton describes a moment of being "jerked clean" into an experience of clarity. It is one of those rare occasions when Merton describes au fond his own interior life. Whether that moment was an aesthetic insight or a moment of mystical intuition or something encompassing both of these elements is difficult to say. What is very clear is that it describes the kind of primal awareness which Merton felt to be the vision of the true contemplative who reached for the deep core of reality.

That experience makes more sense when we consider it in tandem with what Merton was wrestling with in the late 1960s (the deep center of the contemplative life) and the main purposes of his extended trip in the Orient. Those preoccupations run through the two talks he gave in Calcutta which are reproduced below: the role of monasticism in a world that prized relevancy (remember that this was the 1960s); the need—both socio-political and spiritual—for dialogue and comprehension among the spiritual seekers of the world; the search for true understanding and love in the world; stability in a time of upheaval; and, finally, the encounter with ultimate reality.

The prayer which Merton offered was before a group of persons of various religious traditions who were gathered in conference. In a few words Merton summed up, perhaps, the deepest longings of his monastic and Christian vision.

223

During the year 1968 Merton made a number of trips. An earlier one to the West Coast produced the little volume Woods, Shore Desert *(1982) with striking photographs by Merton; a second trip, again to California and then north, resulted in* Thomas Merton in Alaska *(1989). Those volumes make a fine prelude to* The Asian Journal *which, with its excellent notes, is still the book to read about Merton's final year on earth.*

✻

I remember the Moslems' sunset gun going off in Kandy and shaking the bishop's house. And the evening I returned from Polonnaruwa the gun went off as I stepped out of the car and a thousand crows flew up into the rain by the Temple of the Tooth.

Polonnaruwa was such an experience that I could not write hastily of it and cannot write now, or not at all adequately. Perhaps I have spoiled it by trying to talk of it at a dinner party, or to casual acquaintances. Yet when I spoke about it to Walpola Rahula at the Buddhist University I think the idea got across and he said, "Those who carved those statues were not ordinary men."

I visited Polonnaruwa on Monday. Today is Thursday. Heavy rain in Kandy, and on all the valleys and paddy land and jungle and teak and rubber as we go down to the eastern plains. ("We" is the bishop's driver and the vicar general of the Kandy diocese, a Ceylonese Sylvestrine with a Dutch name.) By Dambulla the rain has almost stopped. The nobility and formality of an ancient, moustachioed guide who presents himself under a bo tree. We start up the long sweep of black rock, the vicar general lagging behind, complaining that he dislikes "paganism," telling me I will get much better photos somewhere else, and saying they are all out to cheat me. ("They" being especially the bhikkhus.) Over to the east the black rock of Sigiriya stands up in the distant rain. We do not go there. What I want to see is Polonnaruwa. The high round rock of Dambulla is also quiet, sacred. The landscape is good: miles of scrub, distant "tanks" (artificial lakes dating back to the Middle Ages), distant mountains, abrupt, blue, heads hidden in rain clouds.

At the cave vihara of Dambulla, an undistinguished cloister-like porch fronts the line of caves. The caves are dark. The dirt of the cave floors under bare feet is not quite damp, not quite dry. Dark. The old man has two small candles. He holds them up. I discover that I am right up against an enormous reclining Buddha, somewhere around the knee. Curious effect of big gold Buddha lying down in the dark. I glimpse a few frescoes but those in this first cave are not so exciting. Later, some good ones, but hard to see. The guide is not interested in the frescoes, which are good, only in the rank of Buddhas, which are not good. Lines of stone and sandalwood Buddhas sit and guard the frescoes. The Buddhas in the frescoes are lovely. Frescoes all over the walls and roof of the cave. Scenes. Histories. Myths. Monsters. "Cutting, cutting," says the guide, who consents to show a scene he regards as worthwhile: now sinners being chopped up in hell, now Tamils being chopped up in war. And suddenly I recognize an intent, gold-faced, mad-eyed, black-bearded Ceylonese king I had previously met on a post card. It is a wood sculpture, painted. Some nice primitive fish were swimming on the ceiling, following a line of water in the rock.

Polonnaruwa with its vast area under trees. Fences. Few people. No beggars. A dirt road. Lost. Then we find Gal Vihara and the other monastic complex stupas. Cells. Distant mountains, like Yucatan.

The path dips down to Gal Vihara: a wide, quiet, hollow surrounded with trees. A low outcrop of rock, with a cave cut into it, and beside the cave a big seated Buddha on the left. A reclining Buddha on the right, and Ananda, I guess, standing by the head of the reclining Buddha. In the cave, another seated Buddha. The vicar general, shying away from "paganism," hangs back and sits under a tree reading the guidebook. I am able to approach the Buddhas barefoot and undisturbed, my feet in wet grass, wet sand. Then the silence of the extraordinary faces. The great smiles. Huge and yet subtle. Filled with every possibility, questioning nothing, knowing everything, rejecting nothing, the peace not of emotional resignation but of Madhyamika, of sunyata, that has seen through every question without trying to discredit anyone or anything— *without refutation*—without establishing some other argument. For the doctrinaire, the mind that needs well-established positions, such peace, such silence, can be frightening. I was knocked over with a rush of relief and thankfulness at the *obvious* clarity of the figures, the clarity and fluidity of shape and line, the design of the monumental bodies composed into the rock shape and landscape, figure, rock and tree. And the sweep of bare rock sloping away on the other side of the hollow, where you can go back and see different aspects of the figures.

Looking at these figures I was suddenly, almost forcibly, jerked clean out of the habitual, half-tied vision of things, and an inner clearness, clarity, as if exploding from the rocks themselves, became evident and obvious. The queer *evidence* of the reclining figure, the smile, the sad smile of Ananda standing with arms folded (much more "imperative" than Da Vinci's Mona Lisa because completely simple and straightforward). The thing about all this is that there is no puzzle, no problem, and really no "mystery." All problems are resolved and everything is clear, simply because what matters is clear. The rock, all matter, all life, is charged with dharmakaya . . . everything is emptiness and everything is compassion. I don't know when in my life I have ever had such a sense of beauty and spiritual validity running together in one aesthetic illumination. Surely, with Mahabalipuram and Polonnaruwa my Asian pilgrimage has come clear and purified itself. I mean, I know and have seen what I was obscurely looking for. I don't know what else remains but I have now seen and have pierced through the surface and have got beyond the shadow and the disguise. This is Asia in its purity, not covered over with garbage, Asian or European or American, and it is clear, pure, complete. It says everything; it needs nothing. And because it needs nothing it can afford to be silent, unnoticed, undiscovered. It does not need to be discovered. It is we, Asians included, who need to discover it.

The whole thing is very much a Zen garden, a span of bareness and openness and evidence, and the great figures, motionless, yet with the lines in full movement, waves of vesture and bodily form, a beautiful and holy vision. The rest of the "city," the old palace complex, I had no time for. We just drove around the roads and saw the ruined shapes, and started on the long drive home to Kandy.

INFORMAL TALK DELIVERED AT CALCUTTA, OCTOBER 1968

First, let me struggle with the contradiction that I have to live with, in appearing before you in what I really consider to be a disguise, because I never, never wear this (a clerical collar). What I ordinarily wear is blue jeans and an open shirt; which brings me to the question that people have been asking to a great extent: Whom do you represent? What religion do you represent? And that, too, is a rather difficult question to answer. I came with the notion of perhaps saying something for monks and to monks of all religions because I am supposed to be a monk . . . I may not look like one.

In speaking for monks I am really speaking for a very strange kind of person, a marginal person, because the monk in the modern world is no longer an established person with an established place in society. We realize very keenly in America today that the monk is essentially outside of all establishments. He does not belong to an establishment. He is a marginal person who withdraws deliberately to the margin of society with a view to deepening fundamental human experience. Consequently, as one of these strange people, I speak to you as a representative of all marginal persons who have done this kind of thing deliberately.

Thus I find myself representing perhaps hippies among you, poets, people of this kind who are seeking in all sorts of ways and have absolutely no established status whatever. So I ask you to do me just this one favor of considering me not as a figure representing any institution, but as a statusless person, an insignificant person who comes to you asking your charity and patience while I say one or two things that have nothing to do with my (prepared) paper. If you are interested in the paper, it is there for you to read. I do not think it is a terribly good paper. I think there are a lot of other things you could be better employed in doing.

Are monks and hippies and poets relevant? No, we are deliberately irrelevant. We live with an ingrained irrelevance which is proper to every human being. The marginal man accepts the basic irrelevance of the human condition, an irrelevance which is manifested above all by the fact of death. The marginal person, the monk, the displaced person, the prisoner, all these people live in the presence of death, which calls into question the meaning of life. He struggles with the fact of death in himself, trying to seek something deeper than death; because there is something deeper than death, and the office of the monk or the marginal person, the meditative person or the poet is to go beyond death even in this life, to go beyond the dichotomy of life and death and to be, therefore, a witness to life.

This requires, of course, faith, but as soon as you say faith in terms of this monastic and marginal existence you run into another problem. Faith means doubt. Faith is not the suppression of doubt. It is the overcoming of doubt, and you overcome doubt by going through it. The man of faith who has never experienced doubt is not a man of faith. Consequently, the monk is one who has to struggle in the depths of his being with the presence of doubt, and to go through what some religions call the Great Doubt, to break through beyond doubt into a servitude which is very, very deep because it is not his own personal servitude, it is the servitude of God Himself, in us. The only ultimate reality is God. God lives and dwells in us. We are not justified by any action of our own, but we are called by the voice of God, by the voice of that ultimate being, to pierce through the irrelevance of our life, while accepting and admitting that our life is totally irrelevant, in order to find relevance in Him. And this relevance in Him is not something we can grasp or possess. It is something that can only be received as a gift. Consequently, the kind of life that I represent is a life that is openness to gift; gift from God and gift from others.

It is not that we go out into the world with a capacity to love others greatly. This too we know in ourselves, that our capacity for love is limited. And it has to be completed with the capacity to be loved, to accept love from others, to want to be loved by others, to admit our loneliness and to live with our loneliness because everybody is lonely. This is then another basis for the kind of experience that I am talking about, which is a new approach, a different approach to the external experience of the monk. The monk in his solitude and in his meditation seeks this dimension of life.

But we do have to admit also the value of traditional monastic ways. In the West there is now going on a great upheaval in monasticism, and much that is of undying value is being thrown away irresponsibly, foolishly, in favor of things that are superficial and showy, that have no ultimate value. I do not know how the situation is in the East, but I will say as a brother from the West to Eastern monks, be a little careful. The time is coming when you may face the same situation and your fidelity to your ancient traditions will stand you in good stead. Do not be afraid of that fidelity. I know I need not warn you of this.

Behind, then, all that I have said is the idea that significant contacts are certainly possible and easy on the level of experience, not necessarily institutional monasticism, but among people who are seeking. The basic condition for this is that each be faithful to his own search.

And so I stand among you as one who offers a small message of hope, that first, there are always people who dare to seek on the margin of society, who are not dependent on social acceptance, not dependent on social routine, and prefer a kind of free-floating existence under a state of risk. And among these people, if they are faithful to their own calling, to their own vocation, and to their own message from God, communication on the deepest level is possible.

And the deepest level of communication is not communication, but communion. It is wordless. It is beyond words, and it is beyond speech, and it is beyond concept. Not that we discover a new unity. We discover an older unity. My dear brothers, we are already one. But we imagine that we are not. And what we have to recover is our original unity. What we have to be is what we are.

MONASTIC EXPERIENCE AND EAST-WEST DIALOGUE

1. In all the great world religions there are a few individuals and communities who dedicate themselves in a special way to living out the full consequences and implications of what they believe. This dedication may take a variety of forms, some temporary, some permanent; some active and some intellectual; some ascetic, contemplative and mystical. In this paper the term "monastic" is applied in a broad way to those forms of special contemplative dedication which include:

(a) A certain distance or detachment from the "ordinary" and "secular" concerns of worldly life; a monastic solitude, whether partial or total, temporary or permanent.

(b) A preoccupation with the radical inner depth of one's religious and philosophical beliefs, the inner and experimental "ground" of those beliefs, and their outstanding spiritual implications.

(c) A special concern with inner transformation, a deepening of consciousness toward an eventual breakthrough and discovery of a transcendent dimension of life beyond that of the ordinary empirical self and of ethical and pious observance.

This monastic "work" or "discipline" is not merely an individual affair. It is at once personal and communal. Its orientation is in a certain sense suprapersonal. It goes beyond a merely psychological fulfillment on the empirical level, and it goes beyond the limits of communicable cultural ideals (of one's own national, racial, etc., background). It attains to a certain universality and wholeness which have never yet been adequately described—and probably cannot be described—in terms of psychology. Transcending the limits that separate subject from object and self from not-self, this development achieves a wholeness which is described in various ways by the different religions; a self-realization of atman, of Void, of life in Christ, of fana and baqa (annihilation and reintegration according to Sufism), etc.

This is not necessarily a matter of personal charismata (special divine illuminations or prophetic tasks), but it is usually expected to follow from discipline and initiation into a "traditional religious *way*," that is to say a special mode of life and of consciousness which meets certain unwritten, indeed inexpressible, conditions. The special formation required to meet these conditions is imparted by experienced persons, or judged by a community that has shared something of the traditional consciousness we may call mystical, contemplative, enlightened, or spiritually transformed.

2. At this point—a parenthesis on the problems of language. There are great difficulties inherent in words like "mystical." Lack of agreement on their meaning, etc. Without deciding all these problems here, what matters is to clarify the distinction between the "monastic" type of dedication, the "monastic" quest for a higher type of consciousness, from "active" types of dedication oriented to "good works" like education, care of the sick, etc. Jesuits are not monks (though in fact they include today scholars who have a more sympathetic understanding of monastic questions and problems than many monks have). Missionaries are generally not monks. Confusions on this point are nevertheless present in the Western Church, especially now, when the very notion of the "contemplative life" is under attack even in the (Catholic) monastic milieu. Having referred in a general way to these problems, one might emphasize two points:

(a) Even in the highly active "West" there is nevertheless a monastic tradition which is primarily contemplative, and this tradition is being renewed even in the Protestant milieu which was originally hostile to it.

(b) There is a real possibility of contact on a deep level between this contemplative and monastic tradition in the West and the various contemplative traditions in the East—including the Islamic Sufis, the mystical lay-contemplative societies in Indonesia, etc., as well as the better-known monastic groups in Hinduism and Buddhism.

3. A word on Orthodox as distinguished from Catholic (Western) mysticism. The emphasis on contemplation in Greece and Russia. The Hesychast tradition. Mt. Athos. Problems of Orthodox monasticism today.

Though Catholic monasticism is less frankly contemplative, it is in a better position for dialogue with Asia at the moment because of the climate of openness following Vatican II. Christian monasticism has a tradition of adaptation and comprehension with regard to Greek philosophy, and many Catholics realize that this could also apply very well to Hindu and Buddhist philosophies, disciplines, experiences. An articulate minority exists. It is ready for free and productive communication. Encouragement has been offered by the Vatican Council.

4. To return to our main theme, we can easily see the special value of dialogue and exchange among those in the various religions who seek to penetrate the ultimate ground of their beliefs by a transformation of the religious consciousness. We can see the point of sharing in those disciplines which claim to prepare a way for "mystical" self-transcendence (with due reservations in the use of the term "mystical").

Without asserting that there is complete unity of all religions at the "top," the transcendent or mystical level—that they all start from different dogmatic positions to "meet" at this summit—it is certainly true to say that even where there are irreconcilable differences in doctrine and in formulated belief, there may still be great similarities and analogies in the realm of religious experience. There is nothing new in the observation that holy men like St. Francis and Shri Ramakrishna (to mention only two) have attained to a level of spiritual fulfillment which is at once universally recognizable and relevant to anyone interested in the religious dimension of existence. Cultural and doctrinal differences must remain, but they do not invalidate a very real quality of existential likeness.

5. The purpose of this paper is primarily to make clear that, on this existential level of experience and of spiritual maturity, it is possible to achieve real and significant contacts and perhaps much more besides. We will consider in a moment what this "much more" may be. For the present, one thing above all needs to be emphasized. Such dialogue in depth, at the very ground of monastic and of human experience, is not just a matter of academic interest. It is not just something for which foundation money could be obtained. That is probably true, but this paper is not considering that particular aspect of it. This is not just a matter of "research" and of academic conferences, workshops, study groups, or even of new institutional structuring—producing results that may be fed into the general accumulation of new facts about man, society, culture, and religion.

I speak as a Western monk who is pre-eminently concerned with his own monastic calling and dedication. I have left my monastery to come here not just as a research scholar or even as an author (which I also happen to be). I come as a pilgrim who is anxious to obtain not just information, not just "facts" about other monastic traditions, but to drink from ancient sources of monastic vision and experience. I seek not only to learn more (quantitatively) about religion and about monastic life, but to become a better and more enlightened monk (qualitatively) myself.

I am convinced that communication in depth, across the lines that have hitherto divided religious and monastic traditions, is now not only possible and desirable, but most important for the destinies of Twentieth-Century Man.

I do not mean that we ought to expect visible results of earth-shaking importance, or that any publicity at all is desirable. On the contrary, I am convinced that this exchange must take place under the true monastic conditions of quiet, tranquility, sobriety, leisureliness, reverence, meditation, and cloistered peace. I am convinced that what one might call typically "Asian" conditions of nonhurrying and of patient waiting must prevail over the Western passion for immediate visible results. For this reason I think it is above all important for Westerners like myself to learn what little they can from Asia, *in* Asia. I think we must seek not merely to make superficial reports *about* the Asian traditions, but to live and share those traditions, as far as we can, by living them in their traditional milieu.

I need not add that I think we have now reached a stage of (long-overdue) religious maturity at which it may be possible for someone to remain perfectly faithful to a Christian and Western monastic commitment, and yet to learn in depth from, say, a Buddhist or Hindu discipline and experience. I believe that some of us need to do this in order to improve the quality of our own monastic life and even to help in the task of monastic renewal which has been undertaken within the Western Church.

6. At this point—a parenthesis on the problems of "monastic renewal"—state of confusion resulting from a collapse of formal structures that were no longer properly understood—exterior and formal ritualism, etc., or external observance for its own sake—a traditionalism that was emptied of its truly living traditional content, repudiation of genuine tradition, discipline, contemplation—trivializing the monastic life. This has resulted in a true monastic crisis in the West. It is entirely possible that many hitherto flourishing monastic institutions, which preserved a genuine living continuity with the Middle Ages, may soon cease to exist. Both good and bad in this. Will Asian monasticism sooner or later face the same kind of crisis? Source of the problem: obsession with "relevance" to the new generation—but the problem is only half understood. In reality, the secular quasi-monastic movement of the hippies in America shows that the contemplative dimensions of life (which some monks and clergy are actively repudiating) is definitely relevant to modern youth.

7. In order not to prolong this paper overmuch, let us confine ourselves to two particularly important topics: that of "communication" between monastic traditions, and that of the more obvious "wrong directions" we must avoid. Necessarily, both topics will have to be treated more briefly than we might desire.

8. The question of "communication" is now no longer fraught with too great difficulties. The publication of classical Asian texts and of studies on them, especially in English and in German, has led to the formation of what one might call an inter-traditional vocabulary. We are well on our way to a workable in-

terreligious lexicon of key words—mostly rooted in Sanskrit—which will permit intelligent discussion of all kinds of religious experience in all the religious traditions. This is in fact already being done to some extent, and one of the results of it is that psychologists and psychoanalysts, as well as anthropologists and students of comparative religion, are now able to talk a kind of lingua franca of religious experience. I think this "language," though sometimes pedantic, seems to be fairly reliable, and it is now at the disposition of theologians, philosophers, and plain monks like myself.

This is a first step only, but it is an important step—which will often have to be completed by the services of an interpreter. He in his turn will be more helpful if he knows the "common language," and is interested in the common pursuit of inner enlightenment. Incontestably, however, this kind of communication cannot get far unless it is carried on among people who share some degree of the same enlightenment.

Is it too optimistic to expect the monks themselves to make this contribution? I hope not. And here we come to the "something more" that I referred to above. True communication on the deepest level is more than a simple sharing of ideas, of conceptual knowledge, or formulated truth. The kind of communication that is necessary on this deep level must also be "communion" beyond the level of words, a communion in authentic experience which is shared not only on a "preverbal" level but also on a "postverbal" level.

The "preverbal" level is that of the unspoken and indefinable "preparation," "the predisposition" of mind and heart, necessary for all "monastic" experience whatever. This demands among other things a "freedom from automatisms and routines," and candid liberation from external social dictates, from conventions, limitations, and mechanisms which restrict understanding and inhibit experience of the new, the unexpected. Monastic training must not form men in a rigid mold, but liberate them from habitual and routine mechanisms. The monk who is to communicate on the level that interests us here must be not merely a punctilious observer of external traditions, but a living example of traditional and interior realization. He must be wide open to life and to new experience because he has fully utilized his own tradition and gone beyond it. This will permit him to meet a discipline of another, apparently remote and alien tradition, and find a common ground of verbal understanding with him. The "postverbal" level will then, at least ideally, be that on which they both meet beyond their own words and their own understanding in the silence of an ultimate experience which might conceivably not have occurred if they had not met and spoken . . .

This I would call "communion." I think it is something that the deepest ground of our being cries out for, and it is something for which a lifetime of striving would not be enough.

9. The wrong ways that are to be avoided ought to be fairly evident.

First of all, this striving for intermonastic communion should not become just another way of adding to the interminable empty talk, the endlessly fruitless and trivial discussion of everything under the sun, the inexhaustible chatter with which modern man tries to convince himself that he is in touch with his fellow man and with reality. This contemplative dialogue must be reserved for those who have been seriously disciplined by years of silence and by a long habit of meditation. I would add that it must be reserved for those who have entered with full seriousness into their own monastic tradition and are in authentic contact with the past of their own religious community—besides being open to the tradition and to the heritage of experience belonging to other communities.

Second, there can be no question of a facile syncretism, a mishmash of semireligious verbiage and pieties, a devotionalism that admits everything and therefore takes nothing with full seriousness.

Third, there must be a scrupulous respect for important differences, and where one no longer understands or agrees, this must be kept clear—without useless debate. There are differences that are not debatable, and it is a useless, silly temptation to try to argue them out. Let them be left intact until a moment of greater understanding.

Fourth, attention must be concentrated on what is really essential to the monastic quest: this, I think, is to be sought in the area of true self-transcendence and enlightenment. It is to be sought in the transformation of consciousness in its ultimate ground, as well as in the highest and most authentic devotional love of the bhakti type—but not in the acquisition of extraordinary powers, in miraculous activities, in a special charismata, visions, levitation, etc. These must be seen as phenomena of a different order.

Fifth, questions of institutional structure, monastic rule, traditional forms of cult and observance must be seen as relatively secondary and are not to become the central focus of attention. They are to be understood in their relation to enlightenment itself. However, they are to be given the full respect due to them, and the interests of dialogue and communication should not be allowed to subvert structures that may remain very important helps to interior development.

10. It is time to conclude. The point to be stressed is the importance of serious communication, and indeed of "communion," among contemplatives of different traditions, disciplines, and religions. This can contribute much to the development of man at this crucial point of his history. Indeed, we find ourselves in a crisis, a moment of crucial choice. We are in grave danger of losing a spiritual heritage that has been painfully accumulated by thousands of generations of saints and contemplatives. It is the peculiar office of the monk in the modern world to keep alive the contemplative experience and to keep the way open for modern technological man to recover the integrity of his own inner depths.

Above all, it is important that this element of depth and integrity—this element of inner transcendent freedom—be kept intact as we grow toward the full maturity of universal man. We are witnessing the growth of a truly universal consciousness in the modern world. This universal consciousness may be a consciousness of transcendent freedom and vision, or it may simply be a vast blur of mechanized triviality and ethical cliché.

The difference is, I think, important enough to be of concern to all religions, as well as to humanistic philosophies with no religion at all.

SPECIAL CLOSING PRAYER

(OFFERED AT THE FIRST SPIRITUAL SUMMIT CONFERENCE IN
CALCUTTA BY FATHER THOMAS MERTON)

I will ask you to stand and all join hands in a little while. But first, we realize that we are going to have to create a new language of prayer. And this new language of prayer has to come out of something which transcends all our traditions, and comes out of the immediacy of love. We have to part now, aware of the love that unites us, the love that unites us in spite of real differences, real emotional friction . . . The things that are on the surface are nothing, what is deep is the Real. We are creatures of love. Let us therefore join hands, as we did before, and I will try to say something that comes out of the depths of our hearts. I ask you to concentrate on the love that is in you, that is in us all. I have no idea what I am going to say. I am going to be silent a minute, and then I will say something . . .

Oh God, we are one with You. You have made us one with You. You have taught us that if we are open to one another, You dwell in us. Help us to preserve this openness and to fight for it with all our hearts. Help us to realize that there can be no understanding where there is mutual rejection. Oh God, in accepting one another wholeheartedly, fully, completely, we accept You, and we thank You, and we adore You, and we love You with our whole being, because our being is in Your being, our spirit is rooted in Your spirit. Fill us then with love, and let us be bound together with love as we go our diverse ways, united in this one spirit which makes You present in the world, and which makes You witness to the ultimate reality that is love. Love has overcome. Love is victorious. Amen.

Spiritual Writings

THOUGHTS IN SOLITUDE

In the early 1950s Merton had the use of a small shed on the monastery grounds to which he would repair to think, write, and pray. In the year (1953) The Sign of Jonas was published he began to write out a series of meditations to which he had given the tentative title "Thirty-Seven Meditations." This work would evolve into a short book called Thoughts in Solitude *(1958). The eighteen short meditations which form the last half of that book are reproduced here under the title Merton originally gave them: "The Love of Solitude." Many readers will recognize the second of these meditations as a prayer that is widely reproduced.*

Solitude, of course, is a basic theme in the writings of Thomas Merton. He had been deeply attracted to the solitary life from his early monastic days. His inability to join a solitary monastic congregation like that of the Carthusians led him to campaign, successfully in the end, for solitary opportunities for members of his own order. If there are Cistercian hermits today it is because of the efforts of Thomas Merton.

It is important, however, not to identify Merton's love for solitude with the eremitical life as if they were identical terms. He had a much more sophisticated notion of solitude than that, as these meditations show. One may get a fuller sense of what solitude meant to Merton by understanding what he did not mean by the term.

First of all, solitude should not be confused with physical or social isolation. While it is true that monasteries emphasized separation from large urban centers and a spirit of silence, a solitary in Merton's sense of the term only finds solitude when that solitude is interiorized. Secondly, internalized solitude did not mean absorption into the self or any form of narcissistic self-contemplation with a corresponding rejection of the Other or Others. Solitude, for Merton, was relational, i.e. it was a desire to know who the self truly was, and that form of knowing should lead to the sense of radical dependence on God and an equally radical sense of solidarity with others who are also in God. Solitude, as Merton notes in these pages, can never be renunciation of the community. It can only be a free and full gift by which a person is willing to hand over everything to God. When one does that, one is in solitude even if, as Merton says, one lives in the center of the city.

The fullest treatment of this theme in Thomas Merton is Richard Anthony Cashen's Solitude in the Thought of Thomas Merton *(Kalamazoo: Cistercian Publications, 1981).*

✲

The Love of Solitude

I

To love solitude and to seek it does not mean constantly travelling from one geographical possibility to another. A man becomes a solitary at the moment when, no matter what may be his external surroundings, he is suddenly aware of his own inalienable solitude and sees that he will never be anything but solitary. From that moment, solitude is not potential—it is actual.

However, actual solitude always places us squarely in the presence of an unrealized and even unrealizable possibility of "perfect solitude." But this has to be properly understood: for we lose the actuality of the solitude we already have if we try, with too great anxiety, to realize the material possibility for greater exterior solitude that always seems just out of reach. Actual solitude has, as one of its integral elements, the dissatisfaction and uncertainty that come from being face to face with an unrealized possibility. It is not a mad pursuit of possibilities—it is the humble acquiescence that stabilizes us in the presence of one enormous reality which is in one sense already possessed and in another a "possibility"—an object of hope.

It is only when the solitary dies and goes to heaven that he sees clearly that this possibility was already actualized in his life and he did not know it—for his solitude consisted above all in the "possible" possession of God, and of nothing else but God, in pure hope.

II

My Lord God, I have no idea where I am going. I do not see the road ahead of me. I cannot know for certain where it will end. Nor do I really know myself, and the fact that I think I am following your will does not mean that I am actually doing so. But I believe that the desire to please you does in fact please you. And I hope I have that desire in all that I am doing. I hope that I will never do anything apart from that desire. And I know that if I do this you will lead me by the right road, though I may know nothing about it. Therefore I will trust you always though I may seem to be lost and in the shadow of death. I will not fear, for you are ever with me, and you will never leave me to face my perils alone.

III

In our age everything has to be a "problem." Ours is a time of anxiety because we have willed it to be so. Our anxiety is not imposed on us by force from outside. We impose it on our world and upon one another from within ourselves.

Sanctity in such an age means, no doubt, travelling from the area of anxiety to the area in which there is no anxiety or perhaps it may mean learning, from God, to be without anxiety in the midst of anxiety.

Fundamentally, as Max Picard points out, it probably comes to this: living in a silence which so reconciles the contradictions within us that, although they remain within us, they cease to be a problem (cf World of Silence, pp. 66–67).

Contradictions have always existed in the soul of man. But it is only when we prefer analysis to silence that they become a constant and insoluble problem. We are not meant to resolve all contradictions but to live with them and rise above them and see them in the light of exterior and objective values which make them trivial by comparison.

Silence, then, belongs to the substance of sanctity. In silence and hope are formed the strength of the Saints. (Isaias 30:15.)

When solitude was a problem, I had no solitude. When it ceased to be a problem I found I already possessed it, and could have possessed it all along. Yet still it was a problem because I knew after all that a merely subjective and inward solitude, the fruit of an effort at interiorisation, would never be enough. Solitude has to be objective and concrete. It has to be a communion in something greater than the world, as great as Being itself, in order that in its deep peace we may find God.

We put words between ourselves and things. Even God has become another conceptual unreality in a no-man's land of language that no longer serves as a means of communion with reality.

The solitary life, being silent, clears away the smoke-screen of words that man has laid down between his mind and things. In solitude we remain face to face with the naked being of things. And yet we find that the nakedness of reality which we have feared, is neither a matter of terror nor for shame. It is clothed in the friendly communion of silence, and this silence is related to love. The world our words have attempted to classify, to control and even to despise (because they could not contain it) comes close to us, for silence teaches us to know reality by respecting it where words have defiled it.

When we have lived long enough alone with the reality around us, our veneration will learn how to bring forth a few good words about it from the silence which is the mother of Truth.

Words stand between silence and silence: between the silence of things and the silence of our own being. Between the silence of the world and the silence of God. When we have really met and known the world in silence, words do not separate us from the world nor from other men, nor from God, nor from ourselves because we no longer trust entirely in language to contain reality.

Truth rises from the silence of being to the quiet tremendous presence of the Word. Then, sinking again into silence, the truth of words bears us down into the silence of God.

Or rather God rises up out of the sea like a treasure in the waves, and when language recedes His brightness remains on the shores of our own being.

IV

A man knows when he has found his vocation when he stops thinking about how to live and begins to live. Thus, if one is called to be a solitary, he will stop wondering how he is to live and start living peacefully only when he is in solitude. But if one is not called to a solitary life, the more he is alone the more will he worry about living and forget to live. When we are not living up to our true vocation, thought deadens our life, or substitutes itself for life, or gives in to life so that our life drowns out our thinking and stifles the voice of conscience. When we find our vocation—thought and life are one.

Suppose one has found completeness in his true vocation. Now everything is in unity, in order, at peace. Now work no longer interferes with prayer or prayer with work. Now contemplation no longer needs to be a special "state" that removes one from the ordinary things going on around him for God penetrates all. One does not have to think of giving an account of oneself to anyone but Him.

V

It is necessary that we find the silence of God not only in ourselves but also in one another. Unless some other man speaks to us in words that spring from God and communicate with the silence of God in our souls, we remain isolated in our own silence, from which God tends to withdraw. For inner silence depends on a continual seeking, a continual crying in the night, a repeated bending over the abyss. If we cling to a silence we think we have found forever, we stop seeking God and the silence goes dead within us. A silence in which He is no longer sought ceases to speak to us of Him. A silence from which He does not seem to be absent, dangerously threatens His continued presence. For He is found when He is sought and when He is no longer sought He escapes us. He is heard only when we hope to hear Him, and if, thinking our hope to be fulfilled, we cease to listen, He ceases to speak, His silence ceases to be vivid and becomes dead, even though we recharge it with the echo of our own emotional noise.

VI

Lord, my heart is not exalted. (Ps. 130:1.)

Both pride and humility seek interior silence. Pride, by a forced immobility, seeks to imitate the silence of God. But the silence of God is the perfection of Pure Life and the silence of pride is the silence of death.

Humility seeks silence not in inactivity but in ordered activity, in the activity that is proper to our poverty and helplessness before God. Humility goes to pray and finds silence through words. But because it is natural for us to pass from words to silence, and from silence to words, humility is in all things silent. Even when it speaks, humility listens. The words of humility are so simple, so gentle and so poor that they find their way without effort to the silence of God. Indeed they are the echo of His silence, and as soon as they are spoken His silence is already present in them.

Pride is afraid to go out of itself, for fear of losing what it has produced within itself. The silence of pride is therefore menaced by the action of charity. But since humility finds nothing within itself, (for humility is its own silence), it cannot lose in peace and silence by going out to listen to others or to speak to them for the love of God. In all things humility is silent and at rest and even the labor of humility is rest. *In omnibus requiem quaesivi.**

It is not speaking that breaks our silence, but the anxiety to be heard. The words of the proud man impose silence on all others, so that he alone may be heard. The humble man speaks only in order to be spoken to. The humble man asks nothing but an alms, then waits and listens.

---

* In all things I have sought rest.

Silence is ordered to the ultimate summing up in words of all we have lived for. We receive Christ by hearing in the word of faith. We work out our salvation in silence and hope, but sooner or later comes the time when we must confess Him openly before men, then before all the inhabitants of heaven and earth.

If our life is poured out in useless words, we will never hear anything, will never become anything, and in the end, because we have said everything before we had anything to say we shall be left speechless at the moment of our greatest decision.

But silence is ordered to that final utterance. It is not an end in itself. Our whole life is a meditation of our last decision—the only decision that matters. And we meditate in silence. Yet we are bound to some extent, to speak to others, to help them see their way to their own decision, to teach them Christ. In teaching them Christ, our very words teach them a new silence: the silence of the Resurrection. In that silence they are formed and prepared so that they also may speak what they have heard. *I have believed, therefore have I spoken.* (Ps. 115:1.)

XVII

The great work of the solitary life is gratitude. The hermit is one who knows the mercy of God better than other men because his whole life is one of complete dependence, in silence and in hope, upon the hidden mercy of our Heavenly Father.

The further I advance into solitude the more clearly I see the goodness of all things.

In order to live happily in solitude I must have a compassionate knowledge of the goodness of other men, a reverent knowledge of the goodness of all creation and a humble knowledge of the goodness of my own body and of my own soul. How can I live in solitude if I do not see everywhere the goodness of God, my Creator and Redeemer and the Father of all good?

What is it that has made me evil and hateful to myself? It is my own folly, my own darkness, which have divided me, by sin, against the light which God has placed in my soul to be the reflection of His goodness and the witness of His mercy.

Shall I drive evil out of my soul by wrestling with my own darkness? This is not what God has planned for me. It is sufficient to turn away from my darkness to His light. I do not have to run away from myself; it is sufficient that I find myself, not as I have made myself, by my own stupidity, but as He has made me in His wisdom and remade me in His infinite mercy. For it is His will that my body and soul should be the Temple of His Holy Spirit, that my life should reflect the radiance of His love and my whole being repose in His peace. Then will I truly know Him, since I am in Him and He is truly in me.

XVIII

The Psalms are the true garden of the solitary and the Scriptures are his Paradise. They reveal their secrets to him because, in his extreme poverty and humility, he has nothing else to live by except their fruits. For the true solitary the reading of Scripture ceases to be an "exercise" among other exercises, a means of "cultivating" the intellect or "the spiritual life" or "appreciating the liturgy." To those who read Scripture in an academic or aesthetic or merely devotional way the Bible indeed offers pleasant refreshment and profitable thoughts. But to learn the inner secrets of the Scriptures we must make them our true daily bread, find God in them when we are in greatest need—and usually when we can find Him nowhere else and have nowhere else to look!

In solitude I have at last discovered that You have desired the love of my heart, O my God, the love of my heart as it is—the love of a man's heart.

I have found and have known, by Your great mercy, that the love of a man's heart that is abandoned and broken and poor is most pleasing to You and attracts the gaze of Your pity, and that it is Your desire and Your consolation, O my Lord, to be very close to those who love You and call upon You as their Father. That You have perhaps no greater "consolation" (if I may so speak) than to console Your afflicted children and those who came to You poor and empty handed with nothing but their humanness and their limitations and great trust in Your mercy.

Only solitude has taught me that I do not have to be a god or an angel to be pleasing to You, that I do not have to become a pure intelligence without feeling and without human imperfection before You will listen to my voice.

You do not wait for me to become great before You will be with me and hear me and answer me. It is my lowliness and my humanness that have drawn You to make me Your equal by condescending to my level and living in me by Your merciful care.

And now it is Your desire, not that I give You the thanks and recognition You receive from Your great angels, but the love and gratitude that comes from the heart of a child, a son of woman, Your own Son.

My Father, I know You have called me to live alone with You, and to learn that if I were not a mere man, a mere human being capable of all mistakes and all evil, also capable of a frail and errant human affection for You, I would not be capable of being Your son. You desire the love of a man's heart because Your Divine Son also loves You with a man's Heart and He became Man in order that my heart and His Heart should love You in one love, which is a human love born and moved by Your Holy Spirit.

If therefore I do not love You with a man's love and with a man's simplicity and with the humility to be myself I will never taste the full sweetness of Your Fatherly mercy, and Your Son, as far as my life goes, will have died in vain.

It is necessary that I be human and remain human in order that the Cross of Christ be not made void. Jesus died not for the angels but for men.

This is what I learn from the Psalms in solitude, for the Psalms are full of the human simplicity of men like David who knew God as men and loved Him as men, and therefore knew Him, the One true God, Who would send His only begotten Son to men in the likeness of man that they, while still remaining men, might love Him with a divine love.

And this is the mystery of our vocation: not that we cease to be men in order to become angels or gods, but that the love of my man's heart can become God's love for God and men, and my human tears can fall from my eyes as the tears of God because they well up from the motion of His Spirit in the heart of His incarnate

Son. Hence—the gift of piety grows in solitude, nourished by the Psalms.

When this is learned, then our love of other men becomes pure and strong. We can go out to them without vanity and without complacency, loving them with something of the purity and gentleness and hiddenness of God's love for us.

This is the true fruit and the true purpose of Christian solitude.

NEW SEEDS OF CONTEMPLATION

Thomas Merton's Seeds of Contemplation *was published in 1949. This work on the contemplative life, patterned loosely after the* Pensées *of Pascal, enjoyed an enormous popularity. Twelve years later, Merton, rejecting the possibility of revising that work, rewrote the entire book which was reissued as* New Seeds of Contemplation *(1962). The differences between those two works has been the subject of detailed analysis in Donald Grayston's* Thomas Merton: The Development of a Spiritual Theologian *(New York and Toronto: Edwin Mellen Press, 1985).*

The most significant difference between the two books is that in the latter there has been a shift away from a rigid distinction between nature and grace with a concomitant emphasis on the value of the person (derived from Merton's appreciation of Jacques Maritain's philosophy of personalism) and a greater appreciation of the goodness of religious experience not as an intellectual experience but as a holistic one.

That more incarnational sense is best expressed in the final chapter of New Seeds *which Merton titled "The General Dance." Originally published in* Jubilee *magazine (December 1961), this lyrical essay reflects Merton's encounter with the Russian mystics and his careful study of the Zen tradition. One notes in this essay a sense of the goodness of creation, the gift of Christ's incarnation, and a general sense of the human person as part of the great gift of God which is creation and re-creation. Such an outlook permits Merton to back away from a too negative view of the "external self." He resists the notion that a contemplative person should be a disembodied spirit. In that resistance he eschews the gnostic temptation which his friend and mentor, Jacques Maritain, once referred to as the error of angelism.*

A reliable study of Merton's evolving spiritual theology may be found in two different studies: Anne E. Carr, A Search for Wisdom and Spirit: Thomas Merton's Theology of the Self *(Notre*

Dame: University of Notre Dame, 1988); William Henry Shannon, Thomas Merton's Dark Path, *rev. ed. (New York: Farrar, Straus, & Giroux, 1987).*

⚜

THE GENERAL DANCE

The Lord made His world not in order to judge it, not in order merely to dominate it, to make it obey the dictates of an inscrutable and all-powerful will, not in order to find pleasure or displeasure in the way it worked: such was not the reason for creation either of the world or of man.

The Lord made the world and made man in order that He Himself might descend into the world, that He Himself might become Man. When He regarded the world He was about to make He saw His wisdom, as a man-child, "playing in the world, playing before Him at all times." And He reflected, "my delights are to be with the children of men."

The world was not made as a prison for fallen spirits who were rejected by God: this is the gnostic error. The world was made as a temple, a paradise, into which God Himself would descend to dwell familiarly with the spirits He had placed there to tend it for Him.

The early chapters of Genesis (far from being a pseudo-scientific account of the way the world was supposed to have come into being) are precisely a poetic and symbolic revelation, a completely *true,* though not literal, revelation of God's view of the universe and of His intentions for man. The point of these beautiful chapters is that God made the world as a garden in which He himself took delight. He made man and gave to man the task of sharing in His own divine care for created things. He made man in His own image and likeness, as an artist, a worker, *homo faber,* as the gardener of paradise. He let man decide for himself how created things were to be interpreted, understood and used: for Adam gave the animals their names (God gave them no names at all) and what names Adam gave them, that they were. Thus in his intelligence man, by the act of knowing, imitated something of the creative love of God for creatures. While the love of God, looking upon things, brought them into being, the love of man, looking upon things, reproduced the divine idea, the divine truth, in man's own spirit.

As God creates things by seeing them in His own Logos, man brings truth to life in his mind by the marriage of the divine light, in the being of the object, with the divine light in his own reason. The meeting of these two lights in one mind is truth.

But there is a higher light still, not the light by which man "gives names" and forms concepts, with the aid of the active intelligence, but the dark light in which no names are given, in which God confronts man not through the medium of things, but in His own simplicity. The union of the simple light of God with the simple light of man's spirit, in love, is contemplation. The two simplicities are one. They form, as it were, an emptiness in which there is no addition but rather the taking away of names, of forms, of content, of subject matter, of identities. In this meeting there is not so much a fusion of identities as a disappearance of identities. The Bible speaks of this very simply: "In the breeze after noon God came to walk with Adam in paradise." It is after noon, in the declining light of created day. In the free emptiness of the breeze that blows from where it pleases and goes where no one can estimate, God and man are together, not speaking in words, or syllables or forms. And that was the meaning of creation and of Paradise. But there was more.

The Word of God Himself was the "firstborn of every creature." He "in Whom all things consist" was not only to walk with man in the breeze after noon, but would also become Man, and dwell with man as a brother.

The Lord would not only love His creation as a Father, but He would enter into His creation, emptying Himself, hiding Himself, as if He were not God but a creature. Why should He do this? Because He loved His creatures, and because He could not bear that His creatures should merely adore Him as distant, remote, transcendent and all powerful. This was not the glory that He sought, for if He were merely adored as great, His creatures would in their turn make themselves great and lord it over one another. For where there is a great God, then there are also god-like men, who make themselves kings and masters. And if God were merely a great artist who took pride in His creation, then men too would build cities and palaces and exploit other men for their own glory.

This is the meaning of the myth of Babel, and of the tower builders who would be "as Gods" with their hanging gardens, and with the heads of their enemies hanging in the gardens. For they would point to God and say: "He too is a great builder, and has destroyed all His enemies."

(God said: I do not laugh at my enemies, because I wish to make it impossible for anyone to be my enemy. Therefore I identify myself with my enemy's own secret self.)

So God became man. He took on the weakness and ordinariness of man, and He hid Himself, becoming an anonymous and unimportant man in a very unimportant place. And He refused at any time to Lord it over men, or to be a King, or to be a Leader, or to be a Reformer, or to be in any way Superior to His own creatures. He would be nothing else but their brother, and their counsellor, and their servant, and their friend. He was in no accepted human sense an important person, though since that time we have made Him The Most Important Person. That is another matter: for though it is quite true that He is the King and Lord of all, the conqueror of death, the judge of the living and of the dead, the *Pantokrator,* yet He is also still the Son of Man, the hidden one, unknown, unremarkable, vulnerable. He can be killed. And when the Son of Man was put to death, He rose again from the dead, and was again with us, for He said: "Kill me, it does not matter."

Having died, He dies no more in His own Person. But because He became man and united man's nature to Himself, and died for man, and rose as man from the dead, He brought it about that the sufferings of all men became His own sufferings; their weakness and defenselessness became His weakness and defenselessness; their insignificance became His. But at the same time His own power, immortality, glory and happiness were given to them and could become theirs. So if the God-Man is still great, it is rather for our sakes than for His own that He wishes to be great and strong. For to Him, strength and weakness, life and death are dualities with which He is not concerned, being above them in His transcendent unity. Yet He would raise us also above these dualities by making us one with Him. For though evil and death can touch the evanescent, outer self in which we dwell estranged from Him, in which we

are alienated and exiled in unreality, it can never touch the real
inner self in which we have been made one with Him. For in becoming man, God became not only Jesus Christ but also potentially every man and woman that ever existed. In Christ, God became not only "this" man, but also, in a broader and more mystical
sense, yet no less truly, "every man."

The presence of God in His world as its Creator depends on no
one but Him. His presence in the world as Man depends, in some
measure, upon men. Not that we can do anything to change the
mystery of the Incarnation in itself: but we are able to decide
whether we ourselves, and that portion of the world which is ours,
shall become *aware* of His presence, consecrated by it, and transfigured in its light.

We have the choice of two identities: the external mask which
seems to be real and which lives by a shadowy autonomy for the
brief moment of earthly existence, and the hidden, inner person
who seems to us to be nothing, but who can give himself eternally
to the truth in whom he subsists. It is this inner self that is taken up
into the mystery of Christ, by His love, by the Holy Spirit, so that in
secret we live "in Christ."

Yet we must not deal in too negative a fashion even with the
"external self." This self is not by nature evil, and the fact that it is
unsubstantial is not to be imputed to it as some kind of crime. It is
afflicted with metaphysical poverty: but all that is poor deserves
mercy. So too our outward self: as long as it does not isolate itself in
a lie, it is blessed by the mercy and the love of Christ. Appearances
are to be accepted for what they are. The accidents of a poor and
transient existence have, nevertheless, an ineffable value. They can
be transparent media in which we apprehend the presence of God
in the world. It is possible to speak of the exterior self as a mask: to
do so is not necessarily to reprove it. The mask that each man wears
may well be a disguise not only for that man's inner self but for
God, wandering as a pilgrim and exile in His own creation.

And indeed, if Christ became Man, it is because He wanted to
be any man and every man. If we believe in the Incarnation of the
Son of God, there should be no one on earth in whom we are not
prepared to see, in mystery, the presence of Christ.

What is serious to men is often very trivial in the sight of God. What in God might appear to us as "play" is perhaps what He Himself takes most seriously. At any rate the Lord plays and diverts Himself in the garden of His creation, and if we could let go of our own obsession with what we think is the meaning of it all, we might be able to hear His call and follow Him in His mysterious, cosmic dance. We do not have to go very far to catch echoes of that game, and of that dancing. When we are alone on a starlit night; when by chance we see the migrating birds in autumn descending on a grove of junipers to rest and eat; when we see children in a moment when they are really children; when we know love in our own hearts; or when, like the Japanese poet Bashō we hear an old frog land in a quiet pond with a solitary splash—at such times the awakening, the turning inside out of all values, the "newness," the emptiness and the purity of vision that make themselves evident, provide a glimpse of the cosmic dance.

For the world and time are the dance of the Lord in emptiness. The silence of the spheres is the music of a wedding feast. The more we persist in misunderstanding the phenomena of life, the more we analyze them out into strange finalities and complex purposes of our own, the more we involve ourselves in sadness, absurdity and despair. But it does not matter much, because no despair of ours can alter the reality of things, or stain the joy of the cosmic dance which is always there. Indeed, we are in the midst of it, and it is in the midst of us, for it beats in our very blood, whether we want it to or not.

Yet the fact remains that we are invited to forget ourselves on purpose, cast our awful solemnity to the winds and join in the general dance.

HAGIA SOPHIA

*The prose-poem "Hagia Sophia" had a rather curious origin.
Merton's friend, the artist-typographer Victor Hammer, had a
painting which depicted a woman (Mary) crowning the young
Christ. He was not sure how to explain why Mary should be crowning Christ. In a letter to Hammer dated May 14, 1959, Merton said
that the woman was Holy Wisdom. God, he continued, was both
Father and Mother. This wisdom (Sophia) is the feminine aspect of
God. The Blessed Virgin, who conferred humanity upon the Word,
is the created person who most perfectly manifests the hidden Wisdom of God which is latent in the divine nature.*

*It was from that encounter with Victor Hammer and Merton's
interest in the figure of Wisdom in the biblical book of Proverbs
(especially chapter 8), his own deep devotion to the Blessed Virgin,
and some recurring dreams about a woman whom he identified as
Wisdom, that this poetic meditation arose. Set in the context of the
canonical hours (a device used by other poets like Rilke, Auden,
and Berryman), this is an extended meditation on the feminine
aspect of God through a consideration of the complex symbolism
of Wisdom/Mary/Anima/God as Mother.*

*When Merton finished the poem, Victor Hammer set it in
type in a limited edition under the imprint of his Stamperia del
santuccio. It was later reprinted in the West Coast magazine* Ram-
parts *and, finally, collected in the volume* Emblems of a Season of
Fury *(1963).*

For an analysis of the poem, see Sister Therese Lentfoehr,
Words and Silence: On The Poetry of Thomas Merton *(New
York: New Directions, 1979). For an account of the friendship of
Victor Hammer and Thomas Merton (with an illustration of
Hammer's triptych "Hagia Sophia Crowing the Young Christ"),
see David D. Cooper, "Victor Hammer and Thomas Merton: A*

Friendship Ad Majorem Dei Gloriam," Kentucky Review *VII (1987), pp. 5–28.*

✤

"HAGIA SOPHIA"

I. Dawn. The Hour of Lauds.

There is in all visible things an invisible fecundity, a dimmed light, a meek namelessness, a hidden wholeness. This mysterious Unity and Integrity is Wisdom, the Mother of all, *Natura naturans.* There is in all things an inexhaustible sweetness and purity, a silence that is a fount of action and joy. It rises up in wordless gentleness and flows out to me from the unseen roots of all created being, welcoming me tenderly, saluting me with indescribable humility. This is at once my own being, my own nature, and the Gift of my Creator's Thought and Art within me, speaking as Hagia Sophia, speaking as my sister, Wisdom.

I am awakened, I am born again at the voice of this my Sister, sent to me from the depths of the divine fecundity.

Let us suppose I am a man lying asleep in a hospital. I am indeed this man lying asleep. It is July the second, the Feast of Our Lady's Visitation. A Feast of Wisdom.

At five-thirty in the morning I am dreaming in a very quiet room when a soft voice awakens me from my dream. I am like all mankind awakening from all the dreams that ever were dreamed in all the nights of the world. It is like the One Christ awakening in all the separate selves that ever were separate and isolated and alone in all the lands of the earth. It is like all minds coming back together into awareness from all distractions, cross-purposes and confusions, into unity of love. It is like the first morning of the world (when Adam, at the sweet voice of Wisdom awoke from nonentity and knew her), and like the Last Morning of the world when all the fragments of Adam will return from death at the voice of Hagia Sophia, and will know where they stand.

Such is the awakening of one man, one morning, at the voice of a nurse in the hospital. Awakening out of languor and darkness, out of helplessness, out of sleep, newly confronting reality and finding it to be gentleness.

It is like being awakened by Eve. It is like being awakened by the Blessed Virgin. It is like coming forth from primordial nothingness and standing in clarity, in Paradise.

In the cool hand of the nurse there is the touch of all life, the touch of Spirit.

Thus Wisdom cries out to all who will hear (*Sapientia clamitat in plateis*)* and she cries out particularly to the little, to the ignorant and the helpless.

Who is more little, who is more poor than the helpless man who lies asleep in his bed without awareness and without defense? Who is more trusting than he who must entrust himself each night to sleep? What is the reward of his trust? Gentleness comes to him when he is most helpless and awakens him, refreshed, beginning to be made whole. Love takes him by the hand, and opens to him the doors of another life, another day.

(But he who has defended himself, fought for himself in sickness, planned for himself, guarded himself, loved himself alone and watched over his own life all night, is killed at last by exhaustion. For him there is no newness. Everything is stale and old.)

When the helpless one awakens strong at the voice of mercy, it is as if Life his Sister, as if the Blessed Virgin, (his own flesh, his own sister), as if Nature made wise by God's Art and Incarnation were to stand over him and invite him with unutterable sweetness to be awake and to live. This is what it means to recognize Hagia Sophia.

---

* [Wisdom cries out in the streets.]

II. Early Morning. The Hour of Prime.

O blessed, silent one, who speaks everywhere!

We do not hear the soft voice, the gentle voice, the merciful and feminine.

We do not hear mercy, or yielding love, or nonresistance, or non-reprisal. In her there are no reasons and no answers. Yet she is the candor of God's light, the expression of His simplicity.

We do not hear the uncomplaining pardon that bows down the innocent visages of flowers to the dewy earth. We do not see the Child who is prisoner in all the people, and who says nothing. She smiles, for though they have bound her, she cannot be a prisoner. Not that she is strong, or clever, but simply that she does not understand imprisonment.

The helpless one, abandoned to sweet sleep, him the gentle one will awake: Sophia.

All that is sweet in her tenderness will speak to him on all sides in everything, without ceasing, and he will never be the same again. He will have awakened not to conquest and dark pleasure but to the impeccable pure simplicity of One consciousness in all and through all: one Wisdom, one Child, one Meaning, one Sister.

The stars rejoice in their setting, and in the rising of the Sun. The heavenly lights rejoice in the going forth of one man to make a new world in the morning, because he has come out of the confused primordial dark night into consciousness. He has expressed the clear silence of Sophia in his own heart. He has become eternal.

III. High Morning. The Hour of Tierce.

The Sun burns in the sky like the Face of God, but we do not know his countenance as terrible. His light is diffused in the air and the light of God is diffused by Hagia Sophia.

We do not see the Blinding One in black emptiness. He speaks to us gently in ten thousand things, in which His light is one fulness and one Wisdom.

Thus He shines not on them but from within them. Such is the loving-kindness of Wisdom.

All the perfections of created things are also in God; and therefore He is at once Father and Mother. As Father He stands in solitary might surrounded by darkness. As Mother His shining is diffused, embracing all His creatures with merciful tenderness and light. The Diffuse Shining of God is Hagia Sophia. We call her His "glory." In Sophia His power is experienced only as mercy and as love.

(When the recluses of fourteenth-century England heard their Church Bells and looked out upon the wolds and fens under a kind sky, they spoke in their hearts to "Jesus our Mother." It was Sophia that had awakened in their childlike hearts.)

Perhaps in a certain very primitive aspect Sophia is the unknown, the dark, the nameless Ousia. Perhaps she is even the Divine Nature, One in Father, Son and Holy Ghost. And perhaps she is infinite light unmanifest, not even waiting to be known as Light. This I do not know. Out of the silence Light is spoken. We do not hear it or see it until it is spoken.

In the Nameless Beginning, without Beginning, was the Light. We have not seen this Beginning. I do not know where she is, in this Beginning. I do not speak of her as a Beginning, but as a manifestation.

Now the Wisdom of God, Sophia, comes forth, reaching from "end to end mightily." She wills to be also the unseen pivot of all nature, the center and significance of all the light that is *in* all and *for* all. That which is poorest and humblest, that which is most hidden in all things is nevertheless most obvious in them, and quite manifest, for it is their own self that stands before us, naked and without care.

Sophia, the feminine child, is playing in the world, obvious and unseen, playing at all times before the Creator. Her delights are to be with the children of men. She is their sister. The core of life that exists in all things is tenderness, mercy, virginity, the Light, the Life considered as passive, as received, as given, as taken, as inexhaustibly renewed by the Gift of God. Sophia is Gift, is Spirit, *Donum Dei.** She is God-given and God Himself as Gift. God as all, and God reduced to Nothing: inexhaustible nothingness. *Exinanivit semetipsum.*** Humility as the source of unfailing light.

Hagia Sophia in all things is the Divine Life reflected in them, considered as a spontaneous participation, as their invitation to the Wedding Feast.

Sophia is God's sharing of Himself with creatures. His outpouring, and the Love by which He is given, and known, held and loved.

She is in all things like the air receiving the sunlight. In her they prosper. In her they glorify God. In her they rejoice to reflect Him. In her they are united with him. She is the union between them. She is the Love that unites them. She is life as communion, life as thanksgiving, life as praise, life as festival, life as glory.

Because she receives perfectly there is in her no stain. She is love without blemish, and gratitude without self-complacency. All things praise her by being themselves and by sharing in the Wedding Feast. She is the Bride and the Feast and the Wedding.

The feminine principle in the world is the inexhaustible source of creative realizations of the Father's glory. She is His manifestation in radiant splendor! But she remains unseen, glimpsed only by a few. Sometimes there are none who know her at all.

Sophia is the mercy of God in us. She is the tenderness with which the infinitely mysterious power of pardon turns the darkness of our sins into the light of grace. She is the inexhaustible fountain of

---

* gift of God.
** He emptied himself—Phil 3:7.

kindness, and would almost seem to be, in herself, all mercy. So she does in us a greater work than that of Creation: the work of new being in grace, the work of pardon, the work of transformation from brightness to brightness *tamquam a Domini Spiritu.** She is in us the yielding and tender counterpart of the power, justice and creative dynamism of the Father.

IV. Sunset. The Hour of Compline. Salve Regina.

Now the Blessed Virgin Mary is the one created being who enacts and shows forth in her life all that is hidden in Sophia. Because of this she can be said to be a personal manifestation of Sophia, Who in God is *Ousia* rather than Person.

Natura in Mary becomes pure Mother. In her, *Natura* is as she was from the origin from her divine birth. In Mary *Natura* is all wise and is manifested as an all-prudent, all-loving, all-pure person: not a Creator, and not a Redeemer, but perfect Creature, perfectly Redeemed, the fruit of all God's great power, the perfect expression of wisdom in mercy.

It is she, it is Mary, Sophia, who in sadness and joy, with the full awareness of what she is doing, sets upon the Second Person, the Logos, a crown which is His Human Nature. Thus her consent opens the door of created nature, of time, of history, to the Word of God.

God enters into His creation. Through her wise answer, through her obedient understanding, through the sweet yielding consent of Sophia, God enters without publicity into the city of rapacious men.

She crowns Him not with what is glorious, but with what is greater than glory: the one thing greater than glory is weakness, nothingness, poverty.

---

* As from the Spirit of the Lord.

She sends the infinitely Rich and Powerful One forth as poor and helpless, in His mission of inexpressible mercy, to die for us on the Cross.

The shadows fall. The stars appear. The birds begin to sleep. Night embraces the silent half of the earth.

A vagrant, a destitute wanderer with dusty feet, finds his way down a new road. A homeless God, lost in the night, without papers, without identification, without even a number, a frail expendable exile lies down in desolation under the sweet stars of the world and entrusts Himself to sleep.

THE WISDOM OF THE DESERT

Thomas Merton was intensely involved with the study of monasticism both because he was a master of scholastics in the monastery and because of his own personal life choice to be a monk. During his lifetime he published an enormous number of articles and essays on monastic topics, with the best of them being anthologized in such collections as Contemplation In a World of Action *(1973),* The Monastic Journey *(1977), and* Thomas Merton on Saint Bernard *(1980).*

Among Merton's own favorites (he ranked it "better" on his famous 1967 graph—the highest ranking he allowed himself) was The Wisdom of the Desert *(1961) from which this introductory essay was taken. Merton translated some stories of the early desert solitaries and introduced them with the essay printed below. His original intention was to have the noted Zen scholar, D.T. Suzuki, write an introduction to the book, but this plan fell afoul of the Order's censorship.*

It is easy to see why Merton would have looked to Suzuki for comment. The love of simplicity, the ethos of doing simple things well, the striving for clarity of mind, the absorption of external prayer into the heart, the love of paradox—all of those things which Merton singles out as virtues of these early desert dwellers—resonate with the things which he found attractive in the Zen tradition.

Such a collaboration, alas, was not to be, but Merton's publication of his little book was still an act of homage to his monastic ancestors and an implied tribute to the hiddenness of the contemplative life. In this tightly written essay Merton not only makes an act of pietas *to his monastic tradition but singles out the things which he thought (and continued to think) were essential to the monastic tradition. Much of what he thought monasticism stood for are contained in these pages.*

Merton only translated a small representative sample of the Verba Seniorum *and made no pretension, as he noted, to scholar-*

ship in so doing. For a full translation, see The Sayings of the Desert
Fathers: The Alphabetical Collection, *translated by Benedicta
Ward (Kalamazoo: Cistercian Publications, 1975). The standard
work on this monastic tradition is Derwas Chitty's* The Desert a
City *(New York and London: Oxford, 1966).*

✣

In the fourth century A.D. the deserts of Egypt, Palestine, Arabia and Persia were peopled by a race of men who have left behind
them a strange reputation. They were the first Christian hermits,
who abandoned the cities of the pagan world to live in solitude.
Why did they do this? The reasons were many and various, but they
can all be summed up in one word as the quest for "salvation." And
what was salvation? Certainly it was not something they sought in
mere exterior conformity to the customs and dictates of any social
group. In those days men had become keenly conscious of the
strictly individual character of "salvation." Society—which meant
pagan society, limited by the horizons and prospects of life "in this
world"—was regarded by them as a shipwreck from which each
single individual man had to swim for his life. We need not stop
here to discuss the fairness of this view: what matters is to remember that it was a fact. These were men who believed that to let
oneself drift along, passively accepting the tenets and values of
what they knew as society, was purely and simply a disaster. The
fact that the Emperor was now Christian and that the "world" was
coming to know the Cross as a sign of temporal power only
strengthened them in their resolve.

It should seem to us much stranger than it does, this paradoxical flight from the world that attained its greatest dimensions (I
almost said frenzy) when the "world" became officially Christian.
These men seem to have thought, as a few rare modern thinkers
like Berdyaev have thought, that there is really no such thing as a
"Christian state." They seem to have doubted that Christianity and
politics could ever be mixed to such an extent as to produce a fully
Christian society. In other words, for them the only Christian society was spiritual and extramundane: the Mystical Body of Christ.
These were surely extreme views, and it is almost scandalous to

recall them in a time like ours when Christianity is accused on all sides of preaching negativism and withdrawal—of having no effective way of meeting the problems of the age. But let us not be too superficial. The Desert Fathers did, in fact, meet the "problems of their time" in the sense that *they* were among the few who were ahead of their time, and opened the way for the development of a new man and a new society. They represent what modern social philosophers (Jaspers, Mumford) call the emergence of the "axial man," the forerunner of the modern personalist man. The eighteenth and nineteenth centuries with their pragmatic individualism degraded and corrupted the psychological heritage of axial man with its debt to the Desert Fathers and other contemplatives, and prepared the way for the great regression to the herd mentality that is taking place now.

The flight of these men to the desert was neither purely negative nor purely individualistic. They were not rebels against society. True, they were in a certain sense "anarchists," and it will do no harm to think of them in that light. They were men who did not believe in letting themselves be passively guided and ruled by a decadent state, and who believed that there was a way of getting along without slavish dependence on accepted, conventional values. But they did not intend to place themselves above society. They did not reject society with proud contempt, as if they were superior to other men. On the contrary, one of the reasons why they fled from the world of men was that in the world men were divided into those who were successful, and imposed their will on others, and those who had to give in and be imposed upon. The Desert Fathers declined to be ruled by men, but had no desire to rule over others themselves. Nor did they fly from human fellowship—the very fact that they uttered these "words" of advice to one another is proof that they were eminently social. The society they sought was one where all men were truly equal, where the only authority under God was the charismatic authority of wisdom, experience and love. Of course, they acknowledged the benevolent, hierarchical authority of their bishops: but the bishops were far away and said little about what went on in the desert until the great Origenist conflict at the end of the fourth century.

What the Fathers sought most of all was their own true self, in Christ. And in order to do this, they had to reject completely the false, formal self, fabricated under social compulsion in "the world." They sought a way to God that was uncharted and freely chosen, not inherited from others who had mapped it out before-hand. They sought a God whom they alone could find, not one who was "given" in a set, stereotyped form by somebody else. Not that they rejected any of the dogmatic formulas of the Christian faith: they accepted and clung to them in their simplest and most elemen-tary shape. But they were slow (at least in the beginning, in the time of their primitive wisdom) to get involved in theological contro-versy. Their flight to the arid horizons of the desert meant also a refusal to be content with arguments, concepts and technical verbiage.

We deal here exclusively with hermits. There were also ceno-bites in the desert—cenobites by the hundred and by the thousand, living the "common life" in enormous monasteries like the one founded by St. Pachomius at Tabenna. Among these there was social order, almost military discipline. Nevertheless the spirit was still very much a spirit of personalism and freedom, because even the cenobite knew that his Rule was only an exterior framework, a kind of scaffolding with which he was to help himself build the spiritual structure of his own life with God. But the hermits were in every way more free. There was nothing to which they had to "con-form" except the secret, hidden, inscrutable will of God which might differ very notably from one cell to another! It is very signifi-cant that one of the first of these *Verba* (Number 3) is one in which the authority of St. Anthony is adduced for what is the basic princi-ple of desert life: that God is the authority and that apart from His manifest will there are few or no principles: "Therefore, whatever you see your soul to desire according to God, do that thing, and you shall keep your heart safe."

Obviously such a path could only be travelled by one who was very alert and very sensitive to the landmarks of a trackless wilder-ness. The hermit had to be a man mature in faith, humble and detached from himself to a degree that is altogether terrible. The spiritual cataclysms that sometimes overtook some of the pre-sumptuous visionaries of the desert are there to show the dangers of the lonely life—like bones whitening in the sand. The Desert Fa-ther could not afford to be an illuminist. He could not dare risk attachment to his own ego, or the dangerous ecstasy of self-will. He could not retain the slightest identification with his superficial, transient, self-constructed self. He had to lose himself in the inner, hidden reality of a self that was transcendent, mysterious, half-known, and lost in Christ. He had to die to the values of transient existence as Christ had died to them on the Cross, and rise from the dead with Him in the light of an entirely new wisdom. Hence the life of sacrifice, which started out from a clean break, separating the monk from the world. A life continued in "compunction" which taught him to lament the madness of attachment to unreal values. A life of solitude and labour, poverty and fasting, charity and prayer which enabled the old superficial self to be purged away and permitted the gradual emergence of the true, secret self in which the Believer and Christ were "one Spirit."

Finally, the proximate end of all this striving was "purity of heart"—a clear unobstructed vision of the true state of affairs, an intuitive grasp of one's own inner reality as anchored, or rather lost, in God through Christ. The fruit of this was *quies:* "rest". Not rest of the body, nor even fixation of the exalted spirit upon some point or summit of light. The Desert Fathers were not, for the most part, ecstatics. Those who were have left some strange and misleading stories behind them to confuse the true issue. The "rest" which these men sought was simply the sanity and poise of a being that no longer has to look at itself because it is carried away by the perfection of freedom that is in it. And carried where? Wherever Love itself, or the Divine Spirit, sees fit to go. Rest, then, was a kind of simple no-whereness and no-mindedness that had lost all preoccupation with a false or limited "self." At peace in the possession of a sublime "Nothing" the spirit laid hold, in secret, upon the "All"—without trying to know what it possessed.

Now the Fathers were not even sufficiently concerned with the nature of this rest to speak of it in these terms, except very rarely, as did St. Anthony, when he remarked that "the prayer of the monk is not perfect until he no longer realizes himself or the fact that he is praying." And this was said casually, in passing. For the rest, the Fathers steered clear of everything lofty, everything esoteric, everything theoretical or difficult to understand. That is to say, they refused to talk about such things. And for that matter they were not very willing to talk about anything else, even about the truths of Christian faith, which accounts for the laconic quality of these sayings.

In many respects, therefore, these Desert Fathers had much in common with Indian Yogis and with Zen Buddhist monks of China and Japan. If we were to seek their like in twentieth-century America, we would have to look in strange, out of the way places. Such beings are tragically rare. They obviously do not flourish on the sidewalk at Forty-Second Street and Broadway. We might perhaps find someone like this among the Pueblo Indians or the Navahos: but there the case would be entirely different. You would have simplicity, primitive wisdom: but rooted in a primitive society. With the Desert Fathers, you have the characteristic of a clean break with a conventional, accepted social context in order to swim for one's life into an apparently irrational void.

Though I might be expected to claim that men like this could be found in some of our monasteries of contemplatives, I will not be so bold. With us it is often rather a case of men leaving the society of the "world" in order to fit themselves into another kind of society, that of the religious family which they enter. They exchange the values, concepts and rites of the one for those of the other. And since we now have centuries of monasticism behind us, this puts the whole thing in a different light. The social "norms" of a monastic family are also apt to be conventional, and to live by them does not involve a leap into the void—only a radical change of customs and standards. The words and examples of the Desert Fathers have been so much a part of monastic tradition that time has turned them into stereotypes for us, and we are no longer able to notice their fabulous originality. We have buried them, so to speak, in our own routines, and thus securely insulated ourselves against any form of spiritual shock from their lack of conventionality. Yet it has been my hope that in selecting and editing these "words" I may have presented them in a new light and made their freshness once again obvious.

The Desert Fathers were pioneers, with nothing to go on but the example of some of the prophets, like St. John the Baptist, Elias, Eliseus, and the Apostles, who also served them as models. For the rest, the life they embraced was "angelic" and they walked the untrodden paths of invisible spirits. Their cells were the furnace of

Babylon in which, in the midst of flames, they found themselves with Christ.

They neither courted the approval of their contemporaries nor sought to provoke their disapproval, because the opinions of others had ceased, for them, to be matters of importance. They had no set doctrine about freedom, but they had in fact become free by paying the price of freedom.

In any case these Fathers distilled for themselves a very practical and unassuming wisdom that is at once primitive and timeless, and which enables us to reopen the sources that have been polluted or blocked up altogether by the accumulated mental and spiritual refuse of our technological barbarism. Our time is in desperate need of this kind of simplicity. It needs to recapture something of the experience reflected in these lines. The word to emphasize is *experience*. The few short phrases collected in this volume have little or no value merely as information. It would be futile to skip through these pages and lightly take note of the fact that the Fathers said this and this. What good will it do us to know merely that such things were once *said?* The important thing is that they were lived. That they flow from an experience of the deeper levels of life. That they represent a discovery of man, at the term of an inner and spiritual journey that is far more crucial and infinitely more important than any journey to the moon.

What can we gain by sailing to the moon if we are not able to cross the abyss that separates us from ourselves? This is the most important of all voyages of discovery, and without it all the rest are not only useless but disastrous. Proof: the great travellers and colonizers of the Renaissance were, for the most part, men who perhaps were capable of the things they did precisely because they were alienated from themselves. In subjugating primitive worlds they only imposed on them, with the force of cannons, their own confusion and their own alienation. Superb exceptions like Fray Bartolome de las Casas, St. Francis Xavier, or Father Matthew Ricci, only prove the rule.

These sayings of the Desert Fathers are drawn from a classical collection, the *Verba Seniorum,* in Migne's *Latin Patrology* (Volume 73). The *Verba* are distinguished from the other Desert Fathers' literature by their total lack of literary artifice, their complete and honest simplicity. The *Lives* of the Fathers are much more

grandiloquent, dramatic, stylized. They abound in wonderful
events and in miracles. They are strongly marked by the literary
personalities to whom we owe them. But the *Verba* are the plain,
unpretentious reports that went from mouth to mouth in the Coptic tradition before being committed to writing in Syriac, Greek
and Latin.

Always simple and concrete, always appealing to the experience of the man who had been shaped by solitude, these proverbs
and tales were intended as plain answers to plain questions. Those
who came to the desert seeking "salvation" asked the elders for a
"word" that would help them to find it—a *verbum salutis,* a "word
of salvation." The answers were not intended to be general, universal prescriptions. Rather they were originally concrete and precise
keys to particular doors that had to be entered, at a given time, by
given individuals. Only later, after much repetition and much quotation, did they come to be regarded as common currency. It will
help us to understand these sayings better if we remember their
practical and, one might say, existential quality. But by the time St.
Benedict in his Rule prescribed that the "Words of the Fathers"
were to be read aloud frequently before Compline, they were traditional monastic lore.

The Fathers were humble and silent men, and did not have
much to say. They replied to questions in few words, to the point.
Rather than give an abstract principle, they preferred to tell a concrete story. Their brevity is refreshing, and rich in content. There is
more light and satisfaction in these laconic sayings than in many a
long ascetic treatise full of details about ascending from one "degree" to another in the spiritual life. These words of the Fathers are
never theoretical in our modern sense of the word. They are never
abstract. They deal with concrete things and with jobs to be done in
the everyday life of a fourth-century monk. But what is said serves
just as well for a twentieth-century thinker. The basic realities of the
interior life are there: faith, humility, charity, meekness, discretion,
self-denial. But not the least of the qualities of the "words of salvation" is their common sense.

This is important. The Desert Fathers later acquired a reputation for fanaticism because of the stories that were told about their
ascetic feats by indiscreet admirers. They were indeed ascetics: but
when we read their own words and see what they themselves

thought about life, we find that they were anything but fanatics. They were humble, quiet, sensible people, with a deep knowledge of human nature and enough understanding of the things of God to realize that they knew very little about Him. Hence they were not much disposed to make long speeches about the divine essence, or even to declaim on the mystical meaning of Scripture. If these men say little about God, it is because they know that when one has been somewhere close to His dwelling, silence makes more sense than a lot of words. The fact that Egypt, in their time, was seething with religious and intellectual controversies was all the more reason for them to keep their mouths shut. There were the Neo-Platonists, the Gnostics, the Stoics and Pythagoreans. There were the various, highly vocal, orthodox and heretical groups of Christians. There were the Arians (whom the monks of the Desert passionately resisted). There were the Origenists (and some of the monks were faithfully devoted followers of Origen). In all this noise, the desert had no contribution to offer but a discreet and detached silence.

The great monastic centres of the fourth century were in Egypt, Arabia and Palestine. Most of these stories concern hermits of Nitria and Scete, in northern Egypt, near the Mediterranean coast and west of the Nile. There were also many colonies of monks in the Nile Delta. The Thebaid, near ancient Thebes, further inland along the Nile, was another centre of monastic activity, particularly of the cenobites. Palestine had early attracted monks from all parts of the Christian world, the most famous of them being St. Jerome, who lived and translated the Scriptures in a cave at Bethlehem. Then there was an important monastic colony around Mount Sinai in Arabia: founders of that monastery of St. Catherine which has recently broken into the news with the "discovery" of the works of Byzantine art preserved there.

What kind of life did the Fathers lead? A word of explanation may help us understand their sayings better. The Desert Fathers are usually referred to as "Abbot" (*abbas*) or "Elder" (*senex*). An Abbot was not then, as now, a canonically elected superior of a community, but any monk or hermit who had been tried by years in the desert and proved himself a servant of God. With them, or near them, lived "Brethren" and "Novices"—those who were still in the process of learning the life. The novices still needed the continuous supervision of an elder, and lived with one in order to be instructed by his word and example. The brethren lived on their own, but occasionally resorted to a nearby elder for advice.

Most of the characters represented in these sayings and stories are men who are "on the way" to purity of heart rather than men who have fully arrived. The Desert Fathers, inspired by Clement and Origen, and the Neo-Platonic tradition, were sometimes confident that they could rise above all passion and become impervious to anger, lust, pride and all the rest. But we find little in these sayings to encourage those who believed that Christian perfection was a matter of *apatheia* (impassivity). The praise of monks "beyond all passion" seems indeed to have come from tourists who passed briefly through the deserts and went home to write books about what they had seen, rather than from those who had spent their whole life in the wilderness. These latter were much more inclined to accept the common realities of life and be content with the ordinary lot of man who has to struggle all his life to overcome himself. The wisdom of the *Verba* is seen in the story of the monk John, who boasted that he was "beyond all temptation" and was advised by a shrewd elder to pray to God for a few good solid battles in order that his life might continue to be worth something.

At certain times, all the solitaries and novices would come together for the liturgical *synaxis* (Mass and prayers in common) and after this they might eat together and hold a kind of chapter meeting to discuss communal problems. Then they returned to their solitude, where they spent their time working and praying.

They supported themselves by the labour of their hands, usually weaving baskets and mats out of palm leaves or reeds. These they sold in the nearby towns. There is sometimes question in the *Verba* of matters relating to the work and to the commerce involved. Charity and hospitality were matters of top priority, and took precedence over fasting and personal ascetic routines. The countless sayings which bear witness to this warm-hearted friendliness should be sufficient to take care of accusations that these men hated their own kind. Indeed there was more real love, understanding and kindliness in the desert than in the cities, where, then as now, it was every man for himself.

This fact is all the more important because the very essence of the Christian message is charity, unity in Christ. The Christian mystics of all ages sought and found not only the unification of their own being, not only union with God, but union with one another in the Spirit of God. To seek a union with God that would imply complete separation, in spirit as well as in body from all the rest of mankind, would be to a Christian saint not only absurd but the very opposite of sanctity. Isolation in the self, inability to go out of oneself to others, would mean incapacity for any form of self-transcendence. To be thus the prisoner of one's own selfhood is, in fact, to be in hell: a truth that Sartre, though professing himself an atheist, has expressed in the most arresting fashion in his play *No Exit* (*Huis Clos*).

All through the *Verba Seniorum* we find a repeated insistence on the primacy of love over everything else in the spiritual life: over knowledge, gnosis, asceticism, contemplation, solitude, prayer. Love in fact is the spiritual life, and without it all the other exercises of the spirit, however lofty, are emptied of content and become mere illusions. The more lofty they are, the more dangerous the illusion.

Love, of course, means something much more than mere sentiment, much more than token favours and perfunctory almsdeeds. Love means an interior and spiritual identification with one's brother, so that he is not regarded as an "object" to "which" one "does good." The fact is that good done to another as to an object is of little or no spiritual value. Love takes one's neighbour as one's other self, and loves him with all the immense humility and discretion and reserve and reverence without which no one can presume to enter into the sanctuary of another's subjectivity. From such love all authoritarian brutality, all exploitation, domineering and condescension must necessarily be absent. The saints of the desert were enemies of every subtle or gross expedient by which "the spiritual man" contrives to bully those he thinks inferior to himself, thus gratifying his own ego. They had renounced everything that savoured of punishment and revenge, however hidden it might be.

The charity of the Desert Fathers is not set before us in unconvincing effusions. The full difficulty and magnitude of the task of loving others is recognized everywhere and never minimized. It is hard to really love others if love is to be taken in the full sense of the word. Love demands a complete inner transformation—for without this we cannot possibly come to identify ourselves with our brother. We have to become, in some sense, the person we love.

And this involves a kind of death of our own being, our own self. No matter how hard we try, we resist this death: we fight back with anger, with recriminations, with demands, with ultimatums. We seek any convenient excuse to break off and give up the difficult task. But in these *Verba Seniorum* we read of Abbot Ammonas, who spent fourteen years praying to overcome anger, or rather, more significantly, to be delivered from it. We read of Abbot Serapion, who sold his last book, a copy of the Gospels, and gave the money to the poor, thus selling "the very words which told him to sell all and give to the poor." Another Abbot severely rebuked some monks who had caused a group of robbers to be thrown in jail, and as a result the shamefaced hermits broke into the jail by night to release the prisoners. Time and again we read of Abbots who refuse to join in a communal reproof of this or that delinquent, like Abbot Moses, that great gentle Negro, who walked into the severe assembly with a basket of sand, letting the sand run out through many holes. "My own sins are running out like this sand," he said, "and yet I come to judge the sins of another."

If such protests were made, there was obviously something to protest against. By the end of the fifth century Scete and Nitria had become rudimentary monastic cities, with laws and penalties. Three whips hung from a palm tree outside the church of Scete: one to punish delinquent monks, one to punish thieves and one for vagrants. But there were many monks like Abbot Moses who did not agree: and these were the saints. They represented the primitive "anarchic" desert ideal. Perhaps the most memorable of all were the two old brothers who had lived together for years without a quarrel, who decided to "get into an argument like the rest of men" but simply could not succeed.

Prayer was the very heart of the desert life, and consisted of psalmody (vocal prayer—recitation of the Psalms and other parts of the Scriptures which everyone had to know by heart) and contemplation. What we would call today contemplative prayer is referred to as *quies* or "rest." This illuminating term has persisted in Greek monastic tradition as *hesychia,* "sweet repose." *Quies* is a silent absorption aided by the soft repetition of a lone phrase of the Scriptures—the most popular being the prayer of the Publican: "Lord Jesus Christ, Son of God, have mercy on me a sinner!" In a shortened form this prayer became "Lord have mercy" (*Kyrie elei-*

son)—repeated interiorly hundreds of times a day until it became as spontaneous and instinctive as breathing.

When Arsenius is told to fly from the Cenobium, be silent and rest (*fuge, tace, quiesce*) it is a call to "contemplative prayer." *Quies* is a simpler and less pretentious term, and much less misleading. It suits the simplicity of the Desert Fathers much better than "contemplation" and affords less occasion for spiritual narcissism or megalomania. There was small danger of quietism in the desert. The monks were kept busy, and if *quies* was a fulfilment of all they sought, *corporalis quies* ("bodily rest") was one of their greatest enemies. I have translated *corporalis quies* as "an easy life," so as not to give the impression that agitated action was tolerated in the desert. It was not. The monk was supposed to remain tranquil and stay as much as possible in one place. Some Fathers even frowned on those who sought employment outside their cells and worked for the farmers of the Nile valley during the harvest season.

Finally, in these pages we meet several great and simple personalities. Though the *Verba* are sometimes ascribed only to an unidentified *senex* (elder) they are more often attributed by name to the saint who uttered them. We meet Abbot Anthony, who is no other than St. Anthony the Great. This is the Father of all hermits, whose biography, by St. Athanasius, set the whole Roman world afire with monastic vocations. Anthony was indeed the Father of all the Desert Fathers. But contact with his original thought reminds us that he is not the Anthony of Flaubert—nor do we find here anyone like the Paphnutius of Anatole France. Anthony, it is true, attained *apatheia* after long and somewhat spectacular contests with demons. But in the end he concluded that not even the devil was purely evil, since God could not create evil, and all His works are good. It may come as a surprise to learn that St. Anthony, of all people, thought the devil had some good in him. This was not mere sentimentalism. It showed that in Anthony there was not much room left for paranoia. We can profitably reflect that modern mass-man is the one who has returned so wholeheartedly to fanatical projections of all one's own evil upon "the enemy" (whoever that may be). The solitaries of the desert were much wiser.

Then in these *Verba* we meet others like St. Arsenius, the dour and silent stranger who came to the desert from the far-off court of the Emperors of Constantinople and would not let anybody see his face. We meet the gentle Poemen, the impetuous John the Dwarf, who wanted to "become an angel." Not the least attractive is Abbot Pastor, who appears perhaps most frequently of all. His sayings are distinguished by their practical humility, their understanding of human frailty and their solid common sense. Pastor, we know, was himself very human, and it is said of him that when his own blood brother seemed to grow cold to him and preferred the conversation of another hermit, he became so jealous that he had to go to one of the elders and get his sights adjusted.

These monks insisted on remaining human and "ordinary." This may seem to be a paradox, but it is very important. If we reflect a moment, we will see that to fly into the desert in order to be extraordinary is only to carry the world with you as an implicit standard of comparison. The result would be nothing but self-contemplation, and self-comparison with the negative standard of the world one had abandoned. Some of the monks of the Desert did this, as a matter of fact: and the only fruit of their trouble was that they went out of their heads. The simple men who lived their lives out to a good old age among the rocks and sands only did so because they had come into the desert to be themselves, their *ordinary* selves, and to forget a world that divided them from themselves. There can be no other valid reason for seeking solitude or for leaving the world. And thus to leave the world, is, in fact, to help save it in saving oneself. This is the final point, and it is an important one. The Coptic hermits who left the world as though escaping from a wreck, did not merely intend to save themselves. They knew that they were helpless to do any good for others as long as they floundered about in the wreckage. But once they got a foothold on solid ground, things were different. Then they had not only the power but even the obligation to pull the whole world to safety after them.

This is their paradoxical lesson for our time. It would perhaps be too much to say that the world needs another movement such as that which drew these men into the deserts of Egypt and Palestine. Ours is certainly a time for solitaries and for hermits. But merely to reproduce the simplicity, austerity and prayer of these primitive souls is not a complete or satisfactory answer. We must transcend them, and transcend all those who, since their time, have gone beyond the limits which they set. We must liberate ourselves, in our own way, from involvement in a world that is plunging to disaster.

But our world is different from theirs. Our involvement in it is more complete. Our danger is far more desperate. Our time, perhaps, is shorter than we think.

We cannot do exactly what they did. But we must be as thorough and as ruthless in our determination to break all spiritual chains, and cast off the domination of alien compulsions, to find our true selves, to discover and develop our inalienable spiritual liberty and use it to build, on earth, the Kingdom of God. This is not the place in which to speculate what our great and mysterious vocation might involve. That is still unknown. Let it suffice for me to say that we need to learn from these men of the fourth century how to ignore prejudice, defy compulsion and strike out fearlessly into the unknown.

HERAKLEITOS: A STUDY

Merton wrote the essay "Herakleitos the Obscure" in 1960 and it was first published that year in Jubilee magazine (September 1960) and reprinted in an anthology of his writings: The Behavior of Titans (1961). While the ostensible subject is a Greek philosopher, the close reader will note that it is also a reflection on a kind of spirituality which Merton identified as authentically monastic.

Heraclitus of Ephesus is lost to us except in short fragments of his work which have come down through other authors. Biographical information about him is equally sparse, and some of it is the pure invention of his not always sympathetic critics. Some of the early fathers of the church, as Merton notes in his essay, saw him as a Christian avant la parole, and one, at least, even considered him a saint.

It is not hard to see how Merton—who was reading widely in the Greek classics in this period—would find this enigmatic figure a sympathetic person. Heraclitus is known to us through his arrestingly paradoxical aphorisms and stories of dubious authenticity but not uncharacteristic of his personality (preferring, for example, to play children's games to the public business of politics), and for his doctrine of the Logos. Merton, who consumed literature voraciously, could not help but see in this figure an early representative of the "monastic culture" which so held his own attention—a culture which embraced the Zen paradox and the encounter with that ultimate principle of all that is, whether it be called Tao or Sophia or Logos in the pagan and Johannine sense of the term.

This essay can be read in the context of Merton's studies of Aeschylus and Hesiod which he pursued because of his interest in the figure of Prometheus, but it can also be read in the broader context of Merton's monastic spirituality. It is the latter approach that seems the better. One might well remember that two other poets, greatly loved by Merton, paid their respective tributes to the old Greek philosopher: Gerard Manley Hopkins in the exquisite

Resurrection poem *"That Nature Is a Heraclitean Fire"* and *T.S. Eliot who prefaces* Four Quartets *with two Greek fragments of Heraclitus.*

❖

One of the most challenging, inscrutable and acute of philosophers is Herakleitos of Ephesus, the "dark" *skoteinos, tenebrosus.* He lived in the Ionian Greek city sacred to Artemis, where he flourished at the turn of the fifth century B.C. in the days of the Greek tyrants, and of the Persian wars. He was a contemporary of Pindar and Aeschylus and of the victorious fighters of Marathon, but unlike the poets who wrote and sang in the dawn of the Attic Golden age, Herakleitos was a tight-lipped and cynical pessimist who viewed with sardonic contempt the political fervor of his contemporaries.

He was one of those rare spirits whose prophetic insight enabled them to see far beyond the limited horizons of their society. The Ionian world was the world of Homer and of the Olympian gods. It was a world that believed in static and changeless order, and in the laws of mechanical necessity—basically materialistic. Against this Olympian formalism, against the ritualism and the rigidity of the conventional exterior cult, the static condition of a society that feared all that was not "ordinary," Herakleitos rose up with the protest of the Dionysian mystic. He spoke for the mysterious, the unutterable, and the excellent. He spoke for the logos which was the true law of all being—not a static and rigid form, but a dynamic principle of harmony-in-conflict. This logos-principle was represented by Herakleitos under the symbolic form of fire. However, fire was not only a symbol for Herakleitos. Later philosophers have derided the intuition by which Herakleitos designated fire as the "primary substance" of the cosmos—but perhaps the experience of our time, in which atomic science has revealed the enormous burning energy that can be released from an atom of hydrogen, may prove Herakleitos to have been nearer the truth than was thought by Plato or Aristotle. However, the "fire" of Herakleitos is something more than material. It is spiritual and "divine." It is the key to the spiritual enigma of man. Our spiritual and mystical destiny is to "awaken" to the fire that is within us, and our happiness depends on the harmony-in-conflict that results from this awakening. Our vocation is a call to spiritual oneness in and with the logos. But this interior fulfillment is not to be attained by a false peace resulting from artificial compulsion—a static and changeless "state" imposed by force of will upon the dynamic, conflicting forces with us. True peace is the "hidden attunement of opposite tensions"—a paradox and a mystery transcending both sense and will, like the ecstasy of the mystic.

Herakleitos left no writings of his own. Legend says that he composed a book which he presented to Artemis in her temple, but almost all the stories told of his life and exploits are to be mistrusted. It is much more likely that he wrote nothing at all. His sayings, those cryptic fragments which have so tenaciously survived, have come down to us in the writings of others. Herakleitos is quoted first of all by Plato and Aristotle, but also by later writers like Plotinus, Porphyry, Theophrastus, Philo, and several Christian Fathers such as Clement of Alexandria, Origen and Hyppolitus. Sometimes these philosophers and theologians quote Herakleitos with approval to illustrate a point of their own; more often they bring him up only in order to refute him. But St. Justin Martyr refers to him, along with Socrates, as a "Saint" of pre-Christian paganism. The fact that he is unknown to us except in the context which others have foisted on him makes him even more difficult to understand than he is in himself. Though the fragments which form his whole surviving work can be printed on two or three pages, long and laborious research is needed to untangle their authentic meaning and to liberate the obscure Ionian from the bias imposed on his thought by the interpretation of opponents.

His enigmatic sayings are terse paradoxes, often wearing the sardonic and oracular expression of the Zen *mondo*. The comparison suggests itself quite naturally in our day when Oriental thought has once again found a hearing (perhaps not always an intelligent hearing) in the West. Herakleitos appears at first sight to be more Oriental than Greek, though this appearance can easily be exaggerated, and Herakleitos himself warns us against irresponsible guesses in difficult matters. "Let us not conjecture at random about the greatest things." But it is true that the logos of Herakleitos seems to have much in common with the Tao of Lao-tse as well as with the Word of St. John. His insistence that apparently conflicting opposites are, at bottom, really one is also a familiar theme in Oriental thought. Herakleitos, we must remember, comes *before* Aristotle's principle of identity and contradiction. He does not look at things with the eyes of Aristotelian logic, and consequently he can say that opposites can be, from a certain point of view, the same.

The variations and oppositions between conflicting forces in the world are immediately evident to sense, and are not a complete illusion. But when men become too intent on analyzing and judging these oppositions, and separating them out into good and evil, desirable and undesirable, profitable and useless, they become more and more immersed in illusion and their view of reality is perverted. They can no longer see the deep, underlying connection of opposites, because they are obsessed with their superficial separateness. In reality, the distinction to be made is not between this force which is good and true, as against that force which is evil and false. Rather it is the perception of underlying oneness that is the key to truth and goodness, while the attachment to superficial separateness leads to falsity and moral error. This is why Herakleitos says, "to God all things are good and just and right, but men hold some things wrong and some right." God sees all things as good and right, not in their separateness by which they arc in contrast to everything else, but in their inner harmony with their apparent opposites. But men separate what God has united.

Herakleitos looks on the world not as an abstractionist, but from the viewpoint of experience. However, and this is important, experience for Herakleitos is not merely the uninterpreted datum of sense. His philosophical viewpoint is that of a mystic whose intuition cuts through apparent multiplicity to grasp underlying reality as *one*. This vision of unity which Parmenides was to sum up in the universal concept of being was seen by the poet and mystic, Herakleitos, as "Fire."

We must be very careful not to interpret Herakleitos in a material way. Fire for him is a dynamic, spiritual principle. It is a divine energy, the manifestation of God, the power of God. God, indeed, is for Herakleitos "all things." But this is probably a much more subtle statement than we might be inclined to imagine at first sight, for he says that just as fire when it burns different kinds of aromatical spices becomes a variety of perfumes, so God working in the infinite variety of beings manifests Himself in countless appearances. God, strictly speaking, is then not merely "fire" or "earth" or the other elements, or all of them put together. His energy works, shows itself and hides in nature. He Himself is the Logos, the Wisdom, not so much "at work" in nature but rather "at play" there. In one of the fragments the "dark one" speaks of the logos in the same terms as the sapiential literature of the Bible speaks of the divine Wisdom: as a "child playing in the world":

> When he prepared the heavens, I was present:
> when with a certain law and compass he enclosed the depths:
> When he established the sky above, and poised the fountains
>   of waters:
> When he compassed the sea with its bounds, and set a law to
>   the waters that they should not pass their limits:
> When he balanced the foundations of the earth;
> I was with him forming all things: and was delighted
>   every day, playing before him at all times;
> Playing in the world: and my delights were to be with
>   the children of men.
>   —Proverbs 8:27–31

Herakleitos says: "Time is a child playing draughts. The kingly power is a child's." The reference to the game of draughts is a metaphor for his basic concept that all cosmic things are in a state of becoming and change, and this constant interplay of elements in a state of dynamic flux is the expression of the divine Law, the "justice," "hidden harmony" or "unity" which constantly keeps everything in balance in the midst of conflict and movement.

Wisdom, for Herakleitos, does not consist in that "polymathy"—the "learning of many things"—the scientific research which observes and tabulates an almost infinite number of phenomena. Nor does it consist in the willful, and arbitrary selection of one of many conflicting principles, in order to elevate it above its opposite and to place it in a position of definitive and final superiority. True wisdom must seize upon the very movement itself, and penetrate to the logos or thought within that dynamic harmony. "Wisdom is one thing—it is to know the thought by which all things are steered through all things." We are reminded of the words of the Old Testament Book of Wisdom—the one most influenced by Hellenic thought.

> And all such things as are hid and not foreseen, I have learned: for wisdom, which is the worker of all things, taught me.
>
> For in her is the spirit of understanding: holy, one, manifold, subtile, eloquent, active, undefiled, sure, sweet, loving that which is good, quick, which nothing hindereth, beneficient,
>
> Gentle, kind, steadfast, assured, secure, having all power, overseeing all things, and containing all spirits, intelligible, pure, subtile.
>
> For wisdom is more active than all active things: and reacheth everywhere by reason of her purity.
>
> For she is a vapour of the power of God, and a certain pure emanation of the glory of the almighty God: and therefore no defiled thing cometh into her.
>
> For she is the brightness of eternal light, and the unspotted mirror of God's majesty, and the image of his goodness.
>
> —Wisdom 7:21–26

Here in the inspired language of the sacred writer we find the Scriptural development which perfects and completes the fragmentary intuitions of Herakleitos, elevating them to the sublime level of contemplative theology and inserting them in the economy of those great truths of which Herakleitos could not have dreamt: the Incarnation of the Logos and man's Redemption and Divinization as the supreme manifestation of wisdom and of the "attunement of conflicting opposites."

The heart of Herakleitean epistemology is an implicit contrast between man's wisdom, which fails to grasp the concrete reality of unity-in-multiplicity and harmony-in-conflict, but which instead seizes upon one or other of the conflicting elements and tries to build on this a static and one-sided truth which cannot help but be an artificial fiction. The wisdom of man cannot follow the divine wisdom "one and manifold" in its infinitely varied movement. Yet it aspires to a universal grasp of all reality. In order to "see" our minds seize upon the movement around them and within them, and reduce it to immobility. If it were possible for them to fulfill their deepest wish, our minds would in fact impose on the dynamism of the cosmos a paralysis willed by our own compulsiveness and prejudice: and this would ruin the world. For if things were the way we would have them be, in our arbitrary and shortsighted conception of "order," they would all move in one direction toward their ruin, which would be the supreme disorder. All order based purely on man's conception of reality is merely partial—and partial order leads to chaos. Then all things would be consumed by fire—or by water. The real order of the cosmos is an apparent disorder, the "conflict" of opposites which is in fact a stable and dynamic harmony. The wisdom of man is the product of willfulness, blindness, and caprice and is only the manifestation of his own insensibility to what is right before his eyes. But the eyes and ears tell us nothing if our minds are not capable of interpreting their data.

And so Herakleitos, wielding the sharp weapon of paradox without mercy, seeks to awaken the mind of his disciple to a reality that is right before his eyes but that he is incapable of seeing. He wants to liberate him from the cult of "vanity" and to draw him forth from the sleep of formalism and subjective prejudices. Hence the paradox that Herakleitos, who is an uncompromising aristocrat and individualist in thought as well as in life, maintains that the truth is what is common to all. It is the "fire" which is the life of the cosmos as well as of each man. It is spirit and logos. It is "what is right before your eyes." But each individual loses contact with the One Fire and falls back into the "coldness" and moisture and "sleep" of his little subjective world. The awakening is then a recall from the sleep of individualism in this narrow, infantile sense, to the "common" vision of what is universally true. Unfortunately, the sleep of the individual spreads through society and is encouraged by social life itself when it is lived at a low level of spiritual intensity. The life and thought of the "many" is a conspiracy of sleep, a refusal to struggle for the excellence of wisdom which is hard to find. The "many" are content with the inertia of what is commonplace, "given" and familiar. They do not want anything new: or if they do, it must be a mere novelty, a diversion that confirms them in their comfortable inertia and keeps them from being bored with themselves, no more.

Hence, the "many" are complacently willing to be deluded by "polymathy"—the "learning of many things"—the constant succession of novel "truths," new opinions, new doctrines and interpretations, fresh observations and tabulations of phenomena. This multiplicity beguiles the popular mind with a vain appearance of wisdom. But in reality it is nothing but intellectual and spiritual "sleep" which deadens all capacity for the flash of mighty intuition by which multiplicity is suddenly comprehended as basically one —penetrated through and through by the logos, the divine fire.

The wise man must make tremendous efforts to grasp "the unexpected": that is to say he must keep himself alert, he must constantly "seek for himself" and he must not fear to strive for the excellence that will make him an object of hatred and mistrust in the eyes of the conventional majority—as did Hermodorus, whom the Ephesians threw out of their city on the ground that if he wanted to excel he had better go and do it somewhere else, for "we will have none who is best among us."

The aristocratic contempt of Herakleitos for the conventional verbalizing of his fellow citizens was something other than a pose, or a mad reflex of wounded sensibility. It was a prophetic manifestation of intransigent honesty. He refused to hold his peace and spoke out with angry concern for truth. He who had seen "the One" was no longer permitted to doubt, to hedge, to compromise and to flatter. To treat his intuition as one among many opinions would have been inexcusable. False humility was an infidelity to his deepest self and a betrayal of the fundamental insights of his life. It would have been above all a betrayal of those whom he could not effectively contact except by the shock of paradox. Herakleitos took the same stand as Isaias, who was commanded by God to "blind the eyes of this people" by speaking to them in words that were too simple, too direct, too uncompromising to be acceptable. It is not given to men of compromise to understand parables, for as Herakleitos remarked: "When the things that are right in front of them are pointed out to them, they do not pay attention, though they think they do."

This is the tragedy which most concerns Herakleitos—and which should concern us even more than it did him: the fact that the majority of men think they see, and do not. They believe they listen, but they do not hear. They are "absent when present" because in the act of seeing and hearing they substitute the clichés of familiar prejudice for the new and unexpected truth that is being offered to them. They complacently imagine they are receiving a new light, but in the very moment of apprehension they renew their obsession with the old darkness, which is so familiar that it, and it alone, appears to them to be light.

Divinely impatient with the word-play and imposture of those pseudo-wise men who deceive others by collecting and reshuffling the current opinions, presenting old errors in new disguises, Herakleitos refused to play their pitiable game. Inspired, as Plato said, by the "more severe muses," he sought excellence, in his intuitions, at the cost of verbal clarity. He would go deep, and emerge to express his vision in oracular verses, rather than flatter the crowd by giving it what it demanded and expected of a philosopher, of a professional scholar we would say today. He would be like "the Lord at Delphi who neither utters nor hides his meaning but shows it by a sign." His words would be neither expositions of doctrine nor explanations of mystery, but simply pointers, plunging toward the heart of reality: "fingers pointing at the moon." He knew very well that many would mistake the finger for the moon, but that was inevitable and he did not attempt to do anything about it.

It is interesting to compare Herakleitos with the Prometheus of Aeschylus. In Prometheus, the Firebearer, we see a similar revolt against Olympian formalism. We notice that the Titan, Prometheus, represents the older, more primitive, more "Dionysian" earth gods of archaic Greece, in rebellion against the newly established tyranny of Zeus. Aeschylus was consciously introducing politics into his tragedy, and as a result it strikes the modern reader with a tremendous force. The play is as actual as *Darkness at Noon* and the pressure to conform, exercised upon the chained Titan by Hermes, the agent of Zeus, has a shockingly totalitarian ring about it. A great crux for all interpreters of the Prometheus of Aeschylus, in this context, is whether his fire symbolizes science or wisdom. One might argue the point at length but in the end the only satisfactory solution is that it symbolizes both. For Prometheus, fire is science perfected by wisdom and integrally united with wisdom in a "hidden harmony." For the Olympians it is perhaps true to say that wisdom is not important, and that what they begrudge men is science, because science means power. Our interpretation of Prometheus will be completely perverse if we believe that what he wants is power. On the contrary, he represents the protest of love (which unites gods and men in a single family) against power (by which the gods oppress men and keep them in subjection). In this way Herakleitos rebelled against the accepted Olympian order of things preached by Homer and Hesiod.

As a result, most people found him terribly disturbing. They were "fools who are fluttered by every word," "dogs barking at everyone they do not know." In the end they had their revenge: the revenge that popular mediocrity takes upon singular excellence. They created a legend about Herakleitos—a legend which they could understand, for it consigned him forever to a familiar category and left them in comfort. They dismissed him as a crank, a misanthrope, an eccentic kind of beat who thought he was too good for them and who, as a result, condemned himself to a miserable isolation. He preferred loneliness to the warm security of their collective illusion. They called him "the weeping philosopher," though there is very little evidence of tears in his philosophy. The story developed that he finally retired from Ephesus in disgust and went to live alone in the mountains, "feeding on grass and plants." A writer referred to him as the "crowing, mob-reviling, riddling Herakleitos."

The implication was of course that Herakleitos was proud, that he despised the mob. Certainly contempt for other men is not compatible with humility in so far as it excludes love and empathy. It is altogether possible that Herakleitos was a proud man. But can we be sure of this? Is pride synonymous with an aristocratic insistence upon excellence? It takes humility to confront the prejudice and the contempt of all, in order to cling to an unpopular truth. In the popular mind, any failure to "conform," any aspiration to be different, is labeled as pride. But was Herakleitos exalting himself, his own opinions, or the common truth which transcends individuals and opinions? If we understand his doctrine we will see that this latter was the case.

A biographer (writing eight hundred years after his death), collected every story that might make Herakleitos look like a proud eccentric. Basing himself on the fact that Herakleitos had apparently been a member of the hereditary ruling family of Ephesus and had renounced his responsibilities, Diogenes Laertius recorded that:

> When he was asked by the Ephesians to establish laws he refused to do so because the city was already in the grip of its evil constitution. He used to retire to the temple of Artemis (outside the city) and play at knuckle bones with the children; when the Ephesians stood around him he said: "Why, villains, do you marvel? Is it not better to do this than join you in politics?"

No doubt this story is all that the popular mind was able to retain of his mysterious *logion* about "time being a child, playing draughts." They had taken the finger for the moon, and wanted history to ratify their error.

This story of Herakleitos playing knuckle bones in the temple is completely misleading. Several of his fragments show that he was deeply concerned with man's political life. But, as usual with him, the concern is far below the surface of trivial demagoguery and charlatanism which sometimes passes for "politics." Political life, for Herakleitos, was based on the common understanding of the wise, that is of those who were awake, who were aware of the logos, who were attuned to the inner harmony underlying conflicting opposites. Such men would not be easily deluded by the political passion excited by violence and partisan interest. They would not be swept away by popular prejudices or fears, for they would be able to see beyond the limited horizons of their own petty group. Political life is, substantially, the union of those minds who stand far above their group and their time, and who have a deeper, more universal view of history and of men. Such men are necessarily a minority. Their union is not achieved merely by a speculative participation in philosophical insights. It demands great moral energy and sacrifice. They must not be content to see the logos, they must cling to their vision, and defend their insight into unity with their very lives. "Those who speak with understanding must hold fast to what is common as a city holds fast to its law, and even more strongly."

Herakleitos is certainly not antisocial, certainly not an anarchist. He does not reject all law. On the contrary, wise and objective laws are the reflection of the hidden logos and accord with the hidden harmony underlying the seemingly confused movement on the surface of political life. Hence the function of law is not to impose an abstract arbitrary justice which is nothing but the willfulness of a tyrant guided only by his own fantasy and ambition. Law is an expression of that "justice" which is the living harmony of opposites. It is not the vindication of one part of reality as "good" in opposition to another part considered as "evil." It is the expression of the true good which is the inner unity of life itself, the logos which is common to all. Hence it defends the good of all against usurpation by particular groups and individuals seeking only their own limited advantage under the guise of universal "good."

Because of his aphoristic statements about "war" being the "father of all," Herakleitos has been referred to as a Fascist. The term is ridiculous, since by war he means chiefly the conflict of apparent opposites wherever it may be found, not simply military conflict. One might just as well call him a Marxist because this reconciliation of opposites looks like Hegelian dialectic. In point of fact, Herakleitos holds that political life is both absurd and unjust as long as the more excellent minds are excluded from fruitful participation in political life by the preponderance of mediocrities. Not that the world must be ruled by academic philosophers: but that the leadership must be in the hands of those who, by their well developed political and moral abilities, are able to discern the common justice, the logos, which is the true good of all and which, in fact, is the key to the meaning of life and of history.

Why write of Herakleitos in our day? Not, after twenty-five hundred years, to make him what he cannot be: popular. But he speaks to our age—if only some of us can hear him—he speaks in parables to those of us who are afraid of excellence in thought, in life, in spirit and in intellect. His message to us is spiritual, but few will accept it as such: for we have, by now, got far beyond an Ionian pagan. Or have we? Can it be that some of us who are Christians implicitly use our "faith" as an excuse for not going half as far as Herakleitos went? His thought demands effort, integrity, struggle, sacrifice. It is incompatible with the complacent security which can become for us the first essential in thought and life—we call it "peace." But perhaps Herakleitos is closer than we are to the spiritual and intellectual climate of the Gospel in which the Word that enlightens every man coming into the world is made flesh, enters the darkness which receives Him not: where one must be born again without re-entering the womb; where the Spirit is as the wind, blowing where it pleases, while we do not know where it comes from or where it is going. There was another, far greater than Herakleitos, who spoke in parables. He came to cast fire on the earth. Was He perhaps akin to the Fire of which Herakleitos spoke? The easy way to deny it is to dismiss the Ionian as a pantheist. Tag him with a philosophical label and file him away where he won't make anybody uncomfortable!

But not all Christians have done this. Gerard Manley Hopkins, whose vision of the world is Heraklitean as well as Christian, has wrestled with the thought in a poem that is no complacent evasion of the challenge. For Hopkins, the Cosmos is indeed a "Heraklitean fire." His concept of *inscape* is both Heraklitean and Scotistic. It is an intuition of the patterns and harmonies, the "living character" impressed by life itself revealing the wisdom of the Living God in the mystery of interplaying movements and changes. "*Million fueléd, nature's bonfire burns on.*" The most special, "*clearest-selvéd*" spark of the divine fire is man himself. This spark is put out by death. But is death the end? Does the fire merely burn with another flame? Hopkins reaches further into the mystery, not playing with words but wrestling with the angel of tribulation, to reach the Resurrection when "*world's wildfire leaves but ash*" and "*I am all at once what Christ is . . . immortal diamond.*"

Herakleitos did not know Christ. He could not know that the logos would be made flesh and dwell amongst us. Yet he had some intimation of immortality and of resurrection. Some of his mysterious sayings suggest New Testament texts about the Risen Life of man in Christ: "Man kindles for himself a light in the night time when he has died but is alive . . . he that is awake lights up from sleeping." True, he is talking only of the spiritual and intellectual awakening which is the experience of the enlightened one, discovering the logos. But the mystical quality of this experience makes it also a figure of resurrection and new life, in which Herakleitos evidently believed.

He spoke, as we saw above, of the wise man clinging with all his strength to the "common" thought which unites him with other enlightened minds. The wise man must cling to the logos and to his unity with those who are aware of the logos. He must bear witness to the "common" thought even at the cost of his own life. To die for the truth is then the "greatest death" and wins a "greater portion." What is this portion? "There awaits men when they die such things as they look not for nor dream of." The death of the wise man is the "death of fire"; a passage from darkness into greater light, from confusion into unity. The death of the fool clinging to subjective opinion and self-interest is the "death of earth or water," a sinking into coldness, darkness, oblivion and nonentity. Those who die the death of fire—the death which Christianity was to call martyrdom, and which Herakleitos definitely believed was a "witness" to the Fire and the Logos—become superior beings. They live forever. They take their place among the company of those who watch over the destinies of the cosmos and of men, for they have, in their lives, entered into the secret of the logos. "They who die great deaths rise up to become the wakeful guardians of the living and the dead." The aristocracy in which Herakleitos believed was then not an aristocracy of class, of power, of learning (all these are illusory). It is an aristocracy of the spirit, of wisdom: one might almost say of mysticism and of sanctity.

THE INNER EXPERIENCE

"*The Inner Experience*" *has a checkered background. In the summer of 1959 Merton worked on a rewriting of a little booklet he had published in 1948 under the title* What Is Contemplation? *He wrote a friend that that book—a product of his period as a "rip-roaring Trappist"—was too cerebral and, simultaneously, too superficial. Judging from the drafts in the Merton archives, he decided to write something new rather than try to "patch up"* What Is Contemplation? *"The Inner Experience" is that near book length study.*

In a codicil of his literary will it is stipulated that the complete manuscript that he finally did produce should not be published "as a book." The trustees of the Merton Literary Trust have honored that wish, but there is an edited version of the whole available in a series edited by Brother Patrick Hart, O.C.S.O. in Cistercian Studies *(vols. xviii and xix: nos. 1–4). The selections given below represent the first four parts of "The Inner Experience" as published in* Cistercian Studies.

"The Inner Experience" is an important transitional work of Merton as he struggles with a contemplative doctrine that still honors the Neo-Scholastic formulations of his day (largely described by Jacques Maritain and Reginald Garrigou-LaGrange, O.P.) while incorporating the insights he has gained from his readings in Eastern mystical literature. The impact on his own monastic formation is patent (with the emphasis on spiritual exegesis, the role of the liturgy, and the monastic theology of the Christian tradition), but it is clear that he is trying to restate contemplative themes for a contemporary audience. That he had not fully accomplished the task he set himself may explain his hesitancy about its publication as a finished work.

The best study of this work is in William H. Shannon's

Thomas Merton's Dark Path, *rev. ed. (New York: Farrar, Straus, & Giroux, 1987), pp. 72–141.*

*

I. NOTES ON CONTEMPLATION

The worst thing that can happen to a person who is already divided up into a dozen different compartments is to seal off yet another compartment and tell him that this one is more important than all the others, and that he must henceforth exercise a special care in keeping it separate from them. That is what tends to happen when contemplation is unwisely thrust without warning upon the bewilderment and distraction of Western man. The Eastern traditions have the advantage of disposing the person more naturally for contemplation.

The first thing that you have to do, before you start thinking about such a thing as contemplation, is to try to recover your basic natural unity, to reintegrate your compartmentalized being into a coordinated and simple whole, and learn to live as a unified human person. This means that you have to bring back together the fragments of your distracted existence so that when you say "I" there is really someone present to support the pronoun you have uttered.

Reflect, sometimes, on the disquieting fact that most of your statements of opinions, tastes, deeds, desires, hopes and fears are statements about someone who is not really present. When you say "I think" it is often not you who think, but "they"—it is the anonymous authority of the collectivity speaking through your mask. When you say "I want", you are sometimes simply making an automatic gesture of accepting, and paying for, what has been forced upon you. That is to say, you reach out for what you have been made to want.

Who is this "I" that you imagine yourself to be? An easy and pragmatic branch of psychological thought will tell you that if you can hook up your pronoun with your proper name, and declare that you are the bearer of that name, you know who you are. You are "aware of yourself as a person". Perhaps there is a beginning of truth in this: it is better to describe yourself with a name that is yours alone, than with a noun that applies to a whole species. For then you are evidently aware of yourself as an individual subject, and not just as an object, or as a nameless unit in a multitude. It is true that for modern man even to be able to call himself by his own proper name is an achievement that evokes wonder both in himself and in others. But this is only a beginning, and a beginning that primitive man would perhaps have been able to laugh at. For when a person appears to know his own name, it is still no guarantee that he is aware of the name as representing a real person. On the contrary, it may be the name of a fictitious character occupied in very active self-impersonation in the world of business, of politics, of scholarship or of religion.

This however is not the "I" who can stand in the presence of God and be aware of Him as a "Thou". For this "I" there is perhaps no clear "Thou" at all. Perhaps even other people are merely extensions of the "I", reflections of it, modifications of it, aspects of it. Perhaps for this "I" there is no clear distinction between itself and other objects: it may find itself immersed in the world of objects, and to have lost its own subjectivity, even though it may be very conscious and even aggressively definite in saying "I".

If such an "I" one day hears about "contemplation" he will perhaps set himself to "become a contemplative". That is, he will wish to admire, in himself, something called contemplation. And in order to see it, he will reflect on his alienated self. He will make contemplative faces at himself like a child in front of a mirror. He will cultivate the contemplative look that seems appropriate to him, and that he likes to see in himself. And the fact that his busy narcissism is turned within and feeds upon itself in stillness and secret love, will make him believe that his experience of himself is an experience of God.

But the exterior "I", the "I" of projects, of temporal finalities, the "I" that manipulates objects in order to take possession of them, is alien from the hidden, interior "I" who has no projects and seeks to accomplish nothing, even contemplation. He seeks only to be, and to move (for he is dynamic) according to the secret laws of Being itself, and according to the promptings of a Superior Freedom (that is, of God) rather than to plan and to achieve according to his own desires.

It will be ironical indeed if the exterior self seizes upon something within himself, and slyly manipulates it as if to take possession of some inner contemplative secret, imagining that this manipulation can somehow lead to the emergence of an inner self. The inner self is precisely that self which cannot be tricked or manipulated by anyone, even by the devil. He is like a very shy wild animal that never appears at all whenever an alien presence is at hand, and comes out only when all is perfectly peaceful, in silence, when he is untroubled and alone. He cannot be lured by anyone or anything, because he responds to no lure except that of the divine freedom.

Sad is the case of that exterior self that imagines himself contemplative, and seeks to achieve contemplation as the fruit of planned effort and of spiritual ambition. He will assume varied attitudes, and meditate on the inner significance of his own postures, and try to fabricate for himself a contemplative identity: and all the while there is nobody there. There is only an illusory, fictional "I" which seeks itself, struggles to create itself out of nothing, maintained in being by its own compulsion and is the prisoner of its private illusion.

The call to contemplation is not, and cannot be addressed to such an "I".

The Awakening of the Inner Self

From what has been said, it is clear that there is and can be no special planned technique for discovering and awakening one's inner self, because the inner self is first of all a spontaneity that is nothing if not free. Therefore there is no use in trying to start with a definition of the inner self, and then deducing from its essential properties some appropriate and infallible means of submitting it to control—as if the essence could give us some clue to that which is vulnerable in it, something we can lay hold of, in order to gain power over it. Such an idea would imply a complete misapprehension of the existential reality we are talking about. The inner self is not a part of our being, like a motor in a car. It is our entire substantial reality itself, on its highest and most personal and most existential level. It is like life, and it is life: it is our spiritual life when it is most alive. It is the life by which everything else in us lives and moves. It is in and through and beyond everything that we are. If it is awakened it communicates a new life to the intelligence in which it lives, so that it becomes a living awareness of itself: and this awareness is not so much something that we ourselves have, as something that we are. It is a new and indefinable quality of our living being.

The inner self is as secret as God and, like Him, it evades every concept that tries to seize hold of it with full possession. It is a life that cannot be held and studied as object, because it is not "a thing". It is not reached and coaxed forth from hiding by any process under the sun, including meditation. All that we can do with any spiritual discipline is produce within ourselves something of the silence, the humility, the detachment, the purity of heart and the indifference which are required if the inner self is to make some shy, unpredictable manifestation of his Presence.

At the same time, however, every deeply spiritual experience, whether religious, or moral, or even artistic, tends to have in it something of the presence of the interior self. Only from the inner self does any spiritual experience gain depth, reality and a certain incommunicability. But the depth of ordinary spiritual experience only gives us a derivative sense of the inner self. It reminds us of the forgotten levels of interiority in our spiritual nature, and of our helplessness to explore them.

Nevertheless a certain cultural and spiritual atmosphere favors the secret and spontaneous development of the inner self. The ancient cultural traditions, both of the East and of the West, having a religious and sapiential nature, favored the interior life and indeed transmitted certain common materials in the form of archetypal symbols, liturgical rites, art, poetry, philosophy and myth, which nourished the inner self from childhood to maturity. In such a cultural setting no one needs to be self-conscious about his interior life and subjectivity does not run the risk of being deviated into morbidity or excess. Unfortunately such a cultural setting no longer exists in the West, or is no longer common property. It is something that has to be laboriously recovered by an educated and enlightened minority.

The Example from Zen

Although we are mainly concerned with Christian mysticism, we might profitably pause to consider an example of inner awakening taken from an Oriental text. It is a cryptic and telling instance of interior self-realization, and the elements in the experience are so clearly set out that they provide an almost "clinically perfect" test case in the natural order. This is an account of *Satori,* a spiritual enlightenment, a bursting open of the inner core of the spirit to reveal the inmost self. This takes place in the peace of what we might ordinarily call contemplation, but it breaks through suddenly and by surprise, beyond the level of quiet contemplative absorption, showing that mere interior peace does not suffice to bring us in contact with our deepest liberty.

The thing that is most helpful about this example is that it makes no claims whatever to be supernatural or mystical. Zen is, in a sense, antimystical. Hence it permits us to observe the *natural* working of the inner self. In fact, the chief spokesman for Zen today, D. T. Suzuki, goes to some pains to contrast this spiritual event with Christian mystical experience, laying stress on its "natural" character as a "purely psychological" phenomenon. Hence no one will be offended if we presume to examine this as a psychological case, showing the workings of the inner self presumably without any influence of mystical grace.

Satori, which is the very heart and essence of Zen, is a revolutionary spiritual experience in which, after prolonged purification and trial, and of course after determined spiritual discipline, the monk experiences a kind of inner explosion that blasts his false exterior self to pieces and leaves nothing but "his original face", his "original self before you were born".

This was the experience of a Chinese official of the Sung Dynasty who was a lay-disciple of one of the Zen Masters. Chao-pien, the official, was sitting quietly in his office, at leisure, with his mind at rest in what we would call simple contemplative prayer. According to the Zen theory, he had reached that point of inner maturity where the secret pressure of the inner self was ready to break unexpectedly forth and revolutionize his whole being in *Satori.* When one reaches such a point, say the Zen Masters, any fortuitous sound, word or happening is likely to set off the explosion of "enlightenment" which consists in large part in the sudden, definitive, integral realization of the nothingness of the exterior self and, consequently, the liberation of the real self, the inner "I". Yet these are Western terms. The real self, in Zen language, is beyond the division between self and not-self. Chao-pien was sitting there at peace, when he heard a clap of thunder, and the "mind-doors burst open", in the depths of his silent being, to reveal his "original self", or "suchness". The whole incident is summarized, according to Chinese custom, in a four line poem, and it has rightly become immortal.

> Devoid of thought, I sat quietly by the desk in my official
>   room,
> With my fountain-mind undisturbed, as serene as water;
> A sudden crash of thunder, the mind doors burst open,
> And lo, there sits the old man in all his homeliness.

As an example of spiritual experience this is likely to perplex and even to scandalize those who expect all such things to be quite otherworldly and ethereal. But that is precisely what makes it incomparable for our purpose. Suzuki, incidentally, with his usual love of irony, capitalizes on the dry unsentimental humor of the experience to contrast it with the more affective flights of amorous mysticism with which we are familiar in the West. Unfortunately the lack of erotic or affective notes does not set this experience apart as distinctly "oriental" at all. In all spiritualities there is a contrast between the affective or devotional (*bakhti*) and the intellectual, anoetic type of experience (*raja yoga*). This story may have a distinctly Chinese flavor, but anyone familiar with the *Cloud of Unknowing* and other documents of Western apophatic mysticism will be perfectly at home with it.

And so Chao-pien finds himself with his false self blown to smithereens, and with the fragments carried away as though by a sudden, happy cyclone. There sits *Chao-pien* himself, the same and yet utterly different, for it is the eternal Chao-pien, one with no familiar name, at once humble and mighty, terrible and funny, and utterly beyond description or comparison because he is beyond yes and no, subject and object, self and not-self. It is like the wonderful, devastating and unutterable awe of humble joy with which a Christian realizes: "I and the Lord are One", and when, if one tries to explain this oneness in any way possible to human speech—for instance as the merging of two entities—one must always qualify: "No, not like that, not like that". That is why, of course, Suzuki wants to make quite plain that nothing is really said in this event about union with "Another". Well, all right. Let us assume it is perfectly natural. . . . In any case the event is full of significant elements, and throws much light on what I have been trying to explain.

First of all, even before his *satori* Chao-pien is in a condition of tranquil recollection. This placid unknowing is not yet awareness of the true inner self. But it is a natural climate in which the spiritual life may yield up its secret identity. Suddenly there is a clap of thunder and the "doors" of the inner consciousness fly open. The clap of thunder is just startling enough to create a sudden awareness, a self-realization in which the false, exterior self is caught in all its naked nothingness and immediately dispelled as an illusion. Not only does it vanish, but it is seen never to have been there at all—a pure fiction, a mere shadow of passionate attachment and of self-deception. Instead, the real self stands revealed in all his reality. The term "old man" must of course not be given Pauline connotations. In St Paul's language this would, on the contrary, be the "new man".

But why is this self described as "homely"? In some cases of *satori,* the inner self appears as wonderful or even terrifying, like a roaring lion with a golden mane. Such cases might find analogues in the poetry of William Blake. But here Chao-pien is happy with his "old man in all his homeliness" perhaps because he is thoroughly relieved to discover that the real self is utterly simple, humble, poor, and unassuming. The inner self is not an *ideal* self, especially not an imaginary, perfect creature fabricated to measure up to our compulsive need for greatness, heroism and infallibility. On the contrary the real "I" is just simply ourself and nothing more. Nothing more, nothing less. Our self as we are in the eyes of God, to use Christian terms. Our self in all our uniqueness, dignity, littleness and ineffable greatness: the greatness we have received from God our Father and that we share with Him because He is our Father, and "In Him we live and move and have our being". (Acts 17, 18)

The laconic little poem then expresses the full sense of liberation experienced by one who recognizes, with immense relief, that he is not his false self after all, and that he has all along been nothing else but his real and "homely" self, and nothing more, without glory, without self-aggrandizement, without self-righteousness, and without self-concern.

The Christian Approach

This discovery of the inner self plays a familiar part in Christian mysticism. But there is a significant difference, which is clearly brought out by St Augustine. In Zen there seems to be no effort to get beyond the inner self. In Christianity the inner self is simply a stepping stone to an awareness of God. Man is the image of God, and his inner self is a kind of mirror in which God not only sees Himself, but reveals Himself to the "mirror" in which He is reflected. Thus, through the dark, transparent mystery of our own inner being we can, as it were, see God "through a glass". All this is of course pure metaphor. It is a way of saying that our being somehow communicates directly with the Being of God, Who is "in us". If we enter into ourselves, find our true self, and then pass "beyond" the inner "I", we sail forth into the immense darkness in which we confront the "I AM" of the Almighty. The Zen writers might perhaps contend that they were interested exclusively in what is actually "given" in their experience, and that Christianity is superadding a theological interpretation and extrapolation on top of the experience itself. But here we come upon one of the distinctive features of Christian, Jewish and Islamic mysticisms. For us, there is an infinite metaphysical gulf between the being of God and the being of the soul, between the "I" of the Almighty and our own inner "I". Yet paradoxically our inmost "I" exists in God and God dwells in it. But it is nevertheless necessary to distinguish between the experience of one's own inmost being and the awareness that God has revealed Himself to us in and through our inner self. We must know that the mirror is distinct from the image reflected in it. The difference rests on theological *faith.*

Our awareness of our inner self can at least theoretically be the fruit of a purely natural and psychological purification. Our awareness of God is a supernatural participation in the light by which He reveals Himself interiorly as dwelling in our inmost self. Hence the Christian mystical experience is not only an awareness of the inner self, but also, by a supernatural intensification of faith, it is an experiential grasp of God as present within our inner self. In the interests of brevity, let us proceed without further explanation to a few classical texts, first from St. Augustine:

> Is God then anything of the same nature as the soul? This mind of ours seeks to find something that is God. It seeks to find a Truth not subject to change, a Substance not capable of failing. The mind itself is not of this nature: it is capable of progress and decay, of knowledge and of ignorance, of remembering or forgetting. That mutability is not incident to God.
>
> Having therefore sought to find my God in visible and corporeal things, and found Him not; having sought to find His substance in myself and found Him not, I perceive my God to be something higher than my soul. Therefore that I might attain to Him I thought on these things and poured out my soul above myself. When would my soul attain to that object of its search, which is "above my soul", if my soul were not to pour itself out above itself? For were it to rest in itself, it would not see anything else beyond itself, would not, for all that, see God . . . I have poured forth my soul above myself and there remains no longer any being for me to attain to save my God . . . His dwelling place is above my soul; from thence He beholds me, from thence He governs me and provides for me; from thence He appeals to me, calls me and directs me; leads me in the way and to the end of my way. (*Ennaratio in Psalmum 41*)
>
> And being by them (that is by the Platonists) admonished to return to myself, I entered even to my inmost self, Thou being my guide. I entered and beheld with the eye of the soul, above the same eye of my soul, above my mind, the Light unchangeable . . . And Thou didst beat back the weakness of my sight, streaming forth Thy beams of light

upon me most strongly, and I trembled with love and awe. (*Confessions vii,* 16)[1]

The intellectual and Platonizing speculations of St Augustine put us in a very different experiential climate from what we have just discussed in Zen, and it is therefore not easy to say where to place the "inmost self" of which Augustine speaks. There is always a possibility that what an Eastern mystic describes as Self is what the Western mystic will describe as God because we shall see presently that the mystical union between the soul and God renders them in some sense "undivided" (though metaphysically distinct) in spiritual experience. And the fact that the Eastern mystic, not conditioned by centuries of theological debate, may not be inclined to reflect on the fine points of metaphysical distinction, does not necessarily mean that he has not experienced the presence of God when he speaks of knowing the Inmost Self.

Let us turn to some texts of the Rhenish Dominican mystic, John Tauler. For him, the inner self, the inmost "I" is the "ground" or "center" or "apex" of the soul. Trained in the tradition of Augustine, Tauler is however more concrete and less speculative than his masters, except Eckhart, whose resemblances to Oriental mysticism are being fully studied today: here is Tauler in a passage that reminds one of Chao-pien's "fountain mind":

Now man with all his faculties and also with his soul recollects himself and enters into the temple (his inner self) in which, in all truth, he finds God dwelling and at work. Man then comes to experience God not after the fashion of the senses and of reason, or like something that one understands or reads . . . but he tastes Him, and enjoys Him like something that springs up from the "ground" of the soul as from its own source, or from a fountain, without having been brought there, for a fountain is better than a cistern, the water of cisterns gets stale and evaporates, but the spring flows, bursts out, swells: it

_____
1. Translations taken from *Western Mysticism,* by Dom Cuthbert Butler, pp. 22 and 31.

is true, not borrowed. It is sweet. (Sermon from Thursday before Palm Sunday.)

In another passage, Tauler speaks of the deep contact between the "ground" of the soul and God, following an interior upheaval and purification produced mystically by the action of God. While in the previous quotation there was a resemblance to the fountain in the Chinese text, here is a clap of "mystical thunder".

> After this, one should open the ground of the soul and the deep will to the sublimity of the glorious Godhead, and look upon Him with great and humble fear and denial of oneself. He who in this fashion casts down before God his shadowy and unhappy ignorance then begins to understand the words of Job who said: The spirit passed before me. From this passage of the Spirit is born a great tumult in the soul. And the more this passage has been clear, true, unmixed with natural impressions, all the more rapid, strong, prompt, true and pure will be the work which takes place in the soul, the thrust which overturns it; clearer also will be the knowledge that man has stopped on the path to perfection. The Lord then comes like a flash of lightning; he fills the ground of the soul with light and wills to establish Himself there as the Master Workman. As soon as one is conscious of the presence of the Master, one must, in all passivity, abandon the work to him. (II Sermon for the Exaltation of the Holy Cross, no. 5)

It is obvious that all metaphors are unsatisfactory in this delicate matter. Tauler's "ground" is effective insofar as it conveys the idea of that which is most fundamental in our being, as the rock on which everything else is built as on a foundation. But this is a spiritual "rock" which suddenly ceases to be a rock and becomes transparent and full of light: for it has at the same time the qualities of hardness and solidity, and yet also transparency and penetrability. It is as if it were both rock and air, earth and atmosphere. It can suddenly come alive from within, as with a flash of lightning! Of course the idea of ground also suggests soil from which things grow.

The language of mystics, in short, is always poetic, and claims plenty of license for paradox in dealing freely with symbols, sweeping them far outside the limits of their own capacity to convey a meaning.

According to the Christian mystical tradition, one cannot find one's inner center and know God there as long as one is involved in the preoccupations and desires of the outward self. Tauler, in the lines just quoted, suggests that even the depths of the soul can be troubled with what he calls "natural impressions", which are sense-bound and involved in temporal conflict. Penetration into the depths of our being is then a matter of liberation from the ordinary flow of conscious and half conscious sense impressions, but also and more definitely from the unconscious drives and the clamoring of inordinate passion. Freedom to enter the inner sanctuary of our being is denied to those who are held back by dependence on self-gratification and sense satisfaction, whether it be a matter of pleasure-seeking, love of comfort, or proneness to anger, self-assertion, pride, vanity, greed, and all the rest.

St John of the Cross seems to include all this freedom and more still under the one heading of "faith". Faith is indeed the "dark night" in which we meet God, according to St John of the Cross. "This dark and loving knowledge, which is faith, serves as a means of divine union in this life, even as in the next life the light of glory serves as an intermediary to the clear knowledge of God".[2] Faith in this sense is more than the assent to dogmatic truths proposed for belief by "the authority of God revealing". It is a personal and direct acceptance of God Himself, a "receiving" of the Light of Christ in the soul and a consequent beginning or renewal of spiritual life. But an essential element in this reception of the "light" of Christ is the *rejection* of every other "light" that can appeal to sense, passion, imagination or intellect.

Faith, for St John, is simultaneously a turning to God and a turning away from God's creatures—a blacking out of the visible in order to see the invisible. The two ideas are inseparable for him, and on their inseparability depend his inexorable logic and his pitiless asceticism. But it is important to remember that the mere blacking out of sensible things is not faith, and will not serve as a

---

2. *Ascent of Mount Carmel*, II, xxiv, 4.

means to bring faith into existence. It is the other way round. Faith is a light of such supreme brilliance that it dazzles the mind and darkens all its vision of other realities: but in the end, when we become used to the new light, we gain a new vision of all reality transfigured and elevated in the light itself. As the saint remarks:

> This excessive light of faith which is given to the soul is thick darkness, for it overwhelms that which is great and does away with that which is little, even as the light of the sun overwhelms all other lights whatsoever, so that when it shines and disables our vision they appear to be no lights at all.[3]

This, too, is of course metaphor. The "blindness" to exterior things is a question of interpretation and evaluation. The contemplative does not cease to *know* external objects. But he ceases to be *guided* by them. He ceases to depend on them. He ceases to treat them as ultimate. He evaluates them in a new way, in which they are no longer objects of desire or fear, but remain neutral and as it were empty until such time as they too become filled with the light of God.

During the "dark night" of faith, one must let himself be guided to reality not by visible and tangible things, not by the evidence of sense or the understanding of reason, not by concepts charged with natural hope, or joy, or fear, or desire, or grief, but by "dark faith" that transcends all desire and seeks no human earthly satisfaction, except what is willed by God or connected with His will. Short of this essential detachment, no one can hope to enter into his inmost depths and experience the awakening of that inner self that is the dwelling of God, His hiding place, His temple, His stronghold, and His image.

The one who wants to know how to find God within himself receives the following answer from St John of the Cross:

> Seek Him in faith and love, without desiring to find satisfaction in aught, or to taste and understand more than that which it is well for thee to know, for these two are the

---

3. *Ascent of Mount Carmel*, II, iii, 1.

guides of the blind which will lead thee, by a way that thou knowest not, to the hidden place of God. Because faith, which is the secret that we have mentioned, is like the feet wherewith the soul journeys to God, and love is the guide that directs it . . . Remain thou not therefore either partly or wholly in that which thy faculties can comprehend, I mean be thou never willingly satisfied with that which thou understandest of God, but rather with that which thou understandest not of Him; and do thou never rest in loving and having delight in that which thou understandest or feelest concerning God, but do thou love and have delight in that which thou canst not understand or feel concerning Him; for this, as we have said, is to seek Him in faith. Since God is unapproachable and hidden, . . . however much it seem to thee that thou findest and feelest and understandest Him, thou must ever hold Him as hidden and serve Him after a hidden manner, as one that is hidden.[4]

Yet at the end of this journey of faith and love which brings us into the depths of our own being and releases us that we may voyage beyond ourselves to God, the mystical life culminates in an experience of the presence of God that is beyond all description, and which is only possible because the soul has been completely "transformed in God" so as to become, so to speak "one spirit" with Him. St John of the Cross compares this revelation of God in the depths of our being to the "awakening" of the Word within us, a great stirring of supernatural and divine life, in which the Almighty One Who dwells in us is seen not as an inert "object" but is revealed in spirit and in power as the Ruler and Creator and Mover of all things. St John says:

Even so, when a palace (the center of the soul) is thrown open a man may see at one and the same time the eminence of the person who is within the palace, and also what he is doing. And it is this, as I understand it, that

---

4. *Spiritual Canticle*, I, ii, 12.

happens in this awakening and glance of the soul. Though the soul is substantially in God, as is every creature, He draws back from before it some of the veils and curtains which are in front of it, so that it may see of what nature He is: and then there is revealed to it, and it is able to see (though somewhat darkly since not all the veils are drawn back) that face of His which is full of grace. And since it is moving all things by its power, there appears together with it that which it is doing, and it appears to move in them, and they in it, with continual movement; and for this reason the soul believes that God has moved and awakened, whereas that which has moved and awakened is in reality itself.[5]

These are only a few characteristic texts in which Christian contemplatives have spoken of the awakening of the inner self and the consequent awareness of God. Since our inmost "I" is the perfect image of God, then when that "I" awakens, he finds within himself the Presence of Him Whose image he is. And, by a paradox beyond all human expression, God and the soul seem to have but one single "I". They are (by divine grace) as though one single person. They breathe and live and act as one. "Neither" of the "two" is seen as object.

To anyone who has full awareness of our "exile" from God, our alienation from this inmost self, and our blind wandering in the "region of unlikeness", this claim can hardly seem believable. Yet it is nothing else but the message of Christ calling us to awake from sleep, to return from exile, and find our true selves within ourselves, in that inner sanctuary which is His temple and His heaven, and (at the end of the prodigal's homecoming journey) the "Father's House".

II. SOCIETY AND THE INNER SELF

So far, many of the texts we have quoted on the interior self give the false impression that this inner and spiritual identity is

---

5. *The Living Flame*, IV, 7.

recovered merely by isolation and introversion. This is far from correct. The inner self is not merely what remains when we turn away from exterior reality. It is not mere emptiness, or unconsciousness. On the contrary, if we imagine that our inmost self is purely and simply something in us that is *completely out of contact* with the world of exterior objects we would condemn ourselves in advance to complete frustration in our quest for spiritual awareness. As a matter of fact, though a certain introversion and detachment are necessary in order to reestablish the proper conditions for the "awakening" of what is inmost in ourselves, the spiritual "I" obviously stands in a definite relationship to the world of objects. All the more is it related to the world of other personal "subjects". In seeking to awaken the inner self we must try to learn how this relationship is entirely new and how it gives us a completely different view of things.

Instead of seeing the external world in its bewildering complexity, separateness and multiplicity: instead of seeing objects as things to be manipulated for pleasure or profit: instead of placing ourselves over against objects in a posture of desire, defiance, suspicion, greed or fear, the inner self sees the world from a deeper and more spiritual viewpoint. In the language of Zen, it sees things "without affirmation or denial", that is to say, from a higher vantage point, which is intuitive and concrete and which has no need to manipulate or distort reality by means of slanted concepts and judgments. It simply "sees" what it sees, and does not take refuge behind a screen of conceptual prejudices and verbalistic distortions. Example: the difference between a child's vision of a tree, which is utterly simple, uncolored by prejudice, and "new"—and the lumberman's vision, entirely conditioned by profit motives and considerations of business. The lumberman is no doubt aware that the tree is beautiful, but this is a purely platonic and transient consideration compared with his habitual awareness that it can be reduced to a certain number of board feet at so much per foot. In this case, something is definitely "affirmed" which adds to and modifies one's vision of "a tree", or a forest.

One of the Fathers of the Oriental Church, Philoxenus of Mabbugh, has an original and rather subtle view of original sin as a perversion of faith, in which a false belief was superadded to the "simple" and unspoiled view of truth, so that direct knowledge became distorted by a false affirmation and negation. It is curious to realize that those who most deride religious faith are precisely the ones who interpose between themselves and reality a screen of beliefs based on an illusion of self-interest and of passionate attachment. The fact that these beliefs seem, pragmatically, to "work" is all the more fatal a deception. What, in fact, is the fruit of their working? Largely a perversion of the objects manipulated by the exterior man, and the even greater perversion of man himself. Such belief springs from, and increases, man's inner alienation.

In any case, the idea of Philoxenus presents a striking affinity with the epistemological bases of Zen Buddhism, which seeks above all to clear away the clouds of self-deception which we cast over external reality when we set ourselves to thinking about it. Zen seeks the direct, immediate view in which the experience of a subject-object duality is destroyed. That is why Zen resolutely refuses to answer clearly, or abstractly, or dogmatically any religious or philosophical question whatever. Here is a typical example of one of those question-and-answer illustrations of Zen in which the masters deliberately frustrated all attempts of their disciples to slip an abstract doctrine in between the mind and the "this" which was right before their nose.

> Someone asked Yakusan, who was sitting in meditation:
>   "What are you doing here?"
> He replied, "I am not doing anything".
>   "If so you are sitting in idleness".
>   "Sitting in idleness is doing something".
>   "You say you are not doing anything, but what is this 'anything' that you are not doing?"
>   "Even the ancient sages know not", replied Yakusan.
>   (Suzuki, *Studies in Zen,* p. 59)

And when disciples asked the Zen masters "What is the meaning of Zen?", hoping for a doctrinal exposition, they would get in reply, "How do I know?" or "Ask the post over there" or "Zen is that cypress tree in the courtyard!"

It is at once apparent that the exterior man tends to look at things from an economic or technical or hedonistic viewpoint which, in spite of all its pragmatic advantages, certainly removes the seer from direct contact with the reality which he sees. And this exaggeration of the subject-object relationship by material interest or technical speculation is one of the main obstacles to contemplation, except of course in such notably exceptional cases as the intuitive and synthetic view which crowns and sums up the researches of an Einstein, or of a Heisenberg. Einstein's view of the universe is one of the most notable "contemplative" achievements of our century, though in a special and limited sense of the word contemplation. And here of course the vision was chiefly speculative rather than technological. And yet the atomic bomb owes its origin, in part, to such "contemplatives"!

Nor must we imagine that the inner vision is arrived at purely as the result of individual self-affirmation, in opposition to one's awareness of oneself as a member of a group, or of mankind at large. Here again, the distinction is a matter of perspective. The discovery of our inner self is not arrived at merely by reflection on the fact that we "are not" any of "the others". This may be a part of it, no doubt, but it is not even the most essential part of the awareness. On the contrary, it is probably safe to say that no man could arrive at a genuine inner self-realization unless he had first become aware of himself as a member of a group—as an "I" confronted with a "Thou" who completes and fulfils his own being. In other words, the inner self sees the other not as a limitation upon itself, but as its complement, its "other self", and is even in a certain sense identified with that other, so that the two "are one". This unity in love is one of the most characteristic works of the inner self, so that paradoxically the inner "I" is not only isolated but at the same time united with others on a higher plane, which is in fact the plane of spiritual solitude. Here again, the level of "affirmation and negation" is transcended by spiritual awareness which is the work of love. And this is one of the most characteristic features of Christian contemplative awareness. The Christian is not merely "alone with the Alone" in the neo-platonic sense, but he is One with all his "brothers in Christ." His inner self is, in fact, inseparable from Christ and hence it is in a mysterious and unique way inseparable from all the other "I"s who live in Christ, so that they all form one "mystical Person", which is "Christ."

> That they all may be one as Thou Father in me and I in Thee, that they also may be one in us: that the world may believe that Thou hast sent me . . . I in them and Thou in me, that they may be made perfect in one . . . (John 17)

For this reason it is clear that Christian self-realization can never be a merely individualistic affirmation of one's isolated personality. The inner "I" is certainly the sanctuary of our most personal and individual solitude, and yet paradoxically it is precisely that which is most solitary and personal in ourselves which is united with the "Thou" who confronts us. We are not capable of union with one another on the deepest level until the inner self in each one of us is sufficiently awakened to confront the inmost spirit of the other. This mutual recognition is love "in the Spirit", and is effected, indeed, by the Holy Spirit. According to St Paul, the inmost self of each one of us is our "spirit", or "pneuma", or in other words the Spirit of Christ, indeed Christ Himself, dwelling in us. "For me to live is Christ". And by the spiritual recognition of Christ in our brother, we become "one in Christ" through the "Bond of the Spirit". According to the mysterious phrase of St Augustine, we then become "One Christ loving Himself".

In the same exegesis of Psalm 41 in which we have seen St Augustine, above, speaking of the awakening of the inner self and the realization that God is to be found "above" that self, we also discover this affirmation that God is to be found "through" and "above" the spiritual "self" of the faithful who are united in Him by charity. All these points must be carefully noted if we are not to be misled. First, Augustine nowhere says that God is to be found simply in the collectivity as such. Second, there is question of something more than a merely exterior and juridical society: rather the mystical Christ is a spiritual body or organism, whose life is charity. And by the power of this charity one is raised above and beyond the collective self of the faithful, to God who dwells in and above them all.

How much is there I admire in this tabernacle (the Church):—the self-conquest and the virtues of God's servants. I admire the presence of those virtues in the soul . . . (But he passes beyond the *tabernacle,* to the *House of God,* that is from God dwelling in the saints to God in Himself). And when I come to the House of God I am even struck dumb with astonishment. It is there, in the sanctuary of God, the House of God, is the fountain of understanding. It was going up to the tabernacle that the Psalmist arrived at the house of God: by following the leadings of a certain delight, an inward mysterious and hidden pleasure, as if from the house of God there sounded sweetly some instrument; and he, whilst walking in the tabernacle, hearing a certain inward sound, led on by its sweetness and following the guidance of the sound, withdrawing himself from all noise of flesh and blood, made his way on even to the house of God. (Translation from Butler, *op. cit.* p. 23)

Here it is quite clear that charity, which is the life and the awakening of the inner self, is in fact to a great extent awakened by the presence and the spiritual influence of other selves that are "in Christ". St Augustine speaks of recognizing the inner self of other Christians through the virtuous actions which give evidence of the "Spirit" dwelling in them. It can be said that Christian "edification" is this mutual recognition of the inner spirit in one another, a recognition which is a manifestation of the Mystery of Christ.

In a word, the awakening of the inner self is purely the work of love, and there can be no love where there is not "another" to love. Furthermore, one does not awaken his inmost "I" merely by loving God alone, but by loving other men. Yet here again, as in the case of the inner awareness of contemplation described in the earlier passage, the necessary movement of transcendence must come and lift the spirit "above flesh and blood".

A love that is "above flesh and blood" is not something pale and without passion, but a love in which passion has been elevated and purified by selflessness, so that it no longer follows the inspiration of mere natural instinct. This love is guided by the Spirit of Christ and seeks the good of the other rather than our own momentary interest or pleasure. More, even beyond all opposition between the profit of another and our own profit, it rests in love for love's own sake, and attains, in Christ, to the truth not insofar as it is desirable but above all insofar as it is true, and good in itself. This is at the same time our own highest good and the good of the other, and in such love as this, "all are One".

It would obviously be fatal to seek an inner awakening and self-realization purely and simply by withdrawal. Though a certain movement of withdrawal is necessary if we are to attain the perspective that solitude alone can open up to us, nevertheless this separation is in the interests of a higher union in which our solitude is not lost but perfected, because on this higher level there is no longer question of a love that can be manipulated or brought into subjection by flattery and base motives. Solitude is necessary for spiritual freedom. But once that freedom is acquired, it demands to be put to work in the service of a love in which there is no longer subjection or slavery. Mere withdrawal, without the return to freedom in action, would lead to a static and death-like inertia of the spirit in which the inner self would not awaken at all. There would be no light, no voice within us, only the silence and darkness of the tomb.

In contrast to the paradoxical recovery of unity in and beyond our own inner and solitary "I", is the false withdrawal of the exterior self within its own depths, a withdrawal which imprisons instead of liberating, and which makes impossible all real contact with the inner self of another.

When I speak of the "exterior self" having "depths" of its own, I am perhaps pressing and complicating my metaphor beyond due limits. But I mean to make clear the fact that those recesses of the unconscious in which neurotic and psychotic derangement have their center, belong in reality to man's exterior self: because the exterior self is not limited to consciousness. Freud's concept of the super-ego, as an infantile and introjected substitute for conscience fits very well my idea of the exterior and alienated self. It is at once completely exterior and yet at the same time buried in unconsciousness. So too with the Freudian concept of the "id", in so far as it represents an automatic complex of drives toward pleasure or destruction, in response to external stimuli.

I think this can go far to explain false mysticism and pseudo-religiosity. These are manifestations of a fake interiorization by which, instead of plunging into the depths of one's true freedom and spirituality one simply withdraws into the darker subterranean levels of the exterior self which remains alienated and subject to powers from the outside. The relation between this false inner self and external reality is entirely colored and perverted by a heavy and quasi-magical compulsivity. Instead of the freedom and spontaneity of an inner self that is entirely unpreoccupied with itself and goes forth to meet the other lightly and trustfully, without afterthought of self-concern, we have here the ponderous and obsessive delusion of the paranoid who lays claim to "magical" insight into others, and interprets the portentous "signs" he sees in external reality in favor of his own distended fears, lusts and appetites for power. True Christian charity is stifled in such an atmosphere and contemplation has no place in it. All is heavy, thick, biased, and dark with obsession, even though it lays claim to blinding and supernatural lights. It is a realm of dangerous appetites for command, of false visions and apocalyptic threats, of spiritual sensuality and of a mysticism charged with undertones of sex-perversion.

Just as all sane men instinctively seek, in some way or other, the awakening of their true inner self, so all valid social forms of religion attempt, in some manner, to provide a situation in which each member of the worshipping group can rise above the group and above himself, to find himself and all the rest on a higher level. This implies that all truly serious and spiritual forms of religion aspire at least implicitly to a contemplative awakening both of the individual and of the group. But those forms of religious and liturgical worship which have lost their initial impulse of fervor tend more and more to forget their contemplative purpose, and to attach exclusive importance to rites and forms for their own sake, or for the sake of the effect which they are believed to exercise on the One Who is worshipped.

The highest form of religious worship finds its issue and fulfillment in contemplative awakening and in transcendent spiritual peace—in the quasi experiential union of its members with God, beyond sense and beyond ecstasy. The lowest form is fulfilled in a numinous and magic sense of power which has been "produced" by rites and which gives one momentarily the chance to wring a magical effect from the placated deity. In between these two extremes are various levels of ecstasy, exaltation, ethical self-fulfilment, juridical righteousness and aesthetic intuition. In all these various ways, religion primitive and sophisticated, crude and pure, active and contemplative, seeks to attain to the inner awakening, or at least to produce an apparently satisfactory substitute for it.

But it is evident from what has been said above that few religions ever really penetrate to the inmost soul of the believer, and even the highest of them do not, in their social and liturgical forms invariably reach the inmost "I" of each participant. The common level of inferior religion is situated somewhere in the collective subconscious of the worshippers, and perhaps more often than not in a *collective exterior self.* This is certainly a verifiable fact in modern totalitarian pseudo-religions of state and class. And this is one of the most dangerous features of our modern barbarism: the invasion of the world by a barbarity from within society and within man himself. Or rather, the reduction of man, in technological society, to a level of almost pure alienation in which he can be brought, at will, any time, to a kind of political ecstasy, carried away by the hate, the fear and the crude aspirations centered about a leader, a propaganda slogan or a political symbol. That this sort of ecstasy is to some extent "satisfactory" and produces a kind of pseudo-spiritual catharsis, or at least a release of tension, is unfortunately all too often verified. And it is what modern man is coming more and more to accept as an ersatz for genuine religious fulfilment, for moral activity and for contemplation itself. It is becoming more and more common for the innate aspiration which all men, as images of God, share for the recovery of their inmost self, to be perverted and satisfied by the mere parody of religious mystery, and the evocation of a collective shadow of a "self". The mere fact that the discovery of this ersatz interiority is unconscious seems to be sufficient to make it acceptable. It "feels like" spontaneity, and above all there is the meretricious assurance of greatness and infallibility, and the sweet loss of personal responsibility which one enjoys by abandoning himself to a collective mood, no matter how murderous or how vile it may be in itself. This would seem to be in all technical reality what the New Testament speaks of as Antichrist—that pseudo-Christ in which all real selves are lost and everything is enslaved to a pale, ferocious *imago* inhabiting the maddened group.

It is important at all times to keep clear the distinction between true and false religion, true and false interiority, holiness and possession, love and frenzy, contemplation and magic. In every case, there is an aspiration toward inner awakening, and the same means, good or indifferent in themselves, may be used for good or evil, health or sickness, freedom or obsession.

Symbolism plays a constant and universal part in all religious activity oriented toward some inner awakening. The awakening itself is signified, or myths which express it are represented, in art, rites, sacred gesture, dance, music. Hieratic songs and prayers surround the central act of sacrifice, itself usually deeply symbolic. Higher forms of religion embody the awakening and the union of the spirit with God in a "mystery" where the ritual enactment of a myth serves as "initiation" to a spiritual life, or a consummation in union with the god.

But only in the highest and most spiritual worship does the real connection between exterior rite and inner awakening remain definite and clear. As religion loses its fervor and becomes stereotyped, the worshipper lives and moves on a level where faith is too weak and too diffuse to lead to any inner awakening. Instead of appealing to the inmost self, religion that has thus grown tired is content to stir up the unconscious emotions of the exterior self. In this case there is not a real inner awakening, and the reassurance conceived in ritual worship is no longer spiritual, personal, and free.

The Old Testament prophets inveighed against this more or less exterior worship, which activated the lips but not the heart, and Christ Himself rebuked it in the Pharisees. All genuine revivals of religious fervor aim, in one way or another, at restoring the deeply interior orientation of religious activity, and attempt a renewal and purification of the interior life generated by symbolic rites, mysteries and prayers. It is a question of getting rid of mechanical and compulsive formalism and awakening the inner, spontaneous fervor of "the heart". Generally speaking, the "heart" is used as a more or less adequate symbol of the inner self, though in the Old Testament other physical organs are substituted for it indifferently, for instance the viscera and the "reins". Unfortunately this haphazard use of a physical symbol, to localize the source of religious spontaneity, is no guarantee against emotional, sentimental, erotic and even bacchanalian substitutes for the awakening of the inner self.

As worship degenerates, there is an ever increasing tendency to make use of stimulating agencies to break down the inhibitions generated by routine and restore a semblance of life and power to the symbolic rites. Hence the use of alcohol and of drugs to obtain a spiritual release. But the "inner self" thus released is not necessarily the "I" but rather more usually the subconscious libido held in check automatically by conscience, habit, convention, taboo or magical fear. The release thus achieved is material rather than spiritual, and its effect is an explosion of psychic energy which may be salutary or noxious, painful or happy according to circumstance.

Here too we may remark on the gradual, progressive degeneration and brutalizing of symbols that lose their religious "kick". Study of the religions of Mexico suggests a development that began with a highly spiritualized and refined worship, with cosmic contemplative possibilities and sacrifices of fruits of the earth, and developed bit by bit into the bloodthirsty warrior cult of the Aztecs, centered on war and on human sacrifice. The Aztec sacrifice of the human heart to the sun suggests a kind of frightful parody of the pure and spiritual manifestation of the "inmost self". Here, instead of a man offering to God the "sacrifice" of his exterior self, by self-forgetfulness and love, in order to release and manifest before the face of God the hidden face of his interior soul, a victim is seized by the hieratic representative of collective ferocity, and his heart, cut out with an obsidian knife, is held up bleeding to satisfy the hunger of the sun! This example offers us much food for meditation today as we fall back into collective barbarism in which the individual and his freedom once again lose their meaning and each man is only an expendable unit ready to be immolated to the political idols on which the prosperity and power of the collectivity seem to depend.

Nevertheless it is clear that such examples must not be used to justify rash generalizations about primitive and "pagan" religion. Everywhere, in all kinds of religion, we find the high and the low, the spiritual and the gross, the beautiful and the obscene. If on the one hand there are Bacchic orgies of drunken women, and if temple prostitution substitutes, in certain fertility cults, for the discovery of our own intimate contemplative secret, on the other hand there are pure and sublime mysteries and, especially in the Far East, utterly sophisticated and refined forms of spiritual contemplation. The religion of Abraham indeed was primitive, and it hovered, for a terrible moment, over the abyss of human sacrifice. Yet Abraham walked with God in simplicity and peace and the example of his faith (precisely in the case of Isaac) furnished material for the meditations of the most sophisticated religious thinker of the last century, the Father of Existentialism, Soren Kierkegaard.

Among the Sioux Indians, together with a very rich and varied liturgical life, we find the curiously moving individual and contemplative mystery of "crying for a vision". In this, a young man, following no communal prejudice but only personal and spontaneous inspiration, is prepared by prayers and ceremonies and then goes off to spend several days in prayer and solitude on a mountain, seeking an "answer" from the Great Spirit. It is recorded that deep and genuine examples of inner awakening and even of (natural) quasi-prophetic vocations have been granted to Indians in this primitive spiritual exercise.

It is well known that in the Orient, in China, India, Japan, Indonesia, the religious and contemplative life has been fostered for centuries and has known a development of unparalleled richness. Asia has for centuries been a continent of great monastic communities. At the same time the solitary life has flourished, either in the shadow of the monasteries or in the wilderness of jungle, mountain or desert. Hindu Yoga, in its various forms, has become almost legendary of eastern contemplation. Yoga makes use of a variety of disciplines and ascetic techniques for the "liberation" of man's spirit from the limitations imposed upon him by material, bodily existence. Everywhere in the East, whether in Hinduism or Buddhism, we find that deep, unutterable thirst for the rivers of Paradise. Whatever may be the philosophies and theologies behind these forms of contemplative existence, the striving is always the same: the quest for unity, a return to the inmost self united with the Absolute, a quest for Him Who is above all, and in all, and Who Alone is Alone. Nor is it correct to accuse the oriental mystic of selfishness, as is too frequently done. He too seeks, in his own way, the redemption of all living beings. He too, like St Paul, is well aware of the fact that:

> The expectation of the creature waiteth for the revelation of the sons of God, for the creature was made subject to vanity . . . But the creature also itself shall be delivered from the servitude of corruption, into the liberty of the glory of the children of God (Romans 8:19–21).

Note the analogies between Paul's term "servitude of corruption" and the Hindu concept of *Karma.*

There are other facile generalizations about Hindu religion current in the West, which it would be well to take with extreme reserve: for instance the statement that for the Hindu there is no "personal God". On the contrary, the mysticism of Bakhti Yoga is a mysticism of affective devotion and of ecstatic union with God under the most personal and human forms, sometimes very reminiscent of the "bridal mysticism" of so many western mystics. And it must be said that it is generally neither fair nor enlightening to criticize this or any other form of Yoga purely on a basis of a western and especially an Aristotelian metaphysic since there is perhaps very little common ground between them. This does not mean that the differences between Hinduism and Christianity are of no significance and can be waved aside without further concern, but only that they are difficult to understand and to explain correctly and that the ground for such an explanation has perhaps not yet been fully prepared.

It is certain that the *Bhagavad-Gita* is just as much entitled to a place in a College Course on humanities as Plato or Homer, and it is a wonder that the lofty religious literature of the East has not been numbered among the "Great Books" which now form the basis of a liberal education at least in America. The *Gita,* an ancient Sanskrit philosophical poem, preaches a contemplative way of serenity, detachment, personal devotion to God under the form of the Lord Krishna, and expressed most of all in detached activity—work done without concern for results but with the pure intention of fulfilling the will of God. It is a doctrine of pure love resembling in many points that preached by St Bernard, Tauler, Fenelon and many other Western mystics. It implies detachment even from the joys of contemplation, as from all earthly and temporal achievements. What we have to say later about "masked contemplation" may perhaps be something like the doctrine of contemplation-hidden-in-action which seems to be the very heart of the *Bhagavad Gita.* The contemplative recognition of the inmost self or rather peace in the "unknowing" which emanates from the inmost self, is what the Gita knows as *Yoga:*

> See!
> Steadfast a lamp burns sheltered from the wind;
> Such is the likeness of the Yogi's mind
> Shut from sense storms and burning bright to heaven.
> When the mind broods placid, soothed with holy wont,
> When Self contemplates self, and in itself
> Hath comfort; when it knows the nameless joy
> Beyond all scope of sense, revealed to soul—
> Only to soul, and knowing wavers not
> True to the farther Truth. . . .
>   . . . . Call that state "peace"
> That happy severance "yoga".
>   (Bk. vi, translation of Sir Edward Arnold)

We are in a position, I think, to interpret this text correctly when we reflect that the Yogi is not an exterior self mirrored in his own ego, but one who has found that inner self in whom God Himself dwells and is manifest. The verses can easily be harmonised with St Augustine, due allowance being made for divergences in ontological theory.

This passage of the *Gita* is one which reminds us of Patanjali, the greatest Yogi, whose *Raja Yoga* is the Indian opposite number of the apophatic mysticism of the West, represented by St Gregory of Nyssa, Pseudo-Dionysius and St John of the Cross. The object of *Raja Yoga* is to attain, by control of the thoughts, first to a state of higher spiritual consciousness (*purusha*) and beyond that to *samadhi* (meditation without further "seed" of conceptual thought). Later in this book when we speak of "active contemplation" we refer to something akin to *purusha,* and to what the Greek Fathers called *theoria physica.* And when we speak of infused contemplation we refer to a more supernatural form of *samadhi* which the Greek Fathers called *theologia,* mystical theology or pure contemplation beyond all thought.

In Asia, contemplation has not generally been regarded as an aristocratic privilege. On the contrary, it used to be common for ordinary married people in India to separate, in advancing age, and live in solitary contemplation to prepare for the end of this life. And it is well known that Asia has long been the most thriving home of monastic vocations. Indeed, in Asia it can be said, perhaps not without cause in many cases, that monasticism has become so familiar as to breed contempt.

It may be remarked in parentheses that theologians generally regard the spiritual experiences of oriental religion as occurring on the natural rather than on the supernatural level. However, they have often admitted, with Jacques Maritain and Fr Garrigou-Lagrange, that truly supernatural and mystical contemplation is certainly possible outside the visible church, since God is the master of His gifts and wherever there is sincerity and an earnest desire for truth, He will not deny the gifts of His grace. As we grow in knowledge and appreciation of oriental religion we will come to realize the depth and richness of its varied forms of contemplation. Up to the present, our judgments have been too vague and too undocumented, and have borne witness chiefly to our own ignorance. However, this statement is not intended as an encouragement to the foolish and equally ignorant infatuation with oriental cults which tends to be fashionable in certain circles today.

In Classical Greece, contemplation was definitely aristocratic and intellectual. It was the privilege of a philosophical minority, for whom it was a matter of study and reflection rather than of prayer. But the Classical Greek idea of contemplation, for all its beauty, is one-sided and incomplete. The contemplative, (*theoretikos*), is a man of leisure who devotes himself to study and reasoned reflection in the quest of pure truth. The contemplative life is a life of intellectual speculation, and perhaps of debate. It is the life of the Academy, the University. The contemplative is the professional philosopher. But in such a concept, the essentially religious aspect of contemplation tends to get lost. Furthermore, here the "erotic" desire for contemplation of truth as a "highest good" that can give man "perfect happiness" tends to become too hedonistic and therefore to defeat its own ends. We have seen in the first pages of this essay that a hedonistic quest for contemplation is doomed to frustration.

The Christian contemplative tradition owes much, however, to Classical Greece. The Christian Platonists of Alexandria (especially Origen and Clement) adopted something of the intellectual hedonism of Plato, and as a result we still tend to think of the contemplative life, unconsciously, as one of ease, aestheticism, and speculation.

The great practitioners of contemplation who were the Desert Fathers of Egypt and the Near East, did their best to dispel the illusion. They went into the desert not to seek pure spiritual beauty or an intellectual light, but to see the Face of God. And they knew that before they could see His Face, they would have to struggle, instead, with His adversary. They would have to cast out the devil subtly lodged in their exterior self. They went into the Desert not to study speculative truth but to wrestle with practical evil: not to perfect their analytical intelligence but to purify their hearts. They went into solitude not to *get* something, but in order to *give themselves,* for "He that would save his life must lose it, and he that will lose his life for the sake of Christ, shall save it". By their renunciation of passion and attachment, their crucifixion of the exterior self, they liberated the inner man, the new man "in Christ".

The fact that "contemplation" (*theoria*) is not mentioned in the New Testament should not mislead us. We shall see presently that the teaching of Christ is essentially "contemplative" in a much higher, more practical and less esoteric sense than Plato's.

In the Christian tradition, as we have already observed, contemplation is simply the "experience" (or better, the quasi-experiential knowledge) of God in a luminous darkness which is the perfection of faith illuminating our inmost self. It is the "meeting" of the spirit with God in a communion of love and understanding which is a gift of the Holy Spirit and a penetration into the mystery of Christ. The word "contemplation" suggests lingering enjoyment, timelessness, and a kind of suave passivity. All these elements are there, but they smack rather of pagan *theoria*. The important thing in contemplation is not enjoyment, not pleasure, not happiness, not peace, but the transcendent experience of reality and truth in the act of a supreme and liberated spiritual love. The important thing in contemplation is not gratification and rest but awareness, life, creativity and freedom. In fact, contemplation is man's highest and most essential spiritual activity. It is his most creative and dynamic affirmation of his divine sonship. It is not just the sleepy, suave, restful embrace of "being" in a dark, generalized contentment: it is a flash of the lightning of divinity piercing the darkness of nothingness and sin. Not something general and abstract, but something on the contrary as concrete, particular and "existential" as it can possibly be. It is the confrontation of man with his God, of the Son with his Father. It is the awakening of Christ within us, the establishment of the Kingdom of God in our own soul, the triumph of the Truth and of Divine Freedom in the inmost "I" in which the Father becomes one with the Son in the Spirit who is given to the believer.

III. CHRISTIAN CONTEMPLATION

The story of Adam's fall from Paradise says, in symbolic terms, that man was created as a contemplative. The fall from Paradise was a fall from unity. The Platonizing Greek Fathers even taught that the division of humanity into two sexes was a result of the Fall. St Augustine, in a more cautious and psychological application of the narrative, says that in the Fall Adam, man's interior and spiritual self, his contemplative self, was led astray by Eve, his exterior, material and practical self, his active self. Man fell from the unity of contemplative vision into the multiplicity, complication and distraction of an active, worldly existence.

Since he was now dependent entirely on exterior and contingent things, he became an exile in a world of objects, each one capable of deluding and enslaving him. Centered no longer in God and in his inmost, spiritual self, man now had to *see* and *be aware* of himself as if he were his own god. He had to study himself as a kind of pseudo-object, from which he was estranged. And to compensate for the labors and frustrations of this estrangement, he must try to admire, assert and gratify himself at the expense of others like himself. Hence the complex and painful network of loves and hatreds, desires and fears, lies and excuses in which we are all held captive. In such a condition, man's mind is enslaved by an inexorable concern with all that is exterior, transient, illusory and trivial. And carried away by his pursuit of alien shadows and forms, he can no longer see his own true inner "face", or recognize his identity in the spirit and in God, for that identity is secret, invisible, and incommunicable. But man has lost the courage and the faith without which he cannot be content to be "unseen". He is pitifully dependent on self-observation and self-assertion. That is to say, he is utterly exiled from God and from his own true self, for neither in God nor in our inmost self can there be any aggressive self-assertion: there is only the plain presence of love and of truth.

So man is exiled from God and from his inmost self. He is tempted to seek God, and happiness, outside himself. So his quest for happiness becomes, in fact, a flight from God and from himself: a flight that takes him further and further away from reality. In the end, he has to dwell in the "region of unlikeness"—having lost his inner resemblance to God in losing his freedom to enter his own home, which is the sanctuary of God.

But man must return to Paradise. He must recover himself, salvage his dignity, recollect his lost wits, return to his true identity. There is only one way in which this could be done, says the Gospel of Christ. God Himself must come, like the woman in the parable seeking the lost groat. God Himself must become Man, in order that in the Man-God, man might be able to lose himself as man and find himself as God. God Himself must die on the Cross, leaving man a pattern and a proof of His infinite love. And man, communing with God in the death and resurrection of Christ, must die the spiritual death in which his exterior self is destroyed and his inner self rises from death by faith and lives again "unto God". He must taste eternal life, which is "to know the Father, the one true God, and Jesus Christ whom He has sent".

The Christian life is a return to the Father, the Source, the Ground of all existence, through the Son, the Splendor and the Image of the Father, in the Holy Spirit, the Love of the Father and the Son. And this return is only possible by detachment and "death" in the exterior self, so that the inner self, purified and renewed, can fulfil its function as image of the Divine Trinity.

Christianity is life and wisdom in Christ. It is a return to the Father in Christ. It is a return to the infinite abyss of pure reality in which our own reality is grounded, and in which we exist. It is a return to the source of all meaning and all truth. It is a return to the inmost springs of life and joy. It is a rediscovery of paradise within our own spirit, by self-forgetfulness. And, because of our oneness with Christ, it is the recognition of ourselves as sons of the Father. It is the recognition of ourselves as other Christs. It is the awareness of strength and love imparted to us by the miraculous presence of the Nameless and Hidden One Whom we call the Holy Spirit.

(The Father is a Holy Spirit, but He is named Father. The Son is a Holy Spirit, but He is named Son. The Holy Spirit has a Name which is known only to the Father and the Son. But can it be that when He takes us to Himself, and unites us to the Father through the Son, He takes upon Himself, in us, our own secret name? Is it possible that His ineffable Name becomes our own? Is it possible that we can come to know, for ourselves, the Name of the Holy Spirit when we receive from Him the revelation of our own identity in Him? I can ask these questions, but not answer them.)

1. Contemplation and Theology

Most non-Christians, and probably also many Protestant Christians, probably suppose that the intense preoccupation of the early Church Fathers with the technical details of the dogma of the Incarnation was a matter of arbitrary and subjective wilfulness, and that it had little objective importance. But as a matter of fact, the intricacies of Christology and of the dogma of the hypostatic union were by no means a mere authoritarian web devised to capture the minds and to keep in subjection the wills of the faithful, as rationalism glibly used to declare. Both the theologian and the ordinary believer, in the Patristic age, realized the importance of the correct theological formulation of the mystery of the Incarnation because dogmatic error would in fact imply disastrous practical consequences in the spiritual life of each individual Christian.

One of the main reasons why St Athanasius so stubbornly defended the divinity of Christ against the Arians, who at one time outnumbered the orthodox Christians by a vast majority, was that he saw that if Christ were not God, then it followed that the Christian hope for union with God in and through Christ was a delusion. Everything, as St Paul himself had declared equivalently, depended on faith in Christ as the true Son of God, the Word Incarnate. "For if Christ be not risen again then our preaching is vain, and your faith also is vain. Yea and also we are found false witnesses of God, because we have given testimony against God". (I Corinthians 15:14–15)

It may perhaps not be clear at first sight what this belief in the Resurrection might have to do with contemplation. But in fact the Resurrection and Ascension of Christ, the New Adam, completely restored human nature to its spiritual condition and made possible the divinization of every man coming into the world. This meant that in each one of us the inner self was now able to be awakened and transformed by the action of the Holy Spirit, and this awakening would not only enable us to discover our true identity "in Christ" but would also make the living and Risen Savior present in us. Hence the importance of the Divinity of Christ—for it is as God-Man that He is risen from the dead and as God-Man that He is capable of living and acting in us all by His Spirit, so that in Him we are not only our true personal selves but are also one Mystical Person, one Christ. And thus each one of us is endowed with the creative liberty of the Son of God. Each one of us, in some sense, is able to be completely transformed into the likeness of Christ, to become, as He is, divinely human, and thus to share His spiritual authority and charismatic power in the world.

It is significant that among the minority of Christians who stood with Athanasius, the contemplative Desert Fathers formed a solid and unyielding phalanx of believers in the Divinity of the Second Person, and the Incarnation of the Word. For they believed, with all the orthodox Fathers, what St Athanasius succinctly declared in the formula borrowed from St Irenaeus: "God became man in order that man might become God".

If the Word emerged from the depths of the unknowable mystery of the Father "whom no man hath seen at any time", it was not merely in order to have mankind cast itself down at His feet. He came to be a man like ourselves, and, in His own Person, to unite man to God. As a result of this union of God and Man in the one Person of Christ it was possible for every man to be united to God in his own person, as a true son of God, not by nature but by adoption.

If the "Son of Man came to seek and to save that which was lost" this was not merely in order to reestablish man in a favorable juridical position with regard to God: it was to elevate, change and transform man into God, in order that God might be revealed in Man, and that all men might become One Son of God in Christ. The New Testament texts in which this mystery is stated are unequivocal, and yet they have been to a very great extent ignored not only by the faithful but also by theologians.

The Greek and Latin Fathers never made this mistake! For them, the mystery of the hypostatic union, or the union of the divine and human natures in the One Person of the Word, the God-Man, Jesus Christ, was not only a truth of the greatest, most revolutionary and most existential actuality, but it was the central truth of all being and all history. It was the key which alone could unlock the meaning of everything else, and reveal the inner and spiritual significance of man, of his actions as an individual and in society, of history, of the world, and of the whole cosmos.

If in Christ the assumed human nature, which is in every respect literally and perfectly human, belongs to the Person of the Word of God, then everything human in Christ is by that very fact divine. His thoughts, actions, and his very existence are the works and existence of a divine Person. In Him, we see a Man in every respect identical with ourselves as far as His nature is concerned, thinking and feeling and acting according to our nature, and yet at the very same time living on a completely transcendent and divine level of consciousness and of being. For His consciousness and His being are the consciousness and being of God Himself. Of course, the Living Christ, now enthroned at the right hand of the Father in eternity (according to the metaphorical language of the Scriptures) is indeed in a state of being which to us is beyond all capacity to express or to imagine, and yet in this state of being He is also truly and literally human as well as divine, and there is *no cleavage* between His divine and human natures. Nor was there even the slightest split between the humanity and the divinity of Christ in that other historical state of being in which He lived on this earth. Though the two natures were not confused in any way, they were still completely one in Him, as completely as our own body and soul are one in us.

The very first step to a correct understanding of the Christian theology of contemplation is to grasp clearly the unity of God and man in Christ, which of course presupposes the equally crucial unity of man in himself. For the soul and body are not divided against one another as good and evil principles; and our salvation by no means consists of a rejection of the body in order to liberate the soul from the dominance of an evil material principle. On the contrary, our body is as much ourselves as the soul, and neither one without the other can claim to exist purely in its own right, as a true personal being. It was the same also in Christ in Whom the life, being and actions of His Body were just as much His own, and just as much divine, as the thoughts and aspirations of His soul. So when Christ walked down the roads of Galilee it was not an illusory man or even a real man acting as a temporary "front" for a Divine Agent: the Man Himself who walked there was God.

In the words of St Maximus the Confessor:

> The superessential Word, clothing Himself at the time of His ineffable conception with all that is in our nature, possessed nothing human that was not at the same time divine . . . The knowledge of these things is indemonstrable, being beyond understanding and perceptible only to the faith of those who honor the mystery of Christ in the sincerity of their heart. (*Ambigua*, Patrologia Graeca, 91: 1053.)

And again:

> The mystery of the Incarnation of the Word contains in itself all the meaning of the enigmas and symbols of Scripture, all the significance of visible and intelligible creatures. He who knows the mystery of the Cross and the Sepulchre knows the reason (*logos*) of all things. He who

is initiated into the hidden meaning of the resurrection, knows the end for which, from the beginning, God created all things. (*Centuriae Gnosticae,* Patrologia Graeca, 90: 1108.)

The fact that since the Incarnation God and Man have become inseparable in the One Person of Jesus Christ means that the "supernatural order" has not just been somehow imposed from without upon created nature, but that nature itself has, in man, become transformed and supernaturalized so that in everyone in whom Christ lives and acts, by the Holy Spirit, there is no longer any further division between nature and supernature. The man who lives and acts according to the grace of Christ dwelling in him, acts in that case as another Christ, as a son of God, and thus he prolongs in his own life the effects and the miracle of the Incarnation.

In the words of St Maximus: "God desires at all times to make Himself man in those who are worthy". (*Quaestiones ad Thalassium,* Patrologia Graeca 90, 321)

But this, for the Greek Fathers, clearly means a higher and nobler level of life than we ordinarily lead. It means a life purified, liberated by the action of the Holy Spirit, a life enlightened by supernatural contemplation. Of course, Christ has taken possession of our souls and bodies, and we are already divinized, in the roots of our being, by Baptism. But this divine life remains hidden and dormant within us unless it is more fully developed by a life of asceticism and charity and, on a higher level, of contemplation. We not only passively receive in us the grace of Christ, but we actively renew in our own life the self-emptying and self-transformation by which God became man. Just as the Word "emptied Himself" of His divine and transcendent nobility in order to "descend" to the level of man, so we must empty ourselves of what is human in the ignoble sense of the word, which really means less than human, in order that we may become God. This does not mean the sacrifice or destruction of anything that really belongs to our human nature as it was assumed by Christ, but it means the complete, radical cutting off of everything in us that was *not* assumed by Him because it was not capable of being divinized. And what is this? It is everything that is focussed on our exterior and self-centered passion, as self-assertion, greed, lust; as the desire for the survival and perpetuation

of our illusory and superficial self, to the detriment of our interior
and true self. But our inner man is "renewed in Christ" to become
the "new man". As St Paul says:

> Though our outward man is corrupted, our inward man
> is renewed from day to day . . . while we look not at the
> things which are seen, but at the things which are not
> seen. (2 Corinthians 4:16, 18)
>
> Strip yourselves of the old man, with his deeds and
> put on the new, him who is *renewed unto knowledge*
> according to the image of Him that created him. (Ephe-
> sians 3:9, 10)
>
> That God would grant you . . . to be strengthened by
> His Spirit with might unto the inward man, that Christ
> may dwell by faith in your hearts: that being rooted and
> founded in charity you may be able to comprehend with
> all the saints what is the breadth and length and height
> and depth, to know also the charity of Christ which sur-
> passeth all knowledge that you may be filled unto all the
> fulness of God. (Ephesians 3:16–19)

These texts already give us a full and profound picture of the
idea of contemplation that fills the New Testament everywhere
though the term is never mentioned in this particular sense. It is a
question of the inward man springing to life at the spiritual contact
of God, in faith. This contact brings one face to face with a reality
that is "unseen" first of all, and yet paradoxically, this "seeing" of
the "unseen" brings about an ever deepening renewal of life which
is "according to knowledge", that is to say according to a genuine
experience of Christ, caused by our likeness, or "sonship", by the
gift of the divine Spirit Who makes Christ "dwell in our hearts" or
in our inmost selves. The result of this indwelling of Christ and of
the Holy Spirit is the overflowing fulness of new life, of charity,
divine love, and a spiritual comprehension of the mystery of God's
life within us in all its dimensions, through the experience of
Christ's love for us "which surpasses all understanding".

Later in the book we shall return to these fundamental ideas
about Christian contemplation as an experiential contact with
God, in and through Christ, beyond all knowledge, in the darkness

of the mystery of divine charity, in "unknowing". At the moment, it is sufficient to say categorically that this contemplation is a deep participation in the Christ-life, a spiritual sharing in the union of God and man which is the hypostatic union. This is the whole meaning of the doctrine of divine sonship, of our being sons of God in Christ, and having the Spirit of Christ.

> For whoever are led by the Spirit of God, they are the sons of God. For you have not received the spirit of bondage again in fear, but you have received the spirit of adoption of sons whereby we cry Abba, Father. For the Spirit Himself giveth testimony to our spirit that we are the sons of God. (Romans 8:14–16)

This "testimony of the Spirit" to our inmost self (our own spirit) is in a very broad sense what we call "contemplation", in the Christian context.

2. Contemplation and the Gospels

Let us now briefly and succinctly examine some of the most important Gospel texts related to our subject.

First of all, Jesus declared unequivocally that He and the Father were one, and that He was the Son of God in the strictest and most literal sense of the word. For this He was put to death.

> I and the Father are One . . . I am the Son of God . . . If I do not the works of my Father believe me not. But if I do, though you will not believe me, believe the works: that you may know and believe that the Father is in me and I am in the Father. (John 10:30, 36–38)
>
> I am the light of the world: he that followeth me walketh not in darkness but shall have the light of life . . . I am not alone, but I and the Father that sent me . . . You are of this world, I am not of this world . . . I am the beginning who also speak unto you . . . He that sent me is true, and the things I hear from Him, these same I speak in the world . . . I do nothing of myself, but as the Father hath taught me, these things I speak. And He that sent me

is with me, and he hath not left me alone: for I do always the things that please Him . . . From God I proceeded and came: for I came not of myself, but He sent me . . . If any man keep my word he shall not see death forever . . . If I glorify myself my glory is nothing. It is my Father that glorifieth me, of whom you say that He is your God. And you have not known Him, but I know Him . . . I do know Him, and do keep His word. Abraham your Father rejoiced that he might see my day; he saw it and was glad . . . Amen, amen I say to you, before Abraham was made, *I am* (John, 8)

Have I been so long a time with you and have you not known me? . . . He that seeth me seeth the Father also . . . I am the way, the truth and the life. No man cometh to the Father but by me . . . Do you not believe that I am in the Father and the Father in Me? The words that I speak to you, I speak not of myself. But the Father who abideth in me, He doth the works. (John, 14)

These texts are clear enough. And there is no question about the way they have been interpreted by twenty centuries of Christian tradition. Christian contemplation is based on faith in this mystery. If Christ came into the world as the Son of God, and if the Father was present in Him: if Christ has left the world and gone to the Father, how do we "see" Him, or bridge the gap that remains between us and the transcendental remoteness of His mystery in heaven? The answer is that the Word, in the Father, is not only transcendentally removed at an infinite distance above us, but also and at the same time He is immanent in our world, first of all by nature as the Creator of the world, but then in a special dynamic and mystical presence as the Savior, Redeemer and Lover of the world. The point is then to know how we enter into contact with this special presence of the Lord in His cosmos and in our hearts. If in St John's terms we have to become the sons of God, and in order to become the sons of God we have to receive Christ, then how do we receive Christ? The answer is, *by faith:* and this means not simply by an intellectual assent to certain authoritative dogmatic propositions, but more than that by the *commitment of our whole self and of our whole life to the reality of the presence of Christ in the world.* This act of total surrender is not simply a fantastic intellectual and mystical gamble, it is something much more serious: it is an act of love for this unseen Person who, in the very gift of love by which we surrender ourselves to His reality, also makes Himself present to us. The union of our mind, spirit and life with the Word present within us is effected by the Holy Spirit.

All this is clear in Christ's discourse at the Last Supper, His spiritual testament. First, a distinction is made between the physical presence of the Lord with which the Disciples had become familiar during the period when He lived among them on earth, and the new more intimate invisible presence which would be His when He had died on the Cross, risen from the dead and established His Kingdom.

> But I tell you the truth, it is expedient for you that I go: for if I go not the Paraclete will not come to you: but if I go I will send Him to you . . . When He, the Spirit of Truth is come, He will teach you all truth . . . He shall glorify me because he shall receive of mine and shall show it to you. (John, 16:7, 13, 14)

These words need to be completed by an explanation from the first Epistle of St John: at the same time, we must remember what was said above by St Paul about the Holy Spirit making Christ present to the Christian soul. St John says:

> You have the unction from the Holy One and know all things . . . Let the unction which you have received from Him abide in you. And you have no need that any man teach you; but as His unction teaches you of all things, and is truth and no lie. And as it hath taught you, abide in Him. (I John, 2:20, 27)

It is evident then that the Holy Spirit is given to us as a true and literal gift of God: *Donum Dei altissimi.* He is truly, as St Thomas says, our possession, which means to say He becomes as it were our own spirit, speaking within our own being. It is He that becomes, as it were, our spiritual and divine self, and by virtue of His presence and inspirations we are and we act as other Christs. By Him and through Him we are transformed in Christ. It is clear from the

Gospel and Epistles of the New Testament that the Holy Spirit is truly meant to be given to us as a personal principle of love and activity in the supernatural order, transforming us in Christ. The life of contemplation is then not simply a life of human technique and discipline, it is the life of the Holy Spirit in our inmost souls. The whole duty of the contemplative is to abandon what is base and trivial in his own life, and do all he can to conform himself to the secret and obscure promptings of the Spirit of God. This of course requires a constant discipline of humility, obedience, self-distrust, prudence, and above all of faith.

St Paul earnestly wanted all his Corinthian converts to receive the Holy Spirit and be guided by Him. He tells them in no uncertain words:

> We speak the wisdom of God in mystery, a wisdom which is hidden, which God ordained before the world, unto our glory . . . To us God hath revealed (hidden things) by His Spirit, for the Spirit searcheth all things, even the deep things of God. For what man knoweth the things of a man but the spirit of a man that is in him? So the things also that are of God no man knoweth, but the Spirit of God. Now we have received the spirit not of this world, but the Spirit that is of God; that we may know the things that are given us from God. (I Corinthians, 2:7, 10–12)

This is an important witness to the New Testament idea of what we call contemplation of God. Just as a man knows himself by the testimony of his own inmost self, his own spirit, so God reveals Himself in the love of His Spirit. And this Spirit of God, dwelling in us, given to us, to be as it were our own Spirit, enables us to know and experience, in a mysterious manner, the reality and presence of the divine mercy in ourselves. So the Holy Spirit is intimately united to our own inmost self, and His presence in us makes our "I" the "I" of Christ and of God.

This is the Holy Spirit Whom Christ Himself promised to His disciples and to us at the Last Supper. Too often these texts are merely taken in a broad impersonal sense: the Holy Spirit was given to the Apostles, and hence to the Church. This means that the Holy Spirit protects the Church, and especially the successors of the

Apostles, from dogmatic and moral error. That is true. But it is also much more important to realize that the Holy Spirit is given to each member of the Church to guide him in the truth and to lead him to his supernatural destination, and to open his eyes to the mystery of God's presence and action in his own life.

In the Discourse at the Last Supper, the Savior who was about to die on the Cross returned insistently to the theme of His departure from His disciples in His physical and material presence, in order to live in them mystically and spiritually by His Holy Spirit. But this is not to be understood as the mere substitution of metaphor for reality. Christ was not to be present in His members merely as a memory, as a model, as a good example. Nor would He merely guide and control them from afar, through angels. It is true that the Divine Nature infinitely transcends all that is natural, but in Christ the gap between God and man has been bridged by the Incarnation, and in us the gap is bridged by the invisible presence of the Holy Spirit. Christ is really present in us, more present than if He were standing before us visible to our bodily eyes. For we have become "other Christs".

By virtue of this hidden presence of the Spirit in our inmost self, we need only to deliver ourselves from preoccupation with our external, selfish and illusory self, in order to find God within us. And the Lord has explicitly said that this discovery, a sublime gift of His grace, normally implies some form of spiritual experience.

3. Sacred and Secular

Here we must pause a little to consider the difference between a *sacred* and a *secular* view of life. The expression "the world" is perhaps too vague. It does not merely refer to "what is all around us" or to the created universe. The universe is not evil but good. The "world" in the bad sense certainly does not mean the cosmos, though in certain Christian neo-platonist writings it tends to suggest that meaning. This is due to platonist and gnostic influences which crept into Christianity and persuaded men that the universe was run by more or less fallen angels ("the powers of the air"). Our adjective secular comes from the Latin *saeculum,* which means both "world" and "century". The *saeculum* is that which is temporal, which changes, revolves, and returns again to its starting point. The etymology of the word is uncertain. Perhaps it is related to the Greek *kuklon,* or wheel, from which we get "cycle". So originally, that which is "secular" is that which goes around in interminably recurring cycles. This is what "worldly society" does. Its horizons are those of an ever-recurring sameness:

> One generation passeth away and another generation cometh: but the earth standeth forever. The sun also riseth and goeth down and returneth to his place: and there rising again maketh his round by the south and turneth again to the north: the spirit goeth forward surveying all places round about and returneth to his circuits . . . What is it that hath been? The same thing that shall be. What is it that hath been done? The same that shall be done. Nothing under the sun is new . . . Vanity of vanities, and all is vanity. (Ecclesiastes, ch. 1)

Now all our existence in this life is subject to change and recurrence. That alone does not make it secular. But life becomes secularized when it commits itself completely to the "cycles" of what *appears to be new* but is in fact the same thing over again. Secular life is a life of vain hopes, imprisoned in the illusion of newness and change, an illusion which brings us constantly back to the same old point, the contemplation of our own nothingness. Secular life is a life frantically dedicated to escape, through novelty and variety, from the fear of death. But the more we cherish secular hopes, the more they disappoint us. And the more they disappoint us the more desperately do we return to the attack, and forge new hopes, more extravagant than the last. These too let us down. And we revert to that insufferable condition from which we have vainly tried to escape. In the words of Pascal:

> Nothing is so unbearable to a man as to be completely at rest, without passions, without business, without diversion, without study. He then feels his nothingness, his forlornness, his insufficiency, his dependence, his weakness, his emptiness . . . (*Pensees,* 131)

"Secular" society is by its nature committed to what Pascal calls "diversion", that is, to movement which has, before everything else, the anaesthetic function of quieting our anguish. All society, without exception, tends to be in some respect "secular". But a genuinely secular society is one which cannot be content with innocent escapes from itself. More and more it tends to need and to demand, with insatiable dependence, satisfaction in pursuits that are unjust, evil, or even criminal. Hence the growth of economically useless businesses that exist for profit and not for real production, that create artificial needs which they then fill with cheap and quickly exhausted products. Hence the wars that arise when producers compete for markets and sources of raw material. Hence the nihilism, despair and destructive anarchy that follow war, and then the blind rush into totalitarianism as an escape from despair. Our world has now reached the point when, for the sake of diversion, it is ready to blow itself up. The atomic age is the highest point ever achieved by secularism. And this reminds us, of course, that the real root of secularism is godlessness.

The secular and sacred reflect two kinds of dependence. The secular world depends upon the things it needs to divert itself and escape from its own nothingness. It depends on the creation and multiplication of artificial needs, which it then pretends to "satisfy". Hence the secular world is a world that pretends to exalt man's liberty, but in which man is in fact enslaved by the things on which he depends. In such a society man himself is alienated and becomes a "thing" rather than a person, because he is subject to the rule of what is lower than himself and outside himself. He is subject to his ever increasing needs, to his restlessness, his dissatisfaction, his anxiety and his fear, but above all to the guilt which reproaches him for infidelity to his own inner truth. To escape this guilt, he plunges further into falsity.

In the sacred society, on the other hand, man admits no dependence on anything lower than himself, or even "outside" himself in a spatial sense. His only Master is God. Only when God is our Master can we be free, for God is within ourselves as well as above us. He rules us by liberating us and raising us to union with Himself *from within*. And in so doing He liberates us from our dependence on created things outside us. We use and dominate them, so that they exist for our sakes, and not we for theirs. There is no purely sacred society except in heaven.

But the city of God in heaven is reflected on earth in the

society of those who are united not by "enlightened self-interest" but by sacrificial and Christian love, by mercy and compassion, by selfless and divine pity. They liberate themselves from slavery to "diversion" by renouncing their own pleasure and immediate satisfaction in order to help relieve the needs of others, and in order to help others in turn to become free and to seek their own inner truth, and thus fulfil their destiny on earth.

I have said that even the most sacred of earthly societies tends to have something of a secular character. This is inevitable as soon as we have a visible society of men in the present fallen condition of human nature. The visible and symbolic expressions of the divine tend to become opaque, in their constant use by men, so that we stop at them and no longer go through them to God. Hence Holy Communion, for instance, tends to become a routine and "secularized" activity when it is sought not so much as a mystical contact with the Incarnate Word of God and with all the members of His Mystical Body, but rather as a way of gaining social approval and allaying feelings of anxiety. In this manner even the most sacred realities can be debased and, without totally losing their sacred character, enter into the round of secular "diversion".

The truly sacred attitude toward life is in no sense an escape from the sense of nothingness that assails us when we are left alone with ourselves. On the contrary, it penetrates into that darkness and that nothingness, realizing that the mercy of God has transformed our nothingness into His temple and believing that in our darkness His light has hidden itself. Hence the sacred attitude is one which does not recoil from our own inner emptiness, but rather penetrates into it with awe and reverence, and with the awareness of mystery.

This is a most important discovery in the interior life. For the external self *fears* and recoils from what is beyond it, and above it. It dreads the seeming emptiness and darkness of the interior self. The whole tragedy of "diversion" is precisely that it is a flight from all that is most real and immediate and genuine in ourselves. It is a flight from life and from experience—an attempt to put a veil of objects between the mind and its experience of itself. It is therefore a matter of great courage and spiritual energy to turn away from diversion and prepare to meet, face to face, that *immediate* experience of life which is intolerable to the exterior man. This is only possible when, by a gift of God (St Thomas would say it was the Gift of Fear, or sacred awe) we are able to see our inner selves not as a vacuum but as an *infinite depth,* not as emptiness but as fulness. This change of perspective is impossible as long as we are afraid of our own nothingness, as long as we are afraid of fear, afraid of poverty, afraid of boredom—as long as we run away from ourselves.

What we need is the gift of God which makes us able to find in ourselves not just ourselves but Him: and then our nothingness becomes His all. This is not possible without the liberation effected by compunction and humility. It requires not talent, not mere insight, but *sorrow,* pouring itself out in *love* and *trust.*

The sacred attitude is essentially contemplative, and the secular attitude essentially active. That does not mean that there cannot be an activity that is sacred, (based on love.) But even such activity is sacred only in so far as it tends to contemplation.

The man whose view of life is purely secular, hates himself interiorly, while seeming to love himself. He hates himself in the sense that he cannot stand to be "with" or "by" himself. And because he hates himself, he also tends to hate God, because he cannot abide the inner loneliness which must be suffered and accepted, before God can be found. His rebellion against his own inner loneliness and poverty turns into pride. Pride is the fixation of the exterior self upon itself, and the rejection of all other elements in the self for which it is incapable of assuming responsibility. This includes the rejection of the inmost self, with its apparent emptiness, its indefiniteness, and its general character as that which is dark and unknown. Pride is then a false and evasive self-realization which is in actual fact no realization at all, but only the fabrication of an illusory image. The effort which must then be put into the protection and substantiation of this illusion gives an appearance of strength. But in reality, this fixation upon what does not exist merely exhausts and ruins our being.

There is a subtle but inescapable connection between the "sacred" attitude and the acceptance of one's inmost self. The movement of recognition which accepts our own obscure and unknown self produces the sensation of a "numinous" presence within us. This sacred awe is no mere magic illusion but the real expression of a release of spiritual energy, testifying to our own interior reunion and reconciliation with that which is deepest in us, and, through the inner self, with the transcendent and invisible power of God. This implies humility, or the full acceptance of all that we have tended to reject and ignore in ourselves. The inner self is "purified" by the acknowledgment of sin, not precisely because the inner self is the seat of sin, but because both our sinfulness and our interiority tend to be rejected in one and the same movement by the exterior self, and relegated to the same darkness, so that when the inner self is brought back to light, sin emerges and is liquidated by the assuming of responsibility and by sorrow.

Thus the man with the "sacred" view is one who does not need to hate himself, and is never afraid or ashamed to remain with his own loneliness, for in it he is at peace, and through it he can come to the presence of God. More still, he is able to go out from his own loneliness to find God in other men. That is to say, in his dealings with others he has no need to identify them with their sins and condemn them for their actions: for he is able, in them also, to see below the surface and to guess at the presence of the inner and innocent self that is the image of God. Such a man is able to help other men to find God in themselves, educating them in confidence by the respect he is able to feel for them. Thus he is capable of allaying some of their fears and helping them to put up with themselves, until they become interiorly quiet and learn to see God in the depths of their own poverty.

The basic and most fundamental problem of the spiritual life is this acceptance of our hidden and dark self, with which we tend to identify all the evil that is in us. We must learn by discernment to separate the evil growth of our actions from the good ground of the soul. And we must prepare that ground so that a new life can grow up from it within us, beyond our knowledge and beyond our conscious control. The sacred attitude is then one of reverence, awe, and silence before the mystery that begins to take place within us when we become aware of our inmost self. In silence, hope, expectation, and unknowing, the man of faith abandons himself to the divine will: not as to an arbitrary and magic power whose decrees must be spelt out from cryptic cyphers, but as to the stream of reality and of life itself. The sacred attitude is then one of deep and fundamental respect for the real in whatever new form it may present itself. The secular attitude is one of gross disrespect for reality, upon which the worldly mind seeks only to force its own crude patterns. The secular man is the slave of his own prejudices, preconceptions and limitations. The man of faith is ideally free from prejudice and plastic in his uninhibited response to each new movement of the stream of life. I say "ideally" in order to exclude those whose faith is not pure but is also another form of prejudice enthroned in the exterior man—a preconceived opinion rather than a living responsiveness to the *logos* of each new situation. For there exists a kind of "hard" and rigid religious faith that is not really alive or spiritual, but resides entirely in the exterior self and is the product of conventionalism and systematic prejudice. Speaking of the obedience and docility of the man of faith, Christ made clear that this union with the will of God in action is the necessary step to contemplative awareness of God:

"*If you love me* . . . I will ask the Father and He will give you another Paraclete . . . He that loveth me shall be loved of my Father and I will love him and manifest myself to him . . ." (John xiv, 15 and 21.)

IV. KINDS OF CONTEMPLATION

Strictly speaking contemplation is an immediate and in some sense passive intuition of the inmost reality, of our spiritual self and of God present within us. But there is also an active and mediate form of contemplation, in which this perception is attained in some measure by our own efforts, though with the mysterious and invisible help of grace. The concept of passive or infused contemplation is primarily theological. That is to say, it refers to a reality which is not directly or empirically verifiable, but which is a datum of revelation. This should not be made to sound more mysterious or esoteric than it really is. The revelation of this "passive" intuition seems to be implicit in the statements from St John's Gospel that have been quoted. When Christ says, "I will manifest myself to him", it means that the "activity" is on the side of the Lord, and that the one who contemplates the divine presence is in no position to bring about its manifestation by any effort of his own. Nor is he capable of increasing or modifying it by his efforts. And even, in some cases, he is incapable of *preventing* it. The classical expression for such a grace as this, is that it is effected in us and without us: *in nobis et sine nobis.* Active or mediate contemplation, on the other hand, is effected in us but with our own active cooperation. *In nobis et non sine nobis.**

Normally, a life of active contemplation prepares a man for occasional and unpredictable visits of infused or passive contemplation. Also, active contemplation can never attain the depth and the purity of infused contemplation which, in its purest form, takes place entirely without conceptual mediation. In active contemplation concept and judgment, or at least acts of faith springing from a certain mental activity, serve as a springboard for contemplative intuitions and for states of quietude more or less prolonged.

In active contemplation, there is a deliberate and sustained effort to detect the will of God in events and to bring one's whole self into harmony with that will. Active contemplation depends on ascesis of abandonment, a systematic relaxation of the tensions of the exterior self and a renunciation of its tyrannical claims and demands, in order to move in a dimension that escapes our understanding and overflows in all directions our capacity to plan. The element of dialectic in active contemplation is centered on the discovery of God's will, that is to say the identification of the real direction which events are taking, especially in our own life. But along with this there is a deep concern with the symbolic and ritual enactment of those sacred mysteries which represent the divine actions by which the redemption and sanctification of the world is effected. In other words, active contemplation rests on a deep ground of liturgical, historical and cultural tradition: but a living tradition, not dead convention. And a tradition still in dynamic movement and growth. The contemplative mind is, in fact, not normally ultra-conservative: but neither is it necessarily radical. It transcends both these extremes in order to remain in living contact with that which is genuinely true in any traditional movement. Hence I would say in parentheses that the contemplative mind today will not normally be associated too firmly or too definitively with any "movement" whether political, religious, liturgical, artistic, philosophical or what have you. The contemplative stays clear

---

* "In us and not without us."

of movements, not because they confuse him, but simply because he does not need them and can go farther by himself than he can in their formalized and often fanatical ranks.

Nevertheless active contemplation should be to a great extent in contact with the *logos* of its age. Which means in simple fact that the contemplative today might be expected to have an intuitive grasp of, and even sympathy for, what is most genuine in the characteristic movements of our time—Marxism, existentialism, psychoanalysis, eirenism. They may even at times present a serious temptation for him. But if he is a genuine contemplative he will be able to resist temptation because his contemplation itself will instinctively avoid becoming enmeshed in conceptual systems. I say if he is a genuine contemplative, meaning "if he is sufficiently initiated into the meaning and value of a spiritual life to prefer its simplicity to all the complexities and pretenses of these intellectual fads and campaigns".

In active contemplation, a man becomes able to live within himself. He learns to be at home with his own thoughts. He becomes to a greater and greater degree independent of exterior supports. His mind is pacified not by passive dependence on things outside himself—diversions, entertainments, conversations, business—but by its own constructive activity. That is to say that he derives inner satisfaction from spiritual creativeness: thinking his own thoughts, reaching his own conclusions, looking at his own life and directing it in accordance with his own inner truth, discovered in meditation and under the eyes of God. He derives strength not from what he gets out of things and people, but from giving himself to life and to others. He discovers the secret of life in the *creative energy of love*—not love as a sentimental or sensual indulgence, but as a profound and self-oblative expression of freedom.

Active contemplation is nourished by meditation and reading and, as we shall see, by the sacramental and liturgical life of the Church. But before reading, meditation and worship turn into contemplation, they must merge into a *unified and intuitive vision* of reality.

In reading, for instance, we pass from one thought to another, we follow the development of the author's ideas, and we contribute some ideas of our own if we read well. This activity is discursive.

Reading becomes contemplative when, instead of reasoning,

we abandon the sequence of the author's thoughts in order not only to follow our own thoughts (meditation) but simply *to rise above thought and penetrate into the mystery of truth which is experienced intuitively as present and actual.* We meditate with our mind, which is "part of" our being. But we contemplate with our whole being and not just with one of its parts.

This means that the contemplative intuition of reality is a perception of value: a perception which is not intellectual or speculative, but practical and experiential. It is not just a matter of observation but of realization. It is not something abstract and general, but concrete and particular. It is a personal grasp of the existential meaning and value of reality.

Such personal intuitions may be highly paradoxical and even, sometimes, disturbing. The sense of experiential awareness is very strong, yet there is no discursive intellectual evidence to support this awareness. Hence a peculiar combination of certainty and hazard. One "knows" without knowing how he knows. And this of course can be quite dangerous. It can lead to illusion and to illuminism. The contemplative's only safeguard is humility and self-forgetfulness and the renunciation of all desire to exploit the experience for any purpose whatever. What happens, happens. One accepts it, in humility, and sees it, without inferring anything or instituting any comparison with other experiences. And one walks on in the presence of God. Rightly accepted, contemplative experience has its own proper effect: it increases the intensity and simplicity of a man's love for God and for his fellow men. If it could be said to have a "purpose" then this would be its purpose. But in reality contemplation has no purpose outside itself for, properly understood, it is inseparably joined to love and identified with love. The love which is essential to contemplation is its "purpose" as well as its source. It needs no other.

The beauty of truth seen by the intelligence draws our hearts out of themselves in love and admiration. When the work of thought leads to an intuition of love and of religious awe, then we have "active contemplation".

The religious element in contemplation must be stressed here. There exists also a non-religious and aesthetic contemplation—a kind of aesthetic complacency in the beauty of abstract truth. But unless the note of sacred awe heightens the perception of intellectual beauty, we do not yet have contemplation in the religious sense of the word. And here perhaps we must recognize the limitations and deficiencies of the term. The word "contemplation" is too pale, too vague and too inactive to convey the full spiritual strength of a genuinely religious experience of God. If we are to continue using the word at all, we must strengthen it, forget its purely pagan and intellectual connotations, and think rather of the trembling with which Moses "loosed the shoes from off his feet" on Mount Horeb when God spoke to him out of the burning bush and warned him that he stood upon holy ground. Contemplation, in the Christian context, necessarily implies a sacred "dread"—a holy awe.

Liturgy

Active contemplation is not the mere perception and enjoyment of an abstract spiritual truth. It is a participation in the Church's collective experience in receiving, from God, the concrete revelation of His divine mystery. Hence the liturgy is the ordinary focus of active contemplation. In the sacred liturgy we have, of course, symbolic rites and ceremonies, music, speech, poetry, collective prayer. But to pass through liturgy into contemplation is something much more than mere aesthetic enjoyment of a religious concert or of a very primitive form of sacred drama.

The Christian liturgy is contemplative on two levels: on the level of *spoken revelation* and on the level of *ritual mystery,* or *sacred action.*

On the level of spoken revelation we have the chanting, or at least reading of sacred texts containing not only moral truths and ascetic counsels, but much more, the *formal announcement* (Kerygma) of the *Evangelium,* the mystery of man's salvation. When we stand to listen to the Gospel, we formally and solemnly bear witness to our faith, and by that faith receive into our hearts the very substance of the truth which God reveals to us. We receive the "word of salvation" which is "sharper than any two-edged sword", which enters into the depths of our being with a supernatural and transforming power, and which awakens or renews in us our divine life as sons of God.

To be aware of this inner reality, as the result of our attentive and loving faith, and to "realize" the truth of God's love for us and for the world, is to enter into the way of "active contemplation" which the liturgy lays open to us.

Certain moments in the liturgy of solemn fast days (like the Ember days) remind us of this interconnection between public revelation and private contemplation. At the end of certain scriptural texts the Deacon sings *Flectamus genua* (Let us kneel down) and this is, or should be, followed by a few minutes of silent prayer in which each one supposedly enters into the full awareness of the words that have just been sung. Unfortunately this practice long ago lost its original meaning, and it is only just beginning to come back into liturgical use.

The higher level of liturgical contemplation is in *sacred action,* the ritual of the sacraments and above all of the great mystery, the Holy Eucharist. These rites and divine gifts are more than symbols, they contain the very realities which their symbolism expresses, and bring with them graces to illuminate the eyes of the heart to perceive their inner meaning.

Indeed the sacrament of Baptism was known in ancient times as an "illumination" (*photismos*) and the ritual of this sacrament of Christian initiation still tells us eloquently that it brings not only faith but the power to taste the fulness of faith in contemplation.

Not only does the Church pray God to illuminate the mind of the candidate and drive all blindness from his inmost heart, but all his senses are signed with chrism that he may hear the precepts of God, see the brightness of God, smell the sweet odor of Christ, speak the words of life, and believe in the word of the Lord. The whole being of the baptized Christian is signed in the name of the Holy Trinity, and the mystical senses are awakened in him by the grace of the sacrament. Baptism sanctifies us by bringing to life our inmost self as a "new man in Christ".

At that time one receives the seven Gifts of the Holy Ghost which, according to the teaching of St. Thomas, are spiritual faculties making possible a full mystical life in anyone who completely renounces the world and yields himself completely to the action of God.

But Baptism is only the beginning of the noble and sublime existence of the Christian as son of God. The greatest of the sacraments and the one which perfects and completes all the others is the Blessed Eucharist, the mystery of Christ's love, in which the Christian is sacramentally united to the Risen Lord in Holy Communion. Receiving the Sacred Body of the Savior in the consecrated Host the believer affirms his union with Christ in His Passion, Death and Resurrection from the Dead. He becomes one heart, one mind and one spirit with the Blessed Savior. He becomes lost in the Mystical Christ as a drop of water becomes lost in a chalice of wine. The mystery of the Eucharist both symbolizes and effects the mystical union of the believer with Christ by charity. The grace of contemplation enables him to penetrate into the full meaning of this mystery, to realize its depths and its extent. Contemplation is but a weak word for the great gift which St Paul calls the "spirit of wisdom and revelation in the knowledge of Christ" which leaves us with:

> The eyes of the heart enlightened . . . to know the riches of
> the glory of His inheritance . . . To know also the charity
> of Christ which surpasses all understanding and to be
> filled unto all the fulness of God. (Ephesians 1 and 3)

By active participation in the liturgy the Christian prepares himself to enter into the Church's "contemplation" of the great mysteries of faith. Here least of all is contemplation something merely mental and discursive. It involves man's whole being, body and soul, mind, will, imagination, emotion and spirit. Worship takes man in his wholeness and consecrates him entirely to God, and thence contemplation is the perfection of worship. Without contemplation worship tends to remain lifeless and external. The mere existence of the Church's liturgy is then a call to active contemplation. To remain withdrawn from the liturgy and outside it is to exclude oneself from possibilities of active contemplation that the Church offers to all, with many graces and lights that she alone is privileged to distribute to her children.

At the Last Supper, Jesus gave us more than a sublime doctrine: He gave us Himself, "the way, the truth and the life". The Blessed Sacrament is not a sign or a figure of contemplation; it contains Him Who is the beginning and end of all contemplation. It should not be surprising then that one of the most normal ways of entering into infused prayer is through the graces given in Holy Communion.

Union with God in Activity

The great majority of Christians will never become pure contemplatives on earth. But that does not mean that those whose vocation is essentially active must resign themselves to being excluded from all the graces of a deep interior life and all infused prayer. Christ has promised that the Three Divine Persons will manifest themselves *to all who love Him.* There are many Christians who serve God with great purity of soul and perfect self-sacrifice in the active life. Their vocation does not allow them to find the solitude and silence and leisure in which to empty their minds entirely of created things and to lose themselves in God alone. They are too busy serving Him in His children on earth. At the same time, their minds and temperaments do not fit them for a purely contemplative life: they would know no peace without exterior activity. They would not know what to do with themselves. They would vegetate and *their interior life would grow cold.* Nevertheless they know how to find God by devoting themselves to Him in self-sacrificing labors in which they are able to remain in His presence all day long. They live and work in His company. They realize that He is within them and they taste deep, peaceful joy in being with Him. They lead lives of great simplicity in which they do not need to rise above the ordinary levels of vocal and affective prayer. Without realizing it, their extremely simple prayer is, for them, so deep and interior that it brings them to the threshold of contemplation. They never enter deeply into the contemplative life but they are not unfamiliar with graces akin to contemplation. Although they are active laborers they are also *hidden contemplatives* because of the great purity of heart maintained in them by obedience, fraternal charity, self-sacrifice and perfect abandonment to God's will in all that they do and suffer. They are much closer to God than they realize. They enjoy a kind of "masked" contemplation.

Such Christians as these, far from being excluded from perfection, may reach a higher degree of sanctity than others who have been apparently favored with a deeper interior life. Yet there is all the difference in the world between these hidden contemplatives and the surface Christian whose piety is merely a matter of externals and formal routine. The difference is: *these men live for God and for His love alone.* They cannot help knowing something about Him.

It might be well to point out here that "masked contemplation" has its advantages. Since contemplation is communion with a hidden God in His own hiddenness, it tends to be pure in proportion as it is itself hidden. Obscurity and sincerity seem to go together in the spiritual life. The "masked contemplative" is one whose contemplation is hidden from no one so much as from himself. This may seem like a contradiction in terms. Yet it is a strange and deep truth that the grace of contemplation is most secure and most efficacious when it is no longer sought, or cherished, or desired. It is in a sense most pure when it is barely known. Of course, for it to be contemplation at all, there must be some awareness of it. If there is absolutely no awareness, then there is no contemplation.

Here we speak of an awareness that is present, but utterly un-self-conscious. It is a kind of negative awareness, an "unknowing". According to the classical expression of Pseudo-Dionysius, one knows God by "not-knowing" Him. One reaches Him "apophatically" in the darkness beyond concepts. And one contemplates, so to speak, by forgetting that one is able to contemplate. As soon as one is aware of himself contemplating, the gift is spoiled. This was long ago observed by St Anthony of the Desert who said: "That prayer is most pure in which the monk is no longer aware of himself, or of the fact that he is praying".

Often people think that this remark of St Anthony refers to some curious state of psychological absorption, a kind of mystical sleep. In point of fact it refers to a self-less awareness, a spiritual liberty and lightness and freedom which transcends all special psychological states and is "no state" at all. Would-be contemplatives must be on their guard against a kind of heavy, inert stupor in which the mind becomes swallowed up in itself. To remain immersed in one's own darkness is not contemplation, and no one should attempt to "stop" the functioning of his mind and remain fixed on his own nothingness. Rather we must go out in hope and faith from our own nothingness and seek liberation in God.

The masked contemplative is liberated from temporal concern by his own purity of intention. He no longer seeks himself in action or in prayer, and he has achieved a kind of holy indifference, abandoning himself to the will of God and seeking only to keep in touch with the realities of the present moment. By this of course I mean the inner and spiritual realities, not the surface emotions and excitements which are not reality but illusion.

The life of contemplation in action and purity of heart is then a life of great simplicity and inner liberty. One is not seeking anything special or demanding any particular satisfaction. One is content with what is. One does what is to be done, and the more concrete it is, the better. One is not worried about the results of what is done. One is content to have good motives and not too anxious about making mistakes. In this way one can swim with the living stream of life and remain at every moment in contact with God, in the hiddenness and ordinariness of the present moment with its obvious task.

At such times, walking down a street, sweeping a floor, washing dishes, hoeing beans, reading a book, taking a stroll in the woods—all can be enriched with contemplation and with the obscure sense of the presence of God. This contemplation is all the more pure in that one does not "look" to see if it is there. Such "walking with God" is one of the simplest and most secure ways of living a life of prayer, and one of the safest. It never attracts anybody's attention, least of all the attention of him who lives it. And he soon learns *not to want to see* anything special in himself. This is the price of his liberty.

It has been said above that such people enjoy "graces akin to contemplation" because they are never fully conscious of their "contemplative state". But it must not be thought that they cannot be real mystics. Indeed, a genuine mystical life may be lived in these conditions. The mystical graces given to such souls may be of an active character, but there is a strong undercurrent of contemplative intuition. This will remain pure and vital as long as one is careful not to lose himself in activity, not to become preoccupied with results, and not to lose his purity of intention.

Whether in active or passive contemplation, purity of heart is always the guardian of contemplative truth.

Acquired and Infused Contemplation

So far we have deliberately avoided a classification that divides contemplation into "acquired" and "infused" because the legitimacy of this division has been hotly contested by theologians, and there seems to be little point in resurrecting a controversy which has by now died a natural death.

This battle raged, somewhat fruitlessly, throughout the twenties and thirties of our century. The contestants were trying to determine what were the phenomenological limits of mystical prayer: when did a state of prayer cease to be "natural" or "acquired" and become "supernatural" or "infused"? In other words, when did man cease to be himself the principal agent and yield this primacy to the Spirit of God? At what point does prayer show signs of being truly "mystical"? The other question involved in this was: is it possible by certain sustained efforts, inspired by the grace of God, to prepare oneself for and to enter into genuine contemplation?

The questions which soon became quite complex seem to be, in perspective, rather nugatory disputes about words. In particular everything depended on the way one defined "contemplation" and "mystical". Those who divided contemplation into "natural" and "supernatural" said that (natural) contemplation could be acquired. This natural and acquired contemplation was something like what has been described in these pages as active contemplation: an intuitive perception of supersensory reality, reached after preliminary spiritual efforts of the contemplative himself. But the defenders of acquired contemplation held that this contemplation was not really mystical.

Others, speaking evidently of the same state of prayer, held that it was true and mystical contemplation but that it was not acquired. It was a passive supernatural gift.

Natural Contemplation and Mystical Theology

In these pages, I have decided to ignore the complexities of this now defunct argument, and have simply assumed the existence of a supersensory intuition of the divine which is a gift of grace for which we can, to some extent, prepare ourselves by our own efforts. In this I am basing myself on a distinction made by the Greek Fathers: that between natural contemplation (*theōria physikē*) and theology (*theologia*) or the contemplation of God.

Theōria physikē is the intuition of divine things in and

through the reflection of God in nature and in the symbols of revelation. It presupposes a complete purification of heart by a long ascetic preparation which has delivered the soul from subjection to passion and, consequently, from the illusions generated by passionate attachment to exterior things. When the eye is clear and "single" (that is to say disinterested—having only "one intention") then it can see things as they are. The contemplative at this stage is one whose thoughts are no longer passionate, no longer distorted. They are simple and direct. He sees straight into the nature of things as they are. At the same time he sees into his own nature. And this is a mystical grace from God.

Now the word "natural" in connection with this kind of contemplation, refers not to its origin but to its object. *Theōria physikē* is contemplation of the divine *in nature,* not contemplation of the divine *by our natural powers.* And in fact, "natural contemplation" in this sense is mystical: that is to say it is a gift of God, a divine enlightenment. But it still involves labor and preparation on the part of the contemplative. He has to look about him, see the created world and the symbols with which it is filled. He has to receive, in the sign language of scripture and liturgy, words of God which transform his inner life. Natural contemplation, according to the Greek Fathers, also "sees" and communes with the angelic beings who form a part of created nature. This natural contemplation, which beholds the divine in and through nature, has served me as a prototype for what I have chosen to call "active contemplation"—a contemplation which man seeks and prepares by his own initiative but which, by a gift of God, is completed in mystical intuition.

Theologia, or pure contemplation ("mystical theology" in the language of Pseudo-Denis) is a direct quasi-experiential contact with God beyond all thought, that is to say without the medium of concepts. This excludes not only concepts tinged with passion, or sentimentality, or imagination, but even the simplest intellectual intuitions that require some sort of medium between God and the spirit. Theology in this sense is a direct contact with God. Now this supreme Christian contemplation, according to the Greek Fathers, is a quasi-experiential knowledge of God as He is in Himself, that is to say of God as Three Persons in One Nature: for this is the highest mystery in which He has revealed Himself to us.

Entrance into this supreme mystery is not a matter of spiritual effort, of intellectual subtlety, still less of learning. It is a matter of identification by charity, for charity is the likeness of the soul to God. As St John says:

> Everyone that loveth is born of God, and knoweth God. He that loveth not, knoweth not God, for God is charity . . . In this we know that we abide in Him and He in us, because He hath given us of His Spirit. And we have seen and do testify that the Father hath sent His Son to be the Saviour of the world. (I John 4:7, 14)

This apparently simple text of the Apostle contains in it immense depths of theology: it gives the full justification of the teaching of the Christian mystics on the possibility of our apprehending, in contemplative charity, the very being of God as He is in Himself. For the man who is perfect in love becomes like God who is Love, and in this he is able to experience within himself the presence of the Three Divine Persons, the Father, the source and giver of Love, the Son, the image and glory of Love, and the Spirit Who is the communication of the Father and the Son in Love.

But this theology has one other characteristic that must not be overlooked. It is a contact with God in charity, yes, but also and above all in the darkness of unknowing. This follows necessarily from the fact that it goes beyond the symbols and intuitions of the intellect, and attains to God directly without the medium of any created image. If medium there is, it is not intellectual, not an image or species in the mind, but a disposition of our whole being, brought about by that Love which so likens and conforms us to God that we become able to experience Him mystically in and through our inmost selves, as if He were our very selves. The inner self of the mystic, elevated and transformed in Christ, united to the Father in the Son, through the Holy Spirit, now knows God not so much through the medium of an objective image, as through its own divinized subjectivity. Truly a difficult thing to convey in words, and still more difficult to imagine, if one has not experienced it. The best we can do is read and meditate on the texts of the Masters who are able to speak from experience. Here for instance is St Gregory of Nyssa, interpreting in this sense the symbolism of

Moses' ascent of Sinai into the dark cloud where he is face to face with God. We remember that the "animals and human beings" must be kept away from the foot of the mountain. They must not even touch it, under pain of death. This, says Gregory, suggests the fact that passionate and even simple concepts must be kept away from the mountain of contemplation. The spirit must ascend into the darkness *without any concept at all.*

> The more the spirit in its forward progress arrives, by ever greater and more perfect application, at an understanding of what it means to know these realities, and comes closer and closer to contemplation, the more it sees that the divine nature is invisible. Having left behind all appearances, not only those which are perceived by the senses, but also those which the intelligence believes itself to apprehend, it enters further and further within until, with great struggle of the spirit, it penetrates to the Invisible and Unknowable, and there sees God. (*De Vita Moysi,* ii, 162- "Sources Chretiennes".)

Now this "vision" of God is a vision in darkness, and therefore is not the face to face vision enjoyed by the Blessed in Paradise. Yet it is an equally real and genuine contact with God, the chief distinction being that it takes place without clarity and without "seeing". In fact, the spirit sees God precisely by understanding that He is utterly invisible to it. In this sudden, deep and total acceptance of His invisibility, it casts far from itself every last trace of conceptual meditation, and in so doing rids itself of the spiritual obstacles which stand between it and God. Thoughts, natural light and spiritual images are, so to speak, veils or coverings that impede the direct, naked sensitivity by which the spirit touches the Divine Being. When the veils are removed, then one can touch, or rather be touched by, God, in the mystical darkness. Intuition reaches Him by one final leap beyond itself, an ecstasy in which it sacrifices itself and yields itself to His transcendent presence. In this last ecstatic act of "unknowing" the gap between our spirit as subject and God as object is finally closed, and in the embrace of mystical love we know that we and He are one. This is infused or mystical contemplation in the purest sense of the term.

LEARNING TO LIVE

Every reader of The Seven Storey Mountain *will agree that Merton's experiences at Columbia University in New York City (1935–39) were crucial for his future life. It was there, through his readings and his friendships, that he became interested in, and, finally, a member of, the Catholic Church. It is against the background of his student days that he formed his decision for a religious vocation. In 1961 Columbia honored Merton by awarding him the "University Medal for Excellence" which was presented to Mark Van Doren (Merton was not permitted to leave the cloister for the ceremony) at commencement.*

The essay "Learning to Live" (interestingly enough, the draft copy has the title "Learning to Learn") was written in 1967 for a proposed volume on the university by Columbia's alumni; it was first published after Merton's death in University on the Heights, *edited by Wesley First (New York: Doubleday, 1969) and republished in* Love and Living, *edited by Naomi Burton Stone and Patrick Hart (New York: Farrar, Straus & Giroux, 1979).*

The conceit of the essay is to be found in Merton's observation that the university has, at its best, a kind of monastic quality to it; both can be seen as a paradisis claustralis—*a cloistered paradise. Merton does not wish to evoke an image of ivy and quadrangle by this parallel. He means that both institutions have as their ends the encounter with truth, and, at least in Merton's view, that is an encounter with Truth.*

The particular merit of this short piece of hommage *to his old school is in the way Merton attempts to communicate his monastic culture to a world which would have found it either antique or exotically irrelevant. It was a particular gift that Merton had. There was no attempt to romanticize the monastic life and every attempt to make correlations between the true nature of education and the authentic ends of the contemplative search. True education, like*

357

true contemplation, triggers that deep center at the core of meaning which guarantees the authenticity of the human person.

For a further development of this theme, see Lawrence S. Cunningham, "The Life of Thomas Merton as Paradigm: The View of Academe," in The Message of Thomas Merton, *edited by Brother Patrick Hart (Kalamazoo: Cistercian Publications, 1981), pp. 154–165.*

*

Life consists in learning to live on one's own, spontaneous, freewheeling: to do this one must recognize what is one's own—be familiar and at home with oneself. This means basically learning who one is, and learning what one has to offer to the contemporary world, and then learning how to make that offering valid.

The purpose of education is to show a person how to define himself authentically and spontaneously in relation to his world— not to impose a prefabricated definition of the world, still less an arbitrary definition of the individual himself. The world is made up of the people who are fully alive in it: that is, of the people who can be themselves in it and can enter into a living and fruitful relationship with each other in it. The world is, therefore, more real in proportion as the people in it are able to be more fully and more humanly alive: that is to say, better able to make a lucid and conscious use of their freedom. Basically, this freedom must consist first of all in the capacity to choose their own lives, to find themselves on the deepest possible level. A superficial freedom to wander aimlessly here or there, to taste this or that, to make a choice of distractions (in Pascal's sense) is simply a sham. It claims to be a freedom of "choice" when it has evaded the basic task of discovering who it is that chooses. It is not free because it is unwilling to face the risk of self-discovery.

The function of a university is, then, first of all to help the student to discover himself: to recognize himself, and to identify who it is that chooses.

This description will be recognized at once as unconventional and, in fact, monastic. To put it in even more outrageous terms, the function of the university is to help men and women save their souls and, in so doing, to save their society: from what? From the hell of meaninglessness, of obsession, of complex artifice, of systematic lying, of criminal evasions and neglects, of self-destructive futilities.

It will be evident from my context that the business of saving one's soul means more than taking an imaginary object, "a soul," and entrusting it to some institutional bank for deposit until it is recovered with interest in heaven.

Speaking as a Christian existentialist, I mean by "soul" not simply the Aristotelian essential form but the mature personal identity, the creative fruit of an authentic and lucid search, the "self" that is found after other partial and exterior selves have been discarded as masks.

This metaphor must not mislead: this inner identity is not "found" as an object, but is the very self that finds. It is lost when it forgets to find, when it does not know how to seek, or when it seeks itself as an object. (Such a search is futile and self-contradictory.) Hence the paradox that it finds best when it stops seeking: and the graduate level of learning is when one learns to sit still and be what one has become, which is what one does not know and does not need to know. In the language of Sufism, the end of the ascetic life is *Rida,* satisfaction. Debts are paid (and they were largely imaginary). One no longer seeks something else. One no longer seeks to be told by another who one is. One no longer demands reassurance. But there is the whole infinite depth of *what is* remaining to be revealed. And it is not revealed to those who seek it from others.

Education in this sense means more than learning; and for such education, one is awarded no degree. One graduates by rising from the dead. Learning to be oneself means, therefore, learning to die in order to live. It means discovering in the ground of one's being a "self" which is ultimate and indestructible, which not only survives the destruction of all other more superficial selves but finds its identity affirmed and clarified by their destruction.

The inmost self is naked. Nakedness is not socially acceptable except in certain crude forms which can be commercialized without any effort of imagination (topless waitresses). Curiously, this cult of bodily nakedness is a veil and a distraction, a communion in futility, where all identities get lost in their nerve endings. Everybody claims to like it. Yet no one is really happy with it. It makes money.

Spiritual nakedness, on the other hand, is far too stark to be useful. It strips life down to the root where life and death are equal, and this is what nobody likes to look at. But it is where freedom really begins: the freedom that cannot be guaranteed by the death of somebody else. The point where you become free not to kill, not to exploit, not to destroy, not to compete, because you are no longer afraid of death or the devil or poverty or failure. If you discover this nakedness, you'd better keep it private. People don't like it. But can you keep it private? Once you are exposed . . . Society continues to do you the service of keeping you in disguises, not for your comfort, but for its own. It is quite willing to strip you of this or that outer skin (a stripping which is a normal ritual and which everybody enjoys). The final metaphysical stripping goes too far, unless you happen to be in Auschwitz.

If I say this description is "monastic," I do not necessarily mean "theological." The terms in which it has been stated here are open to interpretation on several levels: theologically, ascetically, liturgically, psychologically. Let's assume that this last is the more acceptable level for most readers. And let's assume that I am simply speaking from experience as one who, from a French lycée and an English public school, has traveled through various places of "learning" and has, in these, learned one thing above all: to keep on going. I have described the itinerary elsewhere, but perhaps a few new ideas may be added here. The journey went from Europe to America, from Cambridge to Columbia. At Columbia, having got the necessary degrees, I crossed the boundary that separates those who learn as students from those who learn as teachers. Then I went to teach English at a Catholic college (St. Bonaventure).* After which I went to be a novice in a Trappist monastery, where I also "learned" just enough theology to renounce all desire to be a theologian. Here also (for I am still in Kentucky) I learned by teaching: not theology as such, but the more hazardous and less charted business of monastic education, which deals with the whole person in a situation of considerable ambiguity and hazard: the novice, the young monk who wants to become a contemplative and who is (you sooner or later discover) trapped both by the institution and

---

* Now St. Bonaventure University.

by his own character in a situation where what he desperately wants beyond all else on earth will probably turn out to be impossible. Perhaps I would have been safer back at Columbia teaching elementary English composition. Fortunately, I am no longer teaching anybody anything.

On the basis of this experience, I can, anyhow, take up an ancient position that views monastery and university as having the same kind of function. After all, that is natural enough to one who could walk about Cambridge saying to himself, "Here were the Franciscans at one time, here the Dominicans, here—at my own college—Chaucer was perhaps a clerk."

A university, like a monastery (and here I have medievalists to back me up, but presume that footnotes are not needed), is at once a microcosm and a paradise. Both monastery and university came into being in a civilization open to the sacred, that is to say, in a civilization which paid a great deal of attention to what it considered to be its own primordial roots in a mythical and archetypal holy ground, a spiritual creation. Thus the *Logos or Ratio** of both monastery and university is pretty much the same. Both are "schools," and they teach not so much by imparting information as by bringing the clerk (in the university) or the monk (in the monastery) to direct contact with "the beginning," the archetypal paradise world. This was often stated symbolically by treating the various disciplines of university and monastic life, respectively, as the "four rivers of paradise." At the same time, university and monastery tended sometimes to be in very heated conflict, for though they both aimed at "participation" in and "experience" of the hidden and sacred values implanted in the "ground" and the "beginning," they arrived there by different means: the university by *scientia,* intellectual knowledge, and the monastery by *sapientia,* or mystical contemplation. (Of course, the monastery itself easily tended to concentrate on scientia—the science of the Scriptures—and in the university there could be mystics like Aquinas, Scotus, and Eckhart. So that in the end, in spite of all the fulminations of the Cistercian St. Bernard, a deeper *sapientia* came sometimes from schools than from monasteries.)

---

* [Purpose.]

The point I am making here is this: far from suggesting that Columbia ought to return to the ideal of Chartres and concentrate on the trivium and quadrivium, I am insinuating that this archetypal approach, this "microcosm-paradise" type of sacred humanism, is basically personalistic.

I admit that all through the Middle Ages men were actively curious about the exact location of the earthly paradise. This curiosity was not absent from the mind of Columbus. The Pilgrim Fathers purified it a little, spiritualized it a little, but New England to them was a kind of paradise: and to make sure of a paradisic institution they created, of all things, Harvard. But the monks of the Middle Ages, and the clerks too, believed that the inner paradise was the ultimate ground of freedom in man's heart. To find it one had to travel, as Augustine had said, not with steps, but with yearnings. The journey was from man's "fallen" condition, in which he was not free not to be untrue to himself, to that original freedom in which, made in the image and likeness of God, he was no longer able to be untrue to himself. Hence, he recovered that nakedness of Adam which needed no fig leaves of law, of explanation, of justification, and no social garments of skins (Gregory of Nyssa). Paradise is simply the person, the self, but the radical self in its uninhibited freedom. The self no longer clothed with an ego.

One must not forget the dimension of relatedness to others. True freedom is openness, availability, the capacity for gift. But we must also remember that the difficult dialectic of fidelity to others in fidelity to oneself requires one to break through the veils of infidelity which, as individual egoists or as a selfish community, we set up to prevent ourselves from living in the truth.

This sacred humanism was, of course, abused and perverted by the sacred institution, and in the end monasticism, by a curious reversal that is so usual in the evolution of societies, identified the fig leaf with the paradise condition and insisted on the monk having at least enough of a self to serve the organization itself pressed into the service of more mundane interests. Freedom, then, consisted in blind obedience, and contemplation consisted in renouncing nakedness in favor of elaborate and ritual vestments. The "person" was only what he was in the eyes of the institution because the institution was, for all intents and purposes, Paradise, the domain of God, and indeed God himself. To be in Paradise, then, consisted in being defined by the paradisic community—or by Academe. Hence, the dogmatic absolutism for which the late Middle Ages are all too well known—and for which they are by no means uniquely responsible.

The original and authentic "paradise" idea, both in the monastery (*paradisus claustralis*)* and in the university, implied not simply a celestial store of theoretic ideas to which the Magistri and Doctores held the key, but the inner self of the student who, in discovering the ground of his own personality as it opened out into the center of all created being, found in himself the light and the wisdom of his Creator, a light and wisdom in which everything comprehensible could be comprehended and what was not comprehensible could nevertheless be grasped in the darkness of contemplation by a direct and existential contact.

Thus, the fruit of education, whether in the university (as for Eckhart) or in the monastery (as for Ruysbroeck) was the activation of that inmost center, that *scintilla animae,* that "apex" or "spark" which is a freedom beyond freedom, an identity beyond essence, a self beyond all ego, a being beyond the created realm, and a consciousness that transcends all division, all separation. To activate this spark is not to be, like Plotinus, "alone with the Alone," but to recognize the Alone which is by itself in everything because there is nothing that can be apart from It and yet nothing that can be with It, and nothing that can realize It. It can only realize itself. The "spark" which is my true self is the flash of the Absolute recognizing itself in me.

This realization at the apex is a coincidence of all opposites (as Nicholas of Cusa might say), a fusion of freedom and unfreedom, being and unbeing, life and death, self and nonself, man and God. The "spark" is not so much a stable entity which one finds but an event, an explosion which happens as all opposites clash within oneself. Then it is seen that the ego is not. It vanishes in its nonseeing when the flash of the spark alone is. When all things are reduced to the spark, who sees it? Who knows it? If you say "God,"

---

* [Cloistered paradise.]

you are destroyed; and if you say no one, you will plunge into hell; and if you say I, you prove you are not even in the ballgame.

The purpose of all learning is to dispose man for this kind of event.

The purpose of various disciplines is to provide ways or paths which lead to this capacity for ignition.

Obviously it would be a grave mistake to do, as some have done and still do, and declare that the only way is to be found in a cloister and the only discipline is asceticism or Zen sitting or, for that matter, turning on with a new drug. The whole of life is learning to ignite without dependence on any specific external means, whether cloistered, Zenist Tantric, psychedelic, or what have you. It is learning that the spark, being a flash at the apex and explosion of all freedoms, can never be subject to control or to enlightenment, can never be got by pressing buttons. A spark that goes off when you swallow something or stick yourself with something may be a fairly passable imitation of the real thing, but it is not the real thing. (I will not argue that it cannot teach you a great deal about the real thing.) In the same way a cloistered complacency—a "peace" that is guaranteed only by getting out of the traffic, turning off the radio, and forgetting the world—is not by itself the real thing either.

The danger of education, I have found, is that it so easily confuses means with ends. Worse than that, it quite easily forgets both and devotes itself merely to the mass production of uneducated graduates—people literally unfit for anything except to take part in an elaborate and completely artificial charade which they and their contemporaries have conspired to call "life."

A few years ago a man who was compiling a book entitled *Success* wrote and asked me to contribute a statement on how I got to be a success. I replied indignantly that I was not able to consider myself a success in any terms that had a meaning to me. I swore I had spent my life strenuously avoiding success. If it so happened that I had once written a best seller, this was a pure accident, due to inattention and naïveté, and I would take very good care never to do the same again. If I had a message to my contemporaries, I said, it was surely this: Be anything you like, be madmen, drunks, and bastards of every shape and form, but at all costs avoid one thing:

success. I heard no more from him and I am not aware that my reply was published with the other testimonials.

Thus, I have undercut all hope of claiming that Columbia made me a success. On the contrary, I believe I can thank Columbia, among so many other things, for having helped me learn the value of unsuccess. Columbia was for me a microcosm, a little world, where I exhausted myself in time. Had I waited until after graduation, it would have been too late. During the few years in which I was there, I managed to do so many wrong things that I was ready to blow my mind. But fortunately I learned, in so doing, that this was good. I might have ended up on Madison Avenue if I hadn't. Instead of preparing me for one of those splendid jobs, Columbia cured me forever of wanting one. Instead of adapting me to the world downtown, Columbia did me the favor of lobbing me half conscious into the Village, where I occasionally came to my senses and where I continued to learn. I think I have sufficiently explained, elsewhere, how much I owed, in this regard, to people like Mark Van Doren (who lived around the corner from me in the Village) and Joseph Wood Krutch (who became, as I have become, a hermit). Such people taught me to imitate not Rockefeller but Thoreau. Of course, I am not trying to say that one has to be Thoreau rather than Rockefeller, nor am I slyly intimating that I have discovered a superior form of resentment, an off-beat way of scoring on everybody by refusing to keep score.

What I am saying is this: the score is not what matters. Life does not have to be regarded as a game in which scores are kept and somebody wins. If you are too intent on winning, you will never enjoy playing. If you are too obsessed with success, you will forget to live. If you have learned only how to be a success, your life has probably been wasted. If a university concentrates on producing successful people, it is lamentably failing in its obligation to society and to the students themselves.

Now I know that even in the thirties, at Columbia, the business of wanting to be a success was very much in the air. There was, in fact, a scandal about the yearbook senior poll. The man who was voted "most likely to succeed" was accused of having doctored the results in his own favor after a surreptitious deal with a yearbook staff member who was voted "best dressed." Incidentally, I was voted best writer. I was not accused of trickery, but everyone understood that the vote, which had been between me and Hank Liebermann, had been decided by my fraternity brothers. (Incidentally, whatever became of the man "most likely to succeed"?)

In any case, no one really cared. Since that time many of my classmates have attained to eminence with all its joys and all its sorrows, and the ones I have seen since then are marked by the signature of anguish. So am I. I do not claim exemption. Yet I never had the feeling that our alma mater just wanted us to become well-paid operators, or to break our necks to keep on the front pages of the *Times.* On the contrary—maybe this is a delusion, but if it is a delusion it is a salutary one—I always felt at Columbia that people around me, half amused and perhaps at times half incredulous, were happy to let me be myself. (I add that I seldom felt this way at Cambridge.) The thing I always liked best about Columbia was the sense that the university was on the whole glad to turn me loose in its library, its classrooms, and among its distinguished faculty, and let me make what I liked out of it all. I did. And I ended up by being turned on like a pinball machine by Blake, Thomas Aquinas, Augustine, Eckhart, Coomaraswamy, Traherne, Hopkins, Maritain, and the sacraments of the Catholic Church. After which I came to the monastery in which (this is public knowledge) I have continued to be the same kind of maverick and have, in fact, ended as a hermit who is also fully identified with the peace movement, with Zen, with a group of Latin American hippie poets, etc., etc.

The least of the work of learning is done in classrooms. I can remember scores of incidents, remarks, happenings, encounters that took place all over the campus and sometimes far from the campus: small bursts of light that pointed out my way in the dark of my own identity. For instance, Mark Van Doren saying to me as we crossed Amsterdam Avenue: "Well, if you have a vocation to the monastic life, it will not be possible for you to decide not to enter" (or words to that effect). I grasped at once the existential truth of this statement.

One other scene, much later on. A room in Butler Hall, overlooking some campus buildings. Daisetz Suzuki, with his great bushy eyebrows and the hearing aid that aids nothing. Mihoko, his beautiful secretary, has to repeat everything. She is making tea. Tea ceremony, but a most unconventional one, for there are no rites and no rules. I drink my tea as reverently and attentively as I can. She goes into the other room. Suzuki, as if waiting for her to go, hastily picks up his cup and drains it.

It was at once as if nothing at all had happened and as if the roof had flown off the building. But in reality nothing had happened. A very very old deaf Zen man with bushy eyebrows had drunk a cup of tea, as though with the complete wakefulness of a child and as though at the same time declaring with utter finality: "This is not important!"

The function of a university is to teach a man how to drink tea, not because anything is important, but because it is usual to drink tea, or, for that matter, anything else under the sun. And whatever you do, every act, however small, can teach you everything—provided you see who it is that is acting.

CONTEMPLATION IN A WORLD OF ACTION

The 1960s—the decade of the civil rights movement, the Vietnam War, the student protest movement in America and Europe, the period of the Second Vatican Council—was a period of tumultuous unrest and change. To say that Thomas Merton was affected by those changes would be to point out a banality. During the 1960s Merton was preoccupied by the place of the monk in a world that demanded engagement, action, commitment, and—to use a catch-phrase of the period—relevancy. The two essays below were part of Merton's response to the exigencies of the time.

"Contemplation in a World of Action" was originally written for a student publication at the University of Louisville in 1968. It is a crisp attempt to disabuse his readership of any naive understanding of prayer but, at the same time, is an apologia for the authentic value of prayer. The careful reader will also note his attempt to sharpen the concept of God as being at the ground of reality rather than Someone "out there." Bishop Robinson's Honest to God, *Dietrich Bonhoeffer's* Letters and Papers from Prison, *and other books of the period are the unspoken partners of his dialogue. The essay is, in the final analysis, a plea for people to be centered—to find a fundamental source and anchor for existence in the midst of an increasingly frenetic world. His parenthetical warning against false mysticism (e.g. through the use of psychedelics—then so popular) reflects the temper of the period.*

Merton wrote "Is the World a Problem?" two years earlier for publication in Commonweal *magazine (June 6, 1966). It is one of a number of pieces Merton wrote in order to recount the radical disjunction he made, in his earliest writing, between the world of nature and the world of grace. His self-parody of the world-denying monk of* The Seven Storey Mountain *in this essay is a vivid description of that shift. Merton was also keenly aware of the world-affirming sentiments of the Pastoral Constitution on the Church in the Modern World* (Gaudium et Spes) *which had been issued at the*

Second Vatican Council just a few years before he wrote, with its call for Christians to take on a more positive view of the world.

Both of these essays were again published posthumously in Contemplation in a World of Action *(Garden City: Doubleday Image, 1973) where many of the themes of these pieces are addressed in other essays of the period.*

*

CONTEMPLATION IN A WORLD OF ACTION

This is not intended merely as another apologia for an official, institutional life of prayer. Nor is it supposed to score points in an outdated polemic. My purpose is rather to examine some basic questions of *meaning.* What does the contemplative life or the life of prayer, solitude, silence, meditation, mean to man in the atomic age? What can it mean? Has it lost all meaning whatever?

When I speak of the contemplative life I do not mean the institutional cloistered life, the organized life of prayer. This has special problems of its own. Many Catholics are now saying openly that the cloistered contemplative *institution* is indefensible, that it is an anachronism that has no point in the modern world. I am not arguing about this—I only remark in passing that I do not agree. Prescinding from any idea of an institution or even of a religious organization, I am talking about a special dimension of inner discipline and experience, a certain integrity and fullness of personal development, which are not compatible with a purely external, alienated, busy-busy existence. This does not mean that they are incompatible with action, with creative work, with dedicated love. On the contrary, these all go together. A certain depth of disciplined experience is a necessary ground for fruitful action. Without a more profound human understanding derived from exploration of the inner ground of human existence, love will tend to be superficial and deceptive. Traditionally, the ideas of prayer, meditation and contemplation have been associated with this deepening of one's personal life and this expansion of the capacity to understand and serve others.

Let us start from one admitted fact: if prayer, meditation and contemplation were once taken for granted as central realities in human life everywhere, they are so no longer. They are regarded, even by believers, as somehow marginal and secondary: what counts is getting things done. Prayer seems to be nothing but "saying words," and meditation is a mysterious process which is not understood: if it has some usefulness, that usefulness is felt to be completely remote from the life of ordinary men. As for contemplation: even in the so-called "contemplative life" it is viewed with suspicion! If "contemplatives" themselves are afraid of it, what will the ordinary lay person think? And, as a matter of fact, the word "contemplation" has unfortunate resonances—the philosophic elitism of Plato and Plotinus.

It is a curious fact that in the traditional polemic between action and contemplation, modern apologists for the "contemplative" life have tended to defend it on pragmatic grounds—in terms of action and efficacy. In other words, monks and nuns in cloisters are not "useless," because they are engaged in a very efficacious kind of spiritual activity. They are not idle, lazy, evasive: they are "getting things done," but in a mysterious and esoteric sort of way, an invisible, spiritual way, by means of their prayers. Instead of acting upon things and persons in the world, they act directly upon God by prayer. This is in fact a "superior kind of activity," a "supreme efficacy," but people do not see it. It has to be believed.

I am not interested, for the moment, in trying to prove anything by this argument. I am concerned only with its meaning to modern people. Obviously there are many who *believe* this in the sense that they accept it "on faith" without quite seeing how it is possible. They accept it on authority without understanding it themselves, and without trying to understand it. The argument is not one which appeals to them. It arouses a curious malaise, but they do not know what to do about it. They put it away on a mental shelf with other things they have no time to examine.

This view of the contemplative life, which is quite legitimate as far as it goes, places a great deal of stress on the prayer of petition, on intercession, on vicarious sacrifice and suffering as work, as action, as "something accomplished" in cloisters. And stress is laid on the idea that the prayers and sacrifices of contemplatives produce certain definite effects, albeit in a hidden manner. They "produce grace" and they also in some way "cause" divine interventions. Thus it happens that a considerable volume of letters arrives in the monastery or convent mailbag requesting prayers on the eve of a serious operation, on the occasion of a lawsuit, in personal and family problems, in sickness, in all kinds of trouble. Certainly, Catholics believe that God hears and answers prayers of petition. But it is a distortion of the contemplative life to treat it as if the contemplative concentrated all his efforts on getting graces and favors from God for others and for himself.

This conception of God and of prayer is one which fits quite naturally into a particular image of the universe, a cause-and-effect mechanism with a transcendent God "outside" and "above" it, acting upon it as Absolute First Cause, Supreme Prime Mover. He is the Uncaused Cause, guiding, planning, willing every effect down to the tiniest detail. He is regarded as a Supreme Engineer. But men can enter into communication with Him, share in His plans, participate in His causation by faith and prayer. He delegates to men a secret and limited share in His activity in so far as they are united with Him.

I am not saying that there is anything "wrong" with this. I have expressed it crudely, but it is perfectly logical and fits in naturally with certain premises. However, the trouble is that it supposes an image of the universe which does not correspond with that of post-Newtonian physics. Now, in the nineteenth century and in the modernist crisis of the early twentieth century there was one response to that: "If our view of the universe does not correspond with that of modern science, then to hell with science. We are right and that's that." But since that time it has been realized that while God is transcendent He is also immanent, and that faith does not require a special ability to imagine God "out there" or to picture Him spatially removed from His Creation as a machine which He directs by remote control. This spatial imagery has been recognized as confusing and irrelevant to people with a radically different notion of the space-time continuum. Teilhard de Chardin is one witness among many—doubtless the best known—to a whole new conception, a dynamic, immanentist conception of God and the world. God is at work in and through man, perfecting an ongoing Creation. This too is to some extent a matter of creating an acceptable image, a picture which we can grasp, which is not totally alien to our present understanding, and it will doubtless be replaced by other images in later ages. The underlying truth is not altered by the fact that it is expressed in different ways, from different viewpoints, as long as these viewpoints do not distort and falsify it.

Now it happens that the immanentist approach, which sees God as directly and intimately present in the very ground of our being (while being at the same time infinitely transcendent), is actually much closer to the contemplative tradition. The real point of the contemplative life has always been a deepening of faith and of the personal dimensions of liberty and apprehension to the point where our direct union with God is realized and "experienced." We awaken not only to a realization of the immensity and majesty of God "out there" as King and Ruler of the universe (which He is) but also a more intimate and more wonderful perception of Him as directly and personally present in our own being. Yet this is not a pantheistic merger or confusion of our being with His. On the contrary, there is a distinct conflict in the realization that though in some sense He is more truly ourselves than we are, yet we are not identical with Him, and though He loves us better than we can love ourselves we are opposed to Him, and in opposing Him we oppose our own deepest selves. If we are involved only in our surface existence, in externals, and in the trivial concerns of our ego, we are untrue to Him and to ourselves. To reach a true awareness of Him as well as ourselves, we have to renounce our selfish and limited self and enter into a whole new kind of existence, discovering an inner center of motivation and love which makes us see ourselves and everything else in an entirely new light. Call it faith, call it (at a more advanced stage) contemplative illumination, call it the sense of God or even mystical union: all these are different aspects and levels of the same kind of realization: the awakening to a new awareness of ourselves in Christ, created in Him, redeemed by Him, to be transformed and glorified in and with Him. In Blake's words, the "doors of perception" are opened and all life takes on a completely new meaning: the real sense of our own existence, which is normally veiled and distorted by the routine distractions of an alienated life, is now revealed in a central intuition. What was lost and dispersed in the relative meaninglessness and triviality of purposeless behavior (living like a machine, pushed around by impulsions and suggestions from others) is brought together in fully integrated conscious significance. This peculiar, brilliant focus is, according to Christian tradition, the work of Love and of the Holy Spirit. This "loving knowledge" which sees everything transfigured "in God," coming from God and working for God's creative and redemptive love and tending to fulfillment in the glory of God, is a contemplative knowledge, a fruit of living and realizing faith, a gift of the Spirit.

The popularity of psychedelic drugs today certainly shows, if nothing else, that there is an appetite for this kind of knowledge and inner integration. The only trouble with drugs is that they superficially and transiently mimic the integration of love without producing it. (I will not discuss here the question whether they may accidentally help such integration, because I am not competent to do so.)

Though this inner "vision" is a gift and is not directly produced by technique, still a certain discipline is necessary to prepare us for it. Meditation is one of the more important characteristic forms of this discipline. Prayer is another. Prayer in the context of this inner awareness of God's direct presence becomes not so much a matter of cause and effect, as a celebration of love. In the light of this celebration, what matters most is love itself, thankfulness, assent to the unbounded and overflowing goodness of love which comes from God and reveals Him in His world.

This inner awareness, this experience of love as an immediate and dynamic presence, tends to alter our perspective. We see the prayer of petition a little differently. Celebration and praise, loving attention to the presence of God, become more important than "asking for" things and "getting" things. This is because we realize that in Him and with Him all good is present to us and to mankind: if we seek first the Kingdom of Heaven, all the rest comes along with it. Hence we worry a great deal less about the details of our daily needs, and we trust God to take care of our problems even if we do not ask Him insistently at every minute to do so. The same applies to the problems of the world. But on the other hand, this inner awareness and openness makes us especially sensitive to urgent needs of the time, and grace can sometimes move us to pray for certain special needs. The contemplative life does not ignore the prayer of petition, but does not overemphasize it either. The contemplative prays for particular intentions when he is strongly and spontaneously inspired to do so, but does not make it his formal purpose to keep asking for this and that all day long.

Now, prayer also has to be seen in the light of another fundamental experience, that of God's "absence." For if God is immanently present He is also transcendent, which means that He is completely beyond the grasp of our understanding. The two ("absence" and "presence") merge in the loving knowledge that "knows by unknowing" (a traditional term of mysticism). It is more and more usual for modern people to be afflicted with a sense of absence, desolation, and incapacity to even "want" to pray or to think of God. To dismiss this superficially as an experience of "the death of God"—as if henceforth God were completely irrelevant— is to overlook one significant fact: that this sense of absence is not a one-sided thing: it is dialectical, and it includes its opposite, namely presence. And while it may be afflicted with doubt it contains a deep need to believe.

The point I want to make is this: experience of the contemplative life in the modern world shows that the most crucial focus for contemplative and meditative discipline, and for the life of prayer, for many modern men, is precisely this so-called sense of absence, desolation, and even apparent "inability to believe." I stress the word "apparent," because though this experience may to some be extremely painful and confusing, and raise all kinds of crucial "religious problems," it can very well be a sign of authentic Christian growth and a point of decisive development in faith, if they are able to cope with it. The way to cope with it is not to regress to an earlier and less mature stage of belief, to stubbornly reaffirm and to "enforce" feelings, aspirations and images that were appropriate to one's childhood and first communion. One must, on a new level of meditation and prayer, live through this crisis of belief and grow to a more complete personal and Christian integration by experience.

This experience of struggle, of self-emptying, "self-naughting," of letting go and of subsequent recovery in peace and grace on a new level is one of the ways in which the *Pascha Christi* (the death and resurrection of Christ) takes hold on our lives and transforms them. This is the psychological aspect of the work of grace which also takes place beyond experience and beyond psychology in the work of the Sacraments and in our objective sharing of the Church's life.

I am of course not talking about "mystical experience" or anything new and strange, but simply the fullness of personal awareness that comes with a total self-renunciation, followed by self-commitment on the highest level, beyond mere intellectual assent and external obedience.

Real Christian living is stunted and frustrated if it remains content with the bare externals of worship, with "saying prayers" and "going to church," with fulfilling one's external duties and merely being respectable. The real purpose of prayer (in the fully personal sense as well as in the Christian assembly) is the deepening of personal realization in love, the awareness of God (even if sometimes this awareness may amount to a negative factor, a seeming "absence"). The real purpose of meditation—or at least that which recommends itself as most relevant for modern man—is the exploration and discovery of new dimensions in freedom, illumination and love, in deepening our awareness of our life in Christ.

What is the relation of this to action? Simply this. He who attempts to act and do things for others or for the world without deepening his own self-understanding, freedom, integrity and capacity to love, will not have anything to give others. He will communicate to them nothing but the contagion of his own obsessions, his aggressiveness, his ego-centered ambitions, his delusions about ends and means, his doctrinaire prejudices and ideas. There is nothing more tragic in the modern world than the misuse of power and action to which men are driven by their own Faustian misunderstandings and misapprehensions. We have more power at our disposal today than we have ever had, and yet we are more alienated and estranged from the inner ground of meaning and of love than we have ever been. The result of this is evident. We are living through the greatest crisis in the history of man; and this crisis is centered precisely in the country that has made a fetish out of action and has lost (or perhaps never had) the sense of contemplation. Far from being irrelevant, prayer, meditation and contemplation are of the utmost importance in America today. Unfortunately, it must be admitted that the official contemplative life as it is lived in our monasteries needs a great deal of rethinking, because it is still too closely identified with patterns of thought that were accepted five hundred years ago, but which are completely strange to modern man.

But prayer and meditation have an important part to play in opening up new ways and new horizons. If our prayer is the expression of a deep and grace-inspired desire for newness of life—and not the mere blind attachment to what has always been familiar and "safe"—God will act in us and through us to renew the Church by preparing, in prayer, what we cannot yet imagine or understand. In this way our prayer and faith today will be oriented toward the future which we ourselves may never see fully realized on earth.

IS THE WORLD A PROBLEM?

Is the world a problem? I type the question. I am tempted to type it over again, with asterisks between the letters, the way H*y*m*a*n K*a*p*l*a*n used to type his name in *The New Yorker* thirty years ago. And as far as I am concerned that would dispose of the question. But the subject is doubtless too "serious" for a chapter title heading a page with "Is the world a problem" running down the middle, full of asterisks. So I have to be serious too, and develop it.

Maybe I can spell this question out politely, admitting that there are still cogent reasons why it should be asked and answered. Perhaps, too, I am personally involved in the absurdity of the question; due to a book I wrote thirty years ago, I have myself become a sort of stereotype of the world-denying contemplative—the man who spurned New York, spat on Chicago, and tromped on Louisville, heading for the woods with Thoreau in one pocket, John of the Cross in another, and holding the Bible open at the Apocalypse. This personal stereotype is probably my own fault, and it is something I have to try to demolish on occasion.

Now that we are all concerned about the Church and the World, the Secular City, and the values of secular society, it was to be expected that someone would turn quizzically to me and ask: "What about you, Father Merton? What do *you* think?"—and then duck as if I were St. Jerome with a rock in my fist.

First of all, the whole question of the world, the secular world, has become extremely ambiguous. It becomes even more ambiguous when it is set up over against another entity, the world of the sacred. The old duality of time-eternity, matter-spirit, natural-supernatural and so on (which makes sense in a very limited and definite context) is suddenly transposed into a totally different context in which it creates nothing but confusion. This confusion is certainly a problem. Whether or not "the world" is a problem, a confused idea of what the world might possibly be is quite definitely a problem and it is that confusion I want to talk about. I want to make clear that I speak not as the author of *The Seven Storey Mountain,* which seemingly a lot of people have read, but as the author of more recent essays and poems which apparently very few people have read. This is not the official voice of Trappist silence, the monk with his hood up and his back to the camera, brooding over the waters of an artificial lake. This is not the petulant and uncanonizable modern Jerome who never got over the fact that he could give up beer. (I drink beer whenever I can lay my hands on any. I love beer, and, by that very fact, the world.) This is simply the voice of a self-questioning human person who, like all his brothers, struggles to cope with turbulent, mysterious, demanding, exciting, frustrating, confused existence in which almost nothing is really predictable, in which most definitions, explanations and justifications become incredible even before they are uttered, in which people suffer together and are sometimes utterly beautiful, at other times impossibly pathetic. In which there is much that is frightening, in which almost everything public is patently phony, and in which there is at the same time an immense ground of personal authenticity that is right there and so obvious that no one can talk about it and most cannot even believe that it is there.

I am, in other words, a man in the modern world. In fact, I am the world just as you are! Where am I going to look for the world first of all if not in myself?

As long as I assume that the world is something I discover by turning on the radio or looking out the window I am deceived from the start. As long as I imagine that the world is something to be "escaped" in a monastery—that wearing a special costume and following a quaint observance takes me "out of this world," I am dedicating my life to an illusion. Of course, I hasten to qualify this. I said a moment ago that in a certain historic context of thought and of life, this kind of thought and action once made perfect sense. But the moment you change the context, then the whole thing has to be completely transposed. Otherwise you are left like the orchestra in the Marx Brothers' *Night at the Opera* where Harpo had inserted "Take Me Out to the Ball Game" in the middle of the operatic score.

The confusion lies in this: on one hand there is a primitive Christian conception of the world as an object of choice. On the other there is the obvious fact that the world is also something about which there is and can be no choice. And, historically, these notions have sometimes got mixed up, so that what is simply "given" appears to have been chosen, and what is there to be chosen, decided for or against, is simply evaded as if no decision were licit or even possible.

That I should have been born in 1915, that I should be the contemporary of Auschwitz, Hiroshima, Viet Nam and the Watts riots, are things about which I was not first consulted. Yet they are also events in which, whether I like it or not, I am deeply and personally involved. The "world" is not just a physical space traversed by jet planes and full of people running in all directions. It is a complex of responsibilities and options made out of the loves, the hates, the fears, the joys, the hopes, the greed, the cruelty, the kindness, the faith, the trust, the suspicion of all. In the last analysis, if there is war because nobody trusts anybody, this is in part because I myself am defensive, suspicious, untrusting, and intent on making other people conform themselves to my particular brand of death wish.

Put in these terms, the world both is and is not a problem. The world is a "problem" in so far as everybody in it is a problem to himself. The world is a problem in so far as we all add up to a big collective question. Starting then from this concept of a world which is essentially problematic because it is full of problematic and self-doubting freedoms, there have been various suggestions made as to what to do about it.

At present the Church is outgrowing what one might call the Carolingian suggestion. This is a world view which was rooted in the official acceptance of the Church into the world of imperial Rome, the world of Constantine and of Augustine, of Charlemagne in the west and of Byzantium in the east. In crude, simple strokes, this world view can be sketched as follows: We are living in the last age of salvation history. A world radically evil and doomed to hell has been ransomed from the devil by the Cross of Christ and is now simply marking time until the message of salvation can be preached to everyone. Then will come the judgment. Meanwhile, men, being evil and prone to sin at every moment, must be prevented by authority from following their base instincts and getting lost.

They cannot be left to their own freedom or even to God's loving grace. They have to have their freedom taken away from them because it is their greatest peril. They have to be told at every step what to do, and it is better if what they are told to do is displeasing to their corrupt natures, for this will keep them out of further subtle forms of mischief. Meanwhile the Empire has become, provisionally at least, holy. As figure of the eschatological kingdom, worldly power consecrated to Christ becomes Christ's reign on earth. In spite of its human limitations the authority of the Christian prince is a guarantee against complete chaos and disorder and must be submitted to—to resist established authority is equivalent to resisting Christ. Thus we have a rigid and stable order in which all values are fixed and have to be preserved, protected, defended against dark forces of impulse and violent passion. War on behalf of the Christian prince and his power becomes a holy war for Christ against the devil. War too becomes a sacred duty.

The dark strokes in the picture have their historical explanation in the crisis of the barbarian invasions. But there are also brighter strokes, and we find in the thought of Aquinas, Scotus, Bonaventure, Dante, a basically world-affirming and optimistic view of man, of his world and his work, in the perspective of the Christian redemption. Here in the more peaceful and flourishing years of the twelfth and thirteenth centuries we see a harmonious synthesis of nature and grace, in which the created world itself is an epiphany of divine wisdom and love, and redeemed in and by Christ, will return to God with all its beauty restored by the transforming power of grace, which reaches down to material creation through man and his work. Already in St. Thomas we find the ground work for an optimistic Christian affirmation of natural and worldly values in the perspective of an eschatological love. However, this view too is static rather than dynamic, hierarchic, layer upon layer, rather than ongoing and self-creating, the fulfillment of a predetermined intellectual plan rather than the creative project of a free and self-building love.

In the Carolingian world view it somehow happened that the idea of the world as an object of choice tended to be frozen. The "world" was identified simply with the sinful, the perilous, the unpredictable (therefore in many cases the new, and even worse the free), and this was what one automatically rejected. Or, if one had the misfortune to choose it, one went at once to confession. The world was therefore what one did not choose. Since society itself was constructed on this concept of the world, Christian society ("Christendom") conceived itself as a world-denying society in the midst of the world. A pilgrim society on the way to another world. It was fitting that there should be in the midst of that society, and in a place of special prominence and choice, certain people who were professional world-deniers, whose very existence was a sign of *contemptus mundi* and of otherworldly aspirations. Thus from a certain point of view this renunciation and unworldliness of monks became a justification of worldly power and of the established social and economic structures. The society that, by its respect for consecrated unworldliness, confessed its own heavenly aspirations, was certainly the realm of Christ on earth, its kings and its mighty were all alike pilgrims with the poor and humble. If all kept their proper place in the procession the pilgrimage would continue to go well. This is all obvious to everyone who has ever read a line about the Middle Ages, and its obviousness is presently being run into the ground by critics of monasticism. What these critics overlook is that though the theory was austere and negative, in practice the "sacred" and basically "clerical" and "monastic" Christendom produced a world-affirming, nature-respecting, life-loving, love-oriented, fruitful and rich culture. It had its limitations and its grave flaws. But the monastic and contemplative ideal of the Middle Ages, based on an ideological rejection of the world, actually recovered and rediscovered the values of the world on a deeper and more imperishable level, not merely somewhere aloft in a card file of Platonic ideas, but in the world itself, its life, its work, its people, its strivings, its hopes and its existential day-to-day reality. The world-denying monastic ethos found itself willy-nilly incorporated in a life-affirming and humanistic climate. No one who has really read Anselm, Thomas, John of Salisbury, Scotus, Bonaventure, Eckhart, and the rest can seriously doubt this.

Nevertheless, this stereotyped hierarchic idea of the world's structure eventually ceased to be really fruitful and productive. It was already sterile and unreal as early as the fifteenth century. And the fact that the Church of the Second Vatican Council has finally admitted that the old immobilism will no longer serve is a bit too overdue to be regarded as a monumental triumph. The Constitution on the Church in the Modern World is salted with phrases which suggest that the fathers were, at least some of them, fully aware of this.

In any case, one of the essential tasks of aggiornamento is that of renewing the whole perspective of theology in such a way that our ideas of God, man and the world are no longer dominated by the Carolingian-medieval imagery of the sacred and hierarchical cosmos, in which everything is decided beforehand and in which the only choice is to accept gladly what is imposed as part of an immobile and established social structure.

In "turning to the world" the contemporary Church is first of all admitting that the world can once again become an object of choice. Not only can it be chosen, but in fact it must be chosen. How? If I had no choice about the age in which I was to live, I nevertheless have a choice about the attitude I take and about the way and the extent of my participation in its living ongoing events. To choose the world is not then merely a pious admission that the world is acceptable because it comes from the hand of God. It is first of all an acceptance of a task and a vocation in the world, in history and in time. In my time, which is the present. To choose the world is to choose to do the work I am capable of doing, in collaboration with my brother, to make the world better, more free, more just, more livable, more human. And it has now become transparently obvious that mere automatic "rejection of the world" and "contempt for the world" is in fact not a choice but the evasion of choice. The man who pretends that he can turn his back on Auschwitz or Viet Nam and act as if they were not there is simply bluffing. I think this is getting to be generally admitted, even by monks.

On the other hand the stereotype of world rejection is now being firmly replaced by a collection of equally empty stereotypes of world affirmation in which I, for one, have very little confidence. They often seem to be gestures, charades, mummery designed to make the ones participating in them feel secure, to make them feel precisely that they are "like participating" and really doing something. So precisely at the moment when it becomes vitally important for the destiny of man that man should learn to choose for himself a peaceful, equitable, sane and humane world the whole question of choice itself becomes a stark and dreadful one. We talk about choosing, yet everything seems more grimly determined than ever before. We are caught in an enormous web of consequences, a net of erroneous and even pathological effects of other men's decisions. After Hitler, how can Germany be anything but a danger to world peace? To choose the world therefore is to choose the anguish of being hampered and frustrated in a situation fraught with frightful difficulties. We can affirm the world and its values all we like, but the complexity of events responds too often with a cold negation of our hopes.

In the old days when everyone compulsively rejected the world it was really not hard at all to secretly make quite a few healthy and positive affirmations of a worldly existence in the best sense of the word, in praise of God and for the good of all men. Nowadays when we talk so much of freedom, commitment, "engagement" and so on, it becomes imperative to ask whether the choices we are making have any meaning whatever. Do they change anything? Do they get us anywhere? Do we really choose to alter the direction of our lives or do we simply comfort ourselves with the choice of making another choice? Can we really decide effectively for a better world?

The "suggestion" that has now most obviously replaced that of the Carolingians is that of Karl Marx. In this view, history is not finished, it has just reached the point where it may, if we are smart, begin. There is no predetermined divine plan (although frankly the messianism in Marx is basically Biblical and eschatological). After a long precarious evolution matter has reached the point, in man, where it can become fully aware of itself, take itself in hand, control its own destiny. And now at last that great seething mass of material forces, the world, will enter upon its true destiny by being raised to a human level. The instruments by which this can be accomplished—technology, cybernetics—are now in our power. But are we in our own power? No, we are still determined by the illusions of thought patterns, superstructures, devised to justify antiquated and destructive economic patterns. Hence if man is to choose to make himself, if he is to become free at last, his duty can be narrowed down to one simple option, one basic commitment: the struggle against the (imperialist) world.

With a shock we find ourselves in a familiar pattern: a predetermined struggle against evil in which personal freedom is viewed with intolerance and suspicion. The world must be changed because it is unacceptable as it is. But the change must be guided by authority and political power. The forces of good are all incarnate in this authority. The forces of evil are on the contrary incarnate in the power of the enemy system. Man cannot be left to himself. He must submit entirely to the control of the collectivity for which he exists. "Man" is not the person but the collective animal. Though he may eventually become free, now is not the time of freedom but of obedience, authority, power, control. Man does not choose to make himself except in the sense that he submits to a choice dictated by the authority of science and the messianic collective—the party which represents the chosen eschatological class. Hence though in theory there are all kinds of possible choices, in reality the only basic choice is that of rejecting and destroying the evil "world"—namely capitalist imperialism and, in the present juncture, the United States. Hence the ambiguities of Communist dogma at the moment: the choice of peace is of course nothing else than the choice of war against the United States. In other words, we have turned the page of *Aïda* and we are now playing "Take Me Out to the Ball Game," but it is the same crazy Marx Brothers' opera. Freedom, humanism, peace, plenty and joy are all enthusiastically invoked, but prove on closer examination to be their opposites. There is only one choice, to submit to the decision handed down from on high by an authoritarian power which defines good and evil in political terms.

This, as I see it, is the present state of the question. The Church has finally realized officially that the classic world view, which began to develop serious flaws five hundred years ago, is no longer viable at all. There is something of a stampede for security in a new world view.

In this endeavor the dialogue with Marxism is going to be of crucial importance not only for Christians but for Marxists. For if it is a true dialogue it will possibly involve some softening and adjustment of doctrinaire positions and an opening to new perspectives and possibilities of collaboration. Obviously, however, the dialogue with official and established Marxism—the Soviets or Red China —is not to be considered yet as a meaningful possibility. But the conversations that have begun with the type of revisionist Marxism represented by the French thinker Roger Garaudy may certainly have some effects. But what effects? Good or bad? It is all too easy for enthusiastic Catholics, having tasted a little of the new wine, to convince themselves that "turning to the world" and "choosing the world" means simply turning to Marx and choosing some varia-tion—Maoist, Soviet, Castroist—of the Communist political line. There is no question that since the Council a few Catholic thinkers and publicists in Europe and South America are tending in this direction. Their tendency is understandable, but I do not find it altogether hopeful.

The majority of Catholic thinkers today are, however, working in the direction of a modern world view in which the demands of the new humanism of Marx, Freud, Teilhard, Bonhoeffer and others are fully respected and often heartily endorsed. For them, the tendency is no longer to regard God as enthroned "out there" at the summit of the cosmos, but as the "absolute future" who will manifest Himself in and through man, by the transformation of man and the world by science oriented to Christ. Though this cer-tainly is not a view which conservative theologians find comfort-ing, it represents a serious attempt to reexpress Christian truths in terms more familiar to modern man. It demands that we take a more dynamic view of man and of society. It requires openness, freedom, the willingness to face risks. It also postulates respect for the human person in the human community. But at the same time it seems to me that it may have serious deficiencies in so far as it may ignore the really deep problems of collective technological and cybernetic society. To assume, for instance, that just because scien-tific and technological humanism can theoretically be seen as "per-fectly biblical" ("nothing is more biblical than technology," says Père Daniélou) does not alter the profound dehumanization that can in fact take place in technological society (as Daniélou also clearly sees). The fact that man can now theoretically control and direct his own destiny does nothing to mitigate the awful determin-ism which in practice makes a mockery of the most realistic plans and turns all men's projects diametrically against their professed humanistic aims. The demonic gap between expressed aims and concrete achievements in the conduct of the Viet Nam war, for instance, should be an object lesson in the impotence of technology to come to grips with the human needs and realities of our time.

I have a profound mistrust of all obligatory answers. The great problem of our time is not to formulate clear answers to neat theoretical questions but to tackle the self-destructive alienation of man in a society dedicated in theory to human values and in practice to the pursuit of power for its own sake. All the new and fresh answers in the world, all the bright official confidence in the collectivity of the secular city, will do nothing to change the reality of this alienation. The Marxist world view is the one really coherent and systematic one that has so far come forward to replace the old medieval Christian and classic synthesis. It has in fact got itself accepted, for better or for worse, by more than half the human race. And yet, while claiming to offer man hope of deliverance from alienation, it has demanded a more unquestioning, a more irrational and a more submissive obedience than ever to its obligatory answers, even when these are manifestly self-contradictory and destructive of the very values they claim to defend.

The dialogue with Marxism is an obvious necessity. But if in the course of it we simply create a vapid brew of neomodernist and pseudoscientific optimism I do not see what has been gained, especially if it leaves people passive and helpless in the presence of dehumanizing forces that no one seems quite able to identify exactly and cope with effectively. In this sense, the world is certainly a problem. Its idea of itself is extremely ambiguous. Its claims to pinpoint and to solve its own greatest problems are, in my opinion, not very convincing. Its obligatory answers are hardly acceptable. I am not in love with them!

When "the world" is hypostatized (and it inevitably is) it becomes another of those dangerous and destructive fictions with which we are trying vainly to grapple. And for anyone who has seriously entered into the medieval Christian, or the Hindu, or the Buddhist conceptions of *contemptus mundi, Mara* and the "*emptiness of the world,*" it will be evident that this means not the rejection of a reality, but the unmasking of an illusion. The world as pure object is something that is not there. It is not a reality outside us for which we exist. It is not a firm and absolute objective structure which has to be accepted on its own inexorable terms. The world has in fact no terms of its own. It dictates no terms to man. We and our world interpenetrate. If anything, the world exists for us, and we exist for ourselves. It is only in assuming full responsibility for our world, for our lives and for ourselves that we can be said to live really for God. The whole human reality, which of course transcends us as individuals and as a collectivity, nevertheless interpenetrates the world of nature (which is obviously "real") and the world of history (also "real" in so far as it is made up of the total effect of all our decisions and actions). But this reality, though "external" and "objective," is not something entirely independent of us, which dominates us inexorably from without through the medium of certain fixed laws which science alone can discover and use. It is an extension and a projection of ourselves and of our lives, and if we attend to it respectfully, while attending also to our own freedom and our own integrity, we can learn to obey its ways and coordinate our lives with its mysterious movements. The way to find the real "world" is not merely to measure and observe what is outside us, but to discover our own inner ground. For that is where the world is, first of all: in my deepest self. But there I find the world to be quite different from the "obligatory answers." This "ground," this "world" where I am mysteriously present at once to my own self and to the freedoms of all other men, is not a visible objective and determined structure with fixed laws and demands. It is a living and self-creating mystery of which I am myself a part, to which I am myself my own unique door. When I find the world in my own ground, it is impossible for me to be alienated by it. It is precisely the obligatory answers which insist on showing me the world as totally other than myself and my brother, which alienate me from myself and from my brother. Hence I see no reason for our compulsion to manufacture ever newer and more shiny sets of obligatory answers.

The questions and the answers surely have their purpose. We are rational and dialectical beings. But even the best answers are themselves not final. They point to something further which cannot be embodied in a verbal ground. They point to life itself in its inalienable and personal ground. They point to that realm of values which, in the eyes of scientific and positivistic thought, has no meaning. But how can we come to grips with the world except in so far as it is a value, that is to say, in so far as it exists for us?

There remains a profound wisdom in the traditional Christian approach to the world as to an object of choice. But we have to admit that the habitual and mechanical compulsions of a certain limited type of Christian thought have falsified the true value-perspective in which the world can be discovered and chosen as it is. To treat the world merely as an agglomeration of material goods and objects outside ourselves, and to reject these goods and objects in order to seek others which are "interior" and "spiritual" is in fact to miss the whole point of the challenging confrontation of the world and Christ. Do we really choose between the world and Christ as between two conflicting realities absolutely opposed? Or do we choose Christ by choosing the world as it really is in him, that is to say created and redeemed by him, and encountered in the ground of our own personal freedom and of our love? Do we really renounce ourselves and the world in order to find Christ, or do we renounce our alienated and false selves in order to choose our own deepest truth in choosing both the world and Christ at the same time? If the deepest ground of my being is love, then in that very love itself and nowhere else will I find myself, and the world, and my brother and Christ. It is not a question of either-or but of all-in-one. It is not a matter of exclusivism and "purity" but of wholeness, wholeheartedness, unity and Meister Eckhart's *Gleichheit* (equality) which finds the same ground of love in everything.

The world cannot be a problem to anyone who sees that ultimately Christ, the world, his brother and his own inmost ground are made one and the same in grace and redemptive love. If all the current talk about the world helps people to discover this, then it is fine. But if it produces nothing but a whole new divisive gamut of obligatory positions and "contemporary answers" we might as well forget it. The world itself is no problem, but we are a problem to ourselves because we are alienated from ourselves, and this alienation is due precisely to an inveterate habit of division by which we break reality into pieces and then wonder why, after we have manipulated the pieces until they fall apart, we find ourselves out of touch with life, with reality, with the world and most of all with ourselves.

RAIN AND THE RHINOCEROS

Merton considered his own writings in the 1960s as taking a decided turn (see the Introduction to this volume for details) toward the more experimental, less "pious," and generously ecumenical. Nowhere is that turn more evident than in the beautiful essay "Rain and the Rhinoceros," written when Merton first began to spend extended periods of time in his hermitage. The essay reflects his long time sympathy for Thoreau, his readings in European literature, and his constant turn to the ancient masters of the monastic and ascetical life. In that sense, this essay is a companion to "Day of a Stranger" which comes from the same period and which strikes similar chords.

"Rain and the Rhinoceros" was first published in 1965 in a popular magazine (Holiday) *and reprinted in* Raids on the Unspeakable *(1966) which is a volume that represents Merton's newer interests at their best. "Mind you," Merton wrote in the introduction to* Raids, *"I do not repudiate the other books. I loved the whole lot of you. But in some way,* Raids, *I think I love you more than the rest."*

Historically, Christian spirituality expresses itself in terms of dialectical tensions (the false self/the true self; self-awareness/self-forgetfulness, etc.) and this essay is replete with them: city versus nature; solitude versus the crowd; nature versus technology; ancient wisdom versus contemporary drama; detachment versus engagement; hope versus despair. Above all, however, is Merton's sense of ironical wit as he meditates on the notion of "having fun" as this notion is tempered by his awareness of the SAC planes flying overhead with their load of atomic weapons (a common note in his writing).

If there is a spirit that hovers behind this essay, it is that of Henry David Thoreau, the archetypical solitary/social critic, to whom Merton pays tribute in the opening pages of his meditation as he had in his writings going back to the early 1950s. For an engaging study of Merton in relation to Thoreau and their mutual concerns, see Brother John Albert, OCSO, "Lights Across the Ridge: Thomas Merton and Henry David Thoreau," in The Thomas Merton Annual, *Volume One (New York: AMS Press, 1988), pp. 271–320.*

*

Let me say this before rain becomes a utility that they can plan and distribute for money. By "they" I mean the people who cannot understand that rain is a festival, who do not appreciate its gratuity, who think that what has no price has no value, that what cannot be sold is not real, so that the only way to make something *actual* is to place it on the market. The time will come when they will sell you even your rain. At the moment it is still free, and I am in it. I celebrate its gratuity and its meaninglessness.

The rain I am in is not like the rain of cities. It fills the woods with an immense and confused sound. It covers the flat roof of the cabin and its porch with insistent and controlled rhythms. And I listen, because it reminds me again and again that the whole world runs by rhythms I have not yet learned to recognize, rhythms that are not those of the engineer.

I came up here from the monastery last night, sloshing through the cornfield, said Vespers, and put some oatmeal on the Coleman stove for supper. It boiled over while I was listening to the rain and toasting a piece of bread at the log fire. The night became very dark. The rain surrounded the whole cabin with its enormous virginal myth, a whole world of meaning, of secrecy, of silence, of rumor. Think of it: all that speech pouring down, selling nothing, judging nobody, drenching the thick mulch of dead leaves, soaking the trees, filling the gullies and crannies of the wood with water, washing out the places where men have stripped the hillside! What a thing it is to sit absolutely alone, in the forest, at night, cherished by this wonderful, unintelligible, perfectly innocent speech, the most comforting speech in the world, the talk that rain makes by itself all over the ridges, and the talk of the watercourses everywhere in the hollows!

Nobody started it, nobody is going to stop it. It will talk as long as it wants, this rain. As long as it talks I am going to listen.

But I am also going to sleep, because here in this wilderness I have learned how to sleep again. Here I am not alien. The trees I know, the night I know, the rain I know. I close my eyes and instantly sink into the whole rainy world of which I am a part, and the world goes on with me in it, for I am not alien to it. I am alien to the noises of cities, of people, to the greed of machinery that does not sleep, the hum of power that eats up the night. Where rain, sunlight and darkness are contemned, I cannot sleep. I do not trust anything that has been fabricated to replace the climate of woods or prairies. I can have no confidence in places where the air is first fouled and then cleansed, where the water is first made deadly and then made safe with other poisons. There is nothing in the world of buildings that is not fabricated, and if a tree gets in among the apartment houses by mistake it is taught to grow chemically. It is given a precise reason for existing. They put a sign on it saying it is for health, beauty, perspective; that it is for peace, for prosperity; that it was planted by the mayor's daughter. All of this is mystification. The city itself lives on its own myth. Instead of waking up and silently existing, the city people prefer a stubborn and fabricated dream; they do not care to be a part of the night, or to be merely of the world. They have constructed a world outside the world, against the world, a world of mechanical fictions which contemn nature and seek only to use it up, thus preventing it from renewing itself and man.

Of course the festival of rain cannot be stopped, even in the city. The woman from the delicatessen scampers along the sidewalk with a newspaper over her head. The streets, suddenly washed, became transparent and alive, and the noise of traffic becomes a plashing of fountains. One would think that urban man in a rainstorm would *have* to take account of nature in its wetness and freshness, its baptism and its renewal. But the rain brings no renewal to the city, only to tomorrow's weather, and the glint of windows in tall buildings will then have nothing to do with the new sky. All "reality" will remain somewhere inside those walls, counting itself and selling itself with fantastically complex determination. Meanwhile the obsessed citizens plunge through the rain bearing the load of their obsessions, slightly more vulnerable than before, but still only barely aware of external realities. They do not see that the streets shine beautifully, that they themselves are walking on stars and water, that they are running in skies to catch a bus or a taxi, to shelter somewhere in the press of irritated humans, the faces of advertisements and the dim, cretinous sound of unidentified music. But they must know that there is wetness abroad. Perhaps they even *feel* it. I cannot say. Their complaints are mechanical and without spirit.

Naturally no one can believe the things they say about the rain. It all implies one basic lie: *only the city is real.* That weather, not being planned, not being fabricated, is an impertinence, a wen on the visage of progress. (Just a simple little operation, and the whole mess may become relatively tolerable. Let business *make* the rain. This will give it meaning.)

Thoreau sat in *his* cabin and criticized the railways. I sit in mine and wonder about a world that has, well, progressed. I must read *Walden* again, and see if Thoreau already guessed that he was part of what he thought he could escape. But it is not a matter of "escaping." It is not even a matter of protesting very audibly. Technology is here, even in the cabin. True, the utility line is not here yet, and so G.E. is not here yet either. When the utilities and G.E. enter my cabin arm in arm it will be nobody's fault but my own. I admit it. I am not kidding anybody, even myself. I will suffer their bluff and patronizing complacencies in silence. I will let them think they know what I am doing here.

They are convinced that *I am having fun.*

This has already been brought home to me with a wallop by my Coleman lantern. Beautiful lamp: It burns white gas and sings viciously but gives out a splendid green light in which I read Philoxenos, a sixth-century Syrian hermit. Philoxenos fits in with the rain and the festival of night. Of this, more later. Meanwhile: what does my Coleman lantern tell me? (Coleman's philosophy is printed on the cardboard box which I have (guiltily) not shellacked as I was supposed to, and which I have tossed in the woodshed behind the hickory chunks.) Coleman says that the light is good, and has a reason: it *"Stretches days to give more hours of fun."*

Can't I just be in the woods without any special reason? Just being in the woods, at night, in the cabin, is something too excellent to be justified or explained! It just *is*. There are always a few people who are in the woods at night, in the rain (because if there were not the world would have ended), and I am one of them. We are not having fun, we are not "having" anything, we are not "*stretching our days,*" and if we had fun it would not be measured by hours. Though as a matter of fact that is what fun seems to be: a state of diffuse excitation that can be measured by the clock and "stretched" by an appliance.

There is no clock that can measure the speech of this rain that falls all night on the drowned and lonely forest.

Of course at three-thirty A.M. the SAC plane goes over, red light winking low under the clouds, skimming the wooded summits on the south side of the valley, loaded with strong medicine. Very strong. Strong enough to burn up all these woods and stretch our hours of fun into eternities.

And that brings me to Philoxenos, a Syrian who had fun in the sixth century, without benefit of appliances, still less of nuclear deterrents.

Philoxenos in his ninth *memra* (on poverty) to dwellers in solitude, says that there is no explanation and no justification for the solitary life, since it is without a law. To be a contemplative is therefore to be an outlaw. As was Christ. As was Paul.

One who is not "alone," says Philoxenos, has not discovered his identity. He seems to be alone, perhaps, for he experiences himself as "individual." But because he is willingly enclosed and limited by the laws and illusions of collective existence, he has no more identity than an unborn child in the womb. He is not yet conscious. He is alien to his own truth. He has senses, but he cannot use them. He has life, but no identity. To have an identity, he has to be awake, and aware. But to be awake, he has to accept vulnerability and death. Not for their own sake: not out of stoicism or despair —only for the sake of the invulnerable inner reality which we cannot recognize (which we can only *be*) but to which we awaken only when we see the unreality of our vulnerable shell. The discovery of this inner self is an act and affirmation of solitude.

Now if we take our vulnerable shell to be our true identity, if we think our mask is our true face, we will protect it with fabrications even at the cost of violating our own truth. This seems to be the collective endeavor of society: the more busily men dedicate themselves to it, the more certainly it becomes a collective illusion, until in the end we have the enormous, obsessive, uncontrollable dynamic of fabrications designed to protect mere fictitious identities—"selves," that is to say, regarded as objects. Selves that can stand back and see themselves having fun (an illusion which reassures them that they are real).

Such is the ignorance which is taken to be the axiomatic foundation of all knowledge in the human collectivity: in order to experience yourself as real, you have to suppress the awareness of your contingency, your unreality, your state of radical need. This you do by creating an awareness of yourself as *one who has no needs that he cannot immediately fulfill.* Basically, this is an illusion of omnipotence: an illusion which the collectivity arrogates to itself, and consents to share with its individual members in proportion as they submit to its more central and more rigid fabrications.

You have needs; but if you behave and conform you can participate in the collective power. You can then satisfy all your needs. Meanwhile, in order to increase its power over you, the collectivity increases your needs. It also tightens its demand for conformity. Thus you can become all the more committed to the collective illusion in proportion to becoming more hopelessly mortgaged to collective power.

How does this work? The collectivity informs and shapes your will to happiness ("have fun") by presenting you with irresistible images of yourself as you would like to be: having *fun that is so perfectly credible that it allows no interference of conscious doubt.* In theory such a good time can be so convincing that you are no longer aware of even a remote possibility that it might change into something less satisfying. In practice, expensive fun always admits of a doubt, which blossoms out into another full-blown need, which then calls for a still more credible and more costly refinement of satisfaction, which again fails you. The end of the cycle is despair.

Because we live in a womb of collective illusion, our freedom remains abortive. Our capacities for joy, peace, and truth are never liberated. They can never be used. We are prisoners of a process, a dialectic of false promises and real deceptions ending in futility.

"The unborn child," says Philoxenos, "is already perfect and fully constituted in his nature, with all his senses, and limbs, but he cannot make use of them in their natural functions, because, in the womb, he cannot strengthen or develop them for such use."

Now, since all things have their season, there is a time to be unborn. We must begin, indeed, in the social womb. There is a time for warmth in the collective myth. But there is also a time to be born. He who is spiritually "born" as a mature identity is liberated from the enclosing womb of myth and prejudice. He learns to think for himself, guided no longer by the dictates of need and by the systems and processes designed to create artificial needs and then "satisfy" them.

This emancipation can take two forms: first that of the active life, which liberates itself from enslavement to necessity by considering and serving the needs of others, without thought of personal interest or return. And second, the contemplative life, which must not be construed as an escape from time and matter, from social responsibility and from the life of sense, but rather, as an advance into solitude and the desert, a confrontation with poverty and the void, a renunciation of the empirical self, in the presence of death, and nothingness, in order to overcome the ignorance and error that spring from the fear of "being nothing." The man who dares to be alone can come to see that the "emptiness" and "usefulness" which the collective mind fears and condemns are necessary conditions for the encounter with truth.

It is in the desert of loneliness and emptiness that the fear of death and the need for self-affirmation are seen to be illusory. When this is faced, then anguish is not necessarily overcome, but it can be accepted and understood. Thus, in the heart of anguish are found the gifts of peace and understanding: not simply in personal illumination and liberation, but by commitment and empathy, for the contemplative must assume the universal anguish and the inescapable condition of mortal man. The solitary, far from enclosing himself in himself, becomes every man. He dwells in the solitude, the poverty, the indigence of every man.

It is in this sense that the hermit, according to Philoxenos, imitates Christ. For in Christ, God takes to Himself the solitude and dereliction of man: every man. From the moment Christ went out into the desert to be tempted, the loneliness, the temptation and the hunger of every man became the loneliness, temptation and hunger of Christ. But in return, the gift of truth with which Christ dispelled the three kinds of illusion offered him in his temptation (security, reputation and power) can become also our own truth, if we can only accept it. It is offered to us also in temptation. "You too go out into the desert," said Philoxenos, "having with you nothing of the world, and the Holy Spirit will go with you. See the freedom with which Jesus has gone forth, and go forth like Him—see where he has left the rule of men; leave the rule of the world where he has left the law, and go out with him to fight the power of error."

And where is the power of error? We find it was after all not in the city, but in *ourselves.*

Today the insights of a Philoxenos are to be sought less in the tracts of theologians than in the meditations of the existentialists and in the Theater of the Absurd. The problem of Berenger, in Ionesco's *Rhinoceros,* is the problem of the human person stranded and alone in what threatens to become a society of monsters. In the sixth century Berenger might perhaps have walked off into the desert of Scete, without too much concern over the fact that all his fellow citizens, all his friends, and even his girl Daisy, had turned into rhinoceroses.

The problem today is that there are no deserts, only dude ranches.

The desert islands are places where the wicked little characters in the *Lord of the Flies* come face to face with the Lord of the Flies, form a small, tight, ferocious collectivity of painted faces, and arm themselves with spears to hunt down the last member of their group who still remembers with nostalgia the possibilities of rational discourse.

When Berenger finds himself suddenly the last human in a rhinoceros herd he looks into the mirror and says, humbly enough, "After all, man is not as bad as all that, is he?" But his world now shakes mightily with the stampede of his metamorphosed fellow citizens, and he soon becomes aware that the very stampede itself is the most telling and tragic of all arguments. For when he considers going out into the street "to try to convince them," he realizes that he "would have to learn their language." He looks in the mirror and sees that *he no longer resembles anyone.* He searches madly for a photograph of people as they were before the big change. But now humanity itself has become incredible, as well as hideous. To be the last man in the rhinoceros herd is, in fact, to be a monster.

Such is the problem which Ionesco sets us in his tragic irony: solitude and dissent become more and more impossible, more and more absurd. That Berenger finally accepts his absurdity and rushes out to challenge the whole herd only points up the futility of a commitment to rebellion. At the same time in *The New Tenant* (*Le Nouveau Locataire*) Ionesco portrays the absurdity of a logically consistent individualism which, in fact, is a self-isolation by the pseudo-logic of proliferating needs and possessions.

Ionesco protested that the New York production of *Rhinoceros* as a farce was a complete misunderstanding of his intention. It is a play not merely against *conformism* but about *totalitarianism.* The rhinoceros is not an amiable beast, and with him around the fun ceases and things begin to get serious. Everything has to make sense and be totally useful to the totally obsessive operation. At the same time Ionesco was criticized for not giving the audience "something positive" to take away with them, instead of just "refusing the human adventure." (Presumably "rhinoceritis" is the latest in human adventure!) He replied: "They [the spectators] leave in a void —and that was my intention. It is the business of a free man to pull himself out of this void by his own power and not by the power of other people!" In this Ionesco comes very close to Zen and to Christian eremitism.

"In all the cities of the world, it is the same," says Ionesco. "The universal and modern man is the man in a rush (i.e. a rhinoceros), a man who has no time, who is a prisoner of necessity, who cannot understand that *a thing might perhaps be without usefulness;* nor does he understand that, at bottom, it is the useful that may be a useless and back-breaking burden. If one does not understand the usefulness of the useless and the uselessness of the useful, one cannot understand art. And a country where art is not understood is a country of slaves and robots. . . ." (*Notes et Contre Notes,* p. 129) Rhinoceritis, he adds, is the sickness that lies in wait "for those who *have lost the sense and the taste for solitude.*"

The love of solitude is sometimes condemned as "hatred of

our fellow men." But is this true? If we push our analysis of collective thinking a little further we will find that the dialectic of power and need, of submission and satisfaction, ends by being a dialectic of hate. Collectivity needs not only to absorb everyone it can, but also implicitly to hate and destroy whoever cannot be absorbed. Paradoxically, one of the needs of collectivity is to reject certain classes, or races, or groups, in order to strengthen its own self-awareness by hating them instead of absorbing them.

Thus the solitary cannot survive unless he is capable of loving everyone, without concern for the fact that he is likely to be regarded by all of them as a traitor. Only the man who has fully attained his own spiritual identity can live without the need to kill, and without the need of a doctrine that permits him to do so with a good conscience. There will always be a place, says Ionesco, *"for those isolated consciences who have stood up for the universal conscience"* as against the mass mind. But their place is solitude. They have no other. Hence it is the solitary person (whether in the city or in the desert) who does mankind the inestimable favor of reminding it of its true capacity for maturity, liberty and peace.

It sounds very much like Philoxenos to me.

And it sounds like what the rain says. We still carry this burden of illusion because we do not dare to lay it down. We suffer all the needs that society demands we suffer, because if we do not have these needs we lose our "usefulness" in society—the usefulness of suckers. We fear to be alone, and to be ourselves, and so to remind others of the truth that is in them.

"I will not make you such rich men as have need of many things," said Philoxenos (putting the words on the lips of Christ), "but I will make you true rich men who have need of nothing. Since it is not he who has many possessions that is rich, but he who has no needs." Obviously, we shall always have *some* needs. But only he who has the simplest and most natural needs can be considered to be without needs, since the only needs he has are real ones, and the real ones are not hard to fulfill if one is a free man!

The rain has stopped. The afternoon sun slants through the pine trees: and how those useless needles smell in the clear air!

A dandelion, long out of season, has pushed itself into bloom between the smashed leaves of last summer's day lilies. The valley resounds with the totally uninformative talk of creeks and wild water.

Then the quails begin their sweet whistling in the wet bushes. Their noise is absolutely useless, and so is the delight I take in it. There is nothing I would rather hear, not because it is a better noise than other noises, but because it is the voice of the present moment, the present festival.

Yet even here the earth shakes. Over at Fort Knox the Rhinoceros is having fun.

A CHRISTIAN LOOKS AT ZEN

"A Christian Looks At Zen" *was first published as a preface to*
John C.H. Wu's book The Golden Age of Zen *(1967) and reprinted*
the following year in Merton's book Zen and the Birds of Appetite
(1968). Merton and Wu had corresponded from the early 1960s
(Wu had also visited Merton at Gethsemani) about the relationship
of Eastern Wisdom and Christianity (Wu was a Catholic). One
close collaboration which derived from that friendship was Mer-
ton's translation (he, in fact, called them "imitations" since he had
little knowledge of Chinese) of writings of the Taoist master
Chaung Tzu. Published under the title The Way of Chaung Tzu
(1965), Merton says, in his Foreword, that John Wu was his "chief
abettor and accomplice."

This essay distills Merton's thinking about Eastern thought. It
represents his decade-long interest in such writings as well as his
friendship with the noted Zen scholar D.T. Suzuki and his apprecia-
tion of those Christians who had initiated a dialogue with such
thought like Aelred Graham, William Johnston, and Peré Dumou-
lin. Those interests, in fact, have deeper roots in Merton's lifelong
concern with the spiritual traditions of the East—a concern which
he manifested even before his conversion to Christianity in the
late 1930s.

It was Merton's strong conviction that an encounter with East-
ern mysticism had the dual effect of enriching the actual practices
of the West by new and useful insights as well as acting as a kind of
prophetic challenge to the contemplative complacency of the West.
He summed up the matter well in a comment to John Wu early in
their correspondence: "One of the defects of a wrong kind of super-
naturalism is that by rejecting those wonderful natural wisdoms
that came before Christ and cried out for fulfillment in the gospel,
they set aside the challenging demands which would make us
Christians strive for the highest purity of our own spiritual wis-
dom." That was written in 1961. A few years later Merton would

probably repent the facile use of "supernaturalism" and "natural wisdom" but not of the insight that stands behind his words.

There are two sources worthwhile reading in tandem with this essay. First is the Merton/Wu correspondence in The Hidden Ground of Love *(New York: Farrar, Straus, & Giroux, 1985), pp. 611–635; second is the exchange between Merton and D.T. Suzuki which reached its full expression in this period, an exchange which began with a 1959 letter from Merton who confessed to Suzuki that he could hardly claim to understand Zen since he could barely understand Christianity; see* Encounter: Thomas Merton and D.T. Suzuki, *edited and introduced by Robert E. Daggy (Monterey: Larkspur, 1988).*

*

Dr. John C.H. Wu is in a uniquely favorable position to interpret Zen for the West. He has given courses on Zen in Chinese and in American universities. An eminent jurist and diplomat, a Chinese convert to Catholicism, a scholar but also a man of profoundly humorous simplicity and spiritual freedom, he is able to write of Buddhism not from hearsay or study alone, but from within. Dr. Wu is not afraid to admit that he brought Zen, Taoism and Confucianism with him into Christianity. In fact in his well-known Chinese translation of the New Testament he opens the Gospel of St. John with the words, "In the beginning was the Tao."

He nowhere feels himself obliged to pretend that Zen causes him to have dizzy spells or palpitations of the heart. Nor does he attempt the complex and frustrating task of trying to conciliate Zen insights with Christian doctrine. He simply takes hold of Zen and presents it without comment. Anyone who has any familiarity with Zen will immediately admit that this is the only way to talk about it. To approach the subject with an intellectual or theological chip on the shoulder would end only in confusion. The truth of the matter is that you can hardly set Christianity and Zen side by side and compare them. This would almost be like trying to compare mathematics and tennis. And if you are writing a book on tennis which might conceivably be read by many mathematicians, there is little point in bringing mathematics into the discussion—best to stick to the tennis. That is what Dr. Wu has done with Zen.

On the other hand, Zen is deliberately cryptic and disconcerting. It seems to say the most outrageous things about the life of the spirit. It seems to jolt even the Buddhist mind out of its familiar thought routines and devout imaginings, and no doubt it will be even more shocking to those whose religious outlook is remote from Buddhism. Zen can sound, at times, frankly and avowedly irreligious. And it is, in the sense that it makes a direct attack on formalism and myth, and regards conventional religiosity as a hindrance to mature spiritual development. On the other hand, in what sense is Zen, as such, "religious" at all? Yet where do we ever find "pure Zen" dissociated from a religious and cultural matrix of some sort? Some of the Zen Masters were iconoclasts. But the life of an ordinary Zen temple is full of Buddhist piety and ritual, and some Zen literature abounds in devotionalism and in conventional Buddhist religious concepts. The Zen of D.T. Suzuki is completely free from all this. But can it be called "typical?" One of the advantages of Dr. Wu's Christian treatment is that he, too, is able to see Zen apart from this accidental setting. It is like seeing the mystical doctrine of St. John of the Cross apart from the somewhat irrelevant backdrop of Spanish baroque. However, the whole study of Zen can bristle with questions like these, and when the well-meaning inquirer receives answers to his questions, then hundreds of other questions arise to take the place of the two or three that have been "answered."

Though much has been said, written and published in the West about Zen, the general reader is probably not much the wiser for most of it. And unless he has some idea of what Zen is all about he may be mystified by Dr. Wu's book, which is full of the classic Zen material: curious anecdotes, strange happenings, cryptic declarations, explosions of illogical humor, not to mention contradictions, inconsistencies, eccentric and even absurd behavior, and all for what? For some apparently esoteric purpose which is never made clear to the satisfaction of the logical Western mind.

Now the reader with a Judeo-Christian background of some sort (and who in the West does not still have some such background?) will naturally be predisposed to misinterpret Zen because he will instinctively take up the position of one who is confronting a "rival system of thought" or a "competing ideology" or an "alien world view" or more simply "a false religion." Anyone who adopts such a position makes it impossible for himself to see what Zen is, because he assumes in advance that it must be something that it expressly refuses to be. Zen is not a systematic explanation of life, it is not an ideology, it is not a world view, it is not a theology of revelation and salvation, it is not a mystique, it is not a way of ascetic perfection, it is not mysticism as this is understood in the West, in fact it fits no convenient category of ours. Hence all our attempts to tag it and dispose of it with labels like "pantheism," "quietism," "illuminism," "Pelagianism," must be completely incongruous, and proceed from a naive assumption that Zen pretends to justify the ways of God to man and to do so falsely. Zen is not concerned with God in the way Christianity is, though one is entitled to discover sophisticated analogies between the Zen experience of the Void (*Sunyata*) and the experience of God in the "unknowing" of apophatic Christian mysticism. However, Zen cannot be properly judged as a mere doctrine, for though there are in it implicit doctrinal elements, they are entirely secondary to the inexpressible Zen experience.

True, we cannot really understand Chinese Zen if we do not grasp the implicit Buddhist metaphysic which it so to speak acts out. But the Buddhist metaphysic itself is hardly doctrinal in our elaborate philosophical and theological sense: Buddhist philosophy is an interpretation of ordinary human experience, but an interpretation which is not revealed by God nor discovered in the access of inspiration nor seen in a mystical light. Basically, Buddhist metaphysics is a very simple and natural elaboration of the implications of Buddha's own experience of enlightenment. Buddhism does not seek primarily to understand or to "believe in" the enlightenment of Buddha as the solution to all human problems, but seeks an existential and empirical participation in that enlightenment experience. It is conceivable that one might have the "enlightenment" without being aware of any discursive philosophical implications at all. These implications are not seen as having any theological bearing whatever, and they point only to the ordinary natural condition of man. It is true that they arrive at certain fundamental deductions which were in the course of time elaborated into complex religious and philosophical systems. But the chief characteristic of Zen is that it rejects all these systematic elaborations in order to get back, as far as possible, to the pure unarticulated and unexplained ground of direct experience. The direct experience of what? Life itself. What it means that I exist, that I live: who is this "I" that exists and lives? What is the difference between an authentic and an illusory awareness of the self that exists and lives? What are and are not the basic facts of existence?

When we in the West speak of "basic facts of existence" we tend immediately to conceive these facts as reducible to certain austere and foolproof propositions—logical statements that are guaranteed to have meaning because they are empirically verifiable. These are what Bertrand Russell called "atomic facts." Now for Zen it is inconceivable that the basic facts of existence should be able to be stated in any proposition however atomic. For Zen, from the moment fact is transferred to a statement it is falsified. One ceases to grasp the naked reality of experience and one grasps a form of words instead. The *verification* that Zen seeks is not to be found in a dialectical transaction involving the reduction of fact to logical statement and the reflective verification of statement by fact. It may be said that long before Bertrand Russell spoke of "atomic facts" Zen had split the atom and made its own kind of statement in the explosion of logic into *Satori* (enlightenment). The whole aim of Zen is not to make foolproof statements about experience, but to come to direct grips with reality without the mediation of logical verbalizing.

But *what* reality? There is certainly a kind of living and non-verbal dialectic in Zen between the ordinary everyday experience of the senses (which is by no means arbitrarily repudiated) and the experience of enlightenment. Zen is not an idealistic rejection of sense and matter in order to ascend to a supposedly invisible reality which alone is real. The Zen experience is a direct grasp of the *unity* of the invisible and the visible, the noumenal and the phenomenal, or, if you prefer, an experiential realization that any such division is bound to be pure imagination.

D.T. Suzuki says: "Tasting, seeing, experiencing, living—all these demonstrate that there is something common to enlightenment-experience and our sense-experience; the one takes place in our innermost being, the other on the periphery of our consciousness. Personal experience thus seems to be the foundation of Buddhist philosophy. In this sense Buddhism is radical empiricism or experientialism, whatever dialectic later developed to probe the meaning of the enlightenment experience." (D.T. Suzuki, *Mysticism: Christian and Buddhist,* N. Y., 1957, p. 48)

Now the great obstacle to mutual understanding between Christianity and Buddhism lies in the Western tendency to focus not on the Buddhist *experience,* which is essential, but on the *explanation,* which is accidental and which indeed Zen often regards as completely trivial and even misleading.

Buddhist meditation, but above all that of Zen, seeks not to *explain* but to *pay attention,* to *become aware,* to *be mindful,* in other words to develop a certain *kind of consciousness that is above and beyond deception* by verbal formulas—or by emotional excitement. Deception in what? Deception in its grasp of itself as it really is. Deception due to diversion and distraction from what is right there—consciousness itself.

Zen, then, aims at a kind of certainty: but it is not the logical certainty of philosophical proof, still less the religious certainty that comes with the acceptance of the word of God by the obedience of faith. It is rather the certainty that goes with an authentic metaphysical intuition which is also existential and empirical. The purpose of all Buddhism is to refine the consciousness until this kind of insight is attained, and the religious implications of the insight are then variously worked out and applied to life in the different Buddhist traditions.

In the *Mahayana* tradition, which includes Zen, the chief implication of this insight into the human condition is *Karuna* or compassion, which leads to a paradoxical reversal of what the insight itself might seem to imply. Instead of rejoicing in his escape from the phenomenal world of suffering, the Bodhisattva elects to remain in it and finds in it his *Nirvana,* by reason not only of the metaphysic which identifies the phenomenal and the noumenal, but also of the compassionate love which identifies all the sufferers in the round of birth and death with the Buddha, whose enlightenment they potentially share. Though there are a heaven and a hell for Buddhists, these are not ultimate, and in fact it would be entirely ambiguous to assume that Buddha is regarded as a Savior who leads his faithful disciples to *Nirvana* as to a kind of negative heaven. (Pure Land Buddhism or Amidism is, however, distinctly a salvation religion.)

It cannot be repeated too often: in understanding Buddhism it would be a great mistake to concentrate on the "doctrine," the formulated philosophy of life, and to neglect the experience, which is absolutely essential, the very heart of Buddhism. This is in a sense the exact opposite of the situation in Christianity. For Christianity begins with revelation. Though it would be misleading to classify this revelation simply as a "doctrine" and an "explanation" (it is far more than that—the revelation of God Himself in the mystery of Christ) it is nevertheless communicated to us in words, in statements, and everything depends on the believer's accepting the truth of these statements.

Therefore Christianity has always been profoundly concerned with these statements: with the accuracy of their transmission from the original sources, with the precise understanding of their exact meaning, with the elimination and indeed the condemnation of false interpretations. At times this concern has been exaggerated almost to the point of an obsession, accompanied by arbitrary and fanatical insistence on hairsplitting distinctions and the purest niceties of theological detail.

This obsession with doctrinal formulas, juridical order and ritual exactitude has often made people forget that the heart of Catholicism, too, is a *living experience* of unity in Christ which far transcends all conceptual formulations. What too often has been overlooked, in consequence, is that Catholicism is the taste and experience of eternal life: "We announce to you the eternal life which was with the Father and has appeared to us. What we have seen and have heard we announce to you, in order that you also may have fellowship with us and that our fellowship may be with the Father and with His Son Jesus Christ." (I John 1:2–3) Too often the Catholic has imagined himself obliged to stop short at a mere correct and external belief expressed in good moral behavior, instead of entering fully into the life of hope and love consummated by union with the invisible God "in Christ and in the Spirit," thus fully sharing in the Divine Nature. (Ephesians 2:18, 2 Peter 1:4, Col. 1:9–17, I John 4:12–12)

The Second Vatican Council has (we hope) happily put an end

to this obsessive tendency in Catholic theological investigation. But the fact remains that for Christianity, a religion of the Word, the understanding of the statements which embody God's revelation of Himself remains a primary concern. Christian experience is a fruit of this understanding, a development of it, a deepening of it.

At the same time, Christian experience itself will be profoundly affected by the idea of revelation that the Christian himself will entertain. For example, if revelation is regarded simply as a system of truths *about* God and an explanation of how the universe came into existence, what will eventually happen to it, what is the purpose of Christian life, what are its moral norms, what will be the rewards of the virtuous, and so on, then Christianity is in effect reduced to a world view, at times a religious philosophy and little more, sustained by a more or less elaborate cult, by a moral discipline and a strict code of Law. "Experience" of the inner meaning of Christian revelation will necessarily be distorted and diminished in such a theological setting. What will such experience be? Not so much a living theological experience of the presence of God in the world and in mankind through the mystery of Christ, but rather a sense of security in one's own correctness: a feeling of confidence that one has been saved, a confidence which is based on the reflex awareness that one holds the correct view of the creation and purpose of the world and that one's behavior is of a kind to be rewarded in the next life. Or, perhaps, since few can attain this level of self-assurance, then the Christian experience becomes one of anxious hope—a struggle with occasional doubt of the "right answers," a painful and constant effort to meet the severe demands of morality and law, and a somewhat desperate recourse to the sacraments which are there to help the weak who must constantly fall and rise again.

This of course is a sadly deficient account of true Christian experience, based on a distortion of the true import of Christian revelation. Yet it is the impression non-Christians often get of Christianity from the outside, and when one proceeds to compare, say, Zen experience in its purity with this diminished and distorted type of "Christian experience," then one's comparison is just as meaningless and misleading as a comparison of Christian philosophy and theology on their highest and most sophisticated level with the myths of a popular and decadent Buddhism.

When we set Christianity and Buddhism side by side, we must try to find the points where a genuinely common ground between the two exists. At the present moment, this is no easy task. In fact it is still practically impossible, as suggested above, to really find any such common ground except in a very schematic and artificial way. After all, what do we mean by Christianity, and what do we mean by Buddhism? Is Christianity Christian Theology? Ethics? Mysticism? Worship? Is our idea of Christianity to be taken without further qualification as the Roman Catholic Church? Or does it include Protestant Christianity? The Protestantism of Luther or that of Bonhoeffer? The Protestantism of the God-is-dead school? The Catholicism of St. Thomas? Of St. Augustine and the Western Church Fathers? A supposedly "pure" Christianity of the Gospels? A demythologized Christianity? A "social Gospel"? And what do we mean by Buddhism? The Theravada Buddhism of Ceylon, or that of Burma? Tibetan Buddhism? Tantric Buddhism? Pure Land Buddhism? Speculative and scholastic Indian Buddhism of the middle ages? Or Zen?

The immense variety of forms taken by thought, experience, worship, moral practice, in both Buddhism and Christianity make all comparisons haphazard, and in the end, when someone like the late Dr. Suzuki announced a study on *Mysticism: Christian and Buddhist,* it turned out to be, rather practically in fact, a comparison between Meister Eckhart and Zen. To narrow the field in this way is at least relevant, though to take Meister Eckhart as representative of Christian mysticism is hazardous. At the same time we must remark that Dr. Suzuki was much too convinced that Eckhart was unusual in his time, and that his statements must have shocked most of his contemporaries. Eckhart's condemnation was in fact due in some measure to rivalry between Dominicans and Franciscans, and his teaching, bold and in some points unable to avoid condemnation, was nevertheless based on St. Thomas to a great extent and belonged to a mystical tradition that was very much alive and was, in fact, the most vital religious force in the Catholicism of his time. Yet to identify Christianity with Eckhart would be completely misleading. That was not what Suzuki intended. He was not comparing the *mystical theology* of Eckhart with the Buddhist philosophy of the Zen Masters, but the *experience* of Eckhart, ontologically and psychologically, with the *experience* of the Zen

Masters. This is a reasonable enterprise, offering some small hope of interesting and valid results.

But can one distill from religious or mystical experience certain pure elements which are common everywhere in all religions? Or is the basic understanding of the nature and meaning of experience so determined by the variety of doctrines that a comparison of experiences involves us inevitably in a comparison of metaphysical or religious beliefs? This is no easy question either. If a Christian mystic has an experience which can be phenomenologically compared with a Zen experience, does it matter that the Christian in fact believes he is personally united with God and the Zen-man interprets his experience as *Sunyata* or the Void being aware of itself? In what sense can these two experiences be called "mystical"? Suppose that the Zen Masters forcefully repudiate any attempt on the part of Christians to grace them with the titles of "mystics"?

It must certainly be said that a certain type of concordist thought today too easily assumes as a basic dogma that "the mystics" in all religions are all experiencing the same thing and are all alike in their liberation from the various doctrines and explanations and creeds of their less fortunate co-religionists. All religions thus "meet at the top," and their various theologies and philosophies become irrelevant when we see that they were merely means for arriving at the same end, and all means are alike efficacious. This has never been demonstrated with any kind of rigor, and though it has been persuasively advanced by talented and experienced minds, we must say that a great deal of study and investigation must be done before much can be said on this very complex question which, once again, seems to imply a purely formalistic view of theological and philosophical doctrines, as if a fundamental belief were something that a mystic could throw off like a suit of clothes and as if his very experience itself were not in some sense modified by the fact that he held this belief.

At the same time, since the personal experience of the mystic remains inaccessible to us and can only be evaluated indirectly through texts and other testimonials—perhaps written and given by others—it is never easy to say with any security that what a Christian mystic and a Sufi and a Zen Master experience is really "the same thing." What does such a claim really mean? Can it be made at all, without implying (quite falsely) that these higher experiences are "experiences of something"? It therefore remains a very serious problem to distinguish in all these higher forms of religious and metaphysical consciousness what is "pure experience" and what is to some extent determined by language, symbol, or indeed by the "grace of a sacrament." We have hardly reached the point where we know enough about these different states of consciousness and about their metaphysical implications to compare them in accurate detail. But there are nevertheless certain analogies and correspondence which are evident even now, and which may perhaps point out the way to a better mutual understanding. Let us not rashly take them as "proofs" but only as significant clues.

Is it therefore possible to say that both Christians and Buddhists can equally well practice Zen? Yes, if by Zen we mean precisely the quest for direct and pure experience on a metaphysical level, liberated from verbal formulas and linguistic preconceptions. On the theological level the question becomes more complex. It will be touched on at the end of this essay.

The best we can say is that in certain religions, Buddhism for instance, the philosophical or religious framework is of a kind that *can* more easily be discarded, because it has in itself a built-in "ejector," so to speak, by which the meditator is at a certain point flung out from the conceptual apparatus into the Void. It is possible for a Zen Master to say nonchalantly to his disciple, "If you meet the Buddha, kill him!" But in Christian mysticism the question whether or not the mystic can get along without the human "form" (*Gestalt*) or the sacred Humanity of Christ is still hotly debated, with the majority opinion definitely maintaining the necessity for the Christ of faith to be present as ikon at the center of Christian contemplation. Here again, the question is confused by the failure to distinguish between the objective theology of Christian experience and the actual psychological facts of Christian mysticism in certain cases. And then one must ask, at what point do the abstract demands of theory take precedence over the psychological facts of experience? Or, to what extent does the theology of a theologian without experience claim to interpret correctly the "experienced theology" of the mystic who is perhaps not able to articulate the meaning of his experience in a satisfactory way?

We keep returning to one central question in two forms: the

relation of objective doctrine to subjective mystic (or metaphysical) experience, and the difference in this relationship between Christianity and Zen. In Christianity the objective doctrine retains priority both in time and in eminence. In Zen the experience is always prior, not in time but in importance. This is because Christianity is based on supernatural revelation, and Zen, discarding all idea of any revelation and even taking a very independent view of sacred tradition (at least written), seeks to penetrate the natural ontological ground of being. Christianity is a religion of grace and divine gift, hence of total dependence on God. Zen is not easily classified as "a religion" (it is in fact easily separable from any religious matrix and can supposedly flourish in the soil either of non-Buddhist religions or no religion at all), and in any event it strives, like all Buddhism, to make man completely free and independent even in his striving for salvation and enlightenment. Independent of what? Of merely external supports and authorities which keep him from having access to and making use of the deep resources in his own nature and psyche. (Note that Chinese and Japanese Zen both in fact flourished in extremely disciplined and authoritarian cultures. Hence their emphasis on "autonomy" meant in fact an ultimate and humble discovery of inner freedom after one had exhausted all the possibilities of an intensely strict and austere authoritarian training—as the methods of the Zen Masters make abundantly clear!)

On the other hand, let us repeat that we must not neglect the great importance of experience in Christianity. But Christian experience always has a special modality, due to the fact that it is inseparable from the mystery of Christ and the collective life of the Church, the Body of Christ. To experience the mystery of Christ mystically or otherwise is always to transcend the merely individual psychological level and to "experience theologically with the Church" (*sentire cum Ecclesia*). In other words, this experience must always be in some way reducible to a theological form that can be shared by the rest of the Church or that shows that it is a sharing of what the rest of the Church experiences. There is therefore in the recording of Christian experiences a natural tendency to set them down in language and symbols that are easily accessible to other Christians. This may perhaps sometimes mean an unconscious translation of the inexpressible into familiar symbols that are always at hand ready for immediate use.

Zen on the other hand resolutely resists any temptation to be easily communicable, and a great deal of the paradox and violence of Zen teaching and practice is aimed at blasting the foundation of ready explanation and comforting symbol out from under the disciple's supposed "experience." The Christian experience is acceptable in so far as it accords with an established theological and symbolic pattern. The Zen experience is only acceptable on the basis of its absolute singularity, and yet it must be in some way communicable. How?

We cannot begin to understand how the Zen experience is manifested and communicated between master and disciple unless we realize *what* is communicated. If we do not know *what* is supposed to be signified, the strange method of signification will leave us totally disconcerted and more in the dark than we were when we started. Now in Zen, what is communicated is not a message. It is not simply a "word," even though it might be the "word of the Lord." It is not a "what." It does not bring "news" which the receiver did not already have, about something the one informed did not yet know. What Zen communicates is an awareness that is potentially already there but is not conscious of itself. Zen is then not Kerygma but realization, not revelation but consciousness, not news from the Father who sends His Son into this world, but awareness of the ontological ground of our own being here and now, right in the midst of the world. We will see later that the supernatural Kerygma and the metaphysical intuition of the ground of being are far from being incompatible. One may be said to prepare the way for the other. They can well complement each other, and for this reason Zen is perfectly compatible with Christian belief and indeed with Christian mysticism (if we understand Zen in its pure state, as metaphysical intuition).

If this is true, then we must admit it is perfectly logical to admit, with the Zen Masters, that "Zen teaches nothing." One of the greatest of the Chinese Zen Masters, the Patriarch, Hui Neng (7th century A.D.), was asked a leading question by a disciple: "Who has inherited the spirit of the Fifth Patriarch?" (i.e., who is Patriarch now?)

Hui Neng replied: "One who understands Buddhism."
The monk pressed his point: "Have you then inherited it?"
Hui Neng said: "No."
"Why not?" asked the monk.
"Because I do not understand Buddhism."

This story is meant precisely to illustrate the fact that Hui Neng *had* inherited the role of Patriarch, or the charism of teaching the purest Zen. He was qualified to transmit the enlightenment of the Buddha himself to disciples. If he had laid claim to an authoritative teaching that made this enlightenment understandable to those who did not possess it, then he would have been teaching *something else,* that is to say a doctrine *about* enlightenment. He would be disseminating the message of his own understanding of Zen, and in that case he would not be awakening others to Zen in themselves, but imposing on them the imprint of his own understanding and teaching. Zen does not tolerate this kind of thing, since this would be incompatible with the true purpose of Zen: awakening a deep ontological awareness, a wisdom-intuition (*Prajna*) in the ground of the being of the one awakened. And in fact, the pure consciousness of *Prajna* would not be pure and immediate if it were a consciousness that one understands *Prajna*.

The language used by Zen is therefore in some sense an anti-language, and the "logic" of Zen is a radical reversal of philosophical logic. The human dilemma of communication is that we cannot communicate ordinarily without words and signs, but even ordinary experience tends to be falsified by our habits of verbalization and rationalization. The convenient tools of language enable us to decide beforehand what we think things mean, and tempt us all too easily to see things only in a way that fits our logical preconceptions and our verbal formulas. Instead of seeing *things* and *facts* as they are we see them as reflections and verifications of the sentences we have previously made up in our minds. We quickly forget how to simply *see* things and substitute our words and our formulas for the things themselves, manipulating facts so that we see only what conveniently fits our prejudices. Zen uses language against itself to blast out these preconceptions and to destroy the specious "reality" in our minds so that we can *see directly.* Zen is saying, as Wittgenstein said, "Don't think: Look!"

Since the Zen intuition seeks to awaken a direct metaphysical consciousness beyond the empirical, reflecting, knowing, willing and talking ego, this awareness must be immediately present to itself and not mediated by either conceptual or reflexive or imaginative knowledge. And yet far from being mere negation, Zen is also entirely positive. Let us hear D.T. Suzuki on the subject:

> "Zen always aims at grasping the central fact of life, which can never be brought to the dissecting table of the intellect. To grasp the central fact of life, Zen is forced to propose a series of negations. Mere negation however is not the spirit of Zen . . ." (Hence, he says, the Zen Masters neither affirm nor negate, they simply act or speak in such a way that the action or speech itself is a plain fact bursting with Zen. . . .) Suzuki continues: "When the spirit of Zen is grasped in its purity, it will be seen what a real thing that (act—in this case a slap) is. For here is no negation, no affirmation, but a plain fact, a pure experience, the very foundation of our being and thought. All the quietness and emptiness one might desire in the midst of most active meditation lies therein. Do not be carried away by anything outward or conventional. Zen must be seized with bare hands, with no gloves on." (D.T. Suzuki, *Introduction to Zen Buddhism, London.* 1960, p. 51)

It is in this sense that "Zen teaches nothing; it merely enables us to wake up and become aware. It does not teach, it points." (Suzuki *Introduction,* p. 38) The acts and gestures of a Zen Master are no more "statements" than is the ringing of an alarm clock.

All the words and actions of the Zen Masters and of their disciples are to be understood in this context. Usually the Master is simply "producing facts" which the disciple either sees or does not see.

Many of the Zen stories, which are almost always incomprehensible in rational terms, are simply the ringing of an alarm clock, and the reaction of the sleeper. Usually the misguided sleeper makes a response which in effect turns off the alarm so that he can go back to sleep. Sometimes he jumps out of bed with a shout of astonishment that it is so late. Sometimes he just sleeps and does not hear the alarm at all!

In so far as the disciple takes the fact to be a sign of something else, he is misled by it. The Master may (by means of some other fact) try to make him aware of this. Often it is precisely at the point where the disciple realizes himself to be utterly misled that he also realizes everything else along with it: chiefly, of course, that there was nothing to realize in the first place except the fact. What *fact?* If you know the answer you are awake. You hear the alarm!

But we in the West, living in a tradition of stubborn ego-centered practicality and geared entirely for the use and manipulation of everything, always pass from one thing to another, from cause to effect, from the first to the next and to the last and then back to the first. Everything always points to something else, and hence we never stop anywhere because we cannot: as soon as we pause, the escalator reaches the end of the ride and we have to get off and find another one. Nothing is allowed just to be and to mean itself: everything has to mysteriously signify something else. Zen is especially designed to frustrate the mind that thinks in such terms. The Zen "fact," whatever it may be, always lands across our road like a fallen tree beyond which we cannot pass.

Nor are such facts lacking in Christianity—the Cross for example. Just as the Buddha's "Fire Sermon" radically transforms the Buddhist's awareness of all that is around him, so the "word of the Cross" in very much the same way gives the Christian a radically new consciousness of the meaning of his life and of his relationship with other men and with the world around him.

In both cases, the "facts" are not merely impersonal and objective, but facts of personal experience. Both Buddhism and Christianity are alike in making use of ordinary everyday human existence as material for a radical transformation of consciousness. Since ordinary everyday human existence is full of confusion and suffering, then obviously one will make good use of both of these in order to transform one's awareness and one's understanding, and to go beyond both to attain "wisdom" in love. It would be a grave error to suppose that Buddhism and Christianity merely offer various *explanations* of suffering, or worse, justifications and mystifications built on this ineluctable fact. On the contrary both show that suffering remains inexplicable most of all for the man who attempts *to explain it in order to evade it,* or who thinks explanation itself is an escape. Suffering is not a "problem" as if it were something we could stand outside and control. Suffering, as both Christianity and Buddhism see, each in its own way, is part of our very ego-identity and empirical existence, and the only thing to do about it is to plunge right into the middle of contradiction and confusion in order to be transformed by what Zen calls the "Great Death" and Christianity calls "dying and rising with Christ."

Let us now return to the obscure and tantalizing "facts" in which Zen deals. In the relation between Zen Master and disciple, the most usually encountered "fact" is the disciple's frustration, his inability to get somewhere by the use of his own will and his own reasoning. Most sayings of the Zen Masters deal with this situation, and try to convey to the disciple that he has a fundamentally misleading experience of himself and of his capacities.

"When the cart stops," said Huai-Jang, the Master of Ma-Tsu, "do you whip the cart or whip the ox?" And he added, "If one sees the Tao from the standpoint of making and unmaking, or gathering and scattering, one does not really see the Tao."

If this remark about whipping the cart or the ox is obscure, perhaps another *Mondo* (question and answer) will suggest the same fact in a different way.

A monk asks Pai-Chang, "Who is the Buddha?"
Pai-Chang answers: "Who are you?"

A monk wants to know what is *Prajna* (the metaphysical wisdom-intuition of Zen). Not only that, but *Mahaprajna,* Great or Absolute Wisdom. The whole works.
The Master answers without concern:
"The snow is falling fast and all is enveloped in mist."
The monk remains silent.
The Master asks: "Do you understand?"
"No, Master, I do not."
Thereupon the Master composed a verse for him:

Mahaprajna
It is neither taking in nor giving up.
If one understands it not,

The wind is cold, the snow is falling.
   (Suzuki, *Introduction,* p. 99–100)

The monk is "trying to understand" when in fact he ought to try to *look.* The apparently mysterious and cryptic sayings of Zen become much simpler when we see them in the whole context of Buddhist "mindfulness" or awareness, which in its most elementary form consists in that "bare attention" which simply *sees* what is right there and does not add any comment, any interpretation, any judgment, any conclusion. It just *sees.* Learning to see in this manner is the basic and fundamental exercise of Buddhist meditation. (See Nyanaponika Thero-Colombo, *The Heart of Buddhist Meditation,* Ceylon, 1956)

If one reaches the point where understanding fails, this is not a tragedy: it is simply a reminder to stop thinking and start looking. Perhaps there is nothing to figure out after all: perhaps we only need to wake up.

A monk said: "I have been with you (Master), for a long time, and yet I am unable to understand your way. How is this?"

The Master said: "Where you do not understand, there is the point for your understanding."

"How is understanding possible when it is impossible?"

The Master said: "The cow gives birth to a baby elephant; clouds of dust rise over the ocean." (Suzuki, *Introduction,* p. 116)

In more technical language, and therefore perhaps more comprehensibly for us, Suzuki says: "Prajna is pure act, pure experience . . . it has a distinct noetic quality . . . but it is not rationalistic . . . it is characterized by immediacy . . . it must not be identified with ordinary intuition . . . for in the case of prajna intuition there is no definable object to be intuited. . . . In prajna intuition the object of intuition is never a concept postulated by an elaborate process of reasoning; it is never 'this' or 'that'; it does not want to attach itself to one particular object." (D.T. Suzuki, *Studies in Zen,* London 1957, p. 87–9) For this reason, Suzuki concludes that *Prajna* intuition is different from "the kind of intuition we have generally in religious and philosophical discourses" in which God or the Absolute are objects of intuition and "the act of intuition is considered complete when a state of identification takes place between the object and the subject." (Suzuki, *Studies* p. 89)

This is not the place to discuss the very interesting and complex question raised here. Let us only say that it is by no means certain that the religious, or at any rate mystical, intuition always sees God "as object." And in fact we shall see that Suzuki qualifies this opinion quite radically by admitting that the mystical intuition of Eckhart is the same as *Prajna.*

Leaving this question aside, it must be said here that if anyone tries to spell out a philosophical or doctrinal interpretation for the Zen sayings like those we have quoted above, he is mistaken. If he seeks to argue that when Pai Chang points to the falling snow as answer to a question about the Absolute, as though to say that the falling snow were identified with the Absolute, in other words that this intuition was a reflexive pantheistic awareness of the *Absolute as object,* seen in the falling snow, then he has entirely missed the point of Zen. To imagine that Zen is "teaching pantheism" is to imagine that it is trying to explain something. We repeat: Zen explains nothing. It just sees. Sees what? Not an Absolute Object but Absolute Seeing.

Though this may seem very remote from Christianity, which is definitely a message, we must nevertheless remember the importance of *direct experience* in the Bible. All forms of "knowing," especially in the religious sphere, and especially where God is concerned, are valid in proportion as they are a matter of experience and of intimate contact. We are all familiar with the Biblical expression "to know" in the sense of to possess in the act of love. This is not the place to examine the possible Zenlike analogies in the experiences of the Old Testament prophets. They were certainly as factual, as existential and as disconcerting as any fact of Zen! Nor can we more than indicate briefly here the well-known importance of direct experience in the New Testament. This is of course to be sought above all in the revelation of the Holy Spirit, the mysterious Gift in which God becomes one with the Believer in order to know and love Himself in the Believer.

In the first two chapters of the first Epistle to the Corinthians St. Paul distinguishes between two kinds of wisdom: one which consists in the knowledge of words and statements, a rational, dialectical wisdom, and another which is at once a matter of paradox and of experience, and goes beyond the reach of reason. To attain to this spiritual wisdom, one must first be liberated from servile dependence on the "wisdom of speech." (I Cor. 1:17) This liberation is effected by the "word of the Cross" which makes no sense to those who cling to their own familiar views and habits of thought and is a means by which God "destroys the wisdom of the wise." (I Cor. 1:18–23) The word of the Cross is in fact completely baffling and disconcerting both to the Greeks with their philosophy and to the Jews with their well-interpreted Law. But when one has been freed from dependence on verbal formulas and conceptual structures, the Cross becomes a source of "power." This power emanates from the "foolishness of God" and it also makes use of "foolish instruments." (the Apostles). (I Cor. 1:27 ff.) On the other hand, he who can accept this paradoxical "foolishness" experiences in himself a secret and mysterious power, which is the power of Christ living in him as the ground of a totally new life and a new being. (I Cor. 2:1–4, cf. Eph. 1:18–23, Gal. 6:14–16)

Here it is essential to remember that for a Christian "the word of the Cross" is nothing theoretical, but a stark and existential experience of union with Christ in His death in order to share in His resurrection. To fully "hear" and "receive" the word of the Cross means much more than simple assent to the dogmatic proposition that Christ died for our sins. It means to be "nailed to the Cross with Christ," so that the ego-self is no longer the principle of our deepest actions, which now proceed from Christ living in us. "I live, now not I, but Christ lives in me." (Gal. 2:19–20; see also Romans 8:5–17) To receive the word of the Cross means the acceptance of a complete self-emptying, a *Kenosis,* in union with the self-emptying of Christ "obedient unto death." (Phil. 2:5–11) It is essential to true Christianity that this experience of the Cross and of self-emptying be central in the life of the Christian so that he may fully receive the Holy Spirit and know (again by experience) all the riches of God in and through Christ. (John 14:16–17, 26; 15:26–27; 16:7–15)

When Gabriel Marcel says: "There are thresholds which thought alone, left to itself, can never permit us to cross. An experience is required—an experience of poverty and sickness . . . ." (Quoted, A. Gelin, *Les Pauvres de Yahvé,* Paris, 1954, p. 57) he is stating a simple Christian truth in terms familiar to Zen.

We must never forget that Christianity is much more than the intellectual acceptance of a religious message by a blind and submissive faith which never understands what the message means except in terms of authoritative interpretations handed down externally by experts in the name of the Church. On the contrary, faith is the door to the full inner life of the Church, a life which includes not only access to an authoritative teaching but above all to a deep personal experience which is at once unique and yet shared by the whole Body of Christ, in the Spirit of Christ. St. Paul compares this knowledge of God, in the Spirit, to the subjective knowledge that a man has of himself. Just as no one can know my inner self except my own "spirit," so no one can know God except God's Spirit; yet this Holy Spirit is given to us, in such a way that God knows Himself in us, and this experience is utterly real, though it cannot be communicated in terms understandable to those who do not share it. (See I Cor. 2:7–15.) Consequently, St. Paul concludes, "we have the mind of Christ." (I Cor. 2:16)

Now when we see that for Buddhism *Prajna* is describable as "having the Buddha mind" we understand that there must surely be some possibility of finding an analogy somewhere between Buddhist and Christian experience, though we are now speaking more in terms of doctrine than of pure experience. Yet the doctrine is about the experience. We cannot push our investigation further here, but it is significant that Suzuki, reading the following lines from Eckhart (which are perfectly orthodox and traditional Catholic theology), said they were *"the same as Prajna intuition."* (D.T. Suzuki, *Mysticism: East and West,* p. 40; the quotation from C. de B. Evans' translation of Eckhart, London, 1924, p. 147)

"In giving us His love God has given us the Holy Ghost so that we can love Him with the love wherewith He loves Himself." The Son Who, in us, loves the Father, in the Spirit, is translated thus by Suzuki into Zen terms: "one mirror reflecting another with no shadow between them." (Suzuki, *Mysticism: East and West,* p. 41)

Suzuki also frequently quotes a sentence of Eckhart's: "The eye wherein I see God is the same eye wherein God sees me" (Suzuki, *Mysticism: East and West,* p. 50) as an exact expression of what Zen means by *Prajna.*

Whether or not Dr. Suzuki's interpretation of the text in Zen terms is theologically perfect in every way remains to be seen, though at first sight there seems to be no reason why it should not be thoroughly acceptable. What is important for us here is that the interpretation is highly suggestive and interesting in itself, reflecting a kind of intuitive affinity for Christian mysticism. Furthermore it is highly significant that a Japanese thinker schooled in Zen should be so open to what is basically the most obscure and difficult mystery of Christian theology: the dogma of the Trinity and the mission of the Divine Persons in the Christian and in the Church. This would seem to indicate that the real area for investigation of analogies and correspondences between Christianity and Zen might after all be theology rather than psychology or asceticism. At least theology is not excluded, but it must be theology as experienced in Christian contemplation, not the speculative theology of textbooks and disputations.

The few words that have been written in this introduction, and the brief, bare suggestions it contains, are by no means intended as an adequate "comparison" between Christian experience and Zen experience. Obviously, we have done little more than express a pious hope that a common ground can some day be found. But at least this should make the Western and Christian reader more ready to enter this book with an open mind, and perhaps help him to suspend judgment for a while, and not decide immediately that Zen is so esoteric and so outlandish that it has no interest or importance for us. On the contrary, Zen has much to teach the West, and recently Dom Aelred Graham, in a book which became deservedly popular (Graham, *Zen Catholicism,* N.Y., 1963), pointed out that there was not a little in Zen that was pertinent to our own ascetic and religious practice. It is quite possible for Zen to be adapted and used to clear the air of ascetic irrelevancies and help us to regain a healthy natural balance in our understanding of the spiritual life.

But Zen must be grasped in its simple reality, not rationalized or imagined in terms of some fantastic and esoteric interpretation of human existence.

Though few Westerners will ever actually come to a real understanding of Zen, it is still worth their while to be exposed to its brisk and heady atmosphere.

A LETTER ON THE CONTEMPLATIVE LIFE

In the summer of 1967 Pope Paul VI asked two monks of the Cistercian abbey of Frattocchie, near Rome, to draft a letter from contemplatives which might be issued "to the world" on the occasion of the bishops' synod which was to be held in Rome that October.

The abbot of Frattocchie, Dom Decroix, and another monk, Filiberto Guala, who was a long-time friend of the pope, contacted Merton to help them with the drafting of such a letter.

"A Letter on the Contemplative Life," written by Merton on the day he received Dom Decroix's request, is his response to this request; as such it is a letter within a letter.

The year 1967 was one of turmoil in the monasteries of the world as they attempted to come to grips with the renewal unleashed by the Second Vatican Council which had been concluded only two years previously. As Merton's correspondence of that period attests (see The School of Charity *for that year) he was impatient with the minutiae of reform and much concerned with the problem of authentic monastic renewal. Merton, above all, wanted no letter to appear which would be triumphalistic in tone, and he very much wanted any such letter to be one which would express solidarity with the general human impulse to search for ultimate meaning; thus his warnings against any "solemn pronouncements."*

"Contemplatives and the Crisis of Faith" is the actual message released at the October synod. It was the joint work of the Carthusian Dom Porion, the French Cistercian Dom Andre Louf, and Thomas Merton. It is striking in its open appeal to the atheistic temptation and its act of faith in the reality of God experienced as God.

Both of these generous documents should be read against Merton's continuing efforts to articulate both what he meant by the contemplative life and its availability to all who are authentic

421

searchers. In a sense these two short pieces distill what Merton was trying to say in the many essays he wrote on the monastic life which are collected in the posthumous volume Contemplation in a World of Action *(1973). For an appreciation of Merton's mature ideas on monasticism, see Tarcisius Conner, "Monk of Renewal," in* Thomas Merton: Monk, *edited by Patrick Hart, OCSO (Garden City: Image, 1976), pp. 173–194.*

＊

A LETTER ON THE CONTEMPLATIVE LIFE

Abbey of Gethsemani, 21 August 1967

Reverend and dear Father,

This morning I received your letter of 14 August and I realize I must answer it immediately in order to get the reply to you before the end of the month. This does not leave me time to plan and think, and hence I must write rapidly and spontaneously. I must also write directly and simply, saying precisely what I think, and not pretending to announce a magnificent message which is really not mine. I will say what I can. It is not much. I will leave the rest of you to frame a document of good theology and clearly inspiring hope which will be of help to modern man in his great trouble.

On the other hand I must begin by saying that I was acutely embarrassed by the Holy Father's request. It puts us all in a difficult position. We are not experts in anything. There are few real contemplatives in our monasteries. We know nothing whatever of spiritual aviation and it would be the first duty of honesty to admit that fact frankly, and to add that we do not speak the language of modern man. There is considerable danger that in our haste to comply with the Holy Father's generous request, based on an even more generous estimate of us, we may come out with one more solemn pronouncement which will end not by giving modern man hope but by driving him further into despair, simply by convincing him that we belong to an entirely different world, in which we have managed, by dint of strong will and dogged refusals, to remain in a past era. I plead with you: we must at all costs avoid this error and act of uncharity. We must, before all else, whatever else we do, speak to modern man as his brothers, as people who are in very much the same difficulties as he is, as people who suffer much of what he suffers, though we are immensely privileged to be exempt from so many, so very many, of his responsibilities and sufferings. And we must not arrogate to ourselves the right to talk down to modern man, to dictate to him from a position of supposed eminence, when perhaps he suspects that our cloister walls have not done anything except confirm us in unreality. The problem of the contemplative orders at present, in the presence of modern man, is a problem of great ambiguity. People look at us, recognize we are sincere, recognize that we have indeed found a certain peace, and see that there may after all be some worth to it: but can we convince them that this means anything to them? I mean, can we convince them professionally and collectively, as 'the contemplatives' in our walled institution, that what our institutional life represents has any meaning for them? If I were absolutely confident in answering yes to this, then it would be simple to draft the message we are asked to draw up. But to me, at least, it is not that simple. And for that reason I am perhaps disqualified from participating in this at all. In fact, this preface is in part a plea to be left out, to be exempted from a task to which I do not in the least recognize myself equal. However, as I said before, I will attempt to say in my own words what I personally, as an individual, have to say and usually do say to my brother who is in the world and who more and more often comes to me with his wounds which turn out to be also my own. The Holy Father, he can be a good Samaritan, but myself and my brother in the world we are just two men who have fallen among thieves and we do our best to get each other out of the ditch.

Hence what I write here I write only as a sinner to another sinner, and in no sense do I speak officially for 'the monastic Order' with all its advantages and its prestige and its tradition.

Let us suppose the message of a so-called contemplative to a so-called man of the world to be something like this:

My dear Brother, first of all, I apologize for addressing you when you have not addressed me and have not really asked me anything. And I apologize for being behind a high wall which you do not understand. This high wall is to you a problem, and perhaps it is also a problem to me, O my brother. Perhaps you ask me why I stay behind it out of obedience? Perhaps you are no longer satisfied with the reply that if I stay behind this wall I have quiet, recollection, tranquility of heart. Perhaps you ask me what right I have to all this peace and tranquility when some sociologists have estimated that within the lifetime of our younger generations a private room will become an unheard-of luxury. I do not have a satisfactory answer: it is true, as an Islamic proverb says 'the hen does not lay eggs in the market place'. It is true that when I came to this monastery where I am, I came in revolt against the meaningless confusion of a life in which there was so much activity, so much movement, so much useless talk, so much superficial and needless stimulation, that I could not remember who I was. But the fact remains that my flight from the world is not a reproach to you who remain in the world, and I have no right to repudiate the world in a purely negative fashion, because if I do that my flight will have taken me not to truth and to God but to a private, though doubtless pious, illusion.

Can I tell you that I have found answers to the questions that torment the man of our time? I do not know if I have found answers. When I first became a monk, yes, I was more sure of 'answers'. But as I grow old in the monastic life and advance further into solitude, I become aware that I have only begun to seek the questions. And what are the questions? Can man make sense out of his existence? Can man honestly give his life meaning merely by adopting a certain set of explanations which pretend to tell him why the world began and where it will end, why there is evil and what is necessary for a good life? My brother, perhaps in my solitude I have become as it were an explorer for you, a searcher in realms which you are not able to visit—except perhaps in the company of your psychiatrist. I have been summoned to explore a desert area of man's heart in which explanations no longer suffice, and in which one learns that only experience counts. An arid, rocky, dark land of the soul, sometimes illuminated by strange fires which men fear and peopled by spectres which men studiously avoid except in their nightmares. And in this area I have learned that one cannot truly know hope unless he has found out how like despair hope is. The language of Christianity has said this for centuries in other less naked terms. But the language of Christianity has been so used and so misused that sometimes you distrust it: you do not know whether or not behind the word 'cross' there stands the experience of mercy and salvation, or only the threat of punishment. If my word means anything to you, I can say to you that I have experienced the cross to mean mercy and not cruelty, truth and not deception; that the news of the truth and love of Jesus is indeed the true good news, but in our time it speaks out in strange places. And perhaps it speaks out in you more than it does in me; perhaps Christ is nearer to you than he is to me. This I say without shame or guilt because I have learned to rejoice that Jesus is in the world in people who know Him not, that He is at work in them when they think themselves far from Him, and it is my joy to tell you to hope though you think that for you of all men hope is impossible. Hope not because you think you can be good, but because God loves us irrespective of our merits and whatever is good in us comes from His love, not from our own doing. Hope because Jesus is with those who are poor and outcast and perhaps despised even by those who should seek them and care for them more lovingly because they act in God's name. . . . No one on earth has reason to despair of Jesus, because Jesus loves man, loves him in his sin, and we too must love man in his sin.

God is not a 'problem' and we who live the contemplative life have learned by experience that one cannot know God as long as one seeks to solve 'the problem of God'. To seek to solve the problem of God is to seek to see one's own eyes. One cannot see one's own eyes because they are that with which one sees and God is the light by which we see—by which we see not a clearly defined 'object' called God, but everything else in the invisible One. God is then the Seer and the Seeing and the Seen. God seeks Himself in us, and the aridity and sorrow of our heart is the sorrow of God who is not known to us, who cannot yet find Himself in us because we do not dare to believe or trust the incredible truth that He could live in us, and live there out of choice, out of preference. But indeed we exist solely for this, to be the place He has chosen for His presence, His manifestation in the world, His epiphany. But we make all this dark and inglorious because we fail to believe it, we refuse to believe it. It is not that we hate God, rather that we hate ourselves, despair of ourselves. If we once began to recognize, humbly but truly, the real value of our own self, we would see that this value was the sign of God in our being, the signature of God upon our being. Fortunately, the love of our fellow man is given us as the way of realizing this. For the love of our brother, our sister, our beloved, our wife, our child, is there to see with the clarity of God Himself that we are good. It is the love of my lover, my brother or my child that sees God in me, makes God credible to myself in me. And it is my love for my lover, my child, my brother, that enables me to show God to him or her in himself or herself. Love is the epiphany of God in our poverty. The contemplative life is then the search for peace not in an abstract exclusion of all outside reality, not in a barren negative closing of the senses upon the world, but in the openness of love. It begins with the acceptance of my own self in my poverty and my nearness to despair, in order to recognize that where God is there can be no despair, and God is in me even if I despair: that nothing can change God's love for me, since my very existence is the sign that God loves me and the presence of His love creates and sustains me. Nor is there any need to understand how this can be or to explain it or to solve the problems it seems to raise. For there is in our hearts and in the very ground of our being a natural certainty that says that insofar as we exist we are penetrated through and through with the sense and reality of God even though we may be utterly unable to believe or experience this in philosophic or even religious terms.

O my brother, the contemplative is not the man who has fiery visions of the cherubim carrying God on their imagined chariot, but simply he who has risked his mind in the desert beyond language and beyond ideas where God is encountered in the nakedness of pure trust, that is to say in the surrender of our own poverty and incompleteness in order no longer to clench our minds in a cramp upon themselves, as if thinking made us exist. The message of hope the contemplative offers you, then, brother, is not that you need to find your way through the jungle of language and problems that today surround God; but that whether you understand or not, God loves you, is present to you, lives in you, dwells in you, calls you, saves you, and offers you an understanding and light which are like nothing you ever found in books or heard in sermons. The contemplative has nothing to tell you except to reassure you and say that if you dare to penetrate your own silence and dare to advance without fear into the solitude of your own heart, and risk the sharing of that solitude with the lonely other who seeks God through you and with you, then you will truly recover the light and the capacity to understand what is beyond words and beyond explanations because it is too close to be explained: it is the intimate union in the depths of your own heart, of God's spirit and your own secret inmost self, so that you and He are in all truth One Spirit. I love you, in Christ.

Such are the few ideas I have had, written in haste—so much more will be said so much better by others.

Yours in Christ Jesus,
br. M. Louis
(Thomas Merton)

CONTEMPLATIVES AND THE CRISIS OF FAITH

While the Synod of Bishops is meeting in Rome, we, a group of contemplative monks, feel ourselves closely united with our bishops in their pastoral cares. We are thinking especially of the difficulties which many Christians are experiencing at the present time concerning their faith—difficulties which even go so far as to lead them to call into question the possibility of attaining to knowledge of the transcendent God who has revealed himself to men.

In this situation, it seems to us that our way of life puts us in a position where we can address a few simple words to all. Since we do not want to make our silence and solitude an excuse for failing to render what may be a service to our brothers, especially to those who are struggling to keep or to find faith in Jesus Christ, we are addressing ourselves in a spirit of sonship to you who are the witnesses to that faith, and the guides and masters of souls, so that you can judge in what measure our message might be useful to the people of God in the world of today.

Our personal qualifications for offering such a testimony are poor indeed. But it is more in the name of the way of life that we lead, rather than in our own names, that we dare to speak.

On the one hand, the cloistered contemplative life is simply the Christian life, but the Christian life lived in conditions which favour the 'experience' of God. It could be described as a sort of specialization in relationship with God which puts us in a position to offer a testimony to this aspect of things.

On the other hand, while the contemplative withdraws from the world, this does not mean that he deserts either it or his fellow-men. He remains wholly rooted in the earth on which he is born, whose riches he has inherited, whose cares and aspirations he has tried to make his own. He withdraws from it in order to place himself more intensely at the divine source from which the forces that drive the world onwards originate, and to understand in this light the great designs of mankind. For it is in the desert that the soul most often receives its deepest inspirations. It was in the desert that God fashioned his people. It was to the desert he brought his people back after their sin, in order to 'allure her, and speak to her tenderly' (Hos. 2.14). It was in the desert, too, that the Lord Jesus, after he had overcome the devil, displayed all his power and fore-shadowed the victory of his Passover.

And in every generation, surely, the people of God has to pass through a similar experience in order to renew itself and to be 'born again'. The contemplative, whose vocation leads him to withdraw into this spiritual desert, feels that he is living at the very heart of the Church. His experience does not seem to him to be esoteric, but, on the contrary, typical of all Christian experience. He can recognize his own situation in the trials and temptations which many of his fellow-Christians are undergoing. He can understand their sufferings and discern the meaning of them. He knows all the bitterness and anguish of the dark night of the soul: *My God, my God, why have you forsaken me?* (Ps. 21.1; cf. Matt. 27.46). But he knows, too, from the story of Christ, that God is the conqueror of sin and death.

The world of today is sorely tempted to fall into atheism—into the denial of this God who cannot be grasped on its own level, and is not accessible to its instruments and calculations. Some Christians, even, moved by the desire to share the condition of their fellow-men in the fullest possible way, are yielding to this outlook when they proclaim the need for a certain measure of unbelief as a necessary basis for any fully human sincerity. According to some of them, it is just not possible to reach a God who is, by definition, transcendent—'wholly other'. To be a Christian, it is enough, they say, to devote oneself generously to the service of mankind.

We are not insensitive to everything that is attractive in such a standpoint, although it leads to absurd results. The contemplative Christian, too, is aware of that fundamental datum, so firmly anchored in mystical tradition, that God who has revealed himself to us in his word, has revealed himself as 'unknown', inasmuch as he is inaccessible to our concepts in this life (Exod. 33.20). He lies infinitely beyond our grasp, for he is beyond all being. Familiar with a God who is 'absent', and, as it were, 'non-existent' as far as the natural world is concerned, the contemplative is, perhaps, better placed than most to understand the attitude of those who are no longer satisfied by a mystery whose presentation is reduced to the level of *things*. But he knows very well, nevertheless, that God does allow the attentive and purified soul to reach him beyond the realm of words and ideas.

In the same way, the contemplative can more readily understand how the temptation to atheism which is confronting many Christians at the present time can affect their faith in a way which may, in the long run, be salutary. For this is a trial which bears a certain analogy with the 'nights' of the mystics. The desert strips our hearts bare. It strips us of our pretensions and alibis; it strips us, too, of our imperfect images of God. It reduces us to what is essential and forces us to see the truth about ourselves, leaving us no way of escape. Now this can be a very beneficial thing for our faith, for it is here, at the very heart of our misery, that the marvels of God's mercy reveal themselves. Grace, that extraordinary power from God, works at the very heart of our dullness and inertia, for 'his power is made perfect in weakness' (2 Cor. 12.9).

It is precisely here that the sympathy and understanding of the contemplative make him want to offer a word of comfort and hope. For his experience is not a negative thing, even though it leads him along the paths of the desert with which the temptation to atheism may well have something in common. The absence of the transcendent God is also, paradoxically, his immanent presence, though it may well be that recollection, silence and a certain measure of withdrawal from the agitation of life are necessary for perceiving this. But all Christians are called to taste God, and we want to proclaim this fact in order to put them on their guard against a certain lassitude and pessimism which might tend to create for them conditions which, from this point of view, are less favourable than our own.

Our Lord was tempted in the desert; but he overcame the tempter. Our faith constantly needs to be purified and disentangled from the false images and ideas which we tend to mix with it. But the night of faith emerges into the unshakable assurance placed in our hearts by God whose will it has been to test us.

The cloistered life in itself bears witness to the reality of this victory. It still attracts hundreds of men and women in our own day. But what meaning would it have if grace did not provide the remedy for our blindness, and if it were not true that the Father, 'after having spoken many times and in many ways to our fathers through the prophets, has spoken to us in these latter days through the Son'? (Heb. 1.1–2). For 'if it is only for this life that we have set our hope in Christ, then we are of all men the most to be pitied' (1 Cor. 15.19).

The truth is that this experience is indescribable. But, fundamentally, it is that which Paul, John and the other Apostles proclaimed as being the experience of every Christian; and it is by using the same expressions as they used that we can best speak about it. We are dealing here with a gift of the Spirit which is, as it were, a guarantee of our inheritance (Eph. 1:14). We are dealing here with a gift of that Spirit through whom love has been poured into our hearts (Rom. 5.5), the Spirit who knows what is of God, because he searches everything, even the depths of God (1 Cor. 2.10), the Spirit whose anointing teaches us all things, so that we have no need for anyone else to teach us (1 John 2.27), the Spirit who unceasingly bears witness to our spirit that we are truly sons of God (Rom. 8.16).

It is in this same Spirit that we have come to understand how true it is that Christ died for our sins and rose again for our justification (Rom. 4.25), and that in him we have access through faith to the Father and are restored to our dignity as sons of God (cf. Rom. 5.2; Heb. 10.19).

The mystical knowledge of the Christian is not only an obscure knowledge of the invisible God. It is also an experience of

God—a personal, loving encounter with the one who has revealed himself to us and saved us, in order to make us sharers in the dialogue of the Father and the Son in the Holy Spirit. For it is surely in the Trinity of Persons that God appears to us most clearly as the 'wholly other', and, at the same time, as closer to us than any being.

This, then, is the good fortune which we have felt it our duty to declare to our Shepherds upon whom the trials of the faith bear most heavily at the present time. We ask them for their blessing, and we remain constantly united with them in prayer. In communion with the whole Church, we unite ourselves to the sufferings of the world, carrying on before God a silent dialogue even with those of our brothers who keep themselves apart from us.

Our message can only end on a note of thanksgiving. For that is the feeling which will always predominate in the hearts of those who have experienced the loving-kindness of God. The Christian, that pardoned sinner whom God's mercy has qualified beyond all expectation to share in the inheritance of the saints in light (Col. 1.12), can only stand before God endlessly proclaiming a hymn of thanksgiving: 'He is good, for his love is eternal' (Ps. 135).

It is our wish to offer our own testimony to this sense of wonder and thankfulness, while inviting our brothers everywhere to share them with us in hope, and in this way to develop the precious seeds of contemplation implanted in their hearts.

A SELECT BIBLIOGRAPHY:
BOOKS BY AND ABOUT THOMAS MERTON

1. BIBLIOGRAPHIES

The Breit/Daggy volume, cited below, is definitive. For works after its publication date, one can consult the running bibliography in *The Merton Seasonal* published at the Thomas Merton Study Center at Bellarmine College (Louisville, Kentucky) and the occasional bibliographical surveys in *The Merton Annual* (New York: AMS Press).

Dell'Isola, Frank *Thomas Merton: A Bibliography* (New York: Farrar, Straus, and Cudahy, 1956)

Dell'Isola, Frank *Thomas Merton: A Bibliography* (Kent: Kent State University, 1974)

Breit, Marquita & Daggy, Robert E. *Thomas Merton: A Comprehensive Bibliography,* new edition (New York: Garland, 1986)

2. BOOKS BY THOMAS MERTON

This listing, based on Robert Daggy's checklist of Merton's books, does not include translations, monastic pamphlets, etc. Books are listed chronologically with American publishers without reference to the many translations.

Thirty Poems (New York: New Directions, 1944)

A Man in the Divided Sea (New York: New Directions, 1946)

Figures for an Apocalypse (New York: New Directions, 1948)

Exile Ends in Glory (Milwaukee: Bruce, 1948)

The Seven Storey Mountain (New York: Harcourt, Brace, 1948)

Seeds of Contemplation (New York: New Directions, 1948)

The Tears of the Blind Lions (New York: New Directions, 1949)
The Waters of Siloe (New York: Harcourt, Brace, 1949)
What Are These Wounds? (Milwaukee: Bruce, 1950)
The Ascent to Truth (New York: Harcourt, Brace, 1951)
The Sign of Jonas (New York: Harcourt, Brace, 1953)
Bread in the Wilderness (New York: New Directions, 1953)
The Last of the Fathers (New York: Harcourt, Brace, 1954)
No Man Is an Island (New York: Harcourt, Brace, 1955)
The Living Bread (New York: Farrar, Straus, 1956)
The Silent Life (New York: Farrar, Straus, 1957)
The Strange Islands: Poems (New York: New Directions, 1957)
Thoughts In Solitude (New York: Farrar, Straus, 1958)
The Secular Journal of Thomas Merton (New York: Farrar, Straus, 1959)
Selected Poems (New York: New Directions, 1959)
Disputed Questions (New York: Farrar, Straus, 1960)
The Wisdom of the Desert (New York: New Directions, 1961)
The Behavior of Titans (New York: New Directions, 1961)
The New Man (New York: Farrar, Straus, 1961)
New Seeds of Contemplation (New York: New Directions, 1962)
Original Child Bomb (New York: New Directions, 1962)
Life and Holiness (New York: Herder, 1963)
Emblems of a Season of Fury (New York: New Directions, 1963)
Seeds of Destruction (New York: Farrar, Straus, 1964)
The Way of Chaung Tzu (New York: New Directions, 1965)
Seasons of Celebration (New York: Farrar, Straus, 1965)
Raids on the Unspeakable (New York: New Directions, 1966)
Conjectures of a Guilty Bystander (Garden City: Doubleday, 1966)
Mystics and Zen Masters (New York: Farrar, Straus, 1967)
Cables to the Ace (New York: New Directions, 1968)
Faith and Violence (Notre Dame: Notre Dame, 1968)
Zen and the Birds of Appetite (New York: New Directions, 1968)
My Argument with the Gestapo (Garden City: Doubleday, 1969)
The Climate of Monastic Prayer (Kalamazoo: Cistercian Publications, 1969)
Contemplative Prayer (New York: Herder, 1969) [same as *Climate*]
The Geography of Lograire (New York: New Directions, 1969)
Opening the Bible (Collegeville: Liturgical Press, 1971)

Contemplation in a World Of Action (Garden City: Doubleday, 1971)

The Collected Poems (New York: Farrar, Straus, 1977)

Thomas Merton on Saint Bernard (Kalamazoo: Cistercian Publications, 1980)

3. WORKS BY THOMAS MERTON EDITED BY OTHERS

A Thomas Merton Reader, edited by Thomas McDonnell (New York: Harcourt, Brace, 1962)

The Asian Journal of Thomas Merton, edited by Naomi Burton, James Laughlin, and Brother Patrick Hart (New York: New Directions, 1973)

The Monastic Journey, edited by Brother Patrick Hart (Kansas City: Sheed, Andrews, 1978)

Loving and Living, edited by Naomi Burton Stone and Brother Patrick Hart (New York: Farrar, Straus, 1979)

Geography of Holiness: The Photography of Thomas Merton, edited by Deba Prasad Patnaik (New York: Pilgrim, 1980)

The Non-Violent Alternative, edited by Gordon C. Zahn (New York: Farrar, Straus, 1980)

Day of a Stranger, edited by Robert E. Daggy (Salt Lake City: Peregrine Smith, 1981)

The Literary Essays of Thomas Merton, edited by Patrick Hart (New York: New Directions, 1981)

Woods, Shore, Desert, edited by Joel Weishaus (Santa Fe: Museum Press, 1983)

Thomas Merton in Alaska, edited by Robert E. Daggy (New York: New Directions, 1988)

A Vow of Conversation: Diary: 1964–1965, edited by Naomi Burton Stone (New York: Farrar, Straus, 1988)

Thomas Merton: "Honorable Reader" Reflections on My Work, edited by Robert E. Daggy (New York: Crossroad, 1989). [First published under title *Introductions East and West* in 1981]

4. THE CORRESPONDENCE OF THOMAS MERTON

The publication of the letters of Thomas Merton is in process. These volumes are in print as of the end of 1990.

A Catch of Anti-Letters: Letters by Thomas Merton and Robert Lax
   (Kansas City: Sheed, Andrews, 1978)
The Hidden Ground of Love: The Letters of Thomas Merton on Religious Experience and Social Concerns, edited by William H. Shannon (New York: Farrar, Straus, 1985)
The Road to Joy: Letters of Thomas Merton to New and Old Friends, edited by Robert E. Daggy (New York: Farrar, Straus, 1989)
The School Of Charity: Letters of Thomas Merton on Religious Renewal and Spiritual Direction, edited by Brother Patrick Hart (New York: Farrar, Straus, 1990)

5. BOOKS ABOUT THOMAS MERTON

There is such a volume of books, monographs, theses, essays, and tributes to Thomas Merton that it is impossible, given space limitations, to note them all. Listed below are works which have influenced this work and which appear regularly in other scholarly studies. More detailed listings of Merton studies may be found in the Breit/Daggy bibliography with the follow-up bibliographies found in *The Merton Seasonal,* and in the reviews of the *Thomas Merton Annual.* Biographies of Merton in the list below are marked with an asterisk (*).

Baker, James Thomas. *Thomas Merton: Social Critic* (Lexington: University of Kentucky Presses, 1971)
Carr, Anne. *A Search for Wisdom and Spirit: Thomas Merton's Theology of the Self* (Notre Dame: University of Notre Dame Press, 1988)
Cooper, David. *Thomas Merton's Art of Denial: The Evolution of a*

Radical Humanist (Athens: University of Georgia Press, 1989)

Forest, James. *Thomas Merton: A Pictorial Biography** (New York: Paulist, 1980)

Furlong, Monica. *Merton: A Biography** (San Francisco: Harper and Row, 1981)

Griffin, John Howard. *The Hermitage Journals* (Garden City: Doubleday Image, 1983)

Hart, Patrick (ed.). *Thomas Merton, Monk: A Monastic Tribute* (Garden City: Doubleday Image, 1976)

Hart, Patrick (ed.). *The Message of Thomas Merton* (Kalamazoo: Cistercian Publications, 1981)

Hart, Patrick (ed.). *The Legacy of Thomas Merton* (Kalamazoo: Cistercian Publications, 1986)

Higgins, John J. *Merton's Theology Of Prayer* (Spencer: Cistercian Publications, 1971)

Kelly, Frederic. *Man Before God: Thomas Merton on Social Responsibility* (Garden City: Doubleday, 1974)

Labrie, Ross. *The Art of Thomas Merton* (Fort Worth: TCU Press, 1979)

Lentfoehr, Therese. *Words and Silence: On The Poetry of Thomas Merton* (New York: New Directions, 1979)

Malits, Elena. *The Solitary Explorer: Thomas Merton's Transforming Journey* (San Francisco: Harper and Row, 1980)

Mott, Michael. *The Seven Mountains of Thomas Merton** (Boston: Houghton Mifflin, 1984) [authorized biography]

Padovano, Anthony. *The Human Journey: Thomas Merton Symbol of a Century* (Garden City: Doubleday, 1982)

Pennington, Basil (ed.). *Towards an Integrated Humanity: Thomas Merton's Journey* (Kalamazoo: Cistercian Publications, 1987)

Pennington, Basil. *Thomas Merton, Brother Monk** (San Francisco: Harper and Row, 1987)

Rice, Edward. *The Man In the Sycamore Tree** (Garden City: Doubleday, 1970)

Shannon, William H. *Thomas Merton's Dark Path*, rev. ed. (New York: Farrar, Straus, 1987)

Twomey, Gerald. *Thomas Merton: Prophet in the Belly of a Paradox* (New York: Paulist, 1978)

Wilkes, Paul (ed.). *Merton: By Those Who Knew Him Best* (San Francisco: Harper and Row, 1984)

Woodcock, George. *Thomas Merton/Monk Poet: A Critical Study* (New York: Farrar, Straus, 1978)

6. OTHER SOURCES

Merton: A Film Biography of Thomas Merton. Produced by Paul Wilkes (1984).

Lectures By Thomas Merton. 19 cassettes (one hour each). Kansas City: Credence Cassettes, 1988.

Lectures By Thomas Merton. 5 cassettes (one hour each). Kansas City: Credence Cassettes, 1990.